MOVING FOR PROSPERITY

GLOBAL MIGRATION AND LABOR MARKETS

Policy Research Report

WORLD BANK GROUP

Contents

Boxes

Figures

Maps

Foreword

Migration made my story possible. I was born in Bulgaria at a time when my future seemed defined within the boundaries of my country. But, with the fall of the iron curtain, I got a chance to travel, study, and work abroad, and eventually moved to the United States to work at the institution of which I am now the CEO.

Research has repeatedly demonstrated that migration is good not just for migrants, but also for the communities they leave behind and for the countries that welcome them. Few economic policies do as much to achieve our goals of ending extreme poverty and sharing prosperity as those that ease labor mobility.

For policy makers, migration represents a dilemma. On the one hand, migration helps millions create a better life for themselves and their families. For some, it is their only hope of escaping poverty, violence, and conflict.

On the other hand, there is considerable resistance to migration in destination countries. Migrants are often portrayed as one of the causes of high unemployment, crime, and poor social services. The hopes of migrants and refugees are increasingly threatened by calls for creating barriers, rather than bridges.

This book encourages a more balanced view of migration, providing fresh analysis and comprehensive data for policy makers as they grapple with how to harness the benefits of this phenomenon for all. Although migration provides large overall benefits to the destination country, local populations often feel the negative effects. Migrants tend to arrive in waves, and they land in certain areas, sectors, or occupations because of strong economic forces. As a result, people in those locations feel a significant impact, moving either to other parts of the country or to other jobs to find employment.

Policies should focus on managing these transitions so that both citizens and migrants can experience and share in the long-term benefits. This means smoothing the sharp peaks of migration patterns, as well as protecting citizens from transitory but often painful economic burdens and dislocations.

It is my hope that the analysis provided in this book can facilitate a change in the conversation about migration. Continued income and opportunity gaps, differences in demographic profiles, and rising aspirations of the world's poor and vulnerable all mean that migration will be a fundamental feature of the world for the foreseeable future. We must act together now to create sustainable migration regimes that can deliver economic and social gains for everyone in the generations to come.

Kristalina Georgieva
Chief Executive Officer
The World Bank

Acknowledgments

This Policy Research Report was authored by Çağlar Özden and Mathis Wagner in the Development Economics Research Group of the World Bank. Michael Packard worked with us throughout the report, and his work, diligence, and ingenuity are reflected on every page.

The work was carried out under the supervision of Shantayanan Devarajan, Senior Director of Development Economics, and Asli Demirgüç-Kunt, Director of Research. We are grateful to both of them for their outspoken advocacy for migration research over the years and their support throughout the entire preparation of the draft. Aaditya Mattoo read, commented on, and corrected multiple versions of the draft. His contributions are too many to list. Substantial contributions were also made by Frederic Docquier, Zovanga Kone, Maggie Liu, David McKenzie, Harry Moroz, Kirsten Schuettler, and Mauro Testaverde. Many other people provided invaluable feedback during the whole process. We would like to thank our discussants at multiple presentations of different sections of the report for their critical feedback: Roberta Gatti, Bill Maloney, Xavier Devictor, and Cyril Muller. Before becoming our senior director, Shanta Devarajan was our internal peer reviewer together with Bill Maloney. Michael Clemens and L. Alan Winters were our gracious and steadfast external reviewers. Many others inside and outside the World Bank provided valuable comments and help: Simon Alder, Erhan Artuc, Simone Bertoli, George Borjas, Xavier Devictor, Christian Dustmann, Jesús Fernández-Huertas Moraga, John Giles, Aart Kraay, Robert E. B. Lucas, Manjula Luthria, Harun Onder, Chris Parsons, Giovanni Peri, Sonia Plaza, Dilip Ratha, Ana Revenga, Jan Stuhler, Paolo Verme, and Soonhwa Yi.

Many of our coauthors influenced our thinking on migration along the years. We are grateful, without implicating them in any shortcoming, to: Erhan Artuc, Michel Beine, George Borjas, Ximena Del Carpio, Frederic Docquier, Bernard Hoekman, William Kerr, Zovanga Kone, Aaditya Mattoo, Anna Maria Mayda, Chris Parsons, Giovanni Peri, Sonia Plaza, Hillel Rapoport, Dilip Ratha, Maurice Schiff, Siddharth Sharma, and Mauro Testaverde.

Despite efforts to be comprehensive, the team apologizes for any oversights and expresses gratitude to all who contributed their thoughts. We are also grateful for a wide range of comments from participants during the review of this report and from the presentation of its working drafts at seminars and workshops.

The World Bank's Formal Publishing Unit coordinated the report design, typesetting, printing, and dissemination. We are grateful to Patricia Katayama, Aziz Gökdemir, and especially Stephen Pazdan for handling a demanding production schedule with great efficiency. All maps were produced by Bruno Bonansea. The report was professionally edited by Nora Mara, whose exceptional writing skills were fully used to correct the errors of two immigrants. Gwenda Larsen proofed the typeset report and caught dozens of errors that managed to evade dozens of people. Ryan Hahn worked with us from the very beginning until the end, helping us with every stage of framing and dissemination of the ideas you will find in this report. Indira Chand, Mikael Ello Reventar, David Sharrock, and Anushka Thewarapperuma worked tirelessly on communication and dissemination. Finally, we are indebted to Michelle Chester and Tourya Tourougui for exceptional administrative support throughout the preparation process and for keeping us on schedule.

About the Team

Çağlar Özden, a Turkish national and a professional migrant, is a Lead Economist in the Development Research Group of the World Bank. Çağlar received his undergraduate degrees in economics and industrial engineering from Cornell University and a PhD in economics from Stanford University. He is a fellow of IZA (Institute of Labor Economics), CReAM (Centre for Research & Analysis of Migration), and ERF (Economic Research Forum). His research explores the nexus of globalization of product and labor markets, government policies, and economic development. He has edited three books and published numerous papers in leading academic journals such as *American Economic Review* and the *Economic Journal.* His current research projects explore the determinants and patterns of global labor mobility; impacts of migrants on destination labor market outcomes; links between migration, trade, and foreign direct investment flows; medical brain drain; and links between aging and global economic integration.

Mathis Wagner is a labor economist and also a migrant. He received his undergraduate degree from the University of Cambridge and a PhD in economics from the University of Chicago. He has worked as an assistant professor at Boston College and as a consultant at the World Bank and is currently at Bates White Economic Consulting. His research focuses on the intersection of labor markets and migration. He has studied the impact of Syrian refugees in Turkey and the consequences of immigration in Malaysia and has evaluated policies to attract high-skilled migrants. His current research is on the economic role of refugees in the United States and in understanding the determinants of worldwide refugee flows.

Michael Packard is a consultant in the Development Research Group at the World Bank. As the son of an immigrant and the grandson of a refugee, he has found working on this report to be especially rewarding. He is currently writing his doctoral dissertation in economics at Georgetown University, where his research focuses on the economic and labor market impacts of migration. He holds a BA summa cum laude from the Department of Economics at the University of Colorado.

Abbreviations

ACS	American Community Survey
ALMP	active labor market policy
CDF	cumulative distribution function
CES	constant elasticity of substitution
DACA	Deferred Action for Childhood Arrivals
DHS	U.S. Department of Homeland Security
DIOC-E	OECD Database on Immigrants in OECD and Non-OECD Countries
EAP	East Asia and Pacific
ECA	Europe and Central Asia
EU	European Union
EU15	Austria, Belgium, Denmark, Finland, France, Germany, Greece, Ireland, Italy, Luxembourg, the Netherlands, Portugal, Spain, Sweden, and the United Kingdom
EULFS	European Union Labour Force Survey
FDI	foreign direct investment
GCC	Gulf Cooperation Council
GDP	gross domestic product
IDP	internally displaced person
IMAGE	Internal Migration Around the Globe (database)
IMPALA	International Migration Policy and Law Analysis
IRCA	Immigration Reform and Control Act
LAC	Latin America and the Caribbean
MENA	Middle East and North Africa
MSA	metropolitan statistical area

NBA	National Basketball Association
OECD	Organisation for Economic Co-operation and Development
OLS	ordinary least squares
PCT	Patent Cooperation Treaty
PISA	Programme for International Student Assessment
PPP	purchasing power parity
PRR	Policy Research Report
SSA	Sub-Saharan Africa
STEM	science, technology, engineering, and mathematics
TFP	total factor productivity
UNHCR	United Nations High Commissioner for Refugees
$NZ	New Zealand dollar
TL	Turkish lira
US$	U.S. dollar

Overview

The rich have many assets; the poor have only one—their labor. Because good jobs are slow to come to the poor, the poor must move to find productive employment. Migration is, therefore, the most effective way to reduce poverty and share prosperity, the twin goals of the World Bank. Not surprisingly, all development experiences and growth episodes in history have involved a reallocation of labor across space and sectors within countries.

Some of the biggest gains, however, come from the movement of people between countries. Migrants' incomes increase three to six times when they move from lower- to higher-income countries. The average income gain for a young unskilled worker moving to the United States is estimated to be about $14,000 per year. If we were to double the number of immigrants in high-income countries by moving 100 million young people from developing countries, the annual income gain would be $1.4 trillion. This global welfare gain dwarfs the gains from the removal of all restrictions on international flows of goods and capital.

These gains remain largely notional because most people cannot move. Only about 3 percent of the world's population live in a country in which they were not born, a proportion that has not changed much over six decades of otherwise unprecedented global integration, via trade, investment, and knowledge flows. Distances in space, culture, and language are inherent impediments to mobility, imposing an estimated 30–50 percent tax on migrant wages. The most important barriers are, however, national borders, the jealous guardians of who can enjoy the privileges and protections of nation-states. The tax equivalent of an international border is over 150 percent for young unskilled workers from most developing countries, more than three times larger than those imposed by physical and cultural dimensions of distance.

The gains for immigrants do not come at the expense of host countries. Farmers in destinations from New Zealand to New Mexico thrive thanks to the hard work of immigrant workers. Institutions at the technology frontier—from CERN (the European Organization for Nuclear Research) in Geneva to Silicon Valley in California—innovate thanks to the ingenuity of immigrants. Native-born workers (those who were born in the destination country) also gain on average, either because they gravitate away from the occupations that immigrants are willing to perform, because they benefit from the complementary skills that immigrants bring, or because they are consumers of the products and services immigrants provide. Almost every empirical study finds that increased labor mobility leads to large gains for the immigrants and positive overall gains for the destination country.

That creates a puzzle. The compelling economic evidence on the economic gains and social benefits of migration sits awkwardly with stark political opposition to immigration. Respondents to political opinion polls rate the arrival of immigrants in their countries as among their worst fears. During the last round of elections in the United States and every Western European country, immigration was invariably one of the top three concerns. Citizens worried about what migrants and refugees would do to jobs and wages, welfare programs, crime, schools, and their national identity. Frustrated by the public's disregard of their empirical findings, many economists attribute political opposition to cultural and social factors, including xenophobia.

This Policy Research Report (PRR), *Moving for Prosperity: Global Migration and Labor Markets*, is an attempt to address this tension between the academic research and the public discourse by focusing on the economic evidence. We suggest a labor market–oriented, economically motivated rationale to the political opposition to migration. Global migration patterns lead to high concentrations of immigrants in certain places, industries, and occupations. For example, the top 10 destination countries account for 60 percent of global immigration. Four states host half of all immigrants in the United States, and 10 counties host half of the immigrants in these four states. Immigrants are further concentrated in a narrow set of industries and occupations in specific geographic regions. The same pattern repeats itself in almost every major destination country. It is these geographic and labor market concentrations of immigrants that lead to increased anxiety, insecurity, and potentially significant short-term disruptions among native-born workers. Furthermore, the positive effects and benefits in the destination labor markets tend to be more diffuse whereas the costs are more concentrated and easily attributable to immigration.

Understanding (and empathizing with) these legitimate economic concerns is critical to informed and effective policy making. The goal should be to ease the costs of short-term dislocations of native-born workers and distribute more widely the economic benefits generated by labor mobility. Proactive interventions to ease the pain and share the gain from immigration are essential to avoid draconian restrictions on immigration that will hurt everybody. Ignoring the massive economic gains of immigration would be akin to leaving billions of hundred dollar bills on the sidewalk.

This PRR aims to inform and stimulate debate, contribute to better policies, facilitate further research, and identify prominent knowledge and data gaps. It presents key facts and findings, research methods and data sources on economic migration and refugees, the determinants of their decisions, and their impact on labor markets in both source and destination countries. We have in mind an audience of policy makers, think tanks, academics, students, the wider public, and, of course, our colleagues in the World Bank. The labor market focus of the PRR is motivated not only by the fact that important development and poverty implications of migration—the World Bank's operational and analytical focus—work through these labor market channels. This focus also reflects space and time constraints, and the absence of rigorous research in certain other areas, which simply do not allow an all-encompassing report that covers every dimension of migration. We believe many of the social, cultural, and political dimensions are highly important; and we are certain future analytical work within and outside the World Bank will address these shortcomings.

This overview is intended to be a stand-alone summary of the main themes and results in the report. It discusses many questions: Who migrates to where? Why do people migrate? What is the impact on the migrants and those they leave behind? What are the short- and long-term labor market, social, and welfare outcomes on native-born citizens in the destination locations? Are there specific implications of high-skilled immigration for both migrant-sending and migrant-receiving countries? How can we address the negative impacts of immigration while sustaining the economic benefits?

The overview also includes a series of policy recommendations based on the evidence presented in the following chapters. As will become clear, there are no easy solutions when it comes to migration policies, hence the presence of vigorous and, at times, harsh debates. Economic considerations are only a part of a complex set of issues, and economics literature does not always provide simple and unambiguous solutions. Nevertheless, we believe that the current economic analysis does contain insights and lessons that need to be placed center stage by policy makers.

The organization of the overview mostly follows the organization of the rest of the report. We start with the description of the size and patterns of global migration and their main determinants, such as wage gaps and geographic distances. We then discuss how these forces and concentrated outcomes shape the economic effects of migration in certain regions, sectors, and occupations. After we present the evidence on the short-term wage and dislocation impact of immigration across different groups, we turn to the question of the policy responses to such impacts. Our focus is on how the gains can be distributed. The next section focuses on long-term impacts, especially on assimilation of immigrants, and the relevant policy measures. The penultimate section is on high-skilled migration, its impact and implications. We conclude with emphasizing the need to develop multilateral and regional frameworks to address the policy conflicts arising in international migration.

The patterns of global migration: Scale

Today's headlines create the impression that we are facing a global migration crisis of extraordinary proportions. However, immigrants' share of the global population has been stable at about 3 percent since the end of the Second World War even though international trade and investment flows have led to an unprecedented integration of the world economy. As of 2015, there were slightly more than 240 million migrants in the world (see figure O.1). Their number has grown throughout the post–World War II period, but only at a rate that has kept an even pace with world population growth.

In current media headlines, "refugees" is probably the only word that surpasses "migrants" in terms of frequency. The civil war in the Syrian Arab Republic has brought renewed attention to the plight of refugees, and the data indicate that total refugee numbers are currently at a 20-year peak. Even though their total number has fluctuated widely, refugees have rarely accounted for more than 10 percent of all migrants (see figure O.2). There were about 15 million refugees[1] in 2015, an increase of about 50 percent from 2004 and the highest level since 1995. Nevertheless, the share of refugees is only about 7 percent of all migrants and about 0.2 percent of the

4

Figure O.1   Global migrants constitute a stable share of world population

World migration, 1960–2015

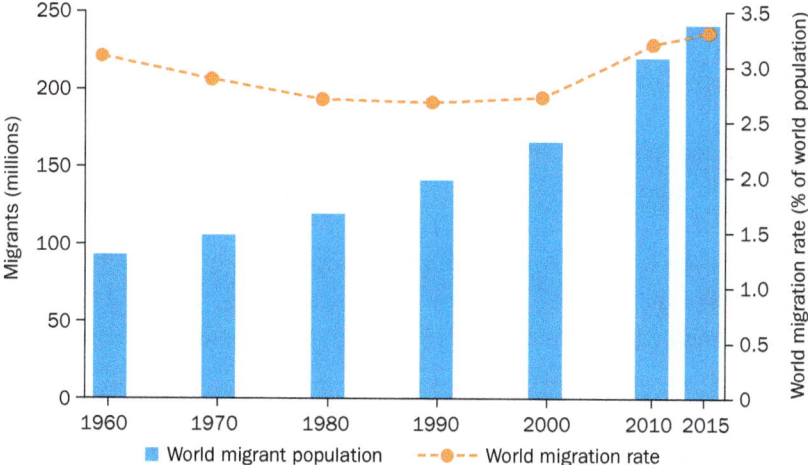

Sources: Data from the World Bank Global Bilateral Migration Database (1960–2000) and the United Nations Global Migration Database (2010–15). Population data from United Nations World Population Prospects.

Figure O.2   Global refugee numbers have grown in recent years but are a small share of migrants and an insignificant share of world population

Refugee numbers and as share of total migrants, 1960–2015

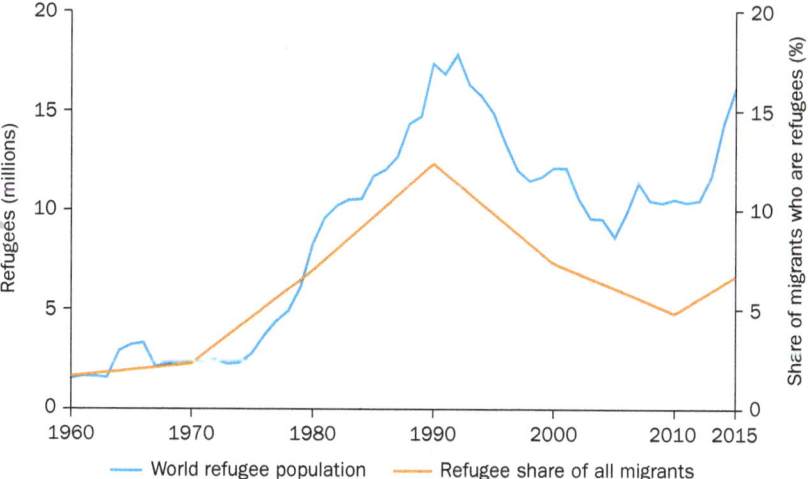

Sources: Refugee data from UNHCR Population Statistics Database. Migration data from the World Bank Global Bilateral Migration Database (1960–2000) and the United Nations Global Migration Database (2010–15).

Note: UNHCR = United Nations High Commissioner for Refugees.

world population. To put it differently, we could fit all the world's refugees in a city roughly the size of Istanbul, Los Angeles, or Moscow.

The patterns of global migration: Concentration

The economic forces that shape global migration and refugee flows have resulted in a situation where immigrants are increasingly concentrated in a few rich destination countries. Two-thirds of the world's immigrants reside in North America, Western Europe, Eastern Europe, and high-income countries of the Middle East and North Africa (see figure O.3). The immigrant shares in most of those regions have increased rapidly since the 1970s. In contrast, East Asia, Latin America and the Caribbean, and Sub-Saharan Africa are notable for their smaller shares of global immigration, especially relative to their local populations. These regions are home to 45 percent of the global population yet host only 15 percent of global migrants.[2]

Figure O.3   **Disproportionately large numbers of migrants move to a few rich countries**

Distribution of global migration, by destination region, 1970, 1990, and 2010

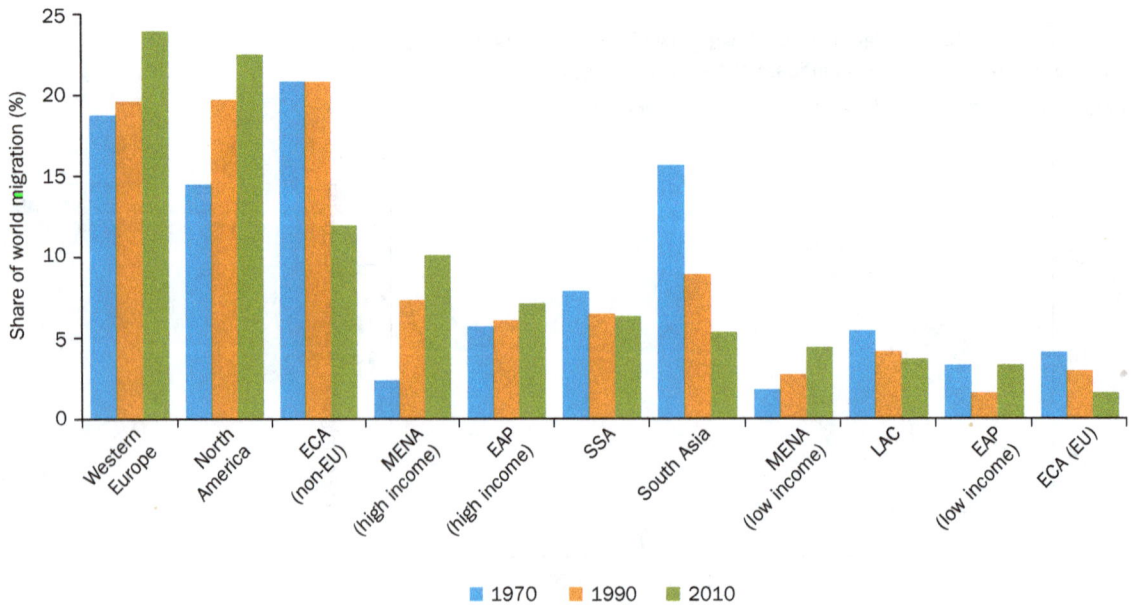

Sources: Data from the World Bank Global Bilateral Migration Database (1960–2000) and the United Nations Global Migration Database (2010–15).

Note: EAP = East Asia and Pacific; ECA = Eastern Europe and Central Asia; EU = European Union; LAC = Latin America and the Caribbean; MENA = Middle East and North Africa; SSA = Sub-Saharan Africa.

What do these patterns imply in terms of the concentration of migration in the source and destination countries? Figure O.4 addresses this question. It presents the cumulative distribution of migrants across destination and origin countries, ranked by the size of the migrant populations. Immigration, depicted by the solid lines, is highly concentrated within the top 10 destination countries: they host about 60 percent of all immigrants in the world. The next 10 largest destination countries, ranked from 11th to 20th, have about 15 percent of the immigrants; and the ratio steadily declines. This pattern has been relatively stable over time, with immigration becoming neither more nor less concentrated from 1970 to 2010. In contrast, emigration, depicted by the dashed lines, is less concentrated and has become even more dispersed over time. By 2010, the top 10 origin countries represented less than 40 percent of total emigration, down from 55 percent in 1970.

Refugee flows are even more concentrated. In 2015, five source countries accounted for 55 percent of all refugees, and five destination countries hosted 40 percent of all refugees. Unlike economic migrants, most refugees, over 80 percent, reside in developing countries. Figure O.5 shows the distribution of

Figure O.4   **Immigration has remained concentrated while emigration is becoming more dispersed**

Cumulative distribution of global migration, 1970, 1990, and 2010

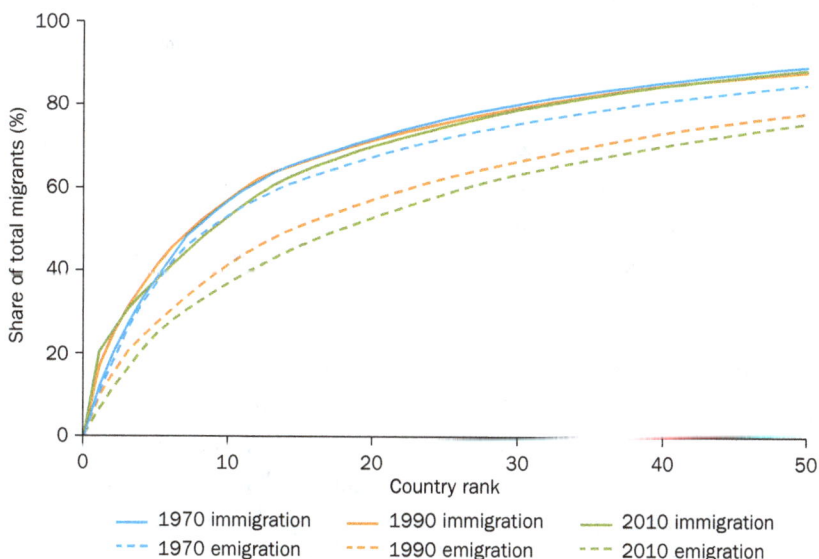

Sources: Data from the World Bank Global Bilateral Migration Database (1960–2000) and the United Nations Global Migration Database (2010–15).

Note: Countries in a given year are ranked by size of their corresponding emigrant or immigrant populations.

Figure 0.5   Refugee flows are more concentrated than overall migration

Destinations of refugees from major crises, 2015

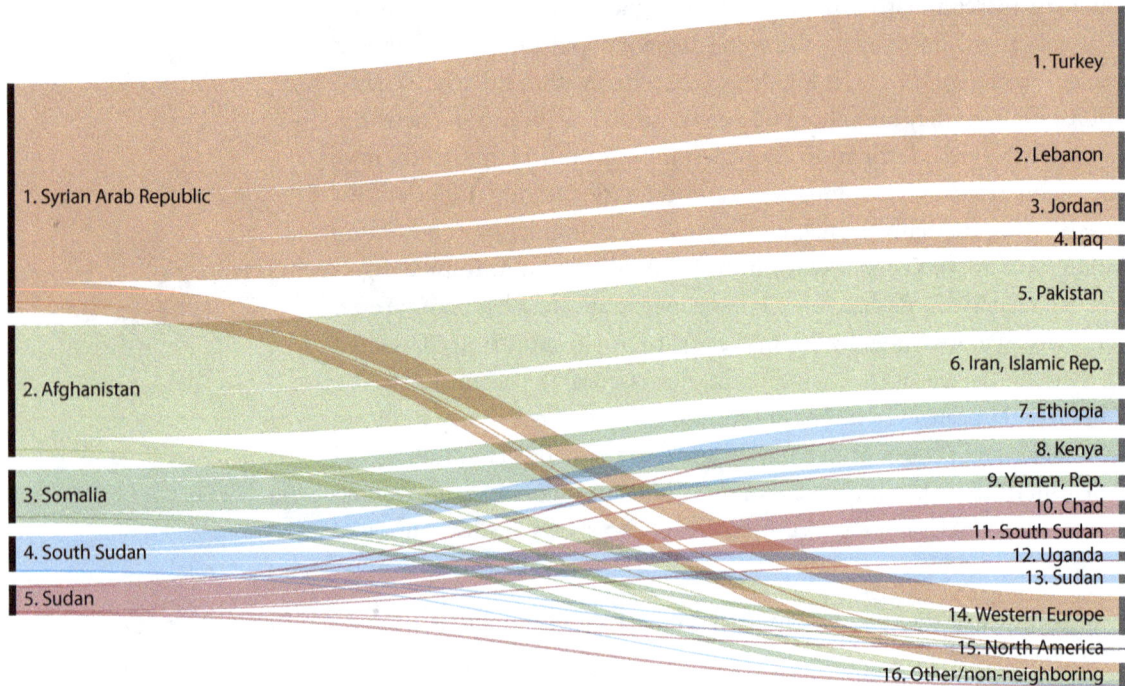

Source: Data from UNHCR Population Statistics Database. Figure made using RAWGraphs visualization platform (Mauri et al. 2017).

Note: Refugees defined as refugees (and those in refugee-like situations) and asylum seekers. UNHCR = United Nations High Commissioner for Refugees.

refugees across different destinations for the five major crises in 2015. For the cases shown, over 87 percent of all refugees and asylum seekers reside in neighboring countries, only 8 percent are in Western Europe, and less than 0.2 percent are in the United States. The result is that, although immigrants account for a large and rising fraction of the population in a small number of wealthier countries, the concentration of refugee flows results in a few poorer countries experiencing very large influxes.

This high concentration of immigration has important implications for populations and labor markets in destination countries. On one hand, concentration is exactly the outcome we expect from an economic realloca-tion and adjustment mechanism like immigration. When there are large wage gaps for the same type of worker in two different labor markets, we observe a large and concentrated flow until wages are equalized. In many ways, this is no different from any other economic flow across markets when sellers take advantage of price differences. This adjustment process yields the productivity gains, wage increases, and poverty reduction discussed earlier. In other words, economic development and market forces are in alignment.

On the other hand, concentration of immigrants in certain destination countries, economic sectors, occupations, and regions as market forces rush to fulfill unmet demand is also the main cause of the economic problems and cultural anxieties of local populations. This is especially the case for those domestic populations who have easily substitutable skills and occupations: they must compete in the labor market with the newly arriving immigrants. The challenge is how to address the adjustment and transition problems caused by this concentration.

The determinants of migration

People move for myriad reasons. In this section, we consider the main benefits and costs of mobility and the role of policy.

Wage gains

Every migrant and every refugee has a unique story, but the common theme is the desire for a better life. For economically motivated migrants, this desire is often realized through better employment opportunities and higher wages. Many migrants, such as refugees or low-skilled economic migrants, might make their choices under severely constrained conditions and limited options, taking considerable personal and financial risks. Yet the evidence indicates that the same basic economic principles underlie the decisions of migrants from a wide array of countries, opportunities, and economic, social, and educational backgrounds.

The most important labor market determinants of migration flows are wage differences between destination and source locations. Empirical evidence unequivocally shows that people tend to move from low-wage to high-wage locations. Figure O.6 plots the wage difference between origin and destination countries against the fraction of emigrants moving from each source country to each destination country. The slope in the graph implies that an emigrant is 10 percent more likely to choose a possible destination country if the mean annual wages are $2,000 higher in that country than in other possible destinations.

Observed patterns and labor market outcomes give more precise measures of the potential wage gains of moving to higher-income destinations.

Figure O.6 **Wage differences drive bilateral migration**

Differences in wages and migration shares between source and destination countries, 2010

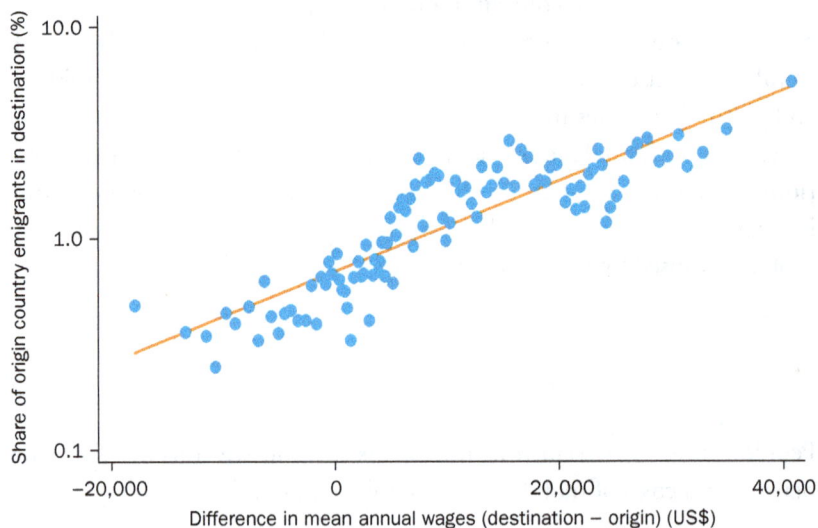

Sources: Data from the 2010/2011 OECD Database on Immigrants in OECD and Non-OECD Countries (DIOC-E) and World Bank International Income Distribution Data (I2D2).

Note: Figure plots the residuals from regressions of the x- and y-axis variables on a set of controls. Controls include origin fixed effects, (log) distance, contiguity, linguistic similarity, and (log) destination population. Dots represent averages over 100 equally sized bins. Sample restricted to all migration corridors with migrant stocks greater than 1,000 with available data. OECD = Organisation for Economic Co-operation and Development.

The preceding discussion gives the wage gains possible when an *average* migrant moves from an origin country and earns the *average* wage in a destination country. A New Zealand visa lottery program, which uses a random ballot to choose among applicants from Tonga, provides some of the clearest evidence on the *actual* economic returns realized when migrants move to a higher-income country. In the first year after winning the lottery and moving to New Zealand, Tongan migrants earn nearly 300 percent more than non-migrants not selected in the lottery (see figure O.7). Importantly, these gains are permanent and persist almost 10 years later. In short, returns to migration are enormous for migrants, regardless of how they are measured.

Distance

When making their migration decisions, people weigh the gains of migration against the costs. This is no different than other critical and

Figure O.7 Wage gains of Tongan migrants to New Zealand are large and permanent

Wage gains due to migration: Quasi-experimental evidence

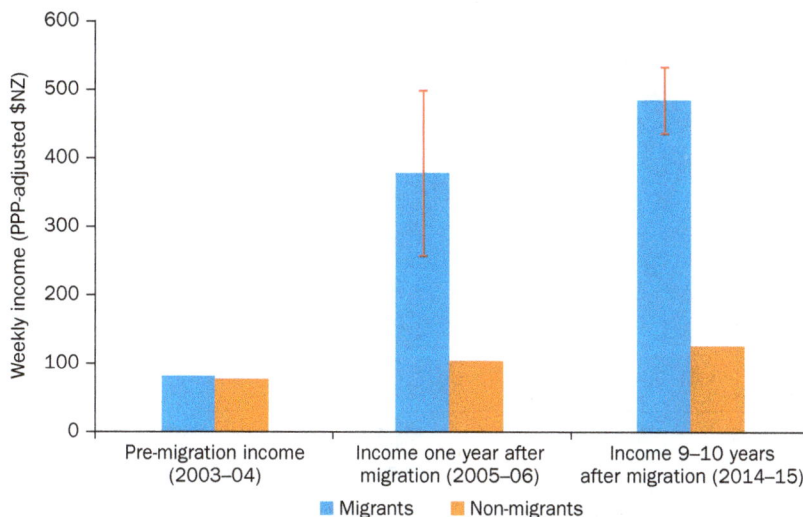

Sources: One-year results from McKenzie, Stillman, and Gibson 2010; long-term results from Gibson et al. 2018. Impacts shown are local average treatment effect estimates for impact of migrating; 95 percent confidence intervals shown for treatment effects.

Note: PPP = purchasing power parity.

life-altering choices that people face regarding their education, careers, families, or investments. They respond to migration's economic benefits—generally revealed through the labor markets in the form of current and future wages—and costs arising from geographic distances, linguistic differences, and cultural divergences.

The most important costs faced by migrants are the monetary, social, and psychological costs of moving, settling, and adapting to a new location with different economic and cultural characteristics. Actual physical distances are powerful deterrents of mobility. Most low-skilled migrants, people with typically limited resources to finance their move, migrate to neighboring countries or to those countries within the same geographic region. And refugees move to the nearest country that will accept them, which, in most cases, is a neighboring country. Figure O.8 shows the cumulative distribution of refugees and low- and high-skilled migrants by distance (where the distance of zero indicates migration to a neighboring country). As we see from the graph, slightly over half of low-skilled migrants and over 80 percent of refugees move to a neighboring country.

Figure 0.8 Most migrants travel to neighboring countries, but the high-skilled travel farther

Cumulative distribution of world migration, by distance, 2000

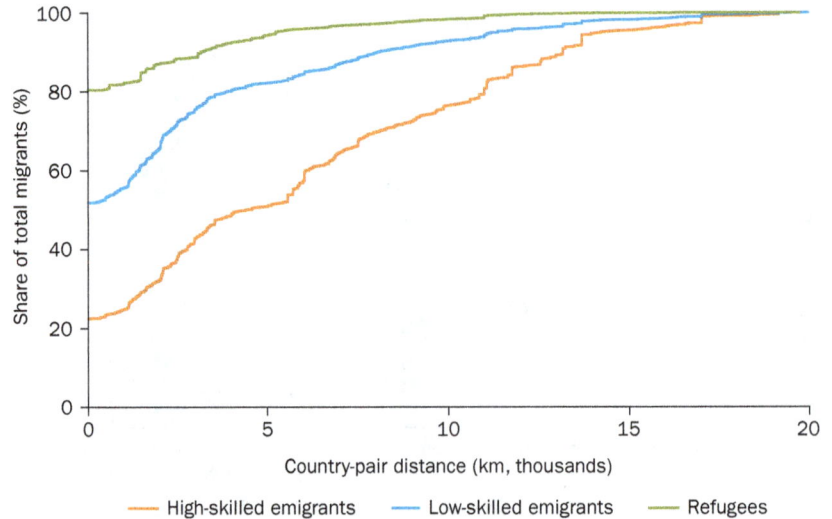

Sources: Figure uses year 2000 migrant stocks from the World Bank Global Bilateral Migration Database (1960–2000) and 2015 refugee stocks from UNHCR Population Statistics Database. Distance and contiguity data derived from the CEPII GeoDist database.

Note: Distance is defined as distance between two most populous cities, and contiguous countries are treated as zero distance. The cumulative distribution function plots the share of all international migrants who reside in a country less than or equal to a given distance from their home country. UNHCR = United Nations High Commissioner for Refugees.

In contrast, high-skilled economic migrants travel much farther than either group, with a median travel distance of 6,000 kilometers.

Migration policies

Every country has the legal right to control who crosses its borders, enters its labor markets, has access to the social benefits offered by the state, and enjoys its legal privileges. When migrants enter a country or a labor market, in addition to embarking on a new life for themselves, they affect the lives of the citizens in numerous ways, some of which are positive and others negative. Government migration policies aim to manage these effects while adhering to certain moral and legal principles. This attempt at balance creates some of the sharpest conflicts at the heart of the debates on destination countries' immigration policies: What policies should be implemented according to the social, economic, and political objectives of the government? How will these policies affect immigration patterns in terms of their composition and size? And which groups within the country will benefit and which ones will be hurt by these policies? Which moral or legal principles should these policies uphold?

A fundamental challenge for immigration policy is that labor markets, mainly through wage differentials across countries, create powerful push and pull forces leading to large-scale demand for migrant labor in many sectors and regions. In most instances, policies are unable to completely withstand the pressure from the economic forces. The result is migration tides, entry of large numbers of undocumented migrants, distorted labor market outcomes, and eventual political conflicts and cultural clashes. Unsurprisingly, these are among the most prominent problems that currently dominate the migration policy debate across the world.

Undocumented or unauthorized immigration is the foremost unintended consequence of governments' legal attempts to control immigration flows. For example, about half of Mexican immigrants in the United States are unauthorized immigrants who entered illegally or overstayed their legal visas. In order to identify effective policies to counter such massive flows, we need to understand how they come into existence. Undocumented Mexican migration to the United States started with a policy decision to end the Bracero Program. Operating from 1942 to 1965, the Bracero Program was an important legal framework for the circular migration of temporary agricultural workers. The program was ended because of various political factors, but the impact, as illustrated in figure O.9, was not exactly what the policy makers intended. Almost immediately afterward, the number of temporary migrants decreased and the number of undocumented migrants skyrocketed. The gap between the demand for unskilled Mexican workers and their supply, as reflected through the wage gaps, was simply too large to sustain in a market economy. Although the legal channel was blocked, market forces prevailed, and undocumented migrants poured in to meet the demand.

In response to the massive inflow after 1965, the U.S. government pursued both external border enforcement and internal labor market controls to discourage illegal immigration. However, there are important limitations to the efficacy of enforcement in deterring unauthorized immigration. First, about one-third of unauthorized immigrants in the United States cross the border legally and then overstay their visas. Second, border enforcement discourages temporary or circular migration and, instead, encourages permanent undocumented migration. Third, enforcement typically does little to reduce the demand for immigrant labor—for example, in construction or agriculture—thereby leaving the main pull factors for immigration intact.

Figure O.9 Restrictions on legal temporary immigration led to an increase in illegal immigration from Mexico to the United States

Mexican migration to the United States, 1955–95

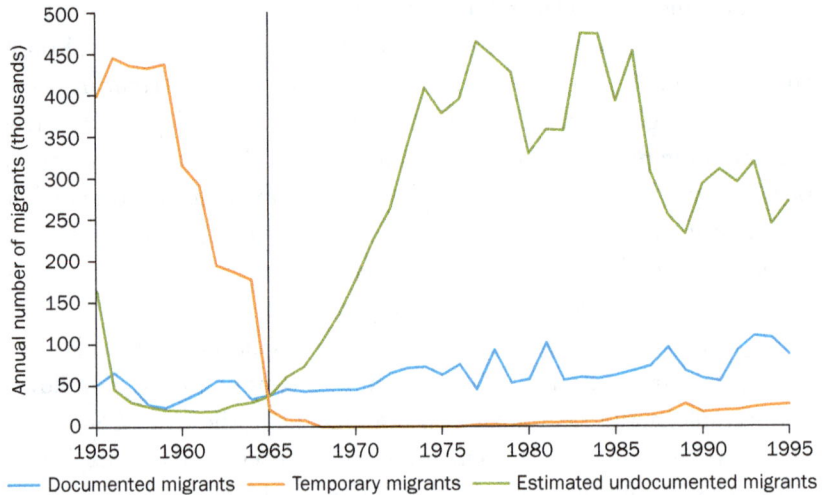

Source: Massey and Pren 2012. Reproduced with permission; further permission required for reuse.

Note: The vertical line (1965) represents the termination of the Bracero Program, which provided a legal framework for the circular migration of temporary agricultural workers.

The difficulty of restricting migration in the presence of large wage differentials, especially between neighboring countries, brings us to our first policy conclusion. It is hard, almost impossible, for governments to implement policies that prevail against such market forces. Instead, *immigration policies should be designed with markets in mind.*

An example of a significant market-oriented policy reform involves temporary migration schemes. When an obvious market demand exists, governments should consider allowing legal, temporary, and sufficiently large programs to meet those shortages—in sectors like agriculture, construction, and tourism, where seasonal and short-term jobs are the norm. *Temporary* migration programs for *temporary* jobs—by divorcing labor market needs from permanent migration—benefit migrants and native populations alike. Such programs would discourage illegal immigration, as well as permanent migration of extended families, by facilitating repeated circular migration.

That temporary migrants would seek to become permanent residents (legally or not) is a valid concern in this context. However, most people in the world prefer to live in their home country and do not actually want to settle permanently in a different country. Temporary migration policies will work as intended only in industries with low turnover costs and substantial seasonal fluctuations in labor demand, such as in agriculture, tourism, or construction. These policies cannot be used to address labor shortages in every industry, as discussed below.

The short-term impact of immigration: Labor markets

Immigrants are frequently blamed for many of the economic woes that countries face and are accused of displacing native-born citizens from their jobs. A large and varied literature addresses the question of whether immigration results in unemployment and lower wages in the destination labor markets. Although no clear consensus has emerged, studies that rely on sudden, relatively unanticipated, and large immigration flows provide the clearest empirical evidence. The major advantage of these studies is that the immigration shocks they document are both large and typically not driven by the availability of jobs, but rather by exogenous supply shocks or push factors. These can be natural disasters, sudden changes in the political environment (such as a crisis), or random selection of migrants through lotteries. Figure O.10 presents a few examples of such natural experiments.

Figure 0.10 **Episodes of sudden migrant inflows can help identify the impact of immigration**

Natural experiments in immigration

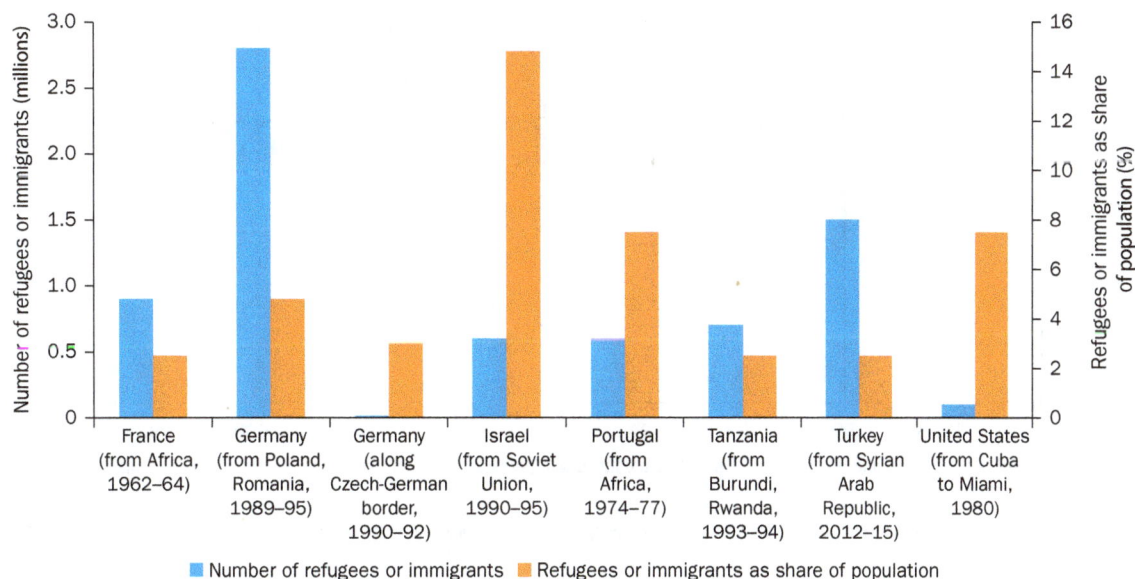

Three stylized facts emerge from these studies. First, immigration results in large displacement effects among groups of native-born citizens who most directly compete with the immigrant labor. These tend to be low-skilled and less-educated workers who are likely to be already struggling in the labor market. Second, groups of native-born citizens that do not directly compete with the immigrants frequently experience significant gains. These groups tend to *complement* the immigrants in the labor markets, and they experience productivity gains. Third, overall wage effects tend to be small compared to the employment and reallocation effects of immigration.

A valuable example is the post-1989 policy that allowed Czech workers to seek employment, but not residency rights, in eligible German border municipalities. Figure O.11 depicts the difference between wage and employment rates in treatment (migrant-receiving) and control (compara-tor) regions over time. By 1993, a 1 percentage point increase in the inflow of Czech workers relative to local employment had led to only about a 0.13 percent decrease in native wages, but we observe an almost one-to-one (0.93 percent) decrease in native local employment. The German workers in migrant-receiving regions simply moved to other parts of the country rather than stay and experience wage losses.

Figure O.11 The arrival of Czech workers in Germany led to low wage but large employment effects as locals relocated to other regions

Wage and employment effects of Czech commuters in Germany, 1986–95

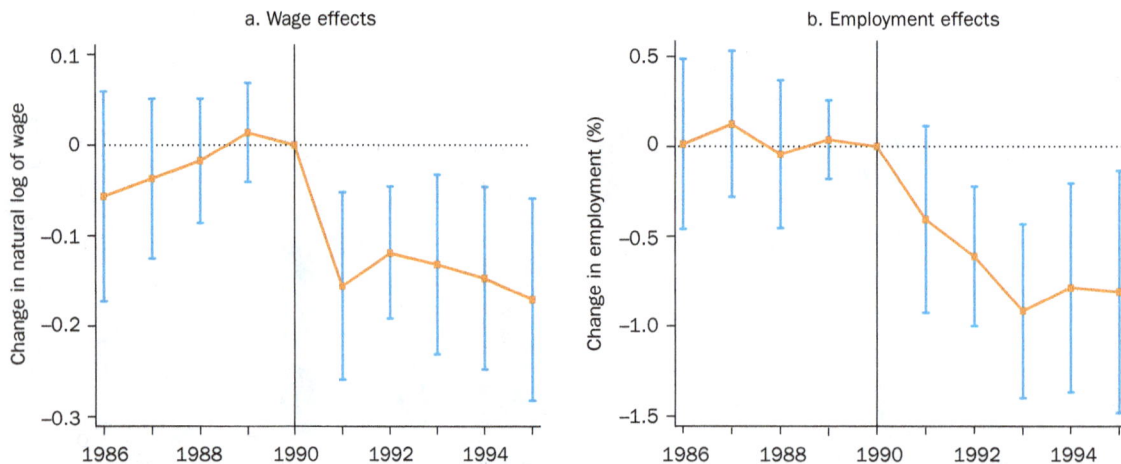

Sources: Dustmann, Schönberg, and Stuhler 2017, figure 4. Reproduced with permission; further permission required for reuse. Data from German social security records, 1986–96.

Note: The vertical black lines represent the implementation of the policy in 1990 that allowed Czech workers in Germany. The blue lines are the confidence intervals.

16

The fact that many of these studies frequently find large displacement effects provides some contrast with much of the literature analyzing voluntary (and gradual) immigration flows. Most of the literature on economic immigration relies on the insight that immigrants change the relative abundance of different skill groups in the economy. An influential strand of this literature considers a whole country as the unit of analysis where immigrants and native-born workers are categorized into different skill groups. The actual supply of workers in a particular skill or education group is compared to the supply that would have prevailed in the absence of immigration. Then the implied change in wages of native-born workers is simulated using estimates of the degree of substitutability between types of workers.

Figure O.12, taken from a 2017 National Academies of Sciences, Engineering, and Medicine report, summarizes the findings of this approach for the United States. It considers the impact of the change in labor supply due to immigration (panel a) and the overall impact of this change on native workers and existing migrants (panel b). The first panel describes the percentage labor supply increase for each education group due to immigration over the period 1990–2010. The economic analysis allows for some degree of imperfect substitutability between immigrants and native workers in the same education group.

Several features of these results are worth highlighting. First, the *average* impact of immigration across *all* workers (native-born workers and already present immigrants) is negligible.[3] Second, when immigrant and native-born workers are *imperfect* substitutes, new immigration flows decrease wages of existing immigrants without exception because they are the closest substitutes to the newly arriving migrants. On the basis of these two observations, on average, wages of native-born workers increase, although only by 0.5 percent. Finally, none of the simulated wage impacts are particularly large. This is primarily because the characteristics of immigrants and natives are not sufficiently dissimilar to result in large relative wage effects, especially in the long run, when other relocation and adjustment mechanisms take place.

How do we reconcile evidence of small wage effects with that of large displacement effects of immigration? The evidence from natural experiments with large labor supply shocks finds substantial dislocation and large-scale native adjustments to an inflow of immigrants. The evidence also suggests that natives' reallocation to other occupations, sectors, or geographic areas as a response to immigrant flows is, in practice,

Figure 0.12 **Immigration has a small impact on overall wages but lowers the wages of those with similar skills**

Simulated wage impacts of 1990–2010 immigrant supply shock in the United States

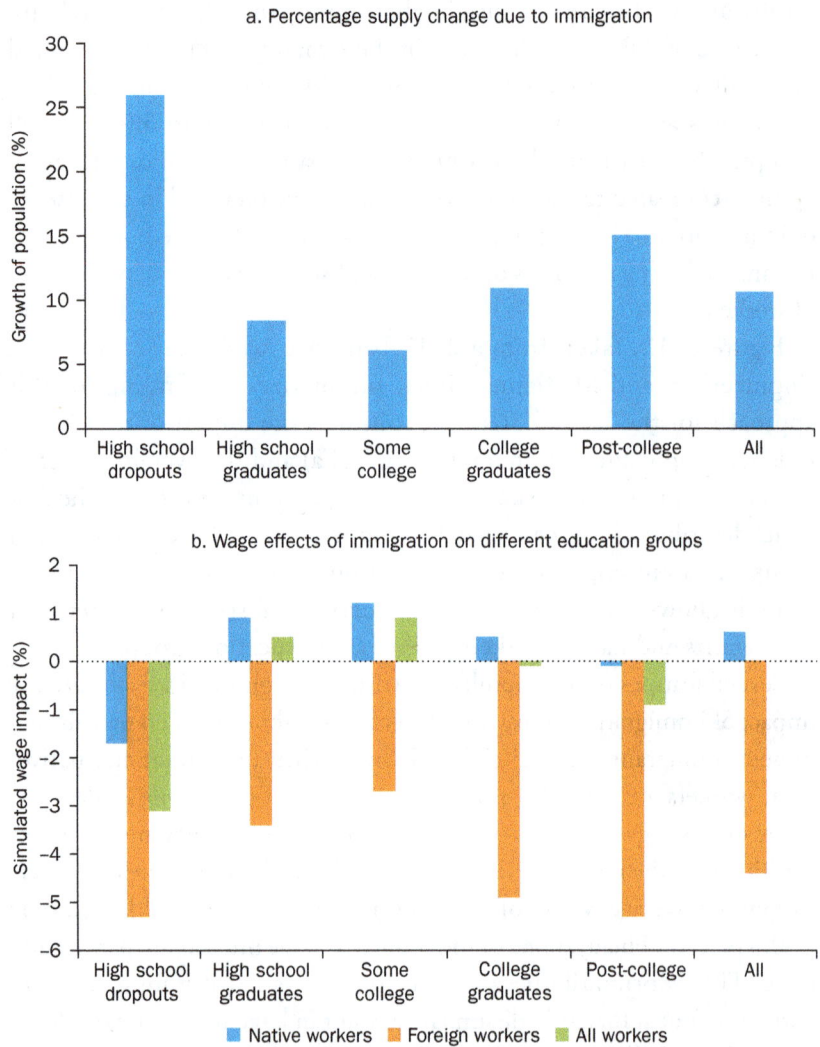

a. Percentage supply change due to immigration

b. Wage effects of immigration on different education groups

■ Native workers   ■ Foreign workers   ■ All workers

Source: National Academies of Sciences, Engineering, and Medicine 2017, table 5-1. Reproduced with permission; further permission required for reuse.

Note: Results from simulations using nested, constant elasticity of substitution framework, set σ_E = 5.0, using a Cobb-Douglas aggregate production function with σ_{KL} = 1.0. The simulations assume that the supply of capital adjusts perfectly to accommodate the arrival of immigrants. In the extreme case where there is no adjustment of capital, all the estimates in the graph should be reduced by 3.2 percentage points.

sufficiently large so that the average wages change only a little. The literature on long-term voluntary migration flows tends to focus on those wage effects and concludes that immigration has little—positive or negative—wage impact for a substantial majority of natives. However, even if relative wage effects are small, the dislocation experienced by some groups of workers (or the fear of such dislocation) because of immigration can explain much of the resentment that many natives exhibit toward immigrants.

Addressing short-term costs: Assistance and adjustment policies

As we saw earlier, in most cases, native workers who most directly compete with immigrant labor locate to other sectors or geographic regions, and the overall wage effects of immigration are small. Concentration of immigration and the resulting dislocation of native-born workers can be large and involve substantial costs. These observations lead us to our next policy recommendation: *policy makers should attempt to aid native-born workers in their adjustment and relocation processes.* The natural question is how to design such policies that help with mostly transitory but potentially disruptive costs. The task is daunting. The existing evidence on similar adjustment assistance mechanisms—aiming to compensate for dislocation due to international trade or technological change—is not encouraging. Yet the current policy of benign neglect is clearly not working either.

The evidence clearly shows that immigration has unequal effects. It benefits many native-born workers as their productivity increases with the arrival of complementary foreign workers. These workers who benefit from immigration tend to be in the high-skilled occupations where the skill complementarities and knowledge spillovers are prevalent. Dislocation and reallocation are, in contrast, especially costly for the less-educated native-born workers who are already more vulnerable to negative economic shocks. Assistance programs can involve retraining programs that would provide more relevant skills. Furthermore, existing education systems for young people need to be modified so native-born youth do not compete with the lower-skilled immigrants who are willing to accept significantly lower wages and more demanding work conditions.

A second component of adjustment policies can be relocation assistance for native-born workers, whether these workers are changing occupations, cities, or sectors of employment. Transitory welfare benefits and unemployment insurance payments are possible components of such assistance programs. However, such programs present many difficulties, such as proper identification of the impacted groups, the extent of the impact, or the ideal duration of the assistance. One option is a minimum income scheme, along the lines implemented by some European countries such as Denmark.

Helping the losers by taxing the winners ...

Once the issue becomes adjustment assistance to those who are affected by immigration, we are immediately confronted with the question of financing. The natural answer is that the beneficiaries of immigration should, at least partially, be responsible for the cost. Currently, legal immigration is practically regulated using quotas, that is, restrictions on the number of immigrants of a certain education/ occupation/sector category allowed to enter and work in a country. The imposition of quotas by the destination country government causes, as in international trade, several specific problems. First, bureaucrats, instead of employers or markets, make the assessment of how many immigrants should be allowed to enter the labor market. Generally, little evidence exists about what type of immigration—by skill, occupation, sector, or experience—most benefits a destination country, especially in the long run. And the needs of the labor market change over time. Second, as is well documented in the literature, quota-based systems are subject to rent-seeking and corruption as firms try to sway government officials to issue quota permits to themselves or to their industries. Finally, and this speaks to the issue of finance, quotas do not generate revenue for the government. Instead, they benefit only those firms (that is, the quota permit holders) lucky enough to hire an immigrant by, for example, obtaining an employment visa, or the intermediary firm who does the recruitment. A possible solution, and our next policy recommendation, is that *governments should start to replace quota regimes with tax regimes to regulate immigration flows.* This might take the form of an additional income tax, a visa fee, or even a visa auction system as proposed by many prominent economists going back to Gary Becker.

Very little is known about the impacts of a visa tax or fee on immigration size or composition. A few countries, such as Singapore and Malaysia, impose levies on immigrants; however, to our knowledge, none of these policies has been rigorously assessed. Nevertheless, given the obvious defects of the existing quota-based policy regimes, the imposition of taxes, fees, or levies instead of quota restrictions has many obvious benefits. Firms will be able to employ the workers they want and provide the government with revenue to aid those who are struggling economically from immigration. Employers will also be able to more rapidly respond to economic fluctuations and hire extra workers right away when needed. In a quota regime, firms cannot expand production quickly even if they are willing to pay for the workers' employment permits. Governments will be able to adjust fees more quickly to respond to changes in the labor markets; quotas seem to be much more inflexible and set for decades at a time. The fee-based regimes may also reduce the hostility to immigrants, who would provide the needed "tax" revenue and could no longer be said to "have a free ride" after they come. A considerable transition period is required as governments learn how to replace quotas with taxes on immigrants. The global trade regime gradually replaced quotas with tariffs, and the same is certainly worth trying in the immigration policy space.

... and by accepting refugees in more countries

Concentration and its impact are more evident in the case of refugees. Most economic migration flows are sufficiently gradual that immigrants can be absorbed into the economy of the host country. Negatively impacted native-born workers tend to adjust by relocating to other sectors or regions. This type of adjustment is, however, often not the case during refugee crises, which typically involve the influx of large numbers of desperate people, in a very short time, into an already poor host country. Since the start of the Syrian refugee crisis in 2013, for example, Jordan and Lebanon have experienced an inflow of refugees equal to 7 percent and 18 percent, respectively, of their populations. In such circumstances, it is unrealistic to expect humanitarian aid to effectively mitigate the economic—as well as the social, cultural, and political—shock of experiencing such a massive influx. Mitigating such shocks is especially important because these destinations are generally other developing countries already suffering from numerous economic problems. In these emergency situations, one of the few viable solutions is to spread the burden of the refugee crisis across the globe.

The number of refugees worldwide is small compared to the world's population or even relative to the world's total migrant population. What turns refugee flows into long-term crises is that both refugee source and destination countries are mostly low- or middle-income developing countries with limited resources. And crises erupt suddenly, requiring prompt action to prevent escalation and suffering. If implemented properly, an active, large-scale refugee settlement policy and coordinated financial assistance would make the impact more easily manageable in host countries, both in the developed and the developing world.

The long-term impact: Immigrant integration and assimilation

The discussion so far has focused on the relative wage and employment impact of immigration on labor markets and possible policy responses. These tend to be mostly static issues. Now we turn to the long-term dynamic issues.

Crucial to understanding the longer-term consequences of immigration is the question of how well immigrants assimilate in their host country. Not all immigration can be temporary; permanent jobs require permanent immigrants. This is especially the case where the job requires training, firm- or location-specific human capital investments, or long-term social and professional relationships. Migrants will need to master the language, customs, and professional and educational requirements in the destination country. The eventual success and overall contributions of immigrants, low- and high-skilled alike, depend on the degree to which they and their employers invest in such location-specific skills and human capital.

At the time of their arrival, immigrants and refugees are, on average, at a severe economic disadvantage, as measured by employment, wages, and occupational quality, compared to natives. Subsequently, immigrants assimilate and catch up with natives in terms of wages and employment. Figures O.13 and O.14 illustrate the pace of assimilation—figure O.13 for employment in the European Union (EU) and figure O.14 for wages in the

Figure 0.13 Refugees start with a bigger disadvantage than economic immigrants, but both groups catch up

Employment assimilation of refugees and immigrants in the European Union

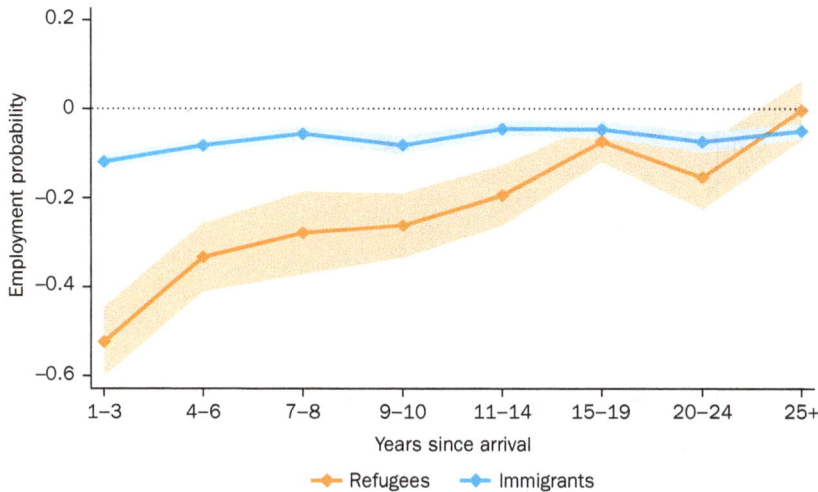

Source: Dustmann et al. 2016 based on 2008 European Union Labour Force Survey data. Reproduced with permission; further permission required for reuse.

Note: The figure displays gaps (together with 90 percent confidence intervals) in the employment probabilities of economic immigrants versus natives, and refugees versus natives, by years since arrival obtained from linear probability models that condition on gender, age (dummy variables for five-year age groups), education (dummy variables for lower-secondary and tertiary education), and host country fixed effects. The sample includes individuals ages 25–64 who are not in full-time education or military service.

United States—by years since arrival. In the EU refugees start with much lower initial employment rates than economic immigrants but subsequently experience much more rapid increases. In the United States, the rate of immigrant wage assimilation is positive but has slowed for more recent immigrant cohorts.

A pathway to permanence can facilitate economic integration

The process of integration and labor market assimilation can be costly and daunting to new immigrants. Adapting to a new work environment, creating a new social and cultural life, and overcoming linguistic barriers take time, effort, and financial resources. Integration requires that immigrants make culture-, employment-, and location-specific human capital investments. This process includes, but is not limited to, language acquisition, technical training, and cultural integration. Crucially, these

Figure 0.14   Immigrant wages converge to native wages, but at a slower rate for recent cohorts

Wage assimilation of immigrants in the United States

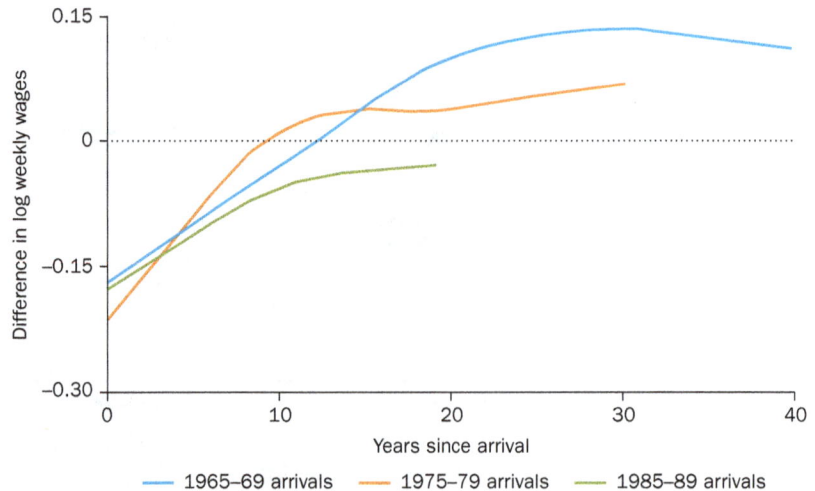

Source: Created using data from table 3-12 in National Academies of Sciences, Engineering, and Medicine 2017 for U.S. wage gaps.

Note: The figure shows U.S. wage gaps as a result of a regression of (log) wages on age (cubic), education, and years since migration, which were binned into groups (0–4, 10–14, 20–24, 30–34, and 40–44 years). Sample is of men, ages 25–64, using U.S. Decennial Census Public Use Microdata Series, 1970, 1980, 1990, 2000, and ACS (American Community Survey) Public Use Microdata Series, 2010–12.

investments depend on the duration of the stay that an immigrant intends in a host country. If immigrants intend to stay only a short time, then they may be reluctant to devote effort and other resources to host country–specific investments. For example, in many European countries, 50 percent of an arrival cohort leave the destination country within 10 years.

Certain destination countries actively discourage integration by providing no pathway to permanence. The motivation is that nonassimilated migrants are more likely to leave once their employment is concluded. However, many of these policies may end up harming the destination countries socially, culturally, and economically. Migrant workers never become fully proficient in their occupations because they remain uncertain about how long they will stay. Culturally and economically insulated immigrant communities, especially their youth, end up posing larger costs in the long run. These issues become especially problematic for immigrants with jobs that require longer-term commitment and specific investments by workers or their employers. The policy implication is that *countries should consider creating a clear path to permanent residency or even citizenship for migrants who obtain such permanent jobs.*

Together with their families, immigrants should have legally secure and protected residency and employment rights. Uncertainty leads to inefficiency and to even greater long-term costs for both the migrants and their employers in the destination countries.

Residency and employment security are especially important for high-skilled workers because their employment-specific investments tend to be very high. Fully aware of this, many destination countries give privileged legal status and priority to high-skilled immigrants. In contrast, low-skilled or undocumented immigrants face some of the greatest barriers to assimilation and integration. Undocumented immigrants and, in many countries, refugees are barred from participating in the formal labor market and enjoy only limited access to public benefits, such as education and health care. Their severely constrained ability to integrate in the host country and the risk of deportation further discourage their investment in host country–specific cultural and social capital. Figure O.15 depicts age-earnings profiles for native-born workers and for legal and undocumented immigrants in the United States. Strikingly, undocumented immigrants experience nearly no wage growth after age thirty, whereas native workers and documented immigrants experience earnings growth well into their forties.

Figure O.15   Wages of undocumented migrants stop increasing at a much younger age

Age-earnings profiles of natives and of immigrants, by legal status

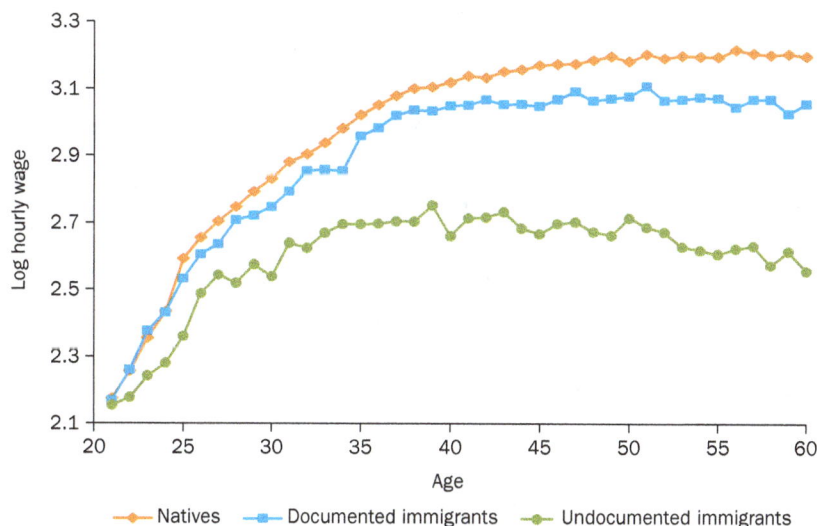

Source: Borjas 2017.

A particularly unfortunate situation is faced by almost half of the world's refugees who find themselves in a country that does not issue work permits to them. Denying the right to work can be detrimental to refugees' welfare and to the host country. As the refugees are absorbed exclusively into informal labor markets, they compete with and harm many of the most economically vulnerable native-born workers. Low-skilled workers, especially women, are most likely to be informally employed and, thus, experience the brunt of the labor market displacement and wage declines due to refugee inflows. The inability to work formally places an additional burden on public finances because of the lost tax revenue or higher welfare benefits that need to be provided to the unemployed native-born workers. Hence, *destination countries should consider granting work permits to allow gradual entry into their labor markets.* Issuing work permits is a politically sensitive topic in most destination countries, but it should be a part of the dialogue. Appropriate labor market insertion policies for the refugees, in short, help the most economically vulnerable natives, the refugees, and the public finances of the host country. And this suggestion is fully consistent with our earlier point that *governments should not fight labor markets but work with them.*

High returns from investing in immigrant children

An area in which immigrant assimilation and integration is particularly important is education. Immigrant students represent a large fraction of school children in a range of countries. Figure O.16 shows the share of 15-year-old students who have an immigrant background. Across Organisation for Economic Co-operation and Development (OECD) economies, 10 percent of students are first- or second-generation immigrants. Dubai has the highest share, with 70 percent.

Both immigrant children and host communities face numerous challenges when active integration policies are not in place in schools. Immigrant children may have limited knowledge of the local language. They are often of different religion and ethnicity than native-born children, and some have parents who are themselves poorly educated. The existing evidence shows that the presence of immigrant children may lower the quality of school education, resulting in lower test scores and higher dropout rates for both natives and migrants.

The policy implication of the existing research in the case of education is rather simple. *Governments should consider investing more heavily than they*

Figure 0.16 Immigrant children constitute a large share of the students in many economies

Share of 15-year-old students with immigrant background, 2012

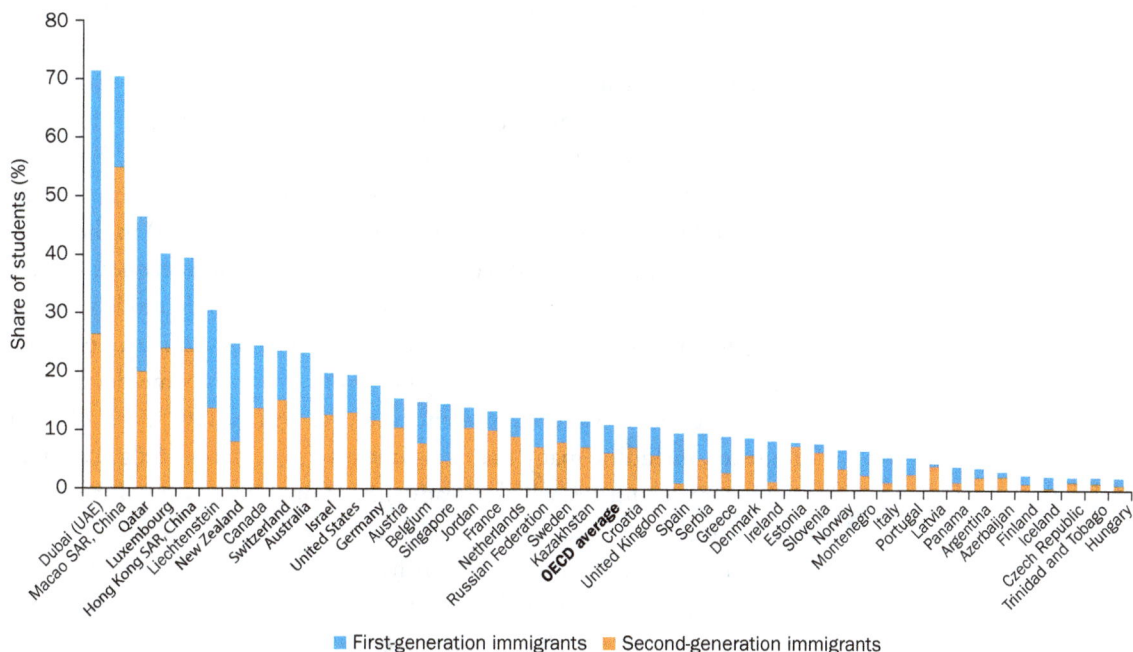

Source: OECD 2012. Reproduced with permission; further permission required for reuse.

Note: OECD = Organisation for Economic Co-operation and Development; UAE = United Arab Emirates.

currently do in integrating immigrant children in schools. Additional investment in schools with many immigrant children benefits both immigrant and native-born children. Such educational investment is possibly the cheapest way to mitigate potential negative spillovers on native classmates and, of course, guarantee the future social and economic success of the immigrant children. This policy answer could be especially important in high-income countries suffering from rapid aging and shrinking labor forces. In the long term these additional investments will pay for themselves. In the short term they could possibly be financed by a tax on immigrant workers as already discussed.

High-skilled migration, agglomeration, and brain drain

Although the arrival of large numbers of undocumented or low-skilled immigrants or refugees leads to much concern in destination countries, the exodus of high-skilled workers to high-income countries—sometimes referred to as brain drain—evokes similar emotions in source countries. This problem is especially severe in low-income countries with skill shortages.

Academic research has demonstrated that the skill composition of migration flows is as important as the overall number of migrants in determining labor market impacts in destination or source countries. But there is more to high-skilled workers and their emigration than simple wage effects, and that is why we devote a whole chapter (chapter 5) to the topic.

High-skilled workers play a central role in today's global economy. They are innovators, entrepreneurs, scientists, teachers, and role models for the next generations. They lead, coordinate, and manage activities of other high-skilled people in complex organizations. High-income destination countries depend on foreign talent to create and sustain many of their industries, including many that are at the forefront of knowledge creation. Low-income countries, which already suffer from human capital shortages, fear the impact of brain drain on their economic growth, public finances, and delivery of key services such as health care and education. It is not surprising that the global mobility of talent is a major policy concern entangling the gains from globalization as well as its pitfalls.

Over time, migration has become increasingly high skilled, presenting new challenges for both host and destination countries. In 1990, the first year for which we have comprehensive data, about 40 million labor-market-age (above age 25) migrants resided in the 27 high-income OECD countries. Migrants with a primary education made up almost half of the total stock, and those with tertiary education accounted for about 27 percent. In 2010, labor-market-age migrants numbered over 85 million, with tertiary-educated migrants accounting for about 43 million—close to 50 percent of the total.

The rapid increase in high-skilled immigration is due to the increase in both the supply of tertiary-educated workers across the world and the demand in OECD countries. Figure O.17 presents the shares of the tertiary educated in the labor forces (blue bars) in OECD and non-OECD countries since 1990. The orange bars show the share of tertiary educated among the emigrants from the same regions to the OECD countries over the same time periods. The patterns in this figure lead to several observations. First, the share of tertiary educated among all emigrants moving to OECD countries has been nearly triple that of the education level of the underlying labor forces in each decade. High-skilled workers are simply far

Figure 0.17 **Migrants and labor forces became more educated across the world**

Share of the high skilled among emigrants and labor forces, 1990–2010

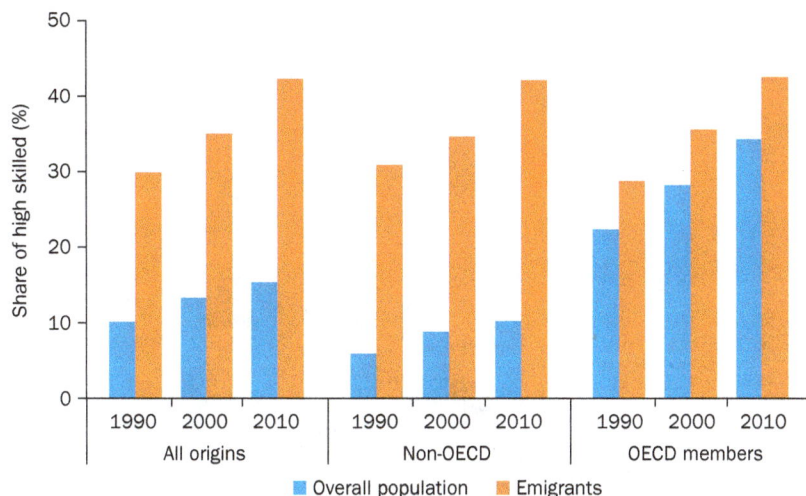

Sources: Migration data for 1990 and 2000 from Docquier, Marfouk, and Lowell 2007; data for 2000 and 2010 from the OECD Database on Immigrants in OECD and Non-OECD Countries (DIOC-E) for 2000/2001 and 2010/2011. Skilled population data from Barro and Lee 2013.

Note: "High skilled" includes those with partially completed tertiary education. Figure shows immigrants to 27 high-income Organisation for Economic Co-operation and Development (OECD) destination countries. Mexico and South Africa are treated as non-OECD origin countries.

more mobile, as shown earlier. Second, the massive increase in high-skilled immigration is driven primarily by the increase in the number of the high skilled in the world population. Since 1990, the share of the high skilled increased more than 60 percent in non-OECD countries. Third, quite remarkably, both OECD and non-OECD origin countries send similar shares of high-skilled migrants to OECD destination countries—over 40 percent as of 2010—despite the fact that the share of tertiary-educated individuals is three to four times higher in OECD countries. Still, it is the non-OECD countries that experience particularly high rates of high-skilled emigration.

The rapid increase in the share of high-skilled migrants, the skill selection, presents itself at the country level as well. Figure O.18 plots the share of the tertiary educated among immigrants, emigrants, and native-born populations for 2010, the latest year of data. The horizontal axis of the left and right panels presents the emigrant and immigrant skill rates, respectively.

Figure O.18 **Both emigrants and immigrants are more skilled than native-born workers in almost every origin and destination country**

Education levels of emigrants, immigrants, and natives, 2010

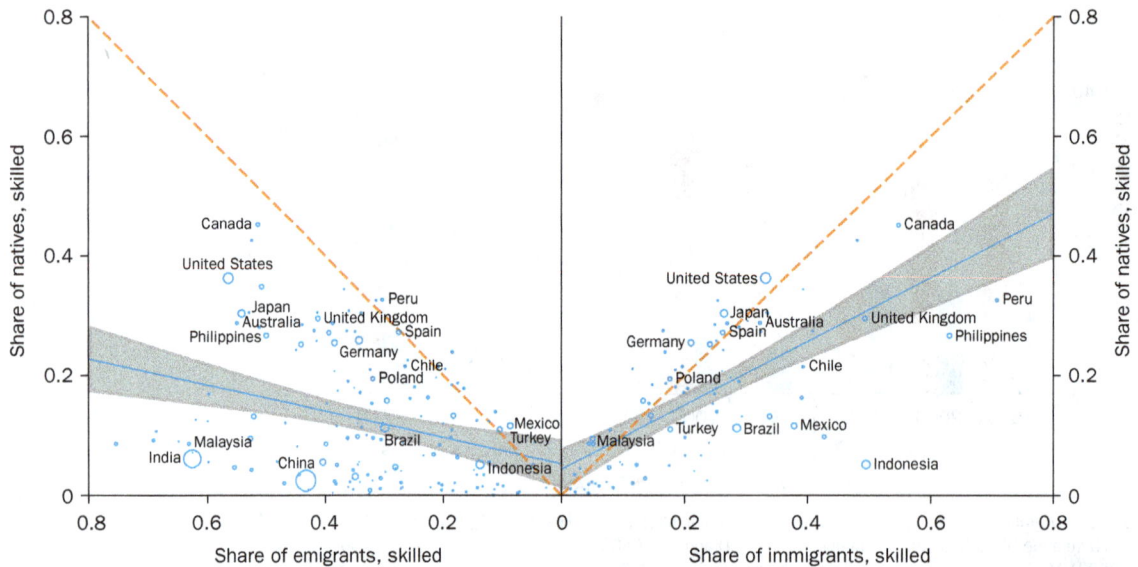

Sources: Migration data from the 2010/2011 OECD Database on Immigrants in OECD and Non-OECD Countries (DIOC-E). Skilled population data from Barro and Lee 2013.

Note: "Skilled" defined as the population with completed tertiary education; shares represent the skilled population divided by the overall population of interest. For the 88 destination countries included in the DIOC-E 2010/2011 dataset, natives' skill rates are calculated from the native-born population; for all other countries skill rates are calculated from the entire population using Barro and Lee 2013 data. Size of circles are scaled by (log) country population. In each panel, the dashed line is the 45-degree line, the blue line is the fitted regression line, and the gray area is the confidence interval around it. OECD = Organisation for Economic Co-operation and Development.

Education levels among the native born or non-migrants are on the left and right vertical axes. Observations below the dashed 45-degree line imply that emigrants (or immigrants) are more educated than the native-born workers. As can be seen, almost every country is below these lines, implying countries send and receive more educated migrants than they retain. Small and lower-income countries are especially exposed to this disproportional emigration of skilled workers. Only in the case of a number of high-income countries—including the United States—is the average immigrant slightly less skilled than the average native worker: these countries lie above the 45-degree line on the right panel.

The extent of concentration emerges even more prominently in the case of high-skilled immigrants who are concentrated in a few destination countries. Figure O.19 presents the cumulative distribution of migrants by skill level. The graph implies that the top 10 destination countries account for

Figure 0.19 High-skilled immigration is more concentrated than low-skilled immigration or emigration

Cumulative distribution of immigration and emigration, by skill level, 2000

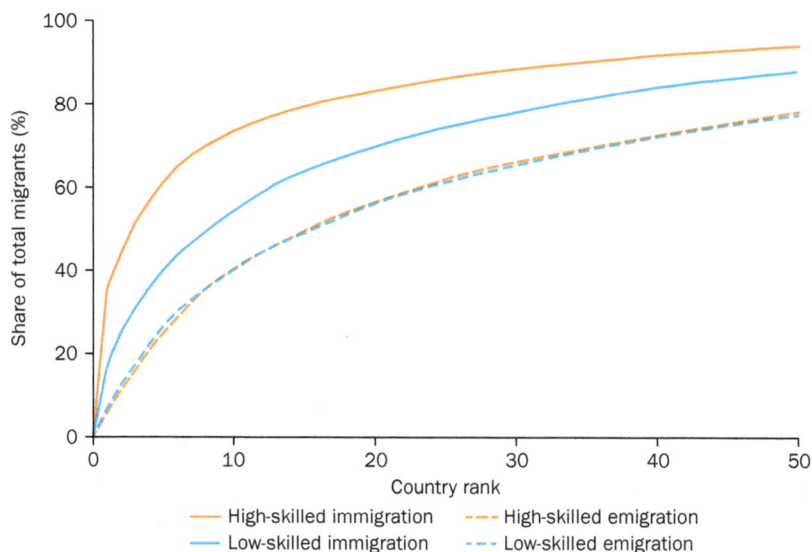

Source: Data from the World Bank Global Bilateral Migration Database (1960–2000).

Note: Countries ranked by size of corresponding population.

75 percent of the high-skilled immigrants in the world. Among these, four Anglo-Saxon destinations—Australia, Canada, the United Kingdom, and the United States—are home to almost two-thirds of all high-skilled migrants. No such concentration exists among source countries.

Economic factors again explain much of this variation in emigration and immigration patterns. Countries with higher returns to education and higher income levels—in other words, high-income OECD countries—attract more-skilled migrants. As an economy rewards education, the composition of immigrant inflows responds by becoming more skilled. Meanwhile, high-skilled migrants can more easily overcome physical distances, linguistic differences, and policy barriers.

Immigrants play an outsized role in contributing to key high-skilled activities. They are disproportionately employed in science, technology, engineering, and mathematics (STEM) fields, and as inventors and innovators. For example, migrants are responsible for about 10 percent of international patents filed under the Patent Cooperation Treaty. Looking across developed countries, figure O.20 shows that immigrants' share

Figure 0.20 Immigrants constitute a high share of inventors in many countries

Share of immigrants among inventors in OECD countries

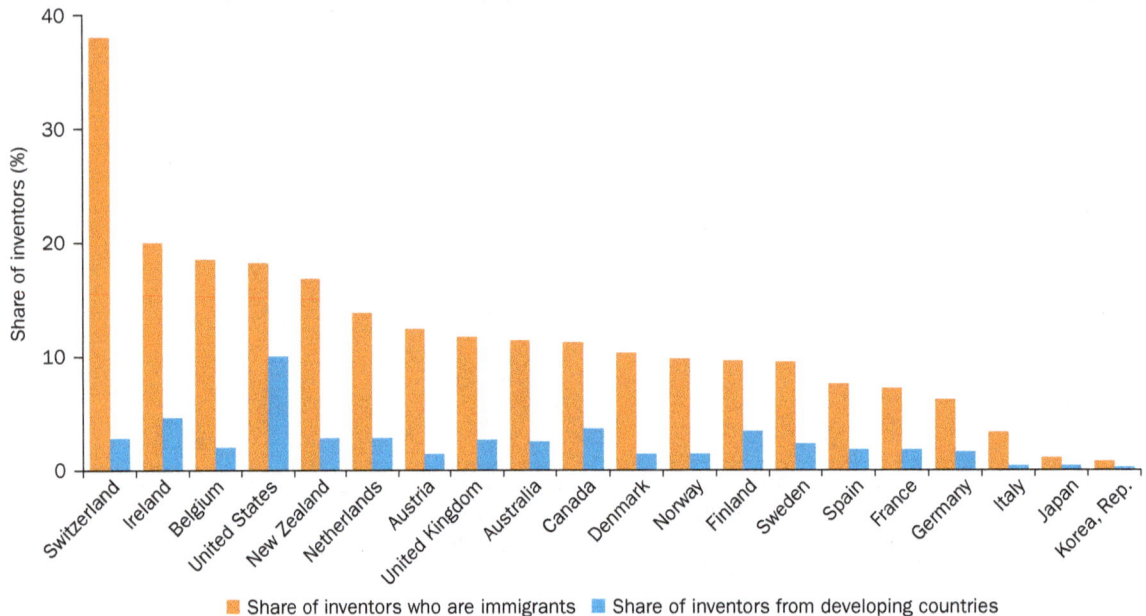

Source: Miguelez 2016, figure 2. Reproduced with permission; further permission required for reuse.

Note: Immigrants are identified via patents filed under the Patent Cooperation Treaty. OECD = Organisation for Economic Co-operation and Development.

among inventors is significantly higher than the overall share of immigrants in nearly every country. Furthermore, inventors from developing countries make up a relatively high share, especially in Canada and the United States.

Policies for high-skilled immigration

Across the globe, countries are increasingly adopting more skill-selective immigration policies that can typically be divided into two broad policy regimes. On one hand, demand-driven policies require that incoming migrants first acquire a job in the destination country. Migrants' almost-immediate employment is therefore prioritized, and potential employers and current labor market conditions play a key role in determining the sectoral and occupational composition of migrants. Supply-driven policies, on the other hand, require incoming migrants to be evaluated by a points-based system. Preference is given to those who possess more desirable labor market characteristics such as younger age, higher education, experience, occupation, and language proficiency. In these regimes, migrants generally obtain employment permits without an actual job offer. The assumption is that they will find employment after their arrival.

The trouble with supply-driven immigration schemes is that—as repeatedly emphasized in this overview—there is little evidence on what type of immigrant most benefits a host country. Personal characteristics—including motivation, creativity, entrepreneurship, and industry-specific knowledge—are difficult to observe but are essential in determining the success of a migrant in the labor market. The best indicator for the contribution of a migrant to the economy of a host country is the evaluation given by the labor market: a job offer. To repeat our previous point once more: *Governments should listen to the voice of labor markets in designing high-skilled immigration policies as well as general immigration policies. Demand- or employer-driven immigration programs, such as the U.S. H-1B, H-2A, and H-2B visas, are preferable over supply- or immigrant-driven point systems that allow for immigration without a job offer.*

The implication is not that different visa categories have no role but rather that governments should *not* try to micromanage work permits or try to guess which skills are more important. Instead, government policies should rely more on market mechanisms. If there are only a limited number of work permits available, the flexibility of an employer-driven scheme is preferable to a system based on hard-to-determine desirable immigrant characteristics. This is true for both high-skilled and low-skilled immigration schemes.

What about the impact on source countries?

Despite the issue's importance and the attention it receives, the evidence on the impact of high-skilled emigration is, however, quite inconclusive. Data constraints—the empirical difficulty of identifying the effects of skill shortages on poverty, growth, or other economic indicators—contribute to the challenge of determining high-skilled emigration's true costs or benefits. One solution is to combine global migration databases with macroeconomic models to simulate the impact of skill-biased emigration on poor countries. The results of this exercise are presented in figure O.21.

The critical determinant of the impact of high-skilled emigration is the extent of productivity spillover that the high skilled generate across the economy. If no such positive productivity spillovers exist, high-skilled

Figure 0.21 High-skilled emigration can hurt poor countries, but diaspora externalities can offset the negative impact

Effect of high-skilled emigration across source countries with different income levels

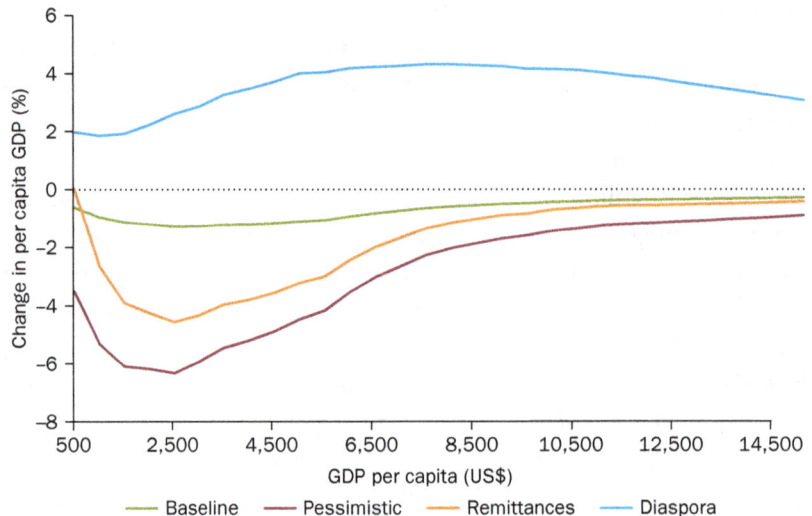

Source: Docquier 2017.

Note: The figure shows the effects of skill-biased emigration by GDP per capita for different channels (see text for more detail). GDP = gross domestic product.

emigration has a relatively small negative impact—about 1 percent—on income levels across the board (green line in figure O.21). In the presence of the spillovers, however, the impact can be quite severe—a decline of almost 6 percent—especially for those origin countries with per capita income levels below $3,000 (red line). Remittances sent back home (orange line) somewhat but not fully compensate for this loss.

One common response of origin countries is to restrict emigration, which brings up several important practical, economic objections to restricting emigration. First, all evidence suggests that high-skilled migrants might be less productive if prevented from migrating. Migrants—high and low skilled—experience huge income gains on migrating. A large part of what makes them productive is the work environment in the destination country. Without the potential income gains from migrating, it is unclear whether these migrants would have acquired these skills in the first place. Second, in practice, it is quite difficult to impose and enforce such mobility restrictions. The same way destination countries cannot seem to prevent entry, in the face of market forces, source countries cannot effectively prevent departure.

If governments cannot impede emigration, what should they do? Recent research highlights at least two promising ways to take advantage of the global market for high-skilled workers and ideas: *First, source countries of high-skilled migrants should engage with their diasporas, and maximize their externalities. Second, they can encourage return migration.*

Emigrants typically continue to be actively engaged—both socially and economically—with their home country. The most common economic engagement takes the form of remittances, which account for an important source of income for many families in developing countries. Diaspora engagement programs also attempt to connect investors and entrepreneurs abroad with investment opportunities at home, and foster the transfer of technology and knowledge from abroad. Promising evidence suggests that countries can successfully encourage the return of their high-skilled diaspora. The idea behind such programs is that it is valuable for people to emigrate and acquire skills abroad. Rather than preventing emigration, these programs seek to subsequently encourage the return of successful emigrants. An example of such a program is the Malaysian Returning Expert Program, which provides tax incentives to successful emigrants who return to Malaysia. The evidence suggests that the program is successful; it encourages more return migration and roughly pays for itself as the return migrants pay taxes (at, albeit, lower rates).

The simulations in the presence of such "brain gain" effects imply that such forces may compensate for the losses from high-skilled emigration and lead to overall economic gains (blue line in figure O.21). Nevertheless, we need to emphasize that the evidence on high-skilled emigration, its impact, and its implications are less than ideal. This is one area where new data and research are desperately and immediately needed.

International coordination of migration policy

The policy recommendations put forth in this overview are primarily described as unilateral policies, designed by the destination countries in most cases, with minimum input from or coordination with origin or other countries. The recommendations reflect the migration policies usually implemented independently by countries. However, we know from a wide range of areas such as international trade, finance, and security that many policies would greatly benefit from international cooperation. Unilateral policies, inherently, generate externalities on partner countries that can be internalized via cooperation and coordination.

Almost no multilateral frameworks exist for regulating economic migration. The main exception is very limited agreements concerning refugees. There are several important exceptions at the regional level, such as the regional labor mobility arrangements within the EU or East Asia. This lack of any multilateral design is in stark contrast to the international trade architecture or financial cooperation where international institutions (such as the World Trade Organization) have contributed to open borders, increase trade, coordinate monetary policies, and improve regulatory enforcement. The absence of formal and established cooperation and coordination between governments in the migration policy space leads to many inefficiencies, conflicts, and crises. Our last observation is that *there is an obvious need for policy coordination—whether at the bilateral, regional, or multilateral level.*

Final thoughts

The debate on the economics of migration needs both sides to be better listeners. Many economists, who believe in the virtue of open markets, are rightly focused on the efficiency gains that would be realized if labor were to move more freely. Despite the large range of estimates, the gains, especially those realized by the migrants, will be substantial—as evidenced by the wage gaps across markets. The mistake is to ignore the distributional impact and dislocation such flows would generate, especially in destination countries, as the efficiency gains are realized.

For those who oppose migration, the reverse is true. Their focus is on the distributional impacts of migration—mostly on migrants taking away jobs and lowering wages. They deny or ignore the significant efficiency gains—or the countless hundred dollar bills—that we are leaving on the sidewalk. Both sides have valid points, and both sides are looking for the solution in the wrong place.

The solutions—the policy measures—need to make the pie as large as possible and, *at the same time,* figure out a way to distribute it more equally. Such redistribution schemes need to include the winning and losing segments of the labor force not only in the destination countries but also in the source countries. This process requires coordination and forward thinking among policy makers. That is the only way we can establish *political* mechanisms to convert *economic* gains into reality. And, we need to add, these challenges are not unique to migration but apply to all other aspects of globalization—from trade to global warming to finance.

We are fully aware these are easy statements to make but daunting tasks to implement. We are hopeful that the analysis and the recommendations in this study will contribute to this process.

Notes

1. Refugees here refer to refugees and people in refugee-like situations as defined by the United Nations High Commissioner for Refugees (UNHCR).
2. Throughout this report we use World Bank regional definitions. Thus, for example, Mexico is considered part of Latin America and the Caribbean and not of North America. Please see table A.1 in the appendix for regional descriptions.
3. This negligible average impact is partially due to the fact that capital is assumed to be fully mobile and adjusts when labor levels increase. This assumption is supposed to represent long-run effects. In the opposite extreme, where there is no capital adjustment, all estimates in the graph would be reduced by about 3.2 percentage points.

References

Barro, R. J., and J. W. Lee. 2013. "A New Data Set of Educational Attainment in the World, 1950–2010." *Journal of Development Economics* 104 (C): 184–98.

Borjas, G. J. 2017. "The Earnings of Undocumented Immigrants." NBER Working Paper 23236, National Bureau of Economic Research, Cambridge, MA.

Docquier, F. 2017. "Note on High Skilled Emigration Externalities." Unpublished working paper, Université Catholique de Louvain, Belgium.

Docquier, F., A. Marfouk, and B. L. Lowell. 2007. "A Gendered Assessment of the Brain Drain." IZA Discussion Paper 3235, Institute for the Study of Labor, Bonn.

Dustmann, C., F. Fasani, T. Frattini, L. Minale, and U. Schönberg. 2016. "On the Economics and Politics of Refugee Migration." *Economic Policy* 32 (91): 497–550.

Dustmann, C., U. Schönberg, and J. Stuhler. 2016. "The Impact of Immigration: Why Do Studies Reach Such Different Results?" *Journal of Economic Perspectives* 30 (4): 31–56.

———. 2017. "Labor Supply Shocks, Native Wages, and the Adjustment of Local Employment." *Quarterly Journal of Economics* 132 (1): 435–83.

Gibson, J., D. McKenzie, H. Rohorua, and S. Stillman. 2018. "The Long-Term Impacts of International Migration: Evidence from a Lottery." *World Bank Economic Review* 32 (1): 127–47.

Massey, D. S., and K. A. Pren. 2012. "Unintended Consequences of U.S. Immigration Policy: Explaining the Post-1965 Surge from Latin America." *Population and Development Review* 38 (1): 1–29.

Mauri, M., T. Elli, G. Caviglia, G. Uboldi, and M. Azzi. 2017. "RAWGraphs: A Visualisation Platform to Create Open Outputs." Article no. 28 in *Proceedings of the 12th Biannual Conference on Italian SIGCHI*, Cagliari, Italy, September 18–20. New York: ACM.

McKenzie, D., S. Stillman, and J. Gibson. 2010. "How Important Is Selection? Experimental vs. Non-experimental Measures of the Income Gains from Migration." *Journal of the European Economic Association* 8 (4): 913–45.

Miguelez, E. 2016. "Inventor Diasporas and the Internationalization of Technology." Policy Research Working Paper 7619, World Bank, Washington, DC.

National Academies of Sciences, Engineering, and Medicine. 2017. *The Economic and Fiscal Consequences of Immigration*. Washington, DC: National Academies Press.

OECD (Organisation for Economic Co-operation and Development). 2012. *Untapped Skills: Realising the Potential of Immigrant Students*. Paris: OECD Publishing.

CHAPTER ONE

Patterns of Global Migration

Today's media headlines create a perception that the world is facing history's most severe migration and refugee crisis. Recent elections and referendums in several high-income Organisation for Economic Co-operation and Development (OECD) countries had migration as one of their leading issues. But what do the data tell us in terms of global migration patterns? Do the migration data support these concerns or suggest a different story? The goal of this chapter is to explore the main patterns of mobility within and across national borders and see how they fit the public perception. The highlighted patterns will be frequently revisited in the following chapters as we delve further into the underlying determinants that give rise to these patterns and as we examine their various impacts.

Migration data reveal a starkly different picture from the commonly held perceptions on global patterns. Since the 1960s, and the earliest collection of globally comparable and comprehensive data, international migration stocks have increased in absolute numbers but still represent a relatively small and stable share of the world population. This measure is in stark contrast to other commonly used indicators of global economic integration, such as international trade, foreign direct investment and capital flows, and number of tourists or international flights. These measures have risen steeply in both absolute and relative terms, whereas migration rates have remained relatively constant in an otherwise rapidly integrating world.

What has changed substantially over time is the *distribution* of migrants across regions of the world, not the total numbers of migrants. Western Europe, North America, and the oil-exporting Gulf Cooperation Council (GCC) countries[1] of the Middle East have become considerably more important as destinations—with the rest of the world losing relative importance. Similarly, the composition of origin countries has changed over the same time frame. It is this compositional change that has led to some of the most profound implications and subsequent political upheavals.

Immigration is now highly concentrated within a few destination countries, but emigration is much less concentrated. In 2010, the top 10 origin countries represented less than 40 percent of the world's emigrants, whereas the top 10 destination countries hosted over 60 percent of the world's immigrants. Since 1970, the number of migrant-sending countries has increased, but the concentration in a limited number of destination countries has remained unchanged.

The movements of refugees are different from those of economic migrants. Refugee flows result from military and civil conflicts, such as the wars in Afghanistan or in the Syrian Arab Republic. Consequently, the number of refugees is far more variable over time than the number of immigrants. Refugees tend to originate from a few conflict areas and reside mostly in neighboring countries and are, thus, far more concentrated than economic migrants.

Finally, a few characteristics of migrants are worth highlighting, especially in the context of labor markets. Migrants are more likely to be young, particularly working-age adults. Men and women tend to migrate in equal proportions. And more-educated people are more likely to migrate and to migrate farther. The main patterns of these characteristics are discussed in this chapter. The causes and implications of such patterns are presented in the following chapters.

Overall migration patterns

Global patterns

As of 2015, there were slightly more than 240 million migrants worldwide, an increase of over 70 percent from the 140 million migrants in 1990 and a 160 percent increase from the 90 million in 1960. Migrant stocks have grown steadily throughout the post–World War II period, at an average annual rate of 2.8 percent since 1990. Growth was strongest between 2000 and 2010, reaching an annual rate of 3.3 percent before declining to 1.9 percent per year between 2010 and 2015. (Please see the discussion of data issues in the appendix for data sources, definitions, and other details.)

Migrant stocks as a percentage of the global population have remained stable throughout this period. As seen in figure 1.1, migrants represented 2.7 percent of the global population in 1990 and 3.3 percent in 2015.

Figure 1.1   Global migrant stocks, 1960–2015

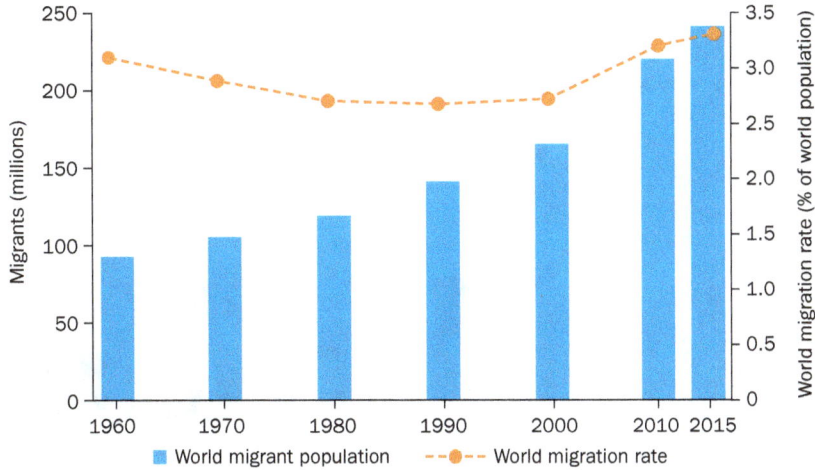

Sources: Data from the World Bank Global Bilateral Migration Database (1960–2000) and the United Nations Global Migration Database (2010–15). Population data from United Nations World Population Prospects.

This slow growth of the global migration-to-population ratio is because the number of migrants broadly rose in line with the world's population. In contrast, the volume of both international trade and capital flows grew exponentially, more than tripling between just 1990 and 2015 as a share of gross domestic product (GDP).

Regional patterns

Underneath the relatively stable global migration shares lie several critical patterns that dominate the overall landscape and shape the ongoing policy debate. The first striking pattern is that migrant stocks are heavily concentrated in several destination regions, especially in wealthier countries with labor shortages and relatively liberal immigration regimes. This concentration is to be expected because wage gaps and income gains are the primary pull factors that determine migration patterns, as will be discussed in greater detail in the following chapter.

Figure 1.2 presents the distribution of international migrants across destination regions. Two-thirds of the world's immigrants reside in North America, Western Europe, Eastern Europe, and high-income countries of the Middle East. The shares in most of these regions have been increasing rapidly since the 1970s. In 2010, almost a quarter of all international migrants were in Western Europe, another quarter in North America, and

Figure 1.2 Distribution of global migrant stocks, by destination region, 1970, 1990, and 2010

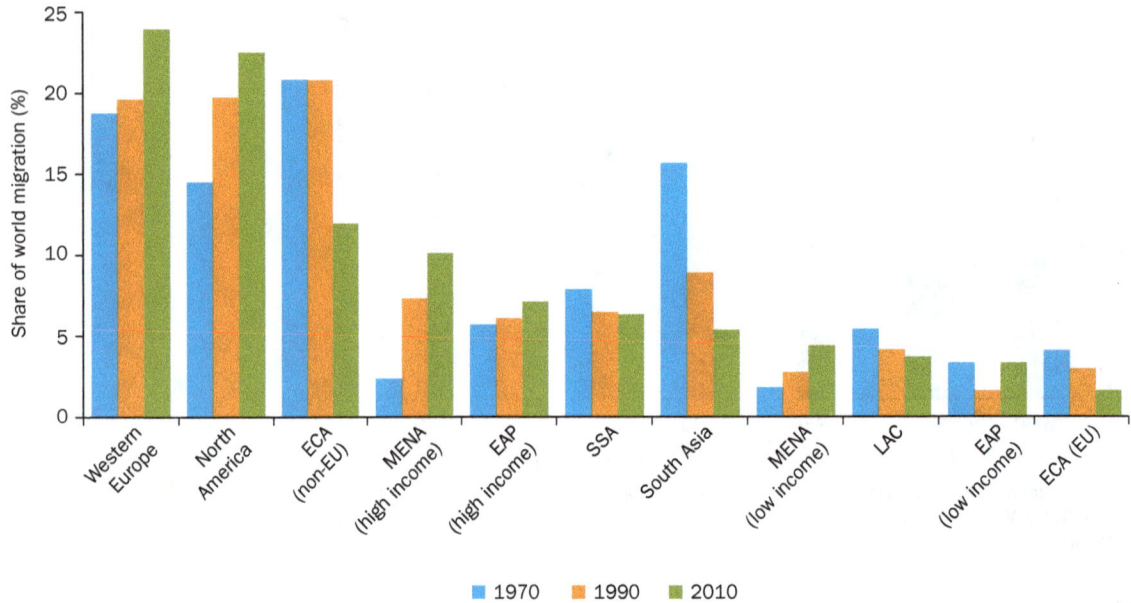

Sources: Data from the World Bank Global Bilateral Migration Database (1960–2000) and the United Nations Global Migration Database (2010–15).

Note: EAP = East Asia and Pacific; ECA = Eastern Europe and Central Asia; EU = European Union; LAC = Latin America and the Caribbean; MENA = Middle East and North Africa; SSA = Sub-Saharan Africa.

about 10 percent in high-income, oil-exporting Middle East and North African (MENA) countries. This concentration emerged alongside a shift in migration away from countries in Eastern Europe and Central Asia (ECA) and South Asia. Relatively large regions like Sub-Saharan Africa (SSA), Latin America and the Caribbean (LAC), and East Asia and Pacific (EAP) are notable for their smaller shares of global migrant stocks. These regions are home to 45 percent of the global population yet host only 15 percent of total migrant stocks.[2]

The increased concentration of immigrants in wealthier regions of the world implies that their share relative to the local populations of these areas has also increased rapidly. This pattern helps to explain the increased attention to the economic, social, and political ramifications of migration flows in these high-income regions. Figure 1.3 depicts immigrant-to-population shares by destination region. From 1970 to 2010, the high-income countries of Western Europe, North America, and the Middle East experienced substantial growth in their immigrant populations. The growth is especially striking for the oil-exporting GCC countries, which

Figure 1.3   Immigrant share of population, by region, 1970, 1990, and 2010

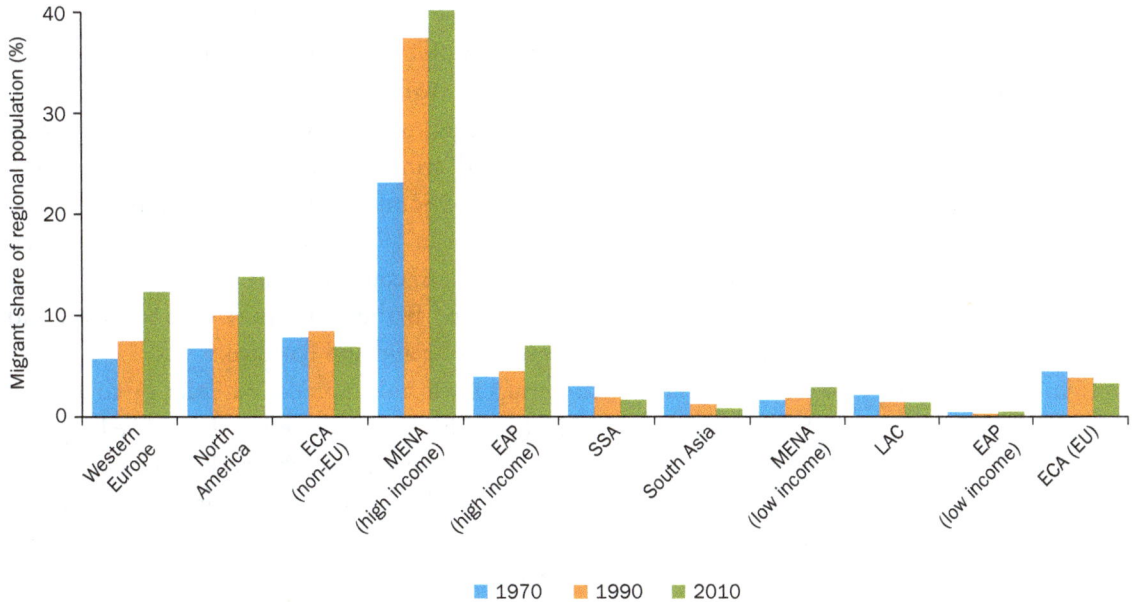

Sources: Data from the World Bank Global Bilateral Migration Database (1960–2000) and the United Nations Global Migration Database (2010–15). Population data from United Nations World Population Prospects.

Note: EAP = East Asia and Pacific; ECA = Eastern Europe and Central Asia; EU = European Union; LAC = Latin America and the Caribbean; MENA = Middle East and North Africa; SSA = Sub-Saharan Africa.

rely on large inflows of foreign labor as their economies have transformed and their income levels have risen rapidly. As of 2010, over 40 percent of the population in these countries was composed of immigrants, implying that there are, on average, two immigrants for every three native-born people. The immigrant-to-population ratio reaches over 75 percent in Kuwait, Qatar, and the United Arab Emirates, where three out of every four people are foreign born. North American and Western European countries have much lower immigration rates, at 14 and 12 percent, respectively. We should note that several high-income economies of the EAP region, such as Singapore and Hong Kong SAR, China, have also become hubs for immigrants in recent decades. The share of migrants in the total population reached 45 and 39 percent in Singapore and Hong Kong SAR, China, respectively, as of 2015. However, given the relatively small populations in these economies, the regional aggregates do not reflect their large shares.

Country-level patterns

Immigration and emigration rates vary significantly across countries and even within the same region. Map 1.1 depicts the emigrant-to-home population ratios by country in 1970 (panel a) and 2015 (panel b). Although fairly stable, emigrant-to-home population ratios have changed substantially in some parts of the world, with rapid increases in emigration rates in regions like South America and Southeast Asia. The result is a relatively more uniform map in 2015 than in 1970. Emigrants represent less than 10 percent of the population in most countries. The exceptions are mostly smaller countries like Antigua and Barbuda, Guyana, and Suriname and some wealthier countries such as Ireland and Portugal.

Map 1.2 shows the immigrant-to-total population ratios by country in 1970 (panel a) and 2015 (panel b). Over this period there have been evident shifts in immigrant-to-population ratios, with declines in some countries and significant increases in others. Strikingly, a handful of countries became significantly darker in the 2015 map. The emergence of the GCC countries as a hub for regional migration from 1970 to 2015—as mentioned in the previous section—is clear. Additionally, in Australia, Canada, and New Zealand, immigrants make up more than 20 percent of the population. In much of Western Europe and the United States, rates are more than 10 percent. However, immigrant-to-population ratios are significantly lower in most of the countries.

Bilateral patterns

Although many migrants still move within their own regions, the share of people moving outside of their region has been gradually increasing. Bilateral global migration data allow us to explore the role of specific migration corridors because we can analyze migrants' origins and destinations. Globalization has helped reduce mobility costs imposed by geographic distances through lower transportation and communication costs, allowing migrants to seek out destinations beyond their immediate neighboring countries. Still, about a third of total global migration remains intraregional, down from 56 percent in 1960, as seen in figure 1.4 (please see the appendix for further details on data).

The decline in intraregional mobility has occurred across almost all regions of the world, with South Asia experiencing a particularly large decline (see figure 1.5). Nearly all (90 percent) of emigration from

Map 1.1 Emigrant-to-home population ratio, 1970 and 2015

a. 1970

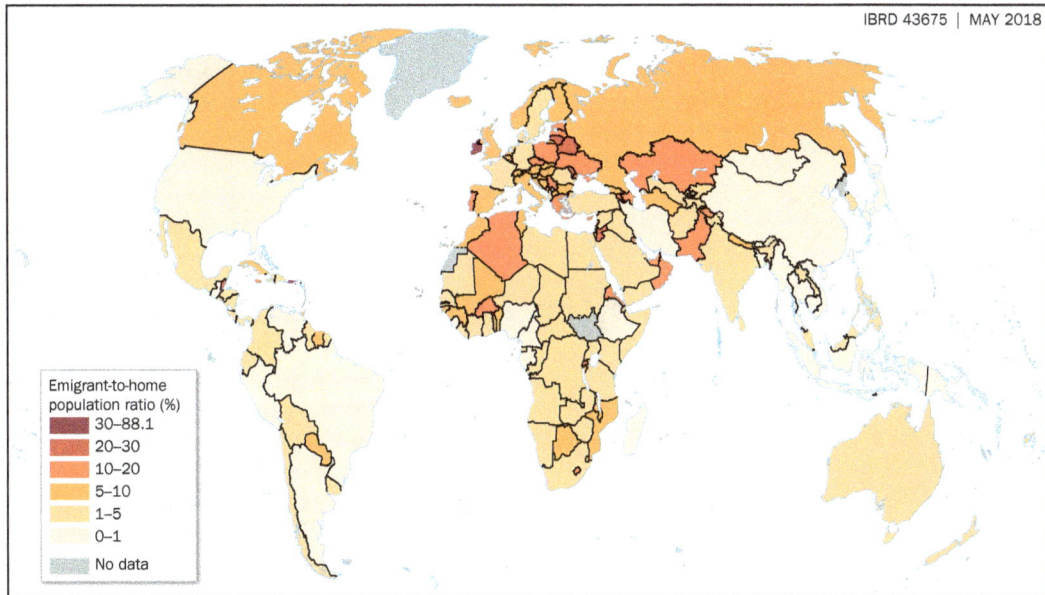

b. 2015

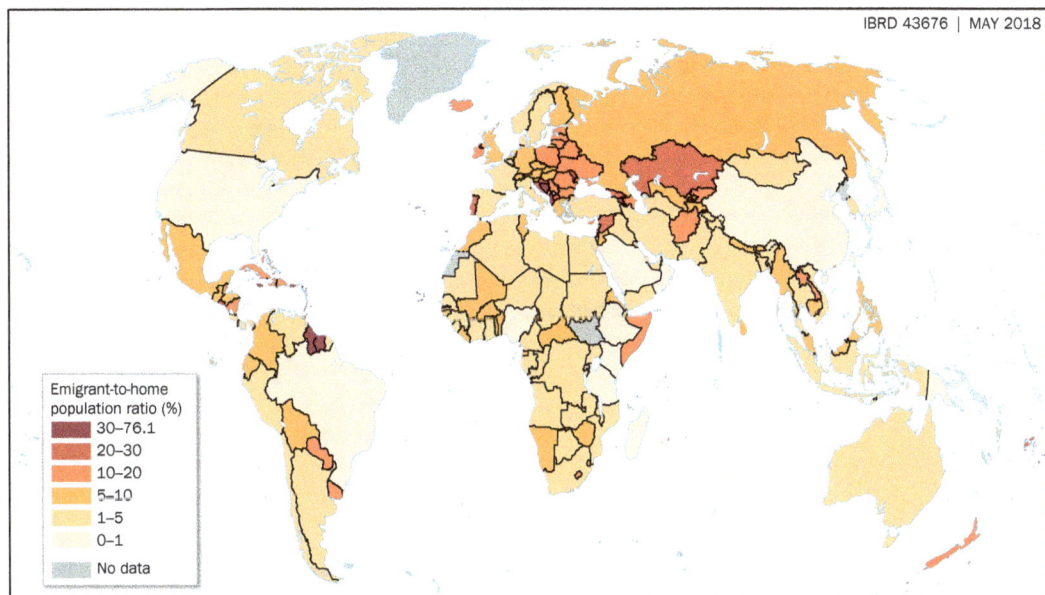

Sources: Data from the World Bank Global Bilateral Migration Database (1960–2000) and the United Nations Global Migration Database (2010–15). Population data from United Nations World Population Prospects.

Map 1.2 Immigrant-to-population ratio, 1970 and 2015

a. 1970

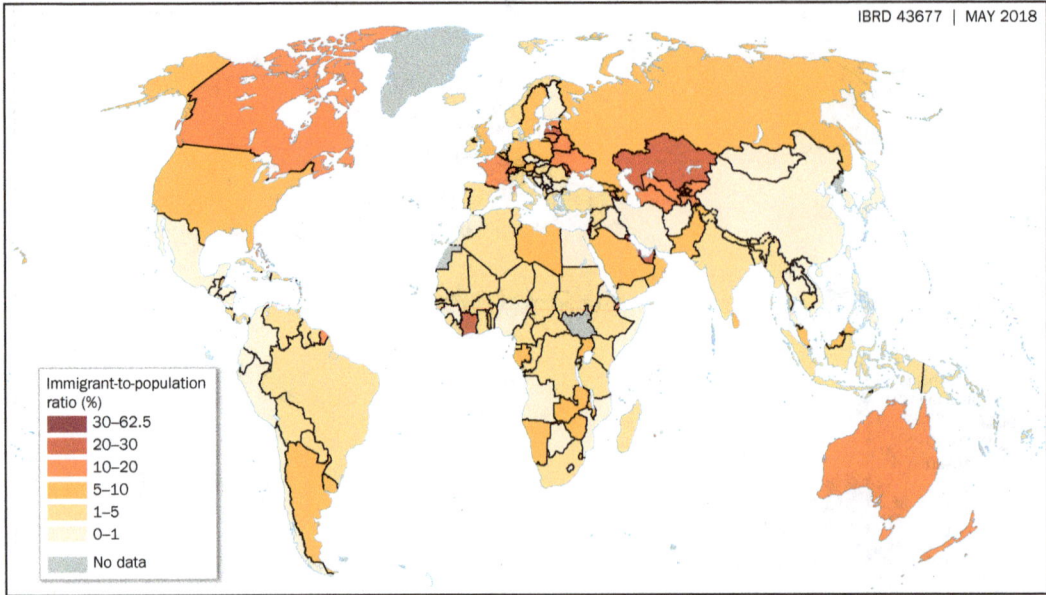

b. 2015

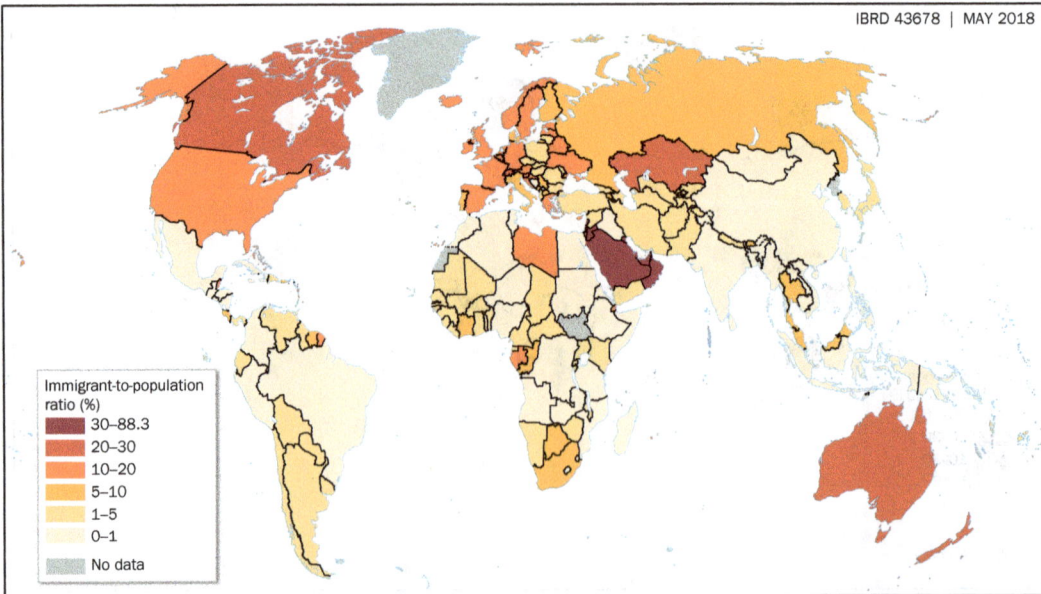

Sources: Data from the World Bank Global Bilateral Migration Database (1960–2000) and the United Nations Global Migration Database (2010–15). Population data from United Nations World Population Prospects.

Figure 1.4 Share of intraregional migration in total migration, 1960–2015

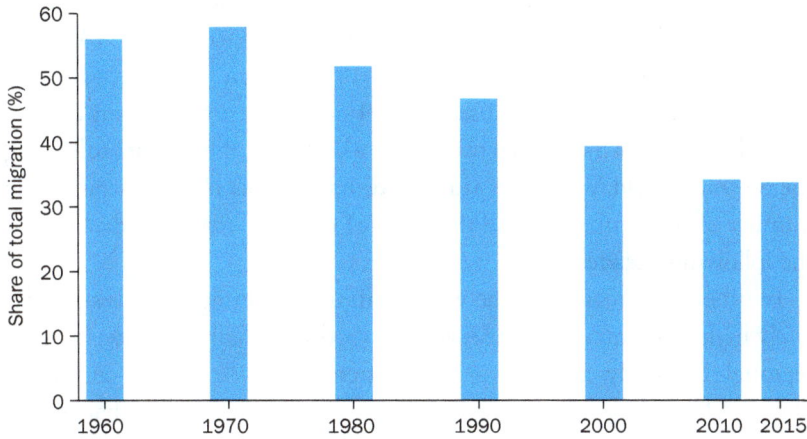

Sources: Data from the World Bank Global Bilateral Migration Database (1960–2000) and the United Nations Global Migration Database (2010–15).

Figure 1.5 Intraregional migration as a share of total emigration, by region, 1970, 1990, and 2010

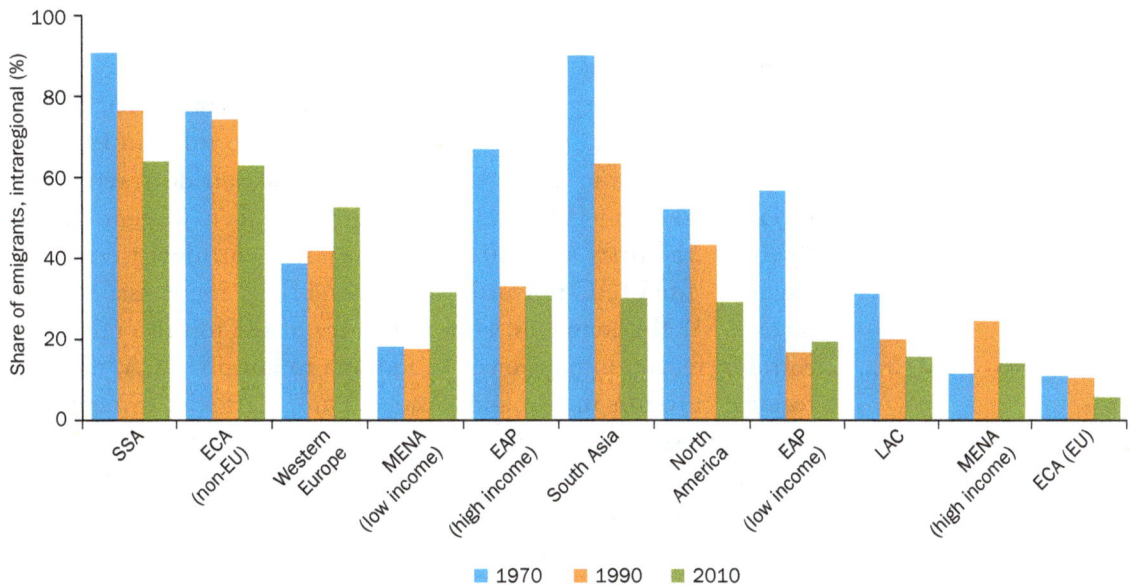

Sources: Data from the World Bank Global Bilateral Migration Database (1960–2000) and the United Nations Global Migration Database (2010–15).

Note: EAP = East Asia and Pacific; ECA = Eastern Europe and Central Asia; EU = European Union; LAC = Latin America and the Caribbean; MENA = Middle East and North Africa; SSA = Sub-Saharan Africa.

South Asian countries was intraregional in 1970, but the ratio declined to about a third in 2010. A significant share of this decline in regional mobility is due to the increased labor migration to high-income MENA countries, the United States, and the United Kingdom. Furthermore, the partition of India and the subsequent refugee flows are the main reasons behind the high intraregional migrant stocks during the decades following the Second World War. Over time, and mainly because of mortality, the number of these migrants and the share of regional migration declined in the following decades.

In other poor regions of the world, intraregional migration is still relatively high. For example, in SSA about two-thirds of all migration is intraregional. Similarly, about two-thirds of emigrants from non–European Union (EU) ECA countries migrate within the region. (A large share of the intraregional migration within the ECA region is also due to the dissolution of the Soviet Union and the overnight creation of new national borders.) As the sole exception, Western Europe's intraregional migration increased steadily between 1970 and 2010. This increase is in most part due to the free labor mobility provisions of the EU that allow people to move freely among the member countries. These flows are especially directed toward higher-income countries such as Germany, the Netherlands, and the United Kingdom.

Some of the top regional migration corridors are now between regions. Table 1.1 shows the 10 largest regional migration corridors in 1970 and 2015. In 1970, four of the five largest regional corridors were intraregional, led by non-EU ECA, then South Asia, then Western Europe. By 2015, the first- and third-largest regional corridors were extraregional—from LAC to North America and from South Asia to high-income MENA countries. However, three of the top five migration corridors remain intraregional. In addition to non-EU ECA, these are regional corridors in SSA and Western Europe. As with intraregional migration patterns overall, the five largest regional flows represent a shrinking share of total global migration, falling from about 55 percent in 1970 to less than 40 percent in 2015.

Figure 1.6 presents the magnitude of every migration corridor between regions in 2010. The thickness of the corridors corresponds to the size of the migrant stock from an origin region (on the left) to a destination region (on the right). In addition to displaying the sheer complexity of global migration, the figure provides many interesting insights into

Table 1.1 Top 10 regional migration corridors, 1970 and 2015

1970			2015		
Origin	Destination	Share of world migration (%)	Origin	Destination	Share of world migration (%)
ECA (non-EU)	ECA (non-EU)	18.76	LAC	North America	10.64
South Asia	South Asia	15.24	ECA (non-EU)	ECA (non-EU)	9.89
W. Europe	W. Europe	8.25	South Asia	MENA (high income)	6.67
SSA	SSA	6.34	SSA	SSA	6.18
W. Europe	North America	6.32	W. Europe	W. Europe	5.24
ECA (EU)	W. Europe	4.23	South Asia	South Asia	4.17
LAC	North America	3.10	ECA (non-EU)	W. Europe	4.04
ECA (non-EU)	ECA (EU)	2.79	ECA (EU)	W. Europe	3.94
W. Europe	LAC	2.71	EAP (low income)	EAP (high income)	3.73
EAP (low income)	EAP (low income)	2.43	EAP (low income)	North America	3.39

Sources: Data from the World Bank Global Bilateral Migration Database (1960–2000) and the United Nations Global Migration Database (2010–15).

Note: EAP = East Asia and Pacific; ECA = Eastern Europe and Central Asia; EU = European Union; LAC = Latin America and the Caribbean; MENA = Middle East and North Africa; SSA = Sub-Saharan Africa; W. Europe = Western Europe.

international migration patterns. First, as previously discussed, in most cases, the most common destinations for migrants from each region are countries in that region itself. Important exceptions are migrants from EU-member ECA countries traveling to Western Europe, migrants from Latin American countries traveling to North America, and migrants from South Asian countries traveling to high-income MENA countries. Additionally, there are very clear net importers and net exporters of international migrants. On the one hand, richer regions such as North America, Western Europe, and the high-income MENA countries attract many more migrants than they send. On the other hand, Latin American, South Asian, and low-income East Asian countries send many more migrants than they receive. For additional discussion of potential migrants, their destinations, and the determinants of their migration decisions, see box 1.1.

Figure 1.6 Region-to-region migration corridors, 2010

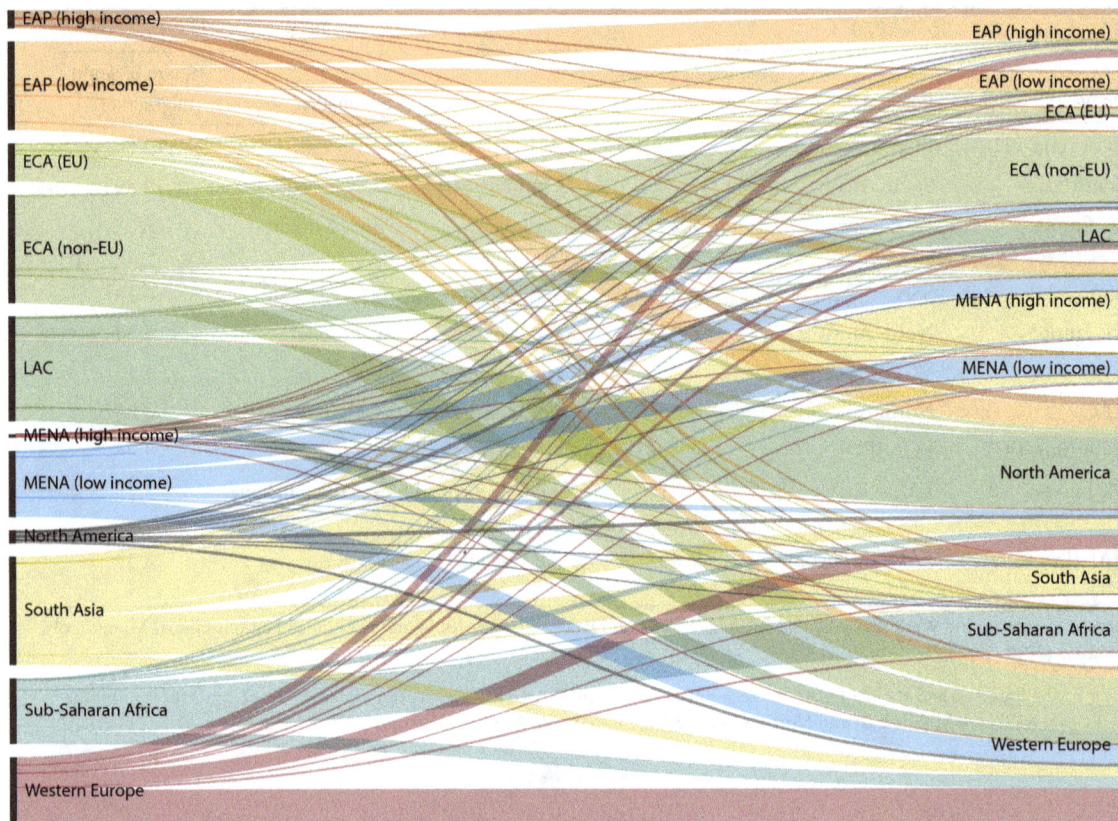

Source: Data from the United Nations Global Migration Database (2010–15). Figure made using RAWGraphs visualization platform (Mauri et al. 2017).

Note: EAP = East Asia and Pacific; ECA = Eastern Europe and Central Asia; EU = European Union; LAC = Latin America and the Caribbean; MENA = Middle East and North Africa; SSA = Sub-Saharan Africa.

Box 1.1   Potential migrants and the desire to move

The Gallup World Poll tries to identify potential migrants by asking respondents in over 150 countries whether they would like to move and, if so, to which country they would go. In surveys taken from 2010 to 2012, Gallup (2017) finds that 13 percent of the world's population would like to migrate but have not done so.

Table B1.1.1 presents the share of potential migrants by region. There is considerable heterogeneity across regions, and much of this variation can be explained by sharp differences in income. For example, 30 percent of the population of Sub-Saharan Africa would like to migrate to another country whereas, in the much richer North America

(continued)

Box 1.1   continued

Table B1.1.1   Potential migrants, by region

Region	Share of the population who would like to migrate, 2010–12 (%)
Sub-Saharan Africa	30
Europe (non-European Union)	21
European Union	20
Middle East and North Africa	19
Latin America and the Caribbean	18
North America	10
Australia/New Zealand/ Oceania	9
South Asia	8
East Asia	8
Southeast Asia	7
Global	13

Source: Gallup 2017.

Table B1.1.2   Top 10 destinations of potential migrants

Country	Share of all potential migrants (%)	Number (millions)
United States	21	147
Germany	6	39
Canada	5	36
United Kingdom	5	35
France	5	32
Australia	4	30
Saudi Arabia	3	25
Spain	3	20
Italy	2	15
Switzerland	2	13
Total	56	392

Source: Gallup 2017.

and Oceania (whose gross population is dominated by Australia and New Zealand), the share is 10 percent or less.

In terms of the most desired destinations, the economic motivations are even more evident. Table B1.1.2 presents the 10 most popular destinations of potential migrants. These top 10 destinations account for 392 million potential migrants, 56 percent of the total. Astonishingly, this is also nearly identical to the share of actual migrants who reside in the world's top 10 destinations (see figure 1.7). Of these destinations, nine are the largest of the high-income western countries. The last, Saudi Arabia, is the largest of the high-income Middle East and North African countries, a popular destination for migrants from South and Southeast Asia.

The concentration of economic migrants

This section digs deeper into the distribution of migrants across origins, destinations, and corridors discussed in the previous section. Global patterns are defined by three facts. First, migration is highly concentrated by destinations as compared to origins, with the concentration remaining relatively constant over time. Second, migrants are now coming from a broader base of origin countries, potentially because globalization and reduced travel costs have made migration a viable option for many more people. Finally, migrants have become less concentrated by corridor, with the largest migration corridors making up a smaller share of the migrant population than ever before.

Concentration by country

Figure 1.7 shows the cumulative distribution of migrants across destination and origin countries, ranked by the size of the migrant population. We construct these figures by ranking the destination (or origin) countries by the number of migrants they receive (or send) and then adding them up as we go down the list. A steeper curve implies more concentration because it takes fewer countries to reach a certain percentage of migration. For example, the 1990 emigration line indicates that the 10 largest migrant-supplying countries in 1990 account for 40 percent of all migrants.

Figure 1.7   Cumulative distribution of global migration, 1970, 1990, and 2010

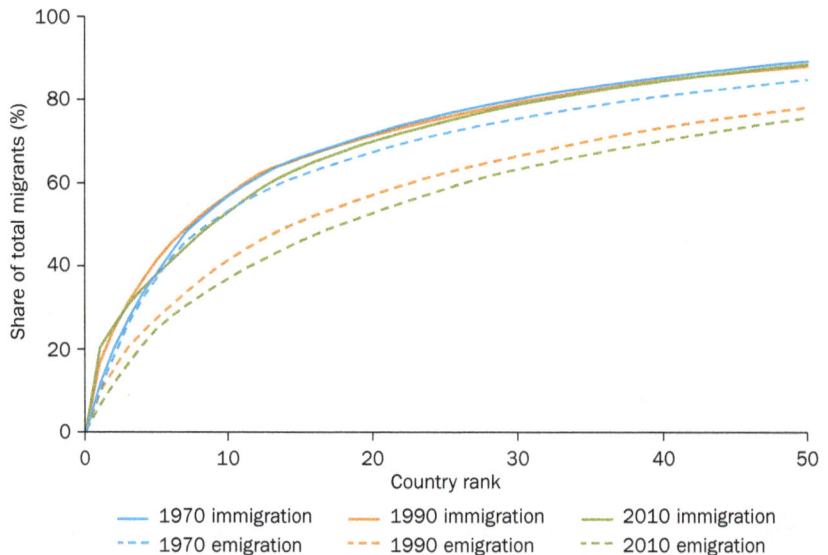

Sources: Data from the World Bank Global Bilateral Migration Database (1960–2000) and the United Nations Global Migration Database (2010–15).

Note: Countries in a given year are ranked by size of their corresponding emigrant or immigrant population.

Immigration is highly concentrated, with the top 10 destination countries representing almost 60 percent of all immigration in the world. This pattern has been relatively constant across time with immigration becoming neither more nor less concentrated from 1970 to 2010.

In every decade, emigration is less concentrated than immigration, and emigration has become even more dispersed over time. More origin countries have become responsible for a larger share of emigration than they were in the past. By 2010, the top 10 origin countries represented less than 40 percent of worldwide emigrants.

A similar pattern plays out within regions. One or two destinations are hubs for intraregional migration, as seen in figure 1.8. This is particularly true for the low-income countries of EAP, among which Thailand receives 62 percent of all intraregional migrants. In South Asia, India receives 52 percent of intraregional migrants. Among the low-income MENA countries (that is, when we exclude the oil-exporting GCC countries), Jordan receives half of intraregional migrants. The Russian Federation is a hub for non-EU Eastern Europe, as are Argentina for Latin America and France and Germany for Western Europe.

Figure 1.8 **Share of intraregional migration of the top destination in each region, 2010**

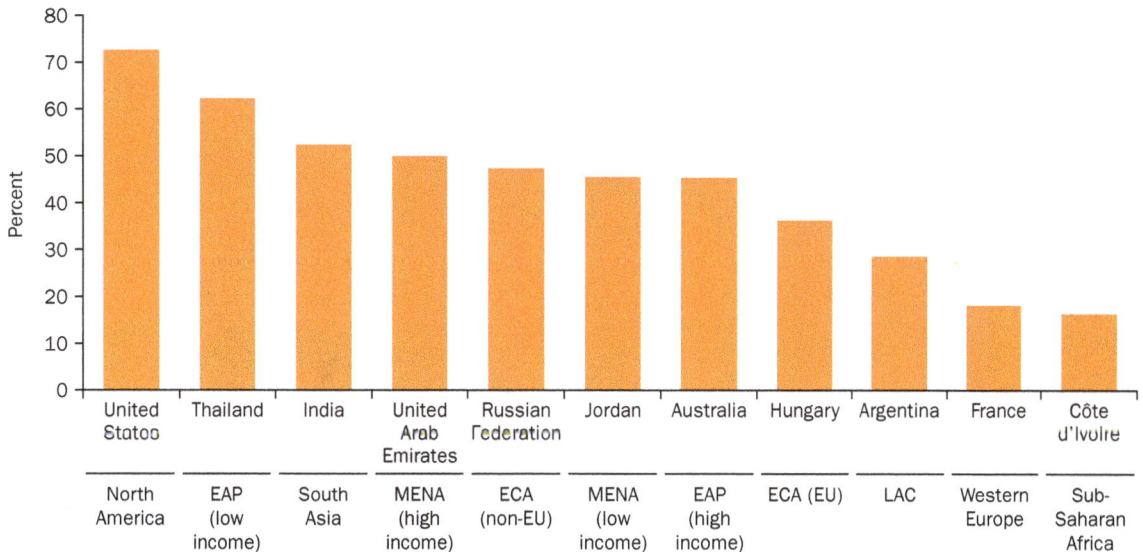

Source: Data from the United Nations Global Migration Database (2010–15).

Note: EAP = East Asia and Pacific; ECA = Eastern Europe and Central Asia; EU = European Union; LAC = Latin America and the Caribbean; MENA = Middle East and North African.

Concentration by corridor

The concentration of migration is even more apparent when we look at bilateral migration corridors. Only about 300 (of the more than 40,000 possible) corridors[3] account for three-quarters of all migrant stock in the world as of 2010.

Like figure 1.7, figure 1.9 also depicts the cumulative share of global migration, but now by individual corridors. The corridors are ranked according to their size, so we can identify the share of global migration in the top 10 (or 20 or 100) corridors. The graph indicates that the top 50 corridors accounted for 40 percent of global migration in 2010. Chapter 2 of this report discusses in detail the reason why particular migration corridors exist with such highly concentrated migration flows. Over time, however, the concentration curve gradually shifts down, indicating that the importance of individual corridors has somewhat diminished as migration has become more dispersed. For example, although the top 300 corridors accounted for 84 percent of global migration in 1970, they accounted for 73 percent in 2010.

Which corridors enter the top 10 list changes over time. Figure 1.10 lists the 10 largest migration corridors in the world in 1970, 1990, and 2010.

Figure 1.9 **Cumulative distribution of global migration, by corridor, 1970, 1990, and 2010**

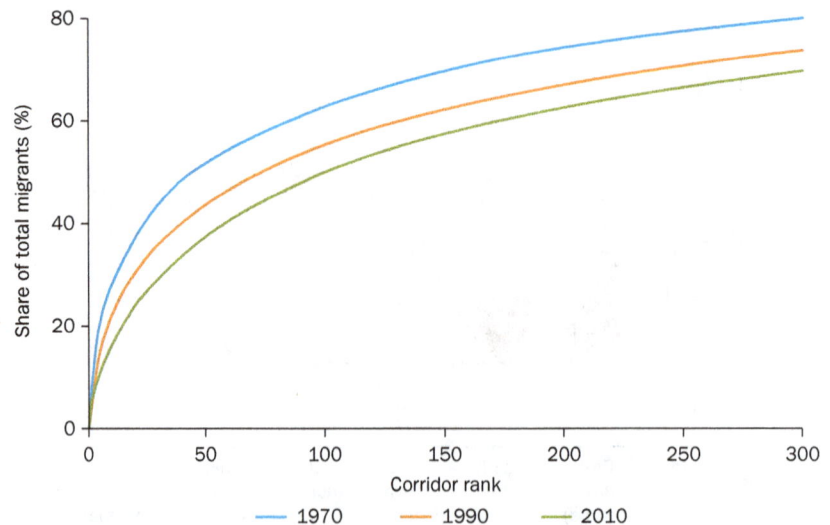

Sources: Data from the World Bank Global Bilateral Migration Database (1960–2000) and the United Nations Global Migration Database (2010–15).

Note: Corridors are ranked by the number of migrants in a given corridor.

Figure 1.10 Top 10 bilateral migration corridors, 1970, 1990, and 2010

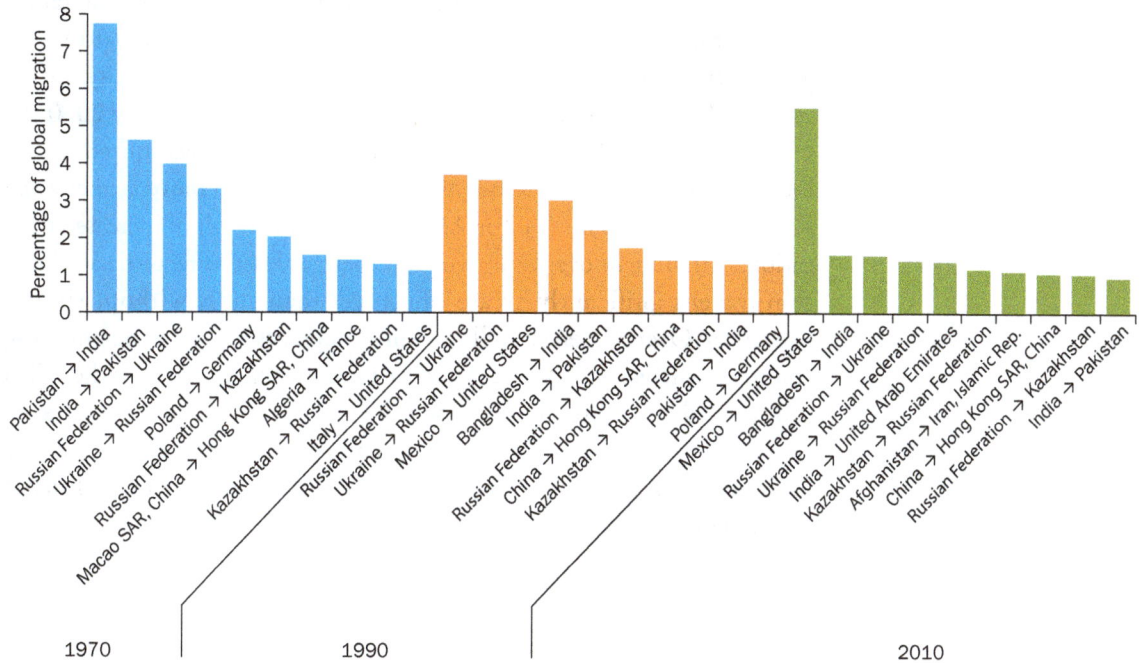

Sources: Data from the World Bank Global Bilateral Migration Database (1960–2000) and the United Nations Global Migration Database (2010–15).

In 1970, the mass migration resulting from the partition of India in 1947 and the internal movements within the Soviet Union shaped the largest migration corridors. Since then, economic forces have changed the composition of the list. Most notably, migration from Mexico to the United States grew from the world's 19th-most important corridor in 1970, when it represented less than 1 percent of global migration, to the largest corridor in 2010, when it represented 6 percent of all migration. Several of the new corridors include nontraditional receiving countries, such as the flows from India to Saudi Arabia, from Myanmar to Thailand, and from Afghanistan to Pakistan.

The largest corridors in the world now contribute less to the global migrant stock than ever before. Although the top corridors are still represented by neighboring countries, western destinations receiving migrants from more distant countries have grown in importance. The United States is the destination for five of the 11th- to 25th-largest corridors (the origins are India, China, the Philippines, Puerto Rico, and Vietnam). Turkey to Germany and Algeria to France are the 19th- and 21st-largest corridors, respectively.

Looking at the distribution of migrants by distance helps to visualize this change. Figure 1.11 shows the cumulative distribution of migration across time periods, and figure 1.12 shows the distribution across skill groups. In 1970, more than half of migrants migrated to a neighboring country. In 1990, this share had declined to 47 percent, and by 2010 the number was below 40 percent. Over time, the curve has shifted down, indicating that a larger number of migrants manage to move farther away from their home countries. Part of this trend is the result of increased educational attainment over time. Migrants with at least some tertiary education travel significantly greater distances than those without similar education. Over 50 percent of low-skilled migrants resided in neighboring countries whereas just over 20 percent of high-skilled migrants did. This shift toward more distant migration explains much of the changing trends seen in concentration in terms of destinations and corridors. The increase in dispersion across migration corridors is overwhelmingly toward richer and more distant countries.

Figure 1.11 Cumulative distribution of global migration, by distance, 1970, 1990, and 2010

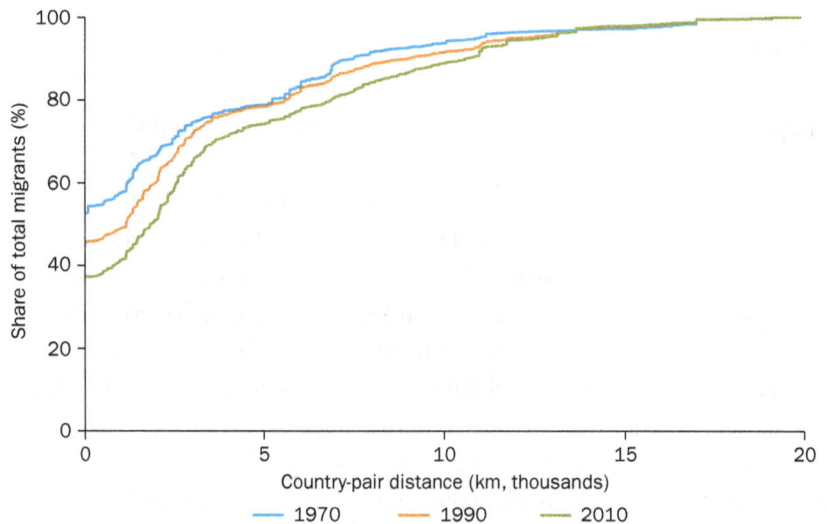

Sources: Data from the World Bank Global Bilateral Migration Database (1960–2000) and the United Nations Global Migration Database (2010–15).

Note: Distance is measured as distance between the two most populous cities, using data from the CEPII GeoDist database. Contiguous countries are treated as zero distance.

Figure 1.12   Cumulative distribution of global migration, by distance and skill, 2000

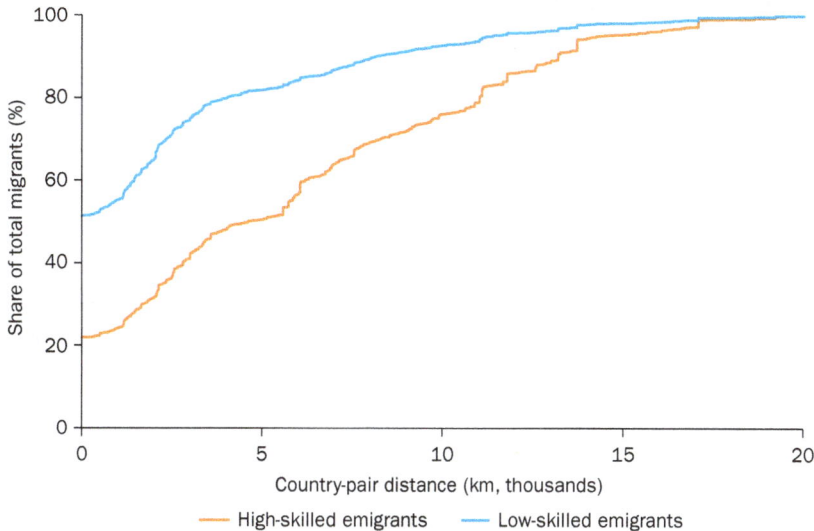

Sources: Figure uses year 2000 migrant stocks from the World Bank Global Bilateral Migration Database (1960–2000). Distance and contiguity data derived from the CEPII GeoDist database.

Note: Distance is defined as distance between two most populous cities, and contiguous countries are treated as zero distance. The cumulative distribution function plots the share of all international migrants who reside in a country less than or equal to a given distance from their home country.

Internal migration

In addition to moving across international borders, people in search of a more prosperous and secure life may also move across regions *within* the same country. Internal migration is often preferable to international migration because it costs less, requires overcoming fewer legal and policy barriers, and may offer better returns to human capital given knowledge of the local language and cultural norms. In this section, we will discuss the difficulties in the measurement of internal migration, describe basic trends over time and across countries, and present the main findings from a few of the world's larger countries.

Measuring internal migration

Measuring and comparing internal migration rates are challenging. In the case of international migration, country borders provide a simple definition of a move. In contrast, multiple levels of administrative divisions generally make it difficult to compare internal migration in one country with that in another. For example, moving across districts within Uttar Pradesh in India might be more difficult than moving across Belgium. Defining internal migration depends on the question at hand and the availability of data. For example, when studying the mobility of labor, a primary interest for many migration economists, internal migration would ideally be defined as movement from one labor market to another; simply moving from one residence to another within the same labor market is not enough.

The definition of a labor market within a country depends also on data availability. National censuses often divide the country into administrative divisions. However, these divisions will not perfectly align with labor markets, and researchers will often have to make a judgment call based on the specifics of their research question in the country of interest. China, for example, could be divided by province, prefecture, or county, which would result in 33, or 333, or 1,464 zones, respectively. In the case of the United States, one could use states, metropolitan areas, counties, or commuting zones, among others. In some cases, the borders or number of zones can change over time.

Another challenge is that administrative divisions might not be comparable across countries. The size and number of zones vary significantly, and thus comparing migration rates can be very misleading. When we make comparisons across countries, should we look at a similar number of zones relative to landmass, or to population, or to some combination of both? In most cases, data availability will dictate the decisions. In other cases, researchers must rely on their expert knowledge of the question and countries at hand.

Table 1.2 Internal migration rates, by number of zones

Country	Number of zones	Five-year internal migration intensity, 2000	Corgeau's k-statistic
Brazil	5	2.2	0.65
	27	3.4	
	1,520	10.0	
Canada	11	3.4	0.99
	288	12.5	
	5,600	16.6	
China	31	2.7	0.53
	347	6.7	
United States	4	4.8	1.22
	9	6.6	
	51	8.9	

Source: Based on Bell and Charles-Edwards 2013, using data from individual country censuses for 70 different countries.

Table 1.2 depicts—for Brazil, Canada, China, and the United States—
five-year internal migration rates, measured as the share of the population
who moved to a different region within the last five years, using several
geographic divisions. Comparing migration rates can be difficult.
Fortunately, in our example, each country has a similar landmass; however,
China is nearly 40 times more densely populated than Canada, with the
others in between. One attempt to make the migration rate consistent
across countries is Corgeau's k-statistic (Corgeau 1973). This statistic relies
on the idea that the migration propensity measured depends on the number of zones. Specifically, the more zones in a country, the more migrations
will be recorded. Corgeau's k-statistic attempts to adjust for this by measuring the variation in migration intensities for different levels of division in
the same country. This k-statistic suggests that the United States experiences the most internal migration, followed by Canada. The internal migration rate in Brazil is about half that in the United States, and the rate is
lower still in China.

Global patterns in internal migration

The Internal Migration Around the Globe (IMAGE) database collects
internal migration data for over 150 countries. Table 1.3, based on data
from Bell and Charles-Edwards (2013), presents five-year and lifetime
internal migration rates across regions for countries in which data are available. More-developed European, North American, and Oceanic countries
exhibit the highest internal migration rates, significantly more than the

Table 1.3   Internal migration rates, by region

Region	Five-year migration rates			Lifetime migration rates		
	Migrants (millions)	Intensity (%)	Number of countries	Migrants (millions)	Intensity (%)	Number of countries
Africa	39.7	4.6	4	113.5	12.5	13
Asia	109.8	2.9	10	282.1	7.2	14
Europe	34.8	5.0	3	166.0	22.7	10
Latin America and the Caribbean	21.9	4.1	16	100.2	18.0	23
North America	21.2	6.8	3	91.5	27.8	6
Oceania	1.8	5.7	3	9.3	29.4	5
Global	229.2	3.7	39	762.6	11.7	66

Source: Based on Bell and Charles-Edwards 2013, using data from individual country censuses for 70 different countries.

less-developed African, Asian, and LAC countries. Looking at five-year transition rates, Asia has especially low internal migration rates, with an average of 2.9 percent, whereas North America (Canada, Mexico, and the United States) has the highest, at 6.8 percent. Identical patterns across regions arise when looking at lifetime migrant stock, which is defined as the share of the population who live in a region different from the one in which they were born.

Internal migration generally flows from poor and rural areas to wealthier urban hubs, which mirrors the patterns of international migration. Figure 1.13 depicts urbanization rates by country income level and individually for Brazil, China, India, and Indonesia over time. Wealthier countries are more urbanized than poorer countries: economic growth and urbanization go together. Over time in practically all countries, rural areas have continued to fall in importance with people continuing to move to urban conurbations. China, for example, experienced a net rural-to-urban migration of 7.9 million people per year from 1978 to 1999, accounting for 75 percent of the growth in the urban population over the same period (Zhang and Song 2003). India, one of the least mobile developing countries, still exhibits substantial migration from less-developed, rural states such as Bihar, Rajasthan, and Uttar Pradesh to more developed, urban destinations such as Delhi, Gujarat, and Maharashtra (Abbas and Varma 2014).

Figure 1.13   Urbanization, 1960–2015

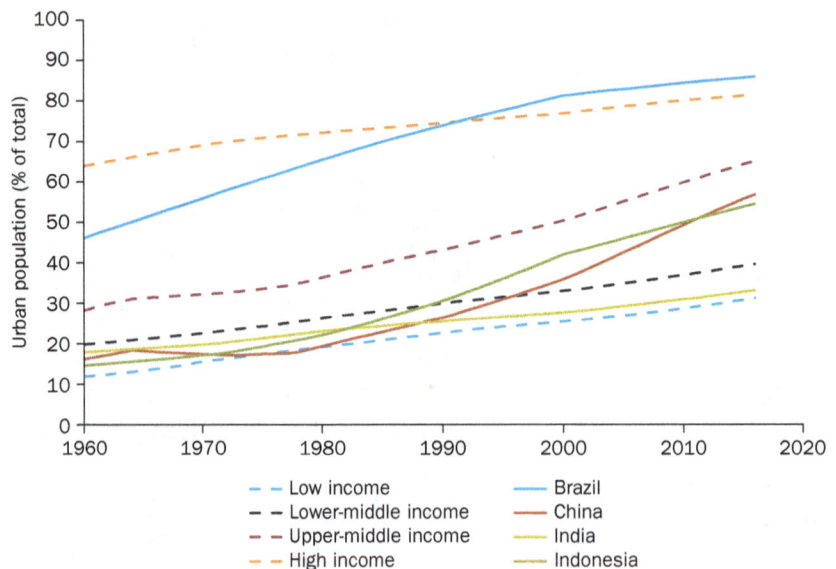

Source: World Bank DataBank.

Refugees

Global refugee patterns

Refugee crises capture much of the attention in the debate on migration, to the extent that refugee crises and migration problems become synonymous. Figure 1.14 presents the global stock of refugees over time: data indicate that total refugee stocks are at a 20-year high. There were about 15 million refugees[4] in 2015, an increase of about 50 percent from 2004 and the highest level since 1995. Worldwide refugee stocks are more volatile than the number of economic migrants because refugee flows arise from political crises, civil conflict, and war. Analyzing figure 1.14 more carefully, we see that refugee stocks peaked in 1990 and declined steadily until 2005, when they reached 8.7 million. Since 2005, however, refugee numbers have increased, with two spikes. The first spike, between 2006 and 2007, is due to conflicts in Iraq and Afghanistan and armed conflict in Colombia. The second spike, between 2013 and 2015, is due to the civil war in Syria and conflict in South Sudan.

As a share of the total migrant stock, refugees dramatically increased in importance from 1960 to 1990, from under 2 percent to about 12 percent. Since that time, the importance of refugees has decreased, plausibly as the world became a more peaceful place, to a low of 5 percent in 2010. The war in Syria has brought renewed attention to the plight of refugees, and, together

Figure 1.14   Global refugee stocks, 1960–2015

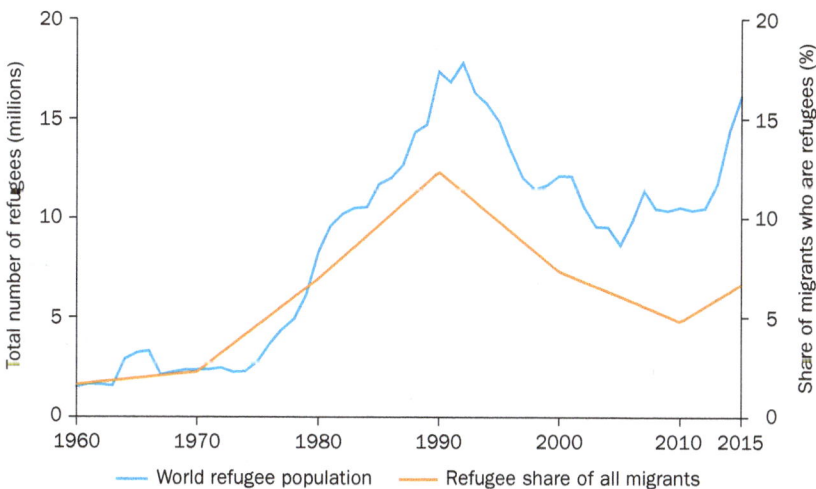

Sources: Refugee data from UNHCR Population Statistics Database. Migration data from the World Bank Global Bilateral Migration Database (1960–2000) and the United Nations Global Migration Database (2010–15).

Note: UNHCR = United Nations High Commissioner for Refugees.

with the increase in the absolute number of refugees, the share has increased to nearly 7 percent.

Regional refugee patterns

Regional refugee trends generally depend on individual crises. Figure 1.15 presents the share of immigrants who are refugees by region and over time. The share of refugees as a percentage of migrants declined or remained constant in all regions of the world between 2000 and 2010, except in LAC, where civil conflict in Colombia led to a spike. From 2010 to 2015, refugee shares increased in SSA and non-EU ECA countries, while remaining almost constant in other regions. Even though we observe trends over time, variation in shares mainly depends on the start and end of individual crises. For example, the drastic rise in the number of refugees in non-EU ECA countries represents the beginning of the Syrian crisis after 2010. Many of these refugees now reside in Turkey. And the fall and subsequent rise in refugee numbers in SSA countries represent the end of conflicts in Angola, Liberia,

Figure 1.15 Refugee stock as a percentage of the migrant stock, by destination region, 2000, 2010, and 2015

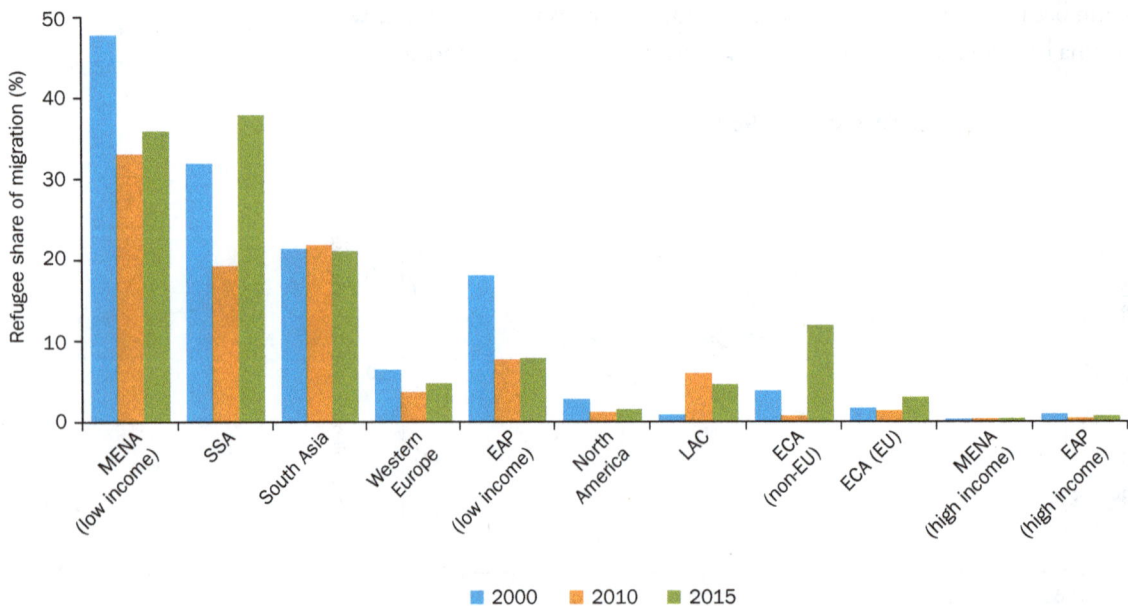

Sources: Refugee data from UNHCR Population Statistics Database. Migration data from the World Bank Global Bilateral Migration Database (1960–2000) and the United Nations Global Migration Database (2010–15).

Note: EAP = East Asia and Pacific; ECA = Eastern Europe and Central Asia; EU = European Union; LAC = Latin America and the Caribbean; MENA = Middle East and North Africa; SSA = Sub-Saharan Africa; UNHCR = United Nations High Commissioner for Refugees.

and Sierra Leone (among others) and new crises arising or becoming worse after 2010 in the Central African Republic, Somalia, and South Sudan.

As mentioned earlier in the chapter, refugees are even more concentrated than economic migrants. However, in stark contrast to economic migrants, and despite the impression emerging in the media, refugees are *not* concentrated in higher-income destination countries in Europe or North America: they are heavily concentrated in poor, neighboring countries. There is a simple explanation for this critical difference. Refugees are often fleeing conflicts and wars that take place, disproportionately, in poorer countries. They have fewer choices about where (or when) to migrate and are typically forced to move to neighboring countries. These neighbors tend to be within the same low-income group.

As of 2010, about 75 percent of the global refugee population was living in low-income countries in MENA, South Asia, and SSA (figure 1.16). These are the same regions where internal conflicts and wars took place during the previous decade. In 2015, non-EU ECA countries hosted about 16 percent of refugees. This large number is simply due to Syrian refugees

Figure 1.16 Distribution of the global refugee stock, by region, 2000, 2010, and 2015

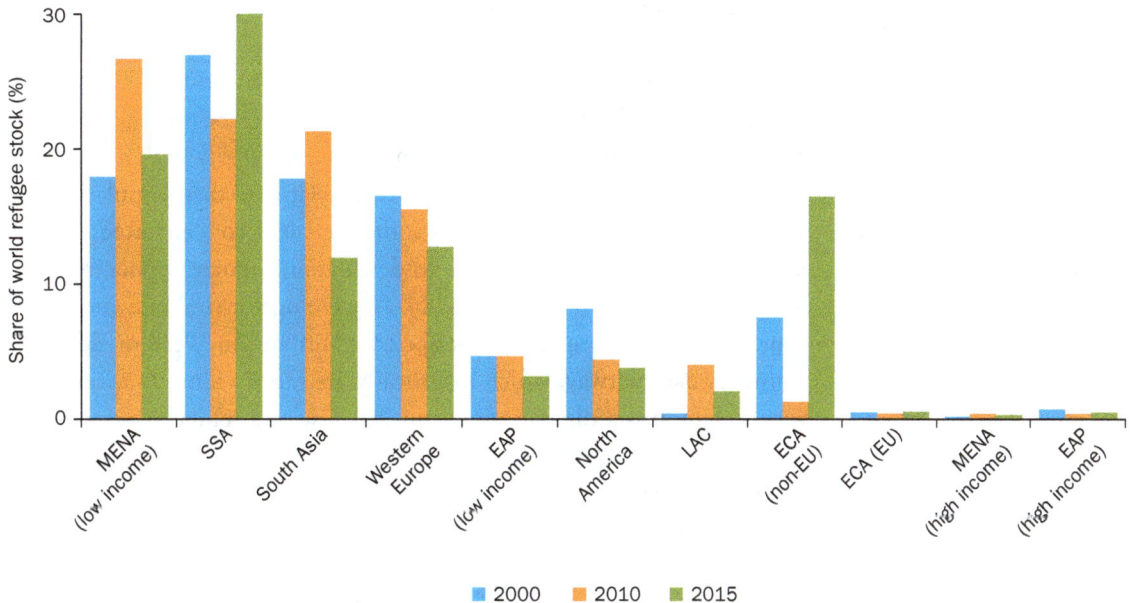

Source: Refugee data from UNHCR Population Statistics Database.

Note: Refugees defined as refugees (and those in refugee-like situations) and asylum seekers. EAP = East Asia and Pacific; ECA = Eastern Europe and Central Asia; EU = European Union; LAC = Latin America and the Caribbean; MENA = Middle East and North Africa; SSA = Sub-Saharan Africa; UNHCR = United Nations High Commissioner for Refugees.

residing in Turkey. The relative size of refugee populations in different regions has changed since 2000 as the conflicts in Afghanistan, Iraq, and Syria have shifted the relative importance away from SSA to the MENA region. Despite the significant public and political attention paid to the influx of refugees to Western Europe in 2015 and 2016, the region's share of the total global refugee stocks declined each year from 2000 to 2010 to 2015. The same pattern holds true for North America.

Country-level refugee patterns

At the country level, refugee departures and arrivals have different patterns than those of economic migrants. Both emigration and immigration rates are more concentrated for refugees than for other types of migrants, with departure ratios more concentrated than arrival ratios. This is due to the concentration of civil conflicts and wars in a few countries that are the sources of a clear majority of the refugees in the world. Refugees fleeing conflicts in Afghanistan, the Central African Republic, Eritrea, Somalia, South Sudan, and Syria made up more than 5 percent of the population of those countries as of 2015. Furthermore, refugees made up more than 5 percent of the total population in more countries in 2000 than in 2015, but more countries sent at least some refugees as of 2015 (see map 1.3, panels a and b). In other words, refugee emigration also became less concentrated and more widespread over time. Still, the overall patterns of refugee emigration are very similar in 2000 and 2015—with a few countries having high rates of refugee departures relative to their population size.

The arrival rate of refugees is somewhat less concentrated, as seen in map 1.4, which depicts refugee-to-destination country population ratios in 2000 (panel a) and 2015 (panel b). High refugee arrival rates are seen in countries neighboring conflict-affected states and in Western European countries like Norway, which historically are more willing to accept refugees. Lebanon is a distinct outlier in 2015, with a refugee-to-population ratio of about 20 percent, more than twice the ratio in Jordan, another neighbor of Syria.

Aside from the Syrian refugee crisis, there is considerable persistence in which countries send and receive refugees because these crises are typically protracted, and frequently refugees neither return home nor move on to another host country. Figure 1.17 shows the distribution of refugees across different destinations for five countries involved in major crises as of 2015. These five origin countries account for 59 percent of all refugees for which

Map 1.3   Refugee-to-origin country population ratio, 2000 and 2015

a. 2000

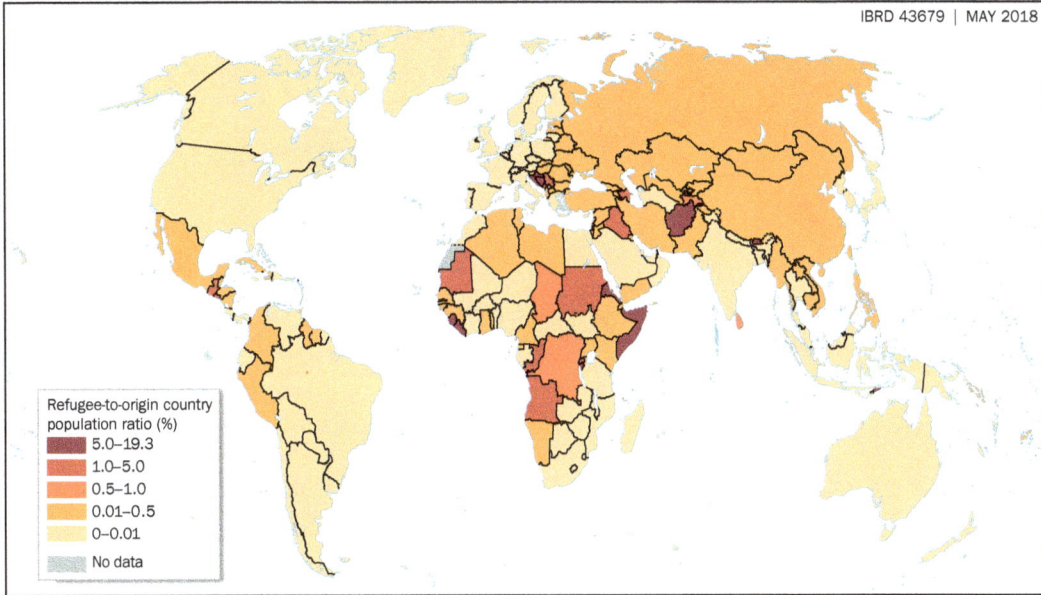

IBRD 43679 | MAY 2018

Refugee-to-origin country
population ratio (%)
- 5.0–19.3
- 1.0–5.0
- 0.5–1.0
- 0.01–0.5
- 0–0.01
- No data

b. 2015

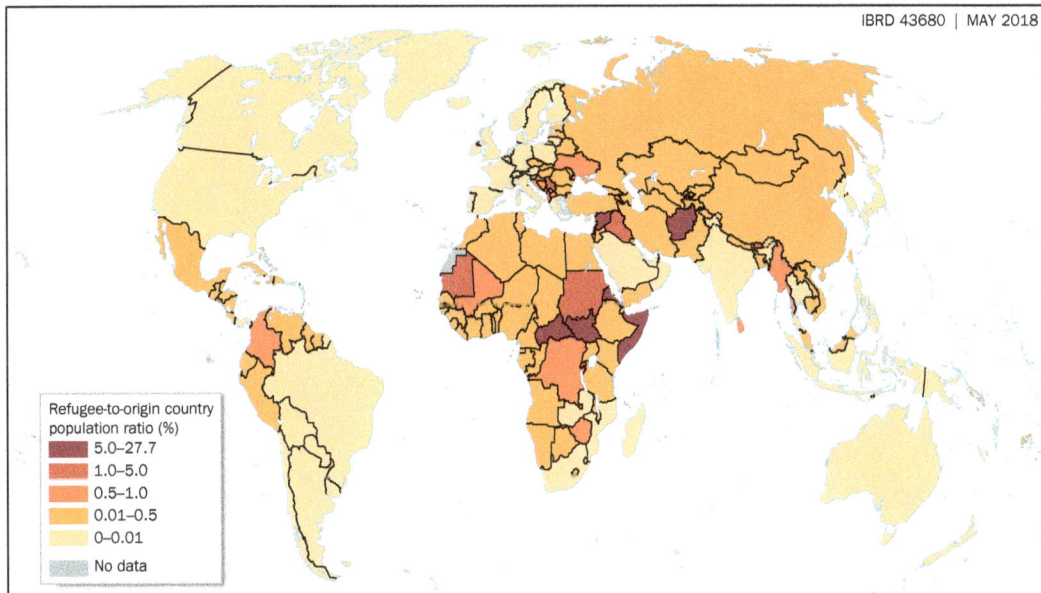

IBRD 43680 | MAY 2018

Refugee-to-origin country
population ratio (%)
- 5.0–27.7
- 1.0–5.0
- 0.5–1.0
- 0.01–0.5
- 0–0.01
- No data

Sources: Data from UNHCR Population Statistics Database. Population data from United Nations World Population Prospects.

Note: Refugees defined as refugees (and those in refugee-like situations) and asylum seekers. UNHCR = United Nations High Commissioner for Refugees.

Map 1.4   Refugee arrival rates in host countries, 2000 and 2015

a. 2000

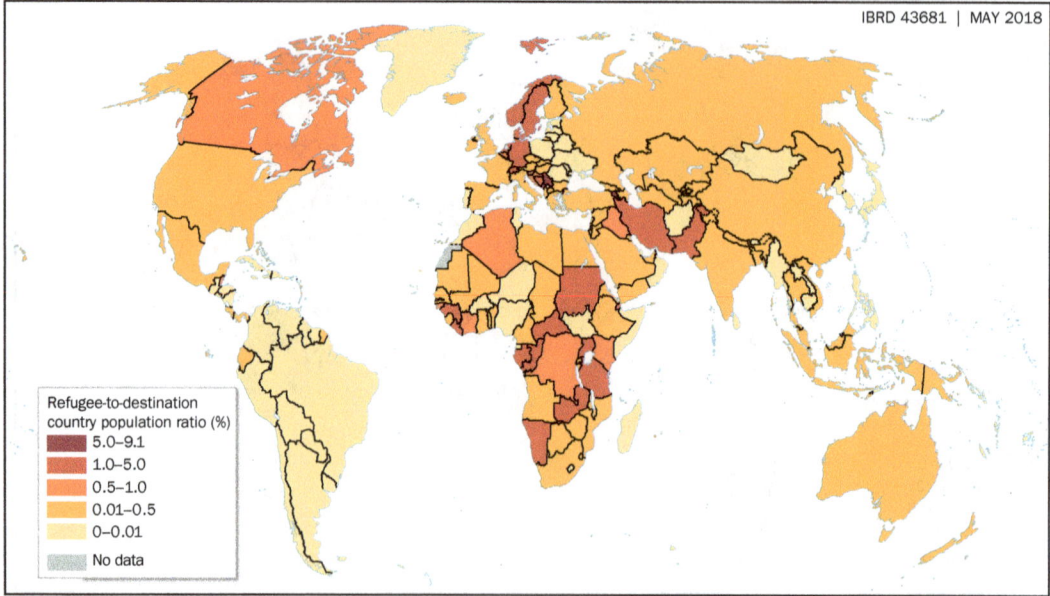

IBRD 43681 | MAY 2018

Refugee-to-destination
country population ratio (%)
- 5.0–9.1
- 1.0–5.0
- 0.5–1.0
- 0.01–0.5
- 0–0.01
- No data

b. 2015

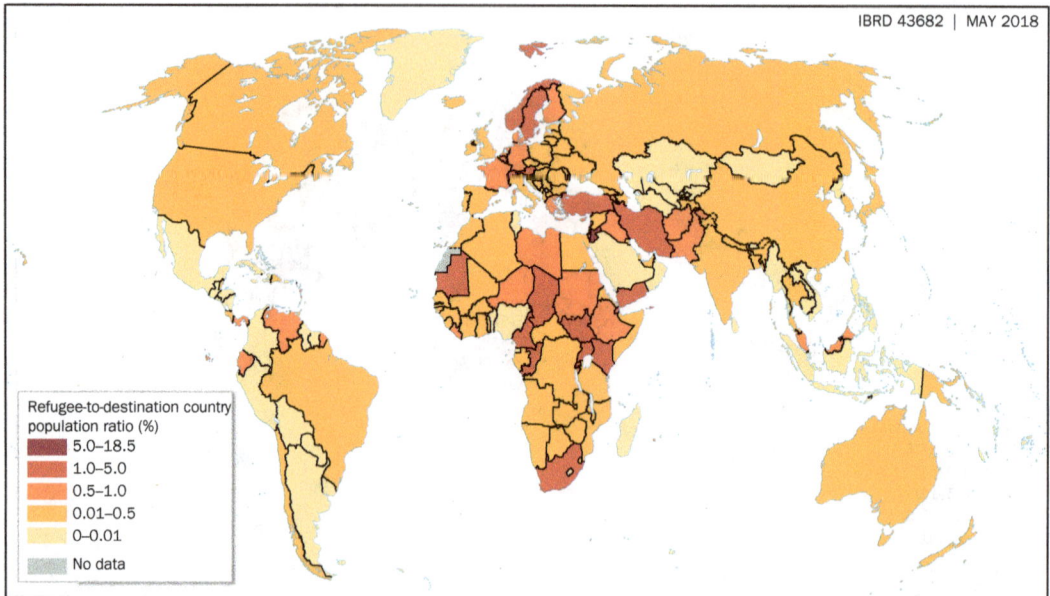

IBRD 43682 | MAY 2018

Refugee-to-destination country
population ratio (%)
- 5.0–18.5
- 1.0–5.0
- 0.5–1.0
- 0.01–0.5
- 0–0.01
- No data

Sources: Data from UNHCR Population Statistics Database. Population data from United Nations World Population Prospects.

Note: Refugees defined as refugees (and those in refugee-like situations) and asylum seekers. UNHCR = United Nations High Commissioner for Refugees.

Figure 1.17   Destinations of refugees from major crises, 2015

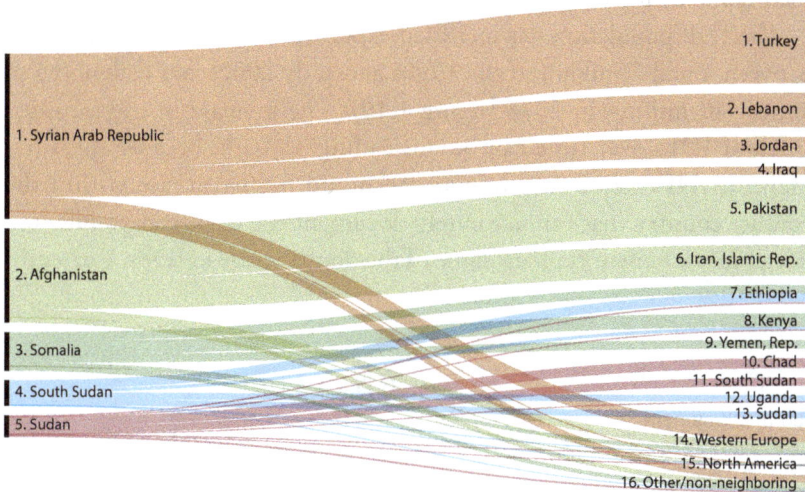

Source: Data from UNHCR Population Statistics Database. Figure made using RAWGraphs visualization platform (Mauri et al. 2017).

Note: Refugees defined as refugees (and those in refugee-like situations) and asylum seekers. UNHCR = United Nations High Commissioner for Refugees.

the data provide a known origin. The destinations are divided into the popular neighboring destinations as well as North America, Western Europe, and other countries. For the five cases shown in figure 1.17, over 87 percent of all refugees and asylum seekers are residing in neighboring countries (for refugees from all origins, that ratio is 71 percent). In contrast, only 8 percent of these refugees reside in Western Europe, and, astonishingly, less than 0.2 percent are in the United States.

Internally displaced people

People displaced by violent conflicts do not always resort to crossing international borders. In many cases, victims of violence seek safety in other regions of their own country. This could be because they lack financing to fund an international move, or because some type of policy restriction prevents a legal border crossing. This population is known as internally displaced persons (IDPs). Figure 1.18 shows the composition of the displaced population for four different humanitarian crises: Afghanistan, Iraq, Somalia, and Syria. In each case the year shown represents the height of the crisis. In three of the four cases, a majority of those displaced remained in their home country.

The IDP population has increased exponentially over time, remaining between 4 and 7 million in the 1990s and early 2000s and ballooning to almost 40 million in 2015 (figure 1.19). The increase in the recorded stock of IDPs over time can be misleading, though, because measurement of IDPs relies on a humanitarian aid infrastructure within the conflict country that can accurately document the displaced population. Better measurement explains some of the dramatic rise in IDPs. Currently,

Figure 1.18   **Composition of forced displacement**

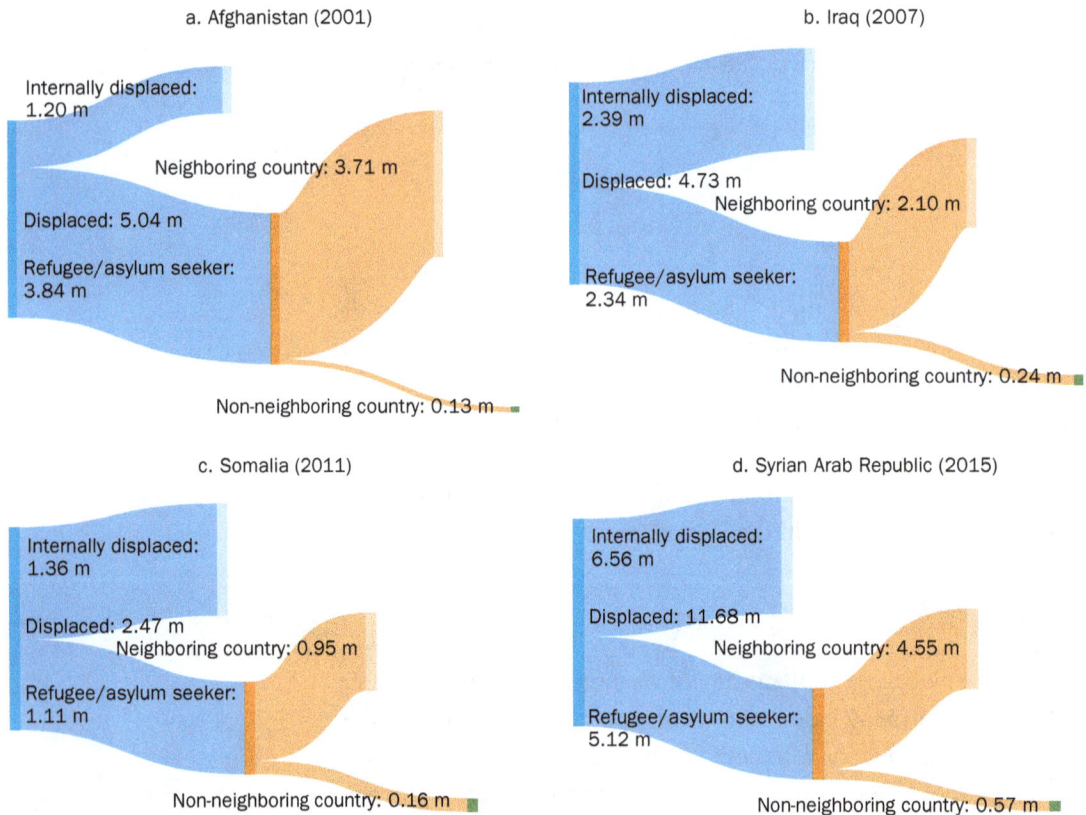

a. Afghanistan (2001)

Internally displaced: 1.20 m

Neighboring country: 3.71 m

Displaced: 5.04 m

Refugee/asylum seeker: 3.84 m

Non-neighboring country: 0.13 m

b. Iraq (2007)

Internally displaced: 2.39 m

Displaced: 4.73 m

Neighboring country: 2.10 m

Refugee/asylum seeker: 2.34 m

Non-neighboring country: 0.24 m

c. Somalia (2011)

Internally displaced: 1.36 m

Displaced: 2.47 m

Neighboring country: 0.95 m

Refugee/asylum seeker: 1.11 m

Non-neighboring country: 0.16 m

d. Syrian Arab Republic (2015)

Internally displaced: 6.56 m

Displaced: 11.68 m

Neighboring country: 4.55 m

Refugee/asylum seeker: 5.12 m

Non-neighboring country: 0.57 m

Source: Data from UNHCR Population Statistics Database.

Note: m = million; UNHCR = United Nations High Commissioner for Refugees.

Figure 1.19 Internally displaced populations, 1993–2015

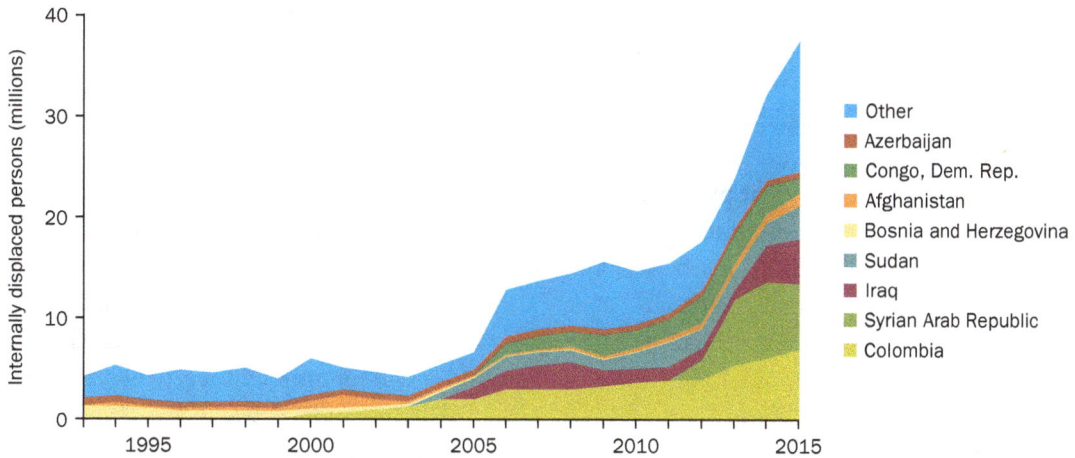

Source: Data from UNHCR Population Statistics Database.

Note: UNHCR = United Nations High Commissioner for Refugees.

the countries with the most IDPs are Colombia and Syria, which account for over one-third of the world's internally displaced population.

Migrant demographics

Migrants' demographic characteristics matter at least as much as their overall numbers in terms of their economic outcomes and their impact on both source and destination countries. Demographic variables, such as age, education, and gender composition, are especially important for labor markets because these variables provide insights about which groups of workers, regions, occupations, and industries will be most directly affected as well as about the overall fiscal ramifications of migration.

Age composition

An important determinant of global migration patterns is the difference in the age distributions of populations in the sending and receiving regions. Specifically, differences in the size of the working-age population—generally taken as the 15–65 age group—matter. High-income countries, the main recipients of economic migrants, have mostly completed their demographic transitions, and so have relatively older and aging populations. Their labor markets exhibit shortages, especially in labor-intensive service sectors. In contrast, many low-income countries, the big senders of migrants, have younger and faster-growing populations. Youth un(der)employment is a chronic problem in these countries and the source of numerous social problems in some cases.

The pyramid chart in figure 1.20 shows this contrast in the age distribution, with sending countries skewed toward younger age groups and receiving countries with much older populations. The population distribution is quite uniform between the ages of zero and 50, forming a pyramid. These countries, basically, no longer exhibit what we think of as the standard age pyramid. The differing patterns across sending and receiving countries confirm our previous statements that migration generally flows from countries with younger populations to those with older populations, which are already experiencing declines in the size of their working-age population.

The missing piece in this demographic picture is the age distribution of the migrants themselves. Migrants tend to be within the working-age cohorts and have different age distribution profiles than locals in the

Figure 1.20   **Age distribution in sending and receiving countries, 2010**

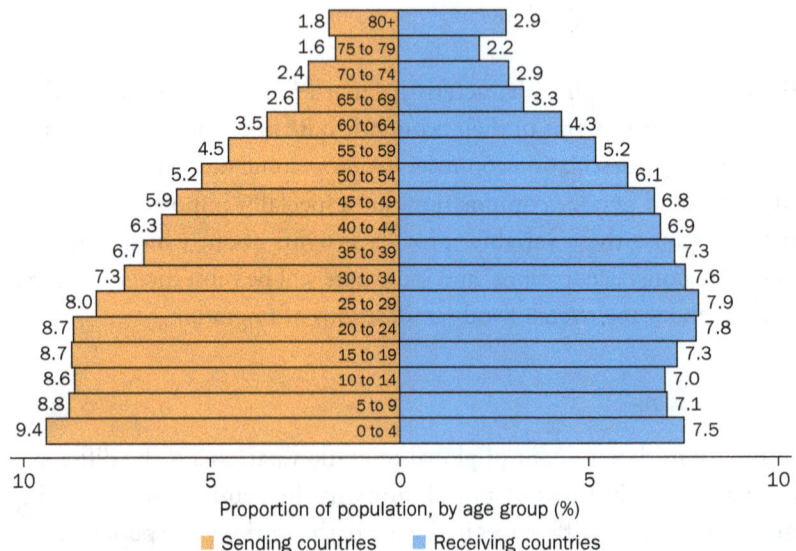

Sources: Migration data from the United Nations Global Migration Database (2010–15). Populations by age from United Nations World Population Prospects.

Note: Sending (receiving) country age group proportions calculated as a weighted mean of country-level age proportions where emigrant (immigrant) stocks are used as weights.

Figure 1.21 Age distribution of immigrants and natives

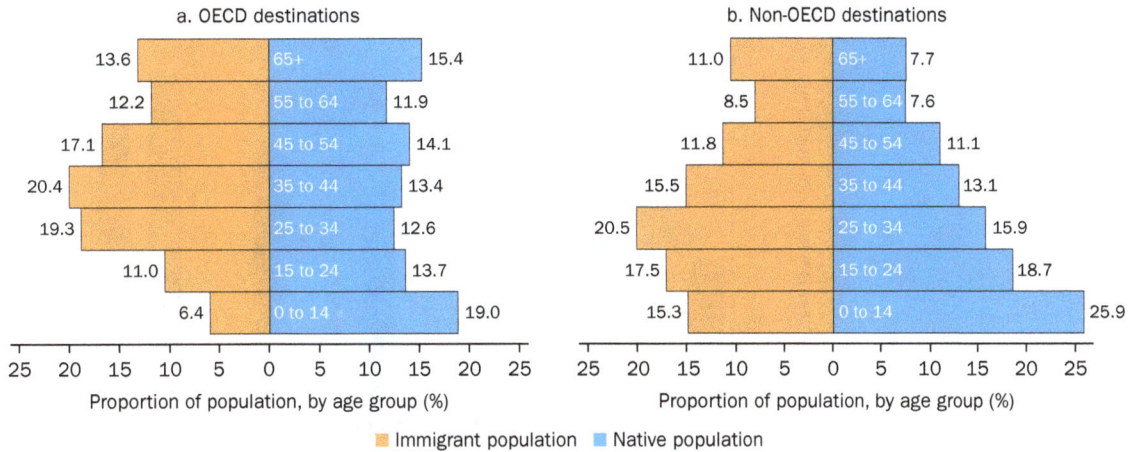

a. OECD destinations

13.6	65+	15.4	
12.2	55 to 64	11.9	
17.1	45 to 54	14.1	
20.4	35 to 44	13.4	
19.3	25 to 34	12.6	
11.0	15 to 24	13.7	
6.4	0 to 14	19.0	

Proportion of population, by age group (%)

b. Non-OECD destinations

11.0	65+	7.7	
8.5	55 to 64	7.6	
11.8	45 to 54	11.1	
15.5	35 to 44	13.1	
20.5	25 to 34	15.9	
17.5	15 to 24	18.7	
15.3	0 to 14	25.9	

Proportion of population, by age group (%)

■ Immigrant population ■ Native population

Source: Data from the 2010/2011 OECD Database on Immigrants in OECD and Non-OECD Countries (DIOC-E).

Note: Country-level age proportions are weighted by size of the immigrant population. OECD = Organisation for Economic Co-operation and Development.

destinations, as seen in figure 1.21. Especially in the case of high-income OECD destination countries with rapidly ageing populations, migrants bolster the working-age population and increase the size of the labor force. Outside of these OECD destinations, migrants again bolster the labor force, but this time because local populations tend to be younger than the migrants. In other words, in both OECD and non-OECD destinations, migrants increase the labor force, reduce the dependency ratio, and increase the relative labor supply. The main difference is the source of the relative labor shortage—too many elderly people in the OECD countries and too many young people in the lower-income non-OECD destinations.

Gender composition

Gender differences in migration rates are relatively small. Female migrants made up 48 percent of the global migrant stock in 2015, about the same level as earlier years and down slightly from a high of 50 percent in 1980. Female migrants make up 3.2 percent of the total female population, just shy of the 3.3 percent overall level (figure 1.22).

Despite the overall gender balance in global migration, notable differences exist in the gender composition of immigrants and emigrants in different regions of the world. Figure 1.23 shows the share of women among emigrants by region and year. Male emigrants dominate the numbers in South Asia, where they make up almost two-thirds of all emigrants

Figure 1.22 Global female migrant stock, 1960–2015

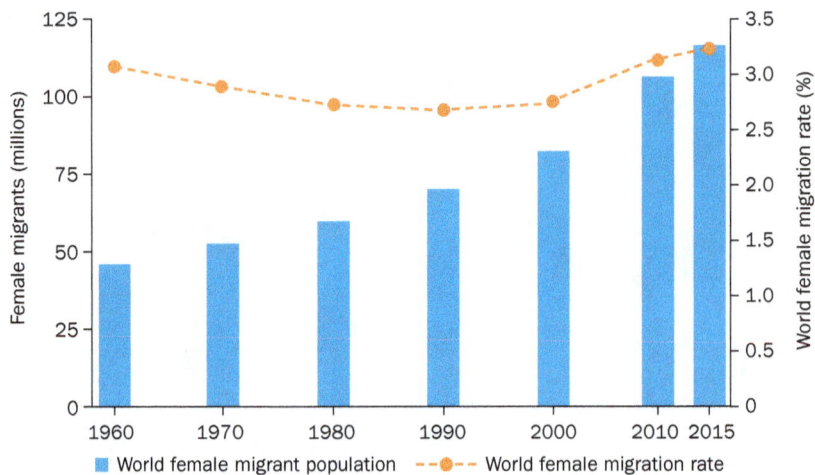

Sources: Data from the World Bank Global Bilateral Migration Database (1960–2000) and the United Nations Global Migration Database (2010–15). Population data from United Nations World Population Prospects.

Figure 1.23 Female share of emigration, by region, 1970, 1990, and 2010

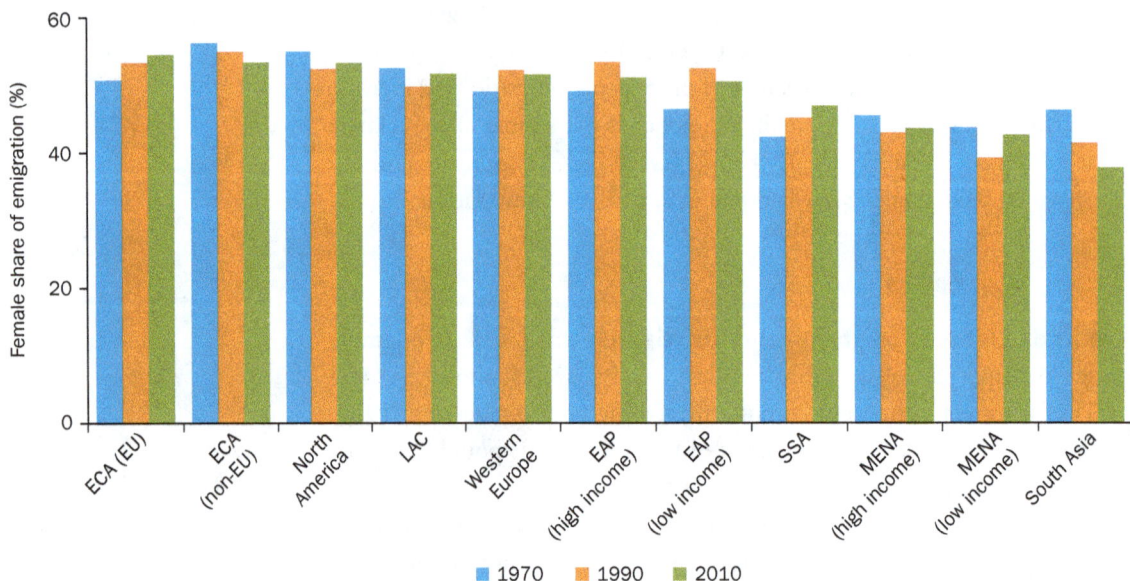

Sources: Data from the World Bank Global Bilateral Migration Database (1960–2000) and the United Nations Global Migration Database (2010–15).

Note: EAP = East Asia and Pacific; ECA = Eastern Europe and Central Asia; EU = European Union; LAC = Latin America and the Caribbean; MENA = Middle East and North Africa; SSA = Sub-Saharan Africa.

from the region. A higher share of the emigrants from MENA and SSA are also men. When we look at trends over time, we see that South Asia and SSA have been on different paths since 1970. The female share of migration has been decreasing significantly in the former and increasing in the latter region. Finally, wealthier regions such as Europe and North America send abroad more women than men.

High-income MENA countries stand out for their low share of female immigrants, who make up just over a quarter of the total in 2010 (figure 1.24). This is a significant change from 1960, when the female share was closer to parity. The large decline in the female share reflects high demand in the region for workers in construction and other relatively low-skilled sectors. In several other regions, women compose most of the immigrant stock, which likely reflects their longer life spans and the predominance of domestic worker immigration in EAP.

In individual countries, gender differences have not changed significantly over time. The x-axis of figure 1.25 shows the share of the 1970 emigrant stock that was female, and the y-axis shows the female share in 2010. The dashed orange 45-degree line indicates points for which there

Figure 1.24   Female share of immigration, by region, 1970, 1990, and 2010

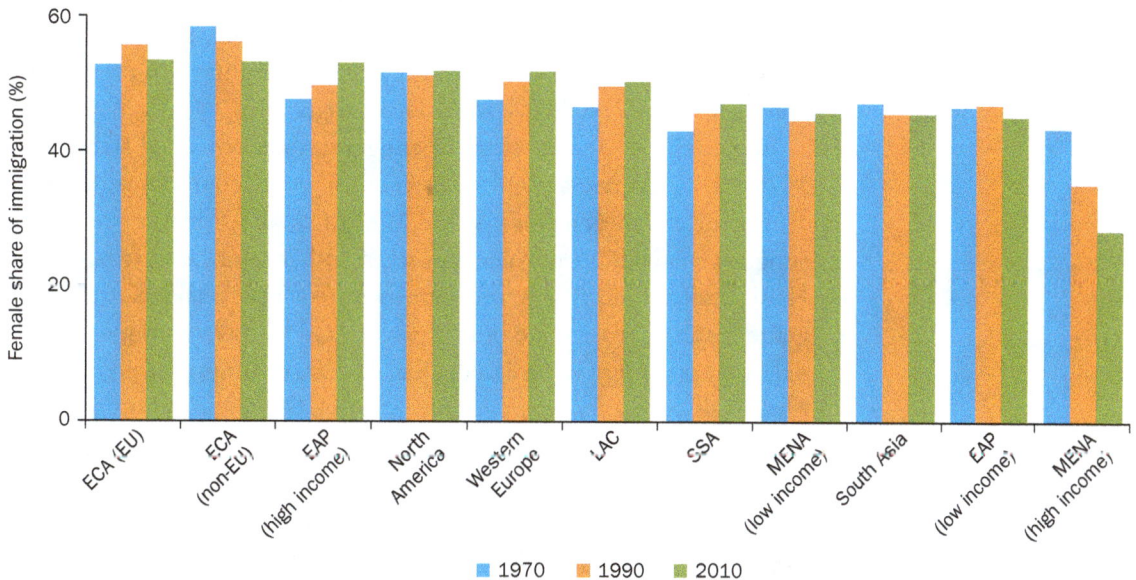

Sources: Data from the World Bank Global Bilateral Migration Database (1960–2000) and the United Nations Global Migration Database (2010–15).

Note: EAP = East Asia and Pacific; ECA = Eastern Europe and Central Asia; EU = European Union; LAC = Latin America and the Caribbean; MENA = Middle East and North Africa; SSA = Sub-Saharan Africa.

Figure 1.25 Female share of emigration, 1970 and 2010

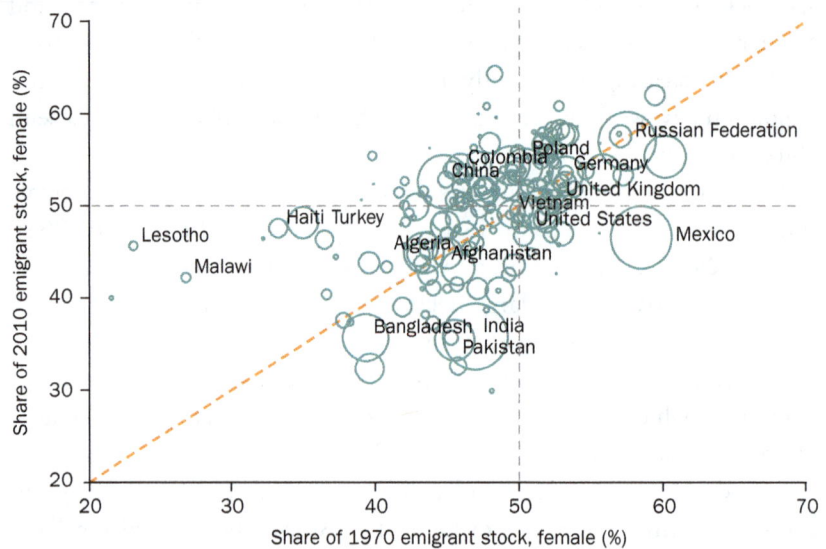

Sources: Data from the World Bank Global Bilateral Migration Database (1960–2000) and the United Nations Global Migration Database (2010–15).

Note: Orange dashed line is the 45-degree line. The size of a circle is proportional to the number of female emigrants from that country.

was no change in the gender ratio between the two periods. Points above the dashed orange line indicate an increasing share, and those points below indicate a decreasing share of female migrants. Figure 1.26 presents the same information on female ratios for immigration.

In general, the female share of emigration has remained stable since 1970 and is clustered around 50 percent. In several countries with significant labor emigration, such as India, Mexico, and Pakistan, the female emigrant share declined whereas in several other source countries, such as Haiti, Lesotho, and Turkey, the share increased. The female share of immigration is also clustered around 50 percent and has been even more stable, reflecting the lack of change in the female share of emigration across countries. As discussed above, the female ratio in GCC destination countries of the Persian Gulf, such as Saudi Arabia, Qatar, and the United Arab Emirates, is rather low but has stayed around the same level since 1970.

Female migrants tend to dominate certain migration corridors (figure 1.27). These corridors tend to consist of a single origin that sends mostly female migrants to several different countries. In 2010, the Philippines was the source country in 3 of the top 10 migration corridors with the highest share of female migrants. Ninety-eight percent of migrants

Figure 1.26 Female share of immigration, 1970 and 2010

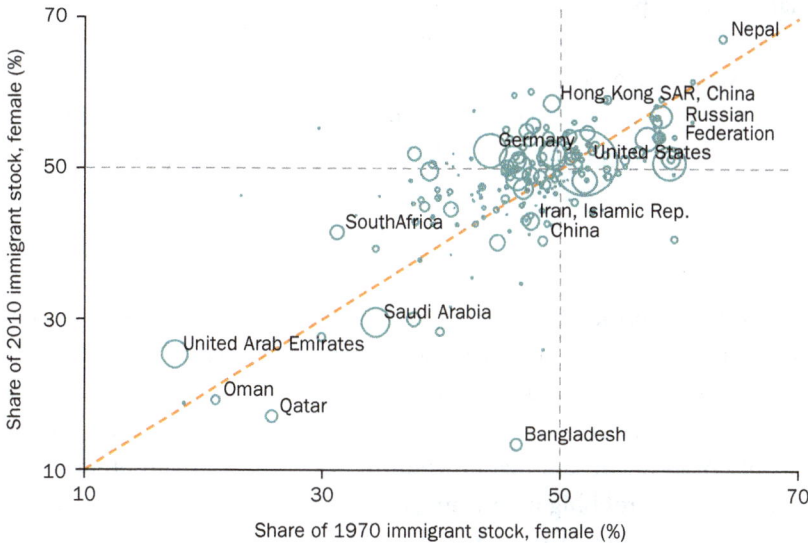

Sources: Data from the World Bank Global Bilateral Migration Database (1960–2000) and the United Nations Global Migration Database (2010–15).

Note: Orange dashed line is the 45-degree line. The size of a circle is proportional to the number of female immigrants in that country.

Figure 1.27 The 10 corridors with the highest share of female migration, 2010

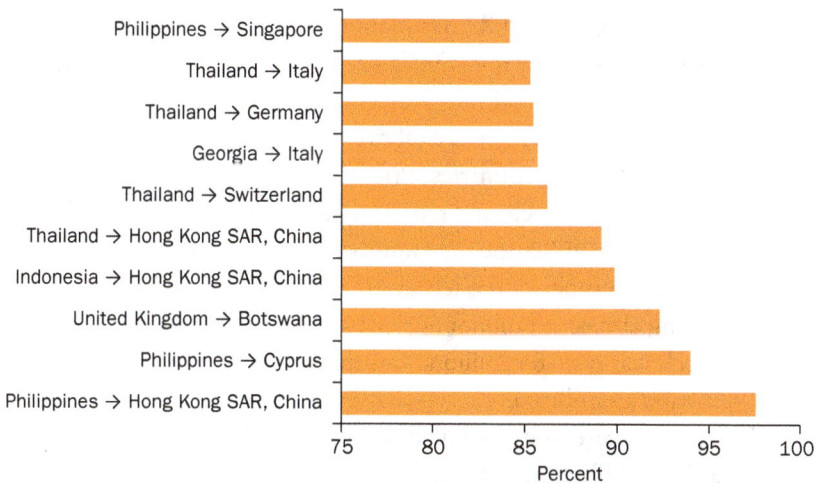

Source: Data from the United Nations Global Migration Database (2010–15).

Note: Limited to corridors with more than 5,000 migrants.

from the Philippines to Hong Kong SAR, China, were women. Other shares were 94 percent to Cyprus and 84 percent to Singapore. The dominance of female migrants in these corridors reflects the demand for domestic workers. Thailand was responsible for another 4 of the top 10 migration corridors, with women making up more than 85 percent of its emigrants to Germany; Hong Kong SAR, China; Italy; and Switzerland.

Skill and education composition

The skill composition of migrants, especially in comparison with the local populations in sending and receiving countries, is perhaps the most critical issue in the academic and policy debates on migration. Whether it is the widely spread claim that "unskilled undocumented migrants are stealing the jobs of locals" in destination countries or that the "brain drain of the highly skilled is robbing poor countries of their future," the skill or educational composition of migration has important economic, social, and political implications. High-skilled migration patterns and their economic implications are discussed in greater detail in chapter 5. The goal in this section is to present some of the more important and relevant patterns, with a focus on regional differences, changes over time, and concentration.

There has been a rapid change in the skill composition of migrant stocks since 1990, the first year for which we have relatively comprehensive data. Figure 1.28 presents the stock of migrants by education level in OECD and non-OECD destination countries, respectively, for 1990, 2000, and 2010. Here we focus only on OECD destination countries because we do not have detailed data for many non-OECD destinations and because a significant majority of high-skilled migrants go to OECD countries. In 1990, about 40 million labor-market-age (above age 25) migrants resided in the 27 high-income OECD countries. Primary-educated migrants made up almost half of the total stock, and tertiary-educated migrants accounted for about 27 percent. In 2000, the total number of immigrants reached almost 60 million. The number of the tertiary-educated migrants increased even faster, reaching almost 20 million, or one-third of the total. By 2010, the migrant stock was over 85 million, and the number of tertiary educated was about half (43 million).

This rapid increase in high-skilled migration is the result of several factors. First, high-skilled migrants can more easily afford the financial costs of migration, earn higher absolute wage gains, and face lower migration policy barriers. Second, the supply of high-skilled migrants has increased

Figure 1.28 Number of migrants by skill level for OECD, non-OECD, and all origins, 1990, 2000, and 2010

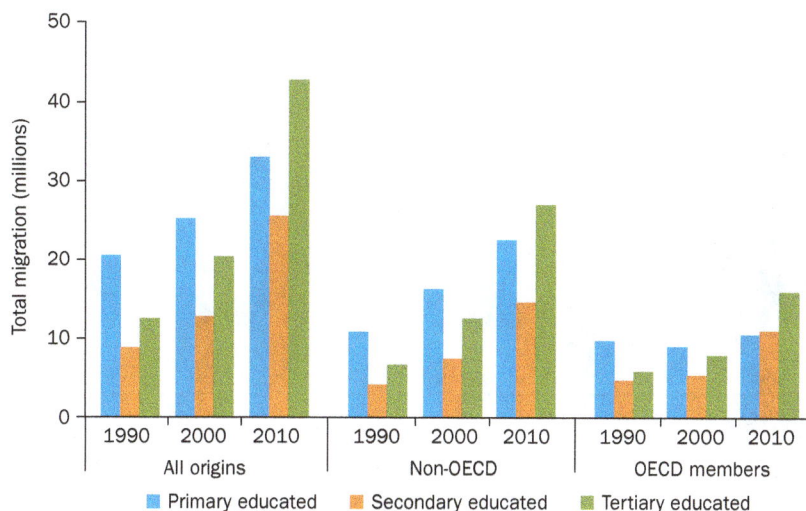

Sources: Data from Docquier, Marfouk, and Lowell 2007 and the 2010/2011 OECD Database on Immigrants in OECD and Non-OECD Countries (DIOC-E).

Note: "Tertiary educated" includes partial tertiary education. Mexico and South Africa treated as non-OECD. OECD = Organisation for Economic Co-operation and Development.

rapidly as overall education levels in the world rose quickly during these two decades. This increase is also evident in the contribution of non-OECD countries to the stock of educated migrants. Non-OECD country emigrants represent about two-thirds of the increase in the tertiary-educated group, which reflects relatively larger increases in the educated population of those countries. Finally, because these figures refer to migrant stocks, they represent the sum of net flows over the previous decades. Therefore, the net migration flows during these time periods are even more skill intensive than what is reflected in the stock figures. That is, more recent migration cohorts have been significantly more skill intensive than existing stocks and previous cohorts.

The skill composition of emigrants shows significant regional variation. Figure 1.29 presents the skill composition for 2010, with several regions having significantly higher-skilled emigrant stocks. For example, most emigrants from high-income EAP, high-income MENA, and North America are tertiary educated: because there is relatively little emigration from these countries, those who do migrate are highly educated and move to high-income OECD countries in the case of the first two regions. For Canada and the United States, the overall education levels of the

Figure 1.29 Distribution of emigrants, by skill level and region, 2010

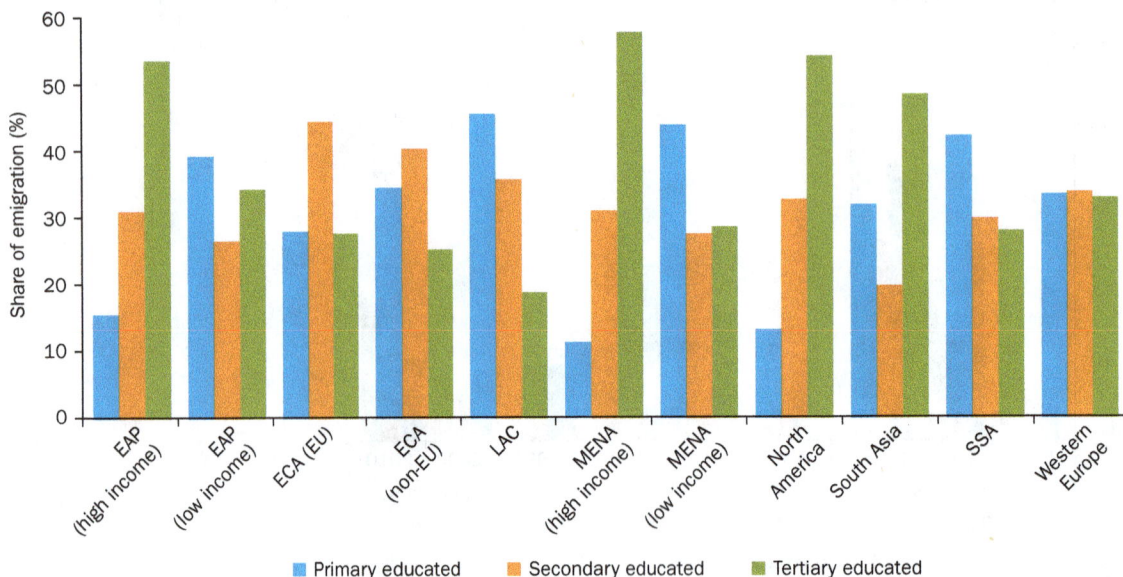

Source: Data from the 2010/2011 OECD Database on Immigrants in OECD and Non-OECD Countries (DIOC-E).

Note: "Tertiary educated" restricted to completed tertiary education. EAP = East Asia and Pacific; ECA = Eastern Europe and Central Asia; EU = European Union; LAC = Latin America and the Caribbean; MENA = Middle East and North Africa; SSA = Sub-Saharan Africa.

underlying populations from which the emigrants are selected are very high to begin with. In contrast to these regions, emigrants from LAC and low-income MENA countries are relatively less educated, and they migrate to neighboring high-income countries to meet the demand for unskilled labor. An interesting case is the South Asian countries: they send low-skilled migrants to GCC countries, send high-skilled migrants to OECD countries, and have relatively few secondary-educated emigrants.

The concentration of migrant stocks, one of our key points, shows interesting variation among different skill levels. Figure 1.30 presents the familiar cumulative distribution of emigrant and immigrant stocks, differentiated by education levels.[5] Earlier, we showed that immigration is significantly more concentrated than emigration. This pattern is true regardless of the education level of the migrants, as seen in figure 1.30. The concentration level of high-skilled immigrants (those with at least some tertiary education) is most striking. The graph implies that top 10 destination countries account for 75 percent of the high-skilled immigrants in the world. Among these, the four most important destinations—Australia, Canada, the United Kingdom, and the United States—are home

Figure 1.30 Cumulative distribution of immigration and emigration, by skill level, 2000

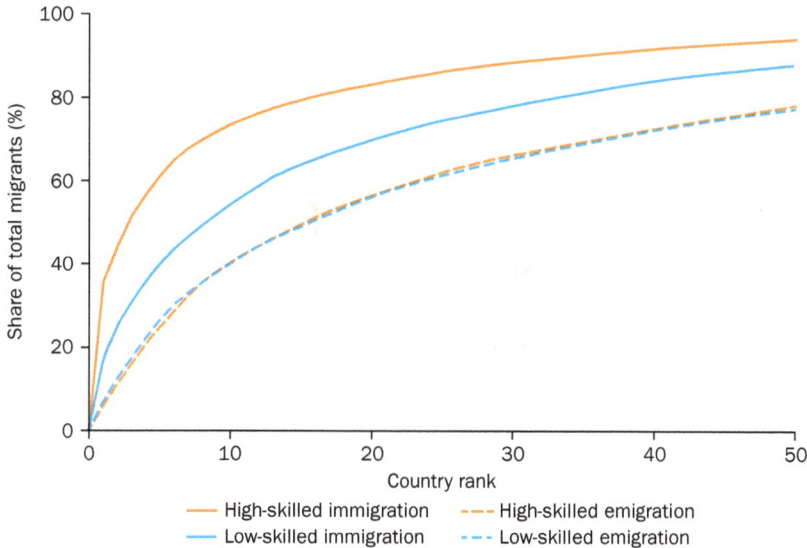

Source: Data from the World Bank Global Bilateral Migration Database (1960–2000).

Note: Countries ranked by size of corresponding population.

to almost two-thirds of high-skilled migrants. Chapter 5 will discuss these issues in greater detail, and the appendix discusses the differences in terms of definitions and data sources.

A related pattern is that certain corridors also are heavily skewed toward high-skilled migration. Table 1.4 lists the corridors with stocks of more than 50,000 people and the largest share of tertiary-educated migrants. Three countries—Canada, the United Kingdom, and the United States—are the destinations in all of these top corridors. Except in the cases of the United States–United Kingdom and Republic of Korea–Canada corridors, the origin country is always a non-OECD country, indicating the extent of skilled migration from the global South to the global North.

Table 1.5 explores the opposite pattern and identifies the corridors with the highest concentration of low-skilled migrants. In this case, these corridors are always between neighboring non-OECD countries, most of which are low-income countries.

Differences in the education level of migrants and non-migrants are quite significant and have important labor market implications, which we discuss in greater detail in chapters 2 and 3. At this point, we will highlight several observations across countries in terms of skill composition of migration.

Table 1.4   Top 10 corridors with the highest share of skilled migrants, 2010

Origin	Destination	Stock skilled	Total stock	Share skilled (%)
Russian Federation	Canada	47,680	59,625	80.0
India	United States	1,198,916	1,533,387	78.2
Taiwan, China	United States	264,379	341,861	77.3
Taiwan, China	Canada	41,165	53,520	76.9
Korea, Rep.	Canada	71,005	95,620	74.3
United States	United Kingdom	99,068	133,916	74.0
Romania	Canada	51,105	70,065	72.9
Iran, Islamic Rep.	Canada	76,360	105,560	72.3
Nigeria	United States	123,094	172,549	71.3
Philippines	Canada	291,220	409,000	71.2

Source: Data from 2010/2011 OECD Database on Immigrants in OECD and Non-OECD Countries (DIOC-E).

Note: Only corridors with more than 50,000 migrants are considered. OECD = Organisation for Economic Co-operation and Development.

Table 1.5   Top 10 corridors with the lowest share of skilled migrants, 2010

Origin	Destination	Stock skilled	Total stock	Share skilled (%)
Malawi	Mozambique	58	65,746	0.1
Mozambique	South Africa	1,339	278,533	0.5
Indonesia	Malaysia	4,746	702,391	0.7
Somalia	Kenya	470	58,680	0.8
Myanmar	Thailand	8,331	896,914	0.9
Afghanistan	Iran, Islamic Rep.	4,467	390,954	1.1
Paraguay	Argentina	4,550	394,770	1.2
Ghana	Togo	1,220	94,664	1.3
Haiti	Dominican Republic	2,860	194,870	1.5
Lao PDR	Thailand	1,725	112,932	1.5

Source: Data from 2010/2011 OECD Database on Immigrants in OECD and Non-OECD Countries (DIOC-E).

Note: Only corridors with more than 50,000 migrants are considered. OECD = Organisation for Economic Co-operation and Development.

The left panel of figure 1.31 shows the proportion of tertiary-educated emigrants on the x-axis and tertiary-educated natives on the y-axis. The right panel shows corresponding information for tertiary-educated immigrants and natives. In other words, this graph allows us to jointly compare the skill ratio of emigrants, immigrants, and non-migrants. The differences between these three ratios, the skill selection patterns, are among the most widely explored issues in the academic literature. The dashed lines indicate parity between the skill composition of natives and immigrants or emigrants. Points below the dashed line imply a higher share of skilled emigrants or immigrants than natives; points above indicate a lower share. The size of the circle is proportional to the size of a country's population.

Starting with the left panel, we note that the skilled are significantly overrepresented among emigrants when compared to natives. Those leaving a country are more likely to be high skilled than those remaining. The gaps are especially large for small and poorer countries with relatively less-educated labor forces. In other words, emigrants are positively selected

Figure 1.31 Education levels of immigrants, emigrants, and natives, 2010

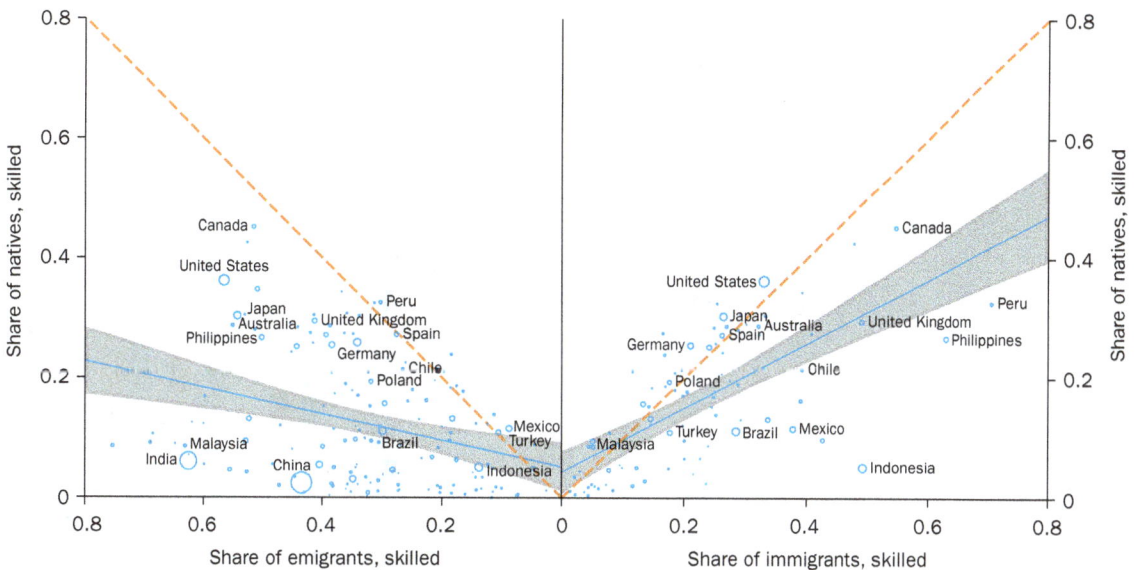

Sources: Migration data from the 2010/2011 OECD Database on Immigrants in OECD and Non-OECD Countries (DIOC-E). Skilled population data from Barro and Lee 2013.

Note: "Skilled" defined as the population with completed tertiary education; shares represent the skilled population divided by the overall population of interest. For the 88 destination countries included in the DIOC-E 2010/2011 dataset, natives' skill rates are calculated from the native-born population; for all other countries skill rates are calculated from the entire population using Barro and Lee 2013 data. Size of circles are scaled by (log) country population. In each panel, the dashed line is the 45-degree line, the blue line is the fitted regression line, and the gray area is the confidence interval around it. OECD = Organisation for Economic Co-operation and Development.

from the skill/education distribution across the board. We see similar patterns for immigrants: they are generally more educated than the natives, but the gaps are smaller. In the case of several countries such as Germany, Japan, and the United States, the points lie slightly above the 45-degree line, indicating that natives are slightly more educated than immigrants.

The final point to emphasize is on the gender composition of high-skilled migration. Women's share of high-skilled migration, particularly when coming from non-OECD countries, has grown more quickly in recent years. Figure 1.32 shows the time trend of the gender composition of migrants by skill level to the 27 high-income OECD countries for which we have detailed data. In 1990, females made up a smaller share of high-skilled migrants, even though they were slightly overrepresented among all migrants. This gap closed slightly but was maintained in 2000. However, in 2010, the share of tertiary-educated women caught up with men and even passed them in many destinations. Like overall migration patterns, the role of non-OECD origin countries played a larger role in the convergence of skill rates between male and female migrants.

Figure 1.32 **Female share of migration, by skill level and origin, 1990, 2000, and 2010**

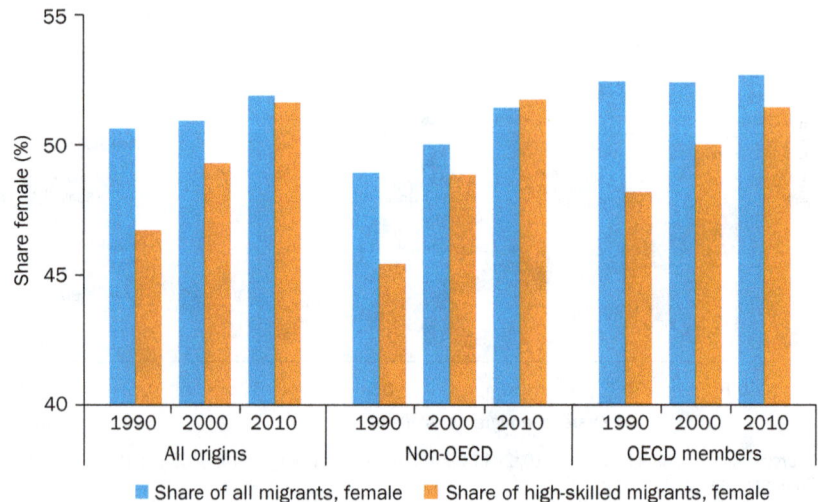

Sources: Data from Docquier, Marfouk, and Lowell 2007 and the 2010/2011 OECD Database on Immigrants in OECD and Non-OECD Countries (DIOC-E).

Note: "High-skilled" includes population with only partially completed tertiary education. Mexico and South Africa treated as non-OECD. OECD = Organisation for Economic Co-operation and Development.

Notes

1. The GCC member states are Bahrain, Kuwait, Oman, Qatar, Saudi Arabia, and the United Arab Emirates.
2. Throughout this report we use World Bank regional definitions. As a result, for example, Mexico is considered part of LAC and not North America. Please see table A.1 in the appendix for regional descriptions.
3. The World Bank recognizes 218 economies, which results in $218 \times 217 = 47,306$ migration corridors.
4. Refugees here refer to refugees and people in refugee-like situations.
5. Figure 1.30 presents the data for 2000 because we wanted to include the information for the whole world, and this is the last year for which this is possible.

References

Abbas, R., and D. Varma. 2014. "Internal Labor Migration in India Raises Integration Challenges for Migrants." *Migration Information Source*, March 3. https://www.migrationpolicy.org/article/internal-labor-migration-india-raises-integration-challenges-migrants.

Barro, R. J., and J. W. Lee. 2013. "A New Data Set of Educational Attainment in the World, 1950–2010." *Journal of Development Economics* 104 (September): 184–98.

Bell, M., and E. Charles-Edwards. 2013. "Cross-National Comparisons of Internal Migration: An Update of Global Patterns and Trends." Technical Paper No. 2013/1, United Nations Department of Economic and Social Affairs, Population Division, New York.

Courgeau, D. 1973. "Migrants et migrations." *Population* (French edition) 28 (1): 95–129.

Docquier, F., A. Marfouk, and B. L. Lowell. 2007. "A Gendered Assessment of the Brain Drain." IZA Discussion Paper 3235, Institute for the Study of Labor, Bonn.

Gallup. 2017. "Number of Potential Migrants Tops 700 Million Worldwide." June 8. http://www.gallup.com/poll/211883/number potential migrants -worldwide-tops-700-million.

Mauri, M., T. Elli, G. Caviglia, G. Uboldi, and M. Azzi. 2017. "RAWGraphs: A Visualisation Platform to Create Open Outputs." Article no. 28 in *Proceedings of the 12th Biannual Conference on Italian SIGCHI*, Cagliari, Italy, September 18–20. New York: ACM.

Zhang, K. H., and S. Song. 2003. "Rural-Urban Migration and Urbanization in China: Evidence from Time-Series and Cross-Section Analyses." *China Economic Review* 14 (4): 386–400.

CHAPTER TWO

The Economic Drivers of Migration Decisions

People move for myriad reasons. Every migrant, whether an economic migrant or a refugee, has a unique story and experience. Our job as economists and researchers is to identify the common themes to these individual stories and migration experiences. What we find is that the search for a better life is foremost among these themes. In other words, the pursuit of higher wages and better jobs is a key determinant of migration for many people. This chapter aims to identify the role of these factors in motivating and shaping international and internal migration decisions. Do people move from low- to high-wage countries? How large are the wage gains associated with migrating? What is the role of different migration costs? How do labor market variables determine various migration outcomes, including the size and the skill composition of migration flows?

Three broad lessons emerge from the existing empirical evidence presented in this chapter. First, economic costs and benefits are critical determinants of migration decisions. Potential migrants weigh these costs and benefits in deciding whether and where to move. The evidence strongly shows that people move from low-wage to high-wage locations and are attracted to labor markets with superior current and future employment opportunities.

Distance, whether physical or cultural, represents a significant cost to potential migrants and shapes observed migration patterns. Physical distances are powerful deterrents and the reason why most low-skilled migrants with tight budget constraints move to neighboring countries or within the same region. The process of assimilation and settlement can be very costly to new immigrants, but existing social networks and linguistic bonds reduce these costs and shape current and future migration flows. Preexisting networks of co-nationals and a common language help new arrivals find jobs, establish a social life, and navigate numerous bureaucratic hurdles. The ability to communicate with natives is essential to maximizing the value of one's human capital and fully benefitting from degrees and credentials that migrants have earned at home.

Policy environment makes a difference, typically as an added cost to migration. Whether it is from preferential treatment of certain groups, tight border security, or granting access to health, welfare, and education benefits, destination countries have a significant impact on the scale and composition of the immigrants they allow to enter.

Second, the skill composition of migration flows, a critical determinant of the economic impact of immigration, varies enormously across origin and destination countries. Economic factors again explain the large variation we observe in skill composition. High-skilled migrants are disproportionately attracted to wealthier countries that have liberal and selective immigration policies and where absolute and relative returns to education and human capital are higher. Physical distances, linguistic differences, and policy barriers are more easily overcome by the high skilled; and social networks are less important in overcoming mobility costs.

Finally, economic factors play an important role in refugees' choices of destination countries. Even though refugees make their choices under much more severely constrained conditions than most economic migrants, their motivations in choosing a particular destination over another are similar. In particular, like economic migrants, refugees are more likely to go to high-wage destination countries, holding other characteristics constant. They still mostly end up in neighboring poorer countries because other factors, such as distance and contiguity, tend to be more important barriers for refugees. Simply put, refugees are also in search of a better life, and economic pull and push factors play similarly important roles in their decisions.

Why migrate? The benefits of migrating

The main economic benefits of migrating come from better employment opportunities and higher wages for most migrants. International migration patterns show that wage differentials between sending and receiving labor markets play an especially important role. Migrants systematically move from low- to high-wage countries, and they typically experience large wage gains over their lifetime.

Wage differentials and migration

Basic economic intuition suggests that we should observe people migrating from low-wage to high-wage locations, as it would be the case with any factor of production. In order to show these patterns, we use the data from the World Bank's International Income Distribution Data (I2D2) dataset (see the appendix for a detailed description of I2D2) to construct mean (log) wages for 88 countries in the world and, then, calculate wage differentials for each pair of countries.[1] Figure 2.1 compares these bilateral annual wage differentials with the (log) share of emigrants from each source country to each destination country.[2]

The figure reveals that people are more likely to move between two countries if the wage differences between the source and destination are greater. The slope in the graph implies that an increase of $2,000 in mean annual wages in the destination country makes an emigrant 10 percent more likely to choose to migrate there. For example, the propensity of Slovenians to migrate to Canada and to the United States can be mostly explained by wage differentials. Annual wages are $21,000 and $30,000

Figure 2.1   **Wage differences and emigrant shares**

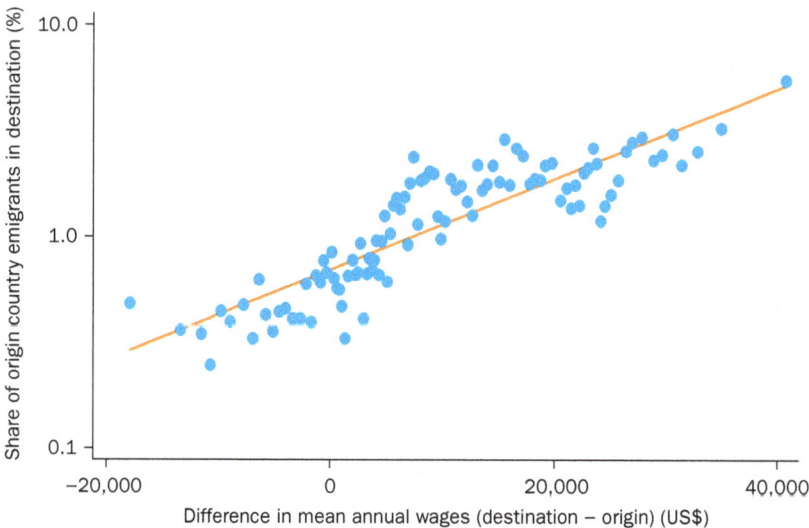

Sources: Data from the 2010/2011 OECD Database on Immigrants in OECD and Non-OECD Countries (DIOC-E) and World Bank International Income Distribution Data (I2D2).

Note: Figure plots the residuals from regressions of the x- and y-axis variables on a set of controls. Controls include origin fixed effects, (log) distance, contiguity, linguistic similarity, and (log) destination population. Dots represent averages over 100 equally sized bins. Sample restricted to all migration corridors with migrant stocks greater than 1,000 with available data. OECD = Organisation for Economic Co-operation and Development.

higher in Canada and the United States, respectively, than in Slovenia; and the fractions of Slovenian emigrants going to these countries are 5.3 and 9 percent, respectively.

The same patterns hold within countries in the case of internal migration. Figure 2.2 shows internal migration between 585 Indian districts using data from the 2001 Census of India.[3] The likelihood of migrating to a particular district increases with the relative (log) wage differential. The relationship is more pronounced and precise than for international migration flows. An increase of 11 percent in mean hourly wages in a district makes an Indian internal migrant 10 percent more likely to migrate to that district.

Using the 2000 Census of China (the Fifth National Population Census), we construct similar migration rates across 334 prefectures. We then combine this information with wage information from the *China City Statistical Yearbook 2001* and *China Statistical Yearbook 2001*. Figure 2.3 compares wage differentials between prefectures with the fraction of emigrants from each source prefecture to each destination prefecture.

Figure 2.2   **Wage differences and Indian internal migration**

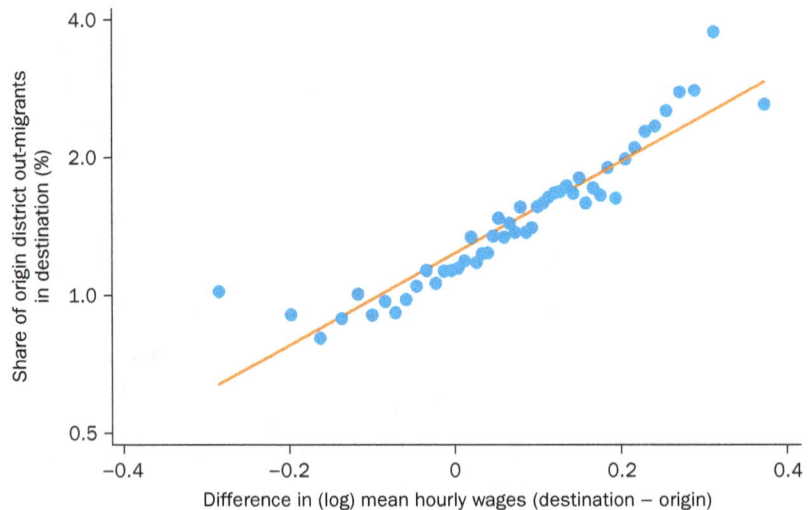

Sources: Data from the 2001 Census of India and the 1999/2000 National Sample Survey (55th round).

Note: Figure plots the residuals from regressions of the x- and y-axis variables on a set of controls. Controls include origin fixed effects, (log) distance, contiguity, linguistic similarity, and (log) destination population. Dots represent averages over 100 equally sized bins. Sample includes males ages 14–65 and district-pair corridors with internal migrant stocks greater than 250.

Figure 2.3   Wage differences and Chinese internal migration

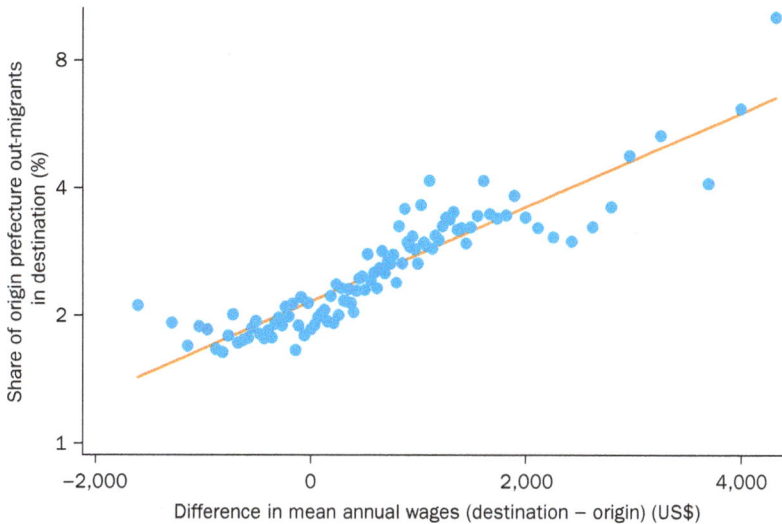

Sources: Data from the Fifth National Population Census 2000, *China City Statistical Yearbook 2001*, and *China Statistical Yearbook 2001*.

Note: Figure plots the residuals from regressions of the x- and y-axis variables on a set of controls. Controls include origin prefecture fixed effects, (log) prefecture-level city distance, within-province migration, and (log) destination population. Dots represent averages over 100 equally sized bins.

The figure shows a clear and tight positive relationship between wages in a prefecture and the probability that a Chinese internal migrant moves there.

Refugees also respond to wage differentials. Refugees flee a country because of wars, violence, ethnic conflict, and persecution.[4] However, wage levels still affect their choices of destination. Figure 2.4 plots the probability that refugees will choose a particular destination country against wage differentials between the home and destination countries. The positive relationship is clear, although less precise than in the case of economic migrants. This is possibly due to other noneconomic factors that enter into refugees' decision process. The data imply a $1,000 increase in mean wages in a given destination makes a refugee 2.8 percent more likely to flee to that destination. This relationship holds when we control for destination population, distance, contiguity, and linguistic similarity between origin and destination countries. In short, refugees, like everyone else, make decisions that are motivated by the search for a better life and are aware that higher-wage countries are more likely to provide that.

Figure 2.4   **Wage differences and refugees and asylum seekers**

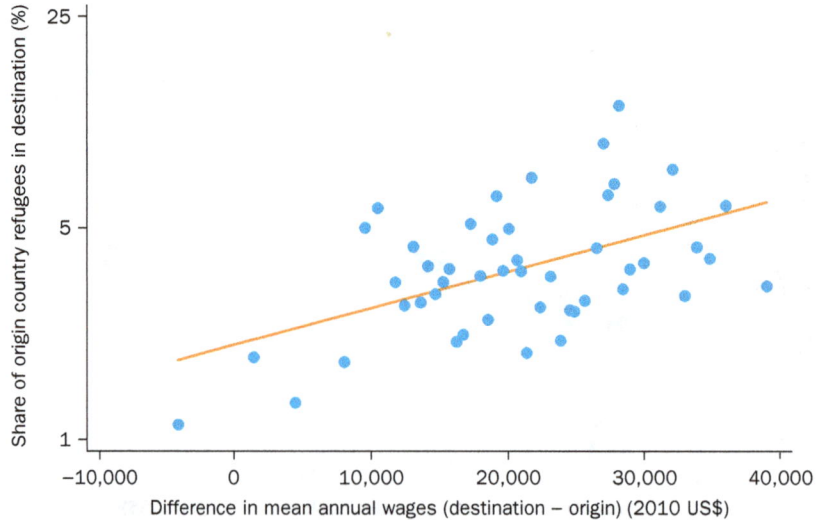

Source: Data from UNHCR Population Statistics Database.

Note: "Refugees" defined as the sum of both refugees (and those in refugee-like situations) and asylum seekers in 2015. Figure plots the residuals from regressions of the x- and y-axis variables on a set of controls. Controls include origin fixed effects, (log) distance, contiguity, linguistic similarity, and (log) destination population. Dots represent averages over 50 equally sized bins. Sample restricted to all corridors with refugee stocks greater than 500 with available data. UNHCR = United Nations High Commissioner for Refugees.

Income gains from migration

Wage differences between origin and destination locations are a major determinant of migration decisions, as shown in the previous section, for international and internal migrants and refugees alike. Do these patterns lead to corresponding wage increases for these migrants when they actually move?

Wages for the same jobs differ dramatically across countries. Even wages of employees at McDonald's differ by as much as a factor of 10 across countries when those employees perform almost identical tasks, using almost identical machinery, to produce almost identical products. Figure 2.5, taken from Ashenfelter (2012), shows a very high degree of correlation between wages and the output of workers at McDonald's across countries. Two important observations are worth highlighting. First, as economic theory suggests, workers are paid the value of their marginal product. Second, workers' marginal productivity levels are likely to differ enormously, even in an entirely standardized production environment. If such wage differences reflect skill differences of workers across countries,

Figure 2.5   Productivity and wages at McDonald's across countries

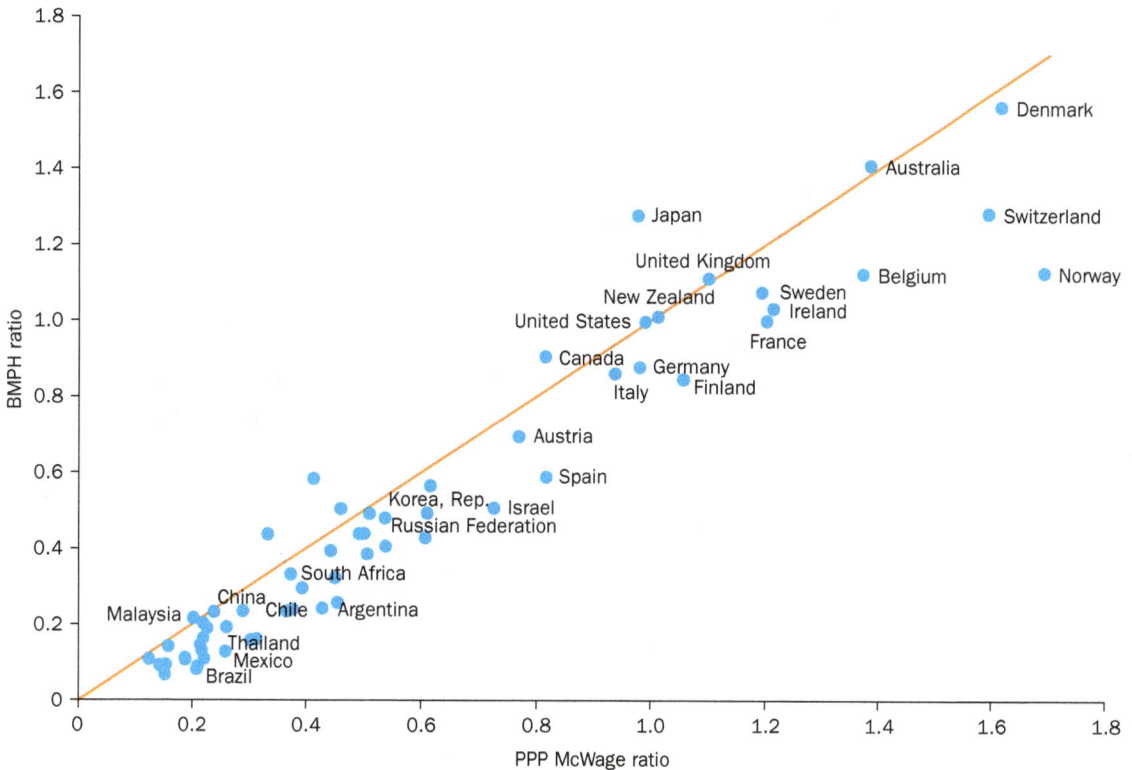

Source: Ashenfelter 2012, figure 2.6. Reproduced with permission; further permission required for reuse.

Note: The McWage is adjusted for purchasing power parity (PPP) prices in 2005, the latest year available. The PPP-adjusted McWage and Big Macs per hour (BMPH) are each expressed relative to the U.S. level, displayed with a 45-degree line.

there is reason to be pessimistic about the ability of migration to increase migrants' incomes.

However, differences in economic and social environments across countries might mean that migrants can increase their wages. While the evidence from McDonald's is suggestive, the ideal comparison is between the wages of identical workers working in different countries to see how much their incomes vary across countries. Although conceptually simple, empirical identification of this thought exercise can be challenging. One approach is to attempt to find non-migrants who "look" identical to migrants on observable characteristics such as gender, age, and education, and then compare the wages of these two groups. This is the approach adopted by Clemens, Montenegro, and Pritchett (2016) using data on immigrants in the United States. Their study estimates that typical individuals from an average developing country should expect to earn four to six times their income upon moving to the United States. Figure 2.6 presents the wage differences between workers in their home countries and in the United States. The fact that these wage differentials are not the result of differences in educational attainment or age suggests that migrants do experience large wage gains upon migrating from poorer to wealthier countries. Many of the factors that make a person productive are not intrinsic but are rather the result of the economic and social environment they work and live in. As a result, migrants, and the world as a whole, are, on average, better off if people are able to move to a wealthier country that has superior institutions, infrastructure, and complementary inputs.

These estimates of wage gains, however, should also be interpreted with caution. First, the wage gains are generally smaller than the gross domestic

Figure 2.6   Wage differences for migrants between the United States and their home countries

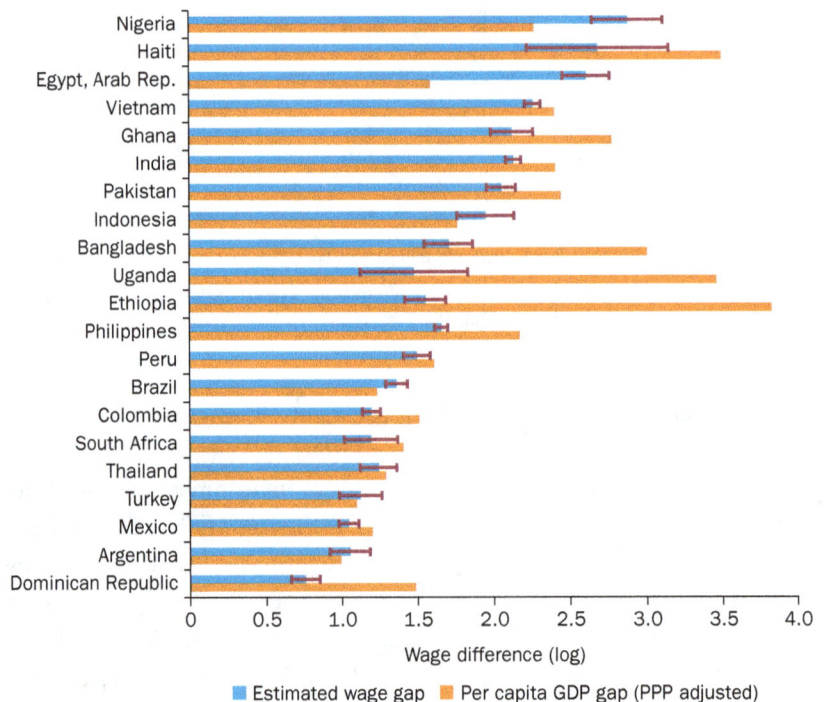

■ Estimated wage gap   ■ Per capita GDP gap (PPP adjusted)

Source: Based on Clemens, Montenegro, and Pritchett 2016, table 1.

Note: GDP per capita are purchasing power parity (PPP) adjusted and from the World Bank. The red lines represent confidence intervals of the estimated (log) wage gaps. The values represent the PPP-adjusted log-wage ratio of U.S. immigrants as compared to their non-migrant counterparts for males ages 35–39 years with 9–12 years of education. For example, in the case of Vietnam, those who migrated to the United States earn, on average, 9.97 (exp(2.3)) times as much as non-migrant Vietnamese.

product (GDP) differentials, suggesting that all productivity differences are not fully eliminated with migration. Second, and more important, is that we do not have precise measures of human capital and other productivity characteristics of workers in most datasets. Migrants are likely to be different from non-migrants in a host of ways that are not easily measured or captured in surveys or censuses.

More convincing evidence that migration results in substantial wage gains comes from immigration lotteries. If the demand to migrate is much greater than the potential migration opportunities, destination countries' governments sometimes offer a lottery to decide who gets to migrate. Such lotteries provide a "natural" experiment with which to measure the actual wage and employment impact of migrating. By comparing individuals who applied to a lottery and won to those who lost, we can isolate the pure effect of migration on wage earnings.

In a series of papers, McKenzie, Stillman, and Gibson (2010) and Gibson et al. (2018) analyze the Pacific Access Category of New Zealand, where a random ballot is used to choose from among applicants from Tonga and several other Pacific Islands. Figure 2.7 shows that winners and losers in the

Figure 2.7   **Wage gains due to migration: Quasi-experimental evidence for Tongans in New Zealand**

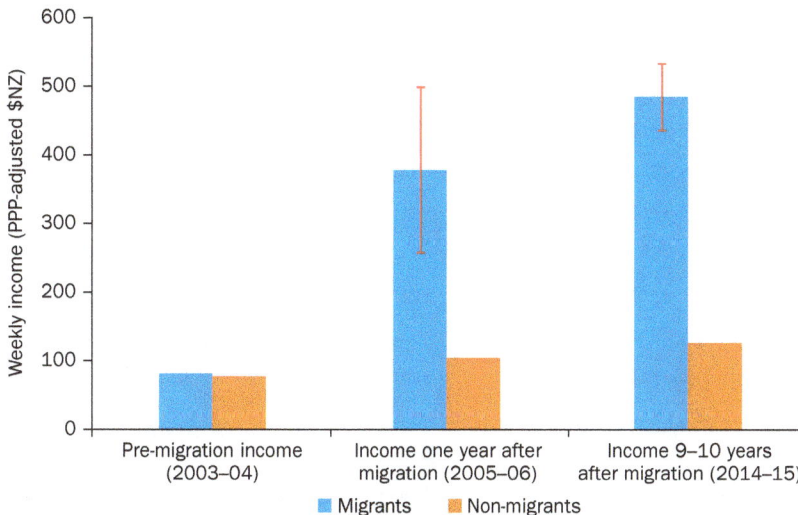

Sources: One-year results from McKenzie, Stillman, and Gibson 2010; long-term results from Gibson et al. 2018. Impacts shown are local average treatment effect estimates for impact of migrating; 95 percent confidence intervals shown for treatment effects.

Note: PPP = purchasing power parity.

lottery had similar incomes in Tonga prior to migration (about $NZ 80, or US$58, per week). In the first year after winning the lottery and moving to New Zealand, the migrants earn 273 percent more than the non-migrants. This relative large wage gap persists almost 10 years later, with migrants earning 284 percent more, or an extra $NZ 359 per week. These wage differences are adjusted for differences in cost of living, and so represent true income gains from migration. Assuming these gains continue through the working lives of migrants, Gibson et al. (2018) estimate that the present discounted value of migrating to New Zealand is $NZ 315,000 (US$237,000) per migrant. This amount is orders of magnitude greater than the income gains from numerous development interventions that are commonly studied. In other words, migrating offers tremendous wage benefits.

Employment differentials and migration

The relationship between migration flows and wage differentials tells only a part of the story on the labor market motivations of migration. Differences in employment rates and opportunities across geographic locations generate another set of important factors.

There is little evidence on the impact of employment rates on international migration flows. Nevertheless, existing data reveal some distinctive patterns. Figure 2.8 shows emigrant and immigrant shares in bilateral

Figure 2.8 **Employment rate differences and international migration**

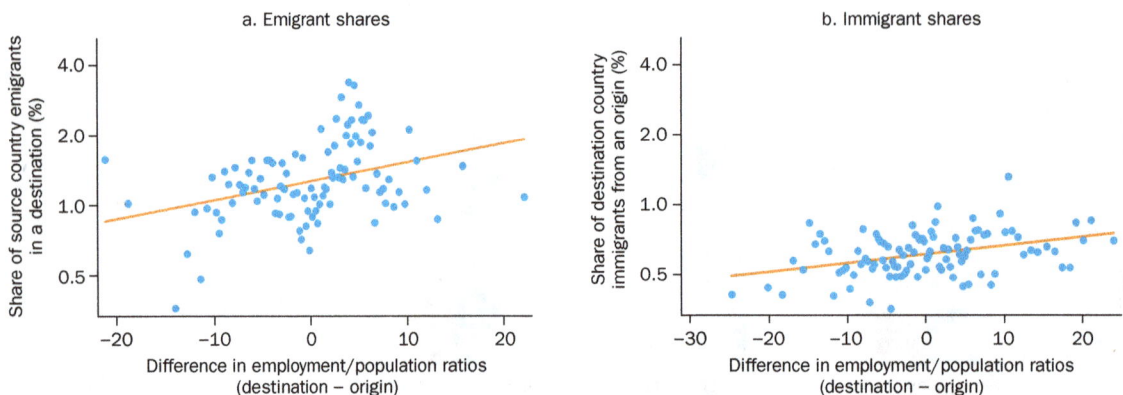

Sources: Data from the 2010/2011 OECD Database on Immigrants in OECD and Non-OECD Countries (DIOC-E) and World Bank International Income Distribution Data (I2D2).

Note: Graphs plot the residuals from regressions of the x- and y-axis variables on a set of controls. Controls for emigrant (immigrant) shares include origin (destination) fixed effects, (log) distance, contiguity, linguistic similarity, (log) GDP differences, and (log) destination (origin) population. Dots represent averages over 100 equally sized bins. Sample restricted to all migration corridors with migrant stocks greater than 1,000 with available data. OECD = Organisation for Economic Co-operation and Development.

corridors plotted against differences in the employment-to-population ratio in destination and source countries. Panel a shows that emigrants, on average, choose higher-employment destination countries. Panel b shows that, again on average, immigrants tend to come from lower-employment countries. Similar evidence exists for refugees who also tend to go to destinations with higher employment rates and lower unemployment, controlling for other factors (see figure 2.9).

Changes in internal migration within a country over time are a rich source of evidence on the employment-related determinants of migration patterns. Especially for the United States, a large literature exists on mobility responses to labor market shocks. A central observation is that U.S. internal migration rates are strongly procyclical (Saks and Wozniak 2011), with most migrants moving to take advantage of opportunities created during good economic years, especially in locations with strong economic growth and job creation. It is less clear, however, whether internal migration smooths the negative shocks in bad times. The fact that aggregate migration rates tend to decline in downturns suggests that U.S. workers do not respond to negative economic shocks by moving to other parts of the country. Instead, people remain in their current locations until the economy starts recovering, even if that location is experiencing higher unemployment (Mian and Sufi 2012; Molloy, Smith, and Wozniak 2011).

Figure 2.9 **Employment and unemployment rate differences and refugees**

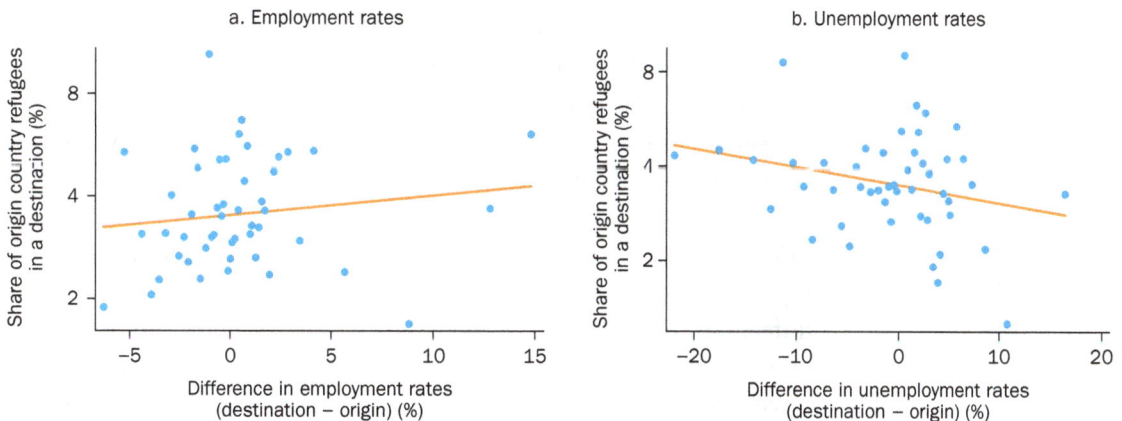

Source: Data from UNHCR Population Statistics Database.

Note: "Refugees" defined as the sum of both refugees (and those in refugee-like situations) and asylum seekers in 2015. Graphs plot the residuals from regressions of the x- and y-axis variables on a set of controls. Controls include origin fixed effects, (log) distance, contiguity, linguistic similarity, (log) GDP differences, and (log) destination population. Dots represent averages over 50 equally sized bins. Sample restricted to all corridors with refugee stocks greater than 500 with available data. UNHCR = United Nations High Commissioner for Refugees.

The financial crisis of 2007–08 and the subsequent "Great Recession" seem to have created slightly different patterns, as argued in a recent paper by Monras (2015). The analysis shows that geographic relocation was important in mitigating negative local economic shocks. However, the relocation mechanism involves decreased in-migration rates into negatively hit locations, rather than increased out-migration.

Addressing the same issue, Ransom (2016) observes that migration rates among unemployed workers were higher than among the employed during 2002–13. More interesting, the migration rates for the unemployed increased during the Great Recession, whereas the migration rate for the employed decreased slightly. The paper finds that the observed differences in migration rates by employment status are primarily due to the asymmetry in the job offer and job destruction rates over the Great Recession. More specifically, job offer rates decreased by about five times more than job destruction rates. Furthermore, employed workers face a steep job-queuing penalty when moving locations, whereas unemployed workers face no such penalty. These two factors together give employed workers an incentive to stay in their current location and keep their jobs, in contrast to unemployed workers, who are more likely to migrate.

Family and migration decisions

An objection to the claim that wage differentials are the main drivers of migration decisions is that many people, especially women, do not migrate for work-related reasons. Research has shown that family-related social reasons are often more prominent in influencing women's migration decisions. For example, according to the 2001 census, Indian women are 2.5 times more likely to migrate internally than men. The reason is that marriage is by far the largest motivation for internal migration by women in India. Migration is nearly universal for women in rural areas, as seen in figure 2.10 (replicated from Fulford 2015). Despite significant regional differences, in most parts of India the norm is for women to be married outside of their natal village, joining their husband's family in his village or town (this is called patrilocal village exogamy). Marriage accounts for 71 percent of all female migration in India. Men have more varied reasons: about 30 percent migrate for work, and a similar number migrate with their families. Over 70 percent of marriage migration is over a short distance and takes place within a district. Hence, women do not migrate far: only

Figure 2.10   Internal migration rates in India, by age and sex

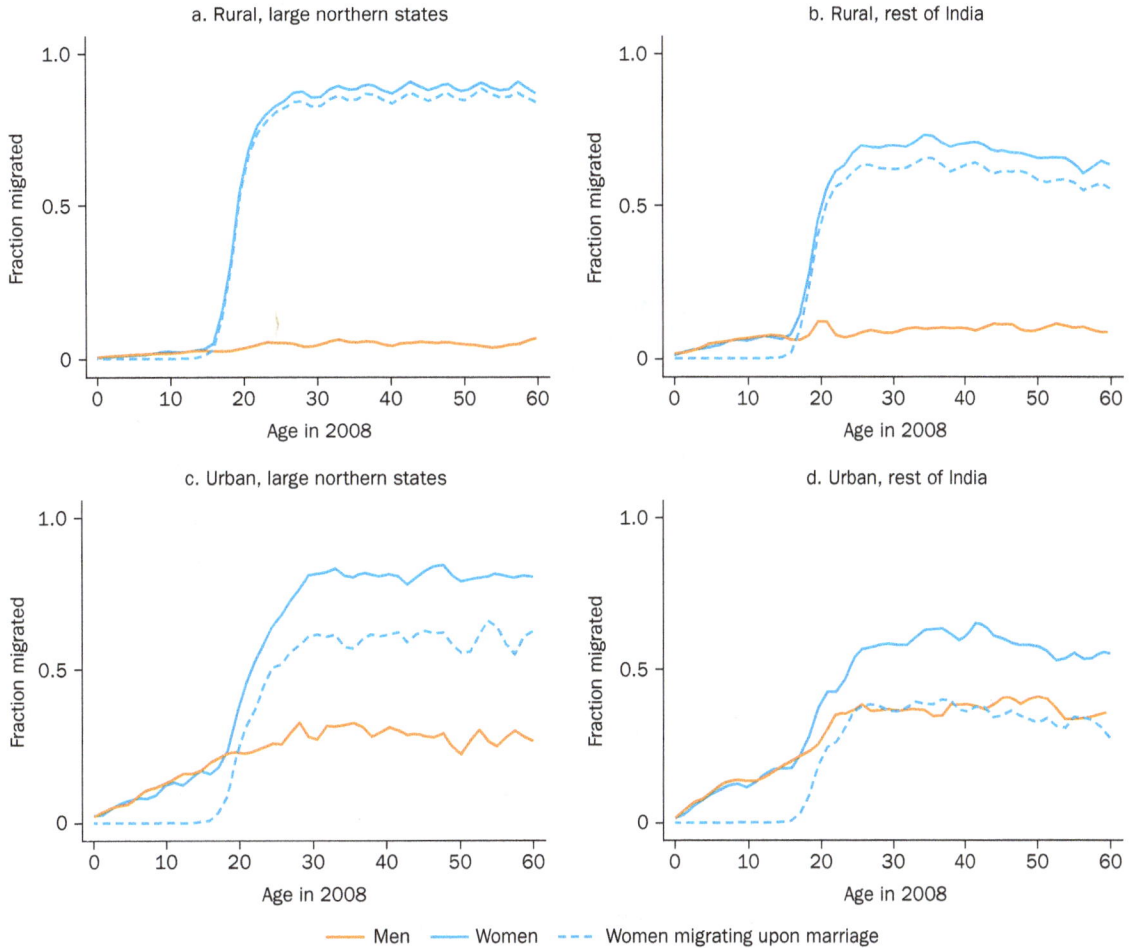

a. Rural, large northern states

b. Rural, rest of India

c. Urban, large northern states

d. Urban, rest of India

——— Men   ——— Women   - - - Women migrating upon marriage

Source: Fulford 2015, figure 2.1. Reproduced with permission; further permission required for reuse.

Note: Weighted to be representative by sector and region. "Sector" is defined as the place of residence at the time of the survey. The large northern states are Bihar, Chhattisgarh, Gujarat, Haryana, Jharkhand, Madhya Pradesh, Orissa, Punjab, Rajasthan, Uttar Pradesh, and Uttaranchal. Data are from the 64th round of the National Sample Survey.

9 percent move across state borders. Meanwhile, 20 percent of male migration in India is across states.

Turning to international migration, using data from the U.S. Office of Immigration Statistics to investigate the characteristics of immigrants to the United States also reveals interesting patterns. Non-work-related reasons seem to motivate a substantial portion of international migration to the United States. Most strikingly, men account for 70 percent of all visas that go to temporary workers and their families,[5] despite the fact that dependents are included in these numbers. Relatively fewer women receive an H-1B visa. For the next stage of the immigration process, permanent residency status or the Green Card, figure 2.11 shows information on persons who obtained permanent residency disaggregated by gender.[6] The data indicate that 48 percent of all female Green Card recipients in 2014 were homemakers, who mostly obtained it through family reunification policies, whereas this was the case for less than 3 percent of men. Meanwhile, 36 percent of men had a management or professional occupation, compared to only 16 percent of women.

Clearly, there are gender differentials in what motivates migration, which raises the question: Do migration patterns related to wage differentials, unemployment rates, distance, and networks differ by gender? The available data suggest that the answer is no. Women and men may often move for distinct reasons, but their aggregate migration patterns are remarkably similar.

Panel a of figure 2.12 shows the emigration-to-population ratio by gender across countries. Practically all countries lie along the 45-degree line, meaning that the same proportion of each gender emigrates. Some of the few exceptions are smaller countries with many female emigrants, and Armenia, Grenada, Jordan, Lebanon, and the Virgin Islands, with many

Figure 2.11 **Occupation of recent permanent residents in the United States, by gender**

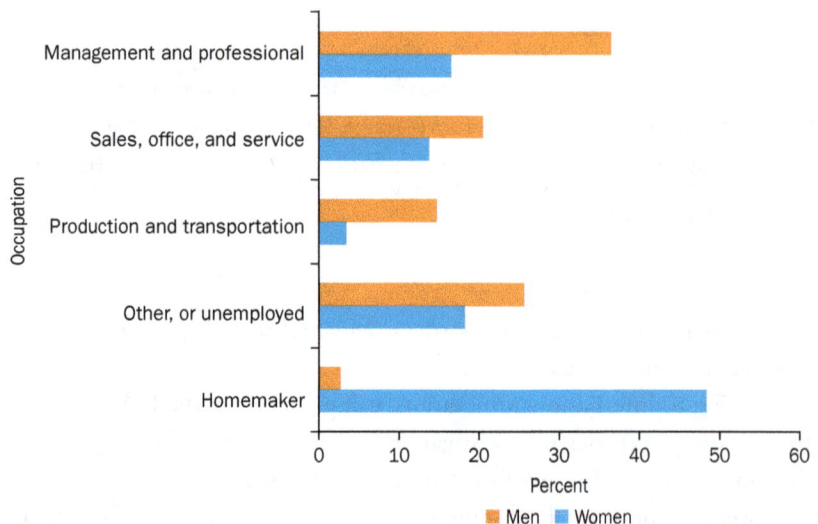

Source: DHS 2016a.

Figure 2.12   International migration rates, by gender

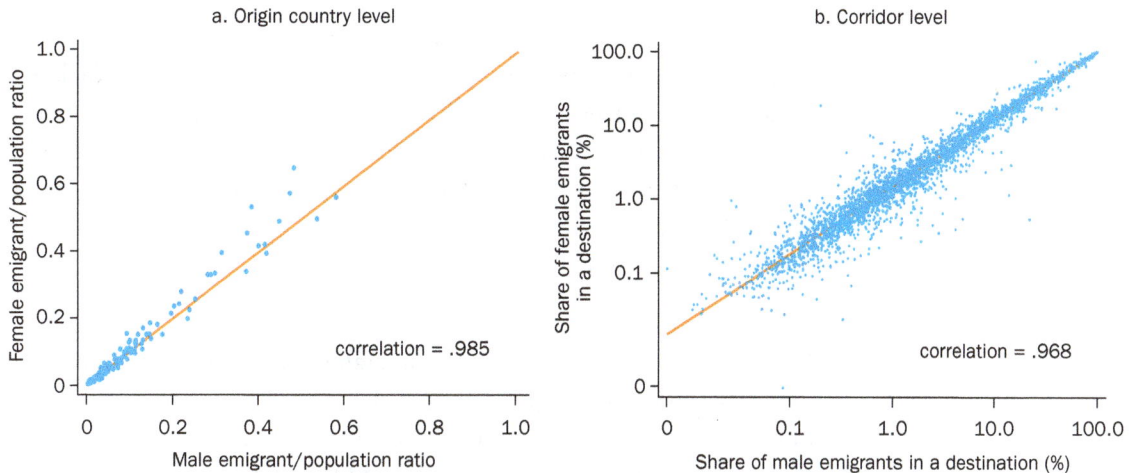

Source: Data from the 2010/2011 OECD Database on Immigrants in OECD and Non-OECD Countries (DIOC-E).

Note: Female (male) migrant shares in panel B defined as the number of female (male) migrants in a given corridor divided by the total number of female (male) emigrants from a given origin country. OECD = Organisation for Economic Co-operation and Development.

more male emigrants. The correlation between male and female emigration rates across the world is a remarkable 0.985.

A similar pattern emerges when we analyze bilateral migration rates according to gender. Simply put, men and women from the same origin country tend to migrate to the same destination countries at the same rates. The scatterplot in panel b of figure 2.12 shows the (natural log) proportion of male migrants from each origin country to each destination country against the proportion of female migrants. The observations are tightly clustered around the 45-degree line, and the correlation across genders is 0.97. Even though male and female migrants from a country migrate to destination countries in very similar proportions, this is not necessarily true for all bilateral flows. For example, migrant flows from Indonesia to Saudi Arabia are disproportionately female (household employees) whereas those from Bangladesh to Oman and Malaysia are disproportionately male (agricultural and construction jobs). But these exceptions are not frequent despite the attention these outlier corridors receive in the media.

An explanation for this seeming puzzle is that both men and women in fact move for employment-related reasons but that women are more likely to be "tied movers." If individuals migrate in search of higher wages and better employment opportunities and their spouses accompany them, then the spouses are indirectly moving for the very same economic reasons.

Why migrate? The costs of migrating

Although the benefits of migration are significant, migration also has high costs. These costs take many different forms and vary across corridors, occupations, genders, education levels, and age groups. The cost of travel, social or economic difficulties in settling in a new country, policy-induced legal barriers, and linguistic adaptation are some of the most common financial and personal costs observed and analyzed.

Distance

Distance is a major determinant of migrants' choice of destination. Even as transportation costs rapidly decline, distance continues to be important in explaining global migration patterns. Figure 2.13 depicts the relationship between emigration probabilities and (natural log) distance between origin and destination countries in 1960 and 2010. The correlation of emigration flows with distance has diminished slightly over time, but it persists and is significant.

The effect of distance is also important for internal migration. For example, Morten and Oliveira (2016) compare migration probabilities with travel times across Brazilian provinces, revealing a strong negative relationship.

Figure 2.13 **Distance and emigrant shares, 1960 and 2010**

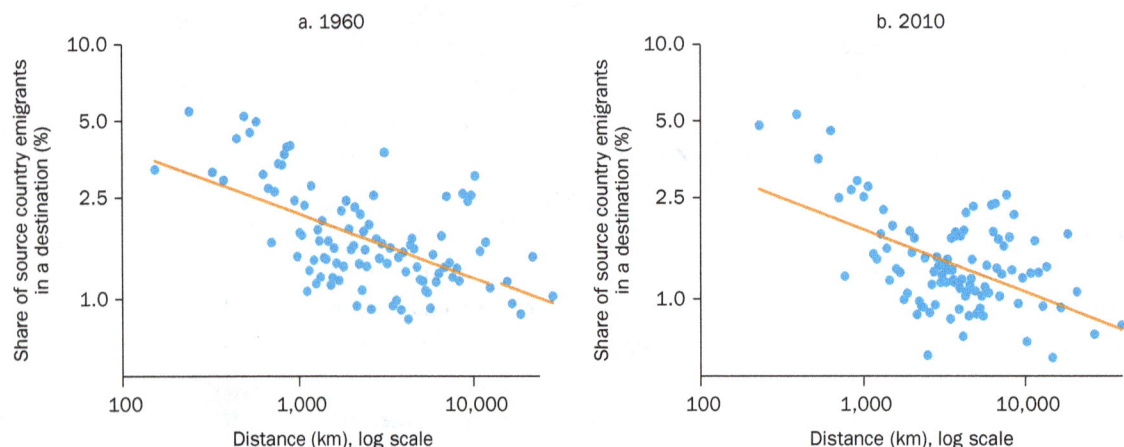

Sources: Data from the World Bank Global Bilateral Migration Database (1960–2000) and the 2010/2011 OECD Database on Immigrants in OECD and Non-OECD Countries (DIOC-E).

Note: Graphs plot the residuals from regressions of the x- and y-axis variables on a set of origin country fixed effects. OECD = Organisation for Economic Co-operation and Development.

Figure 2.14   **Distance and Indian internal migration**

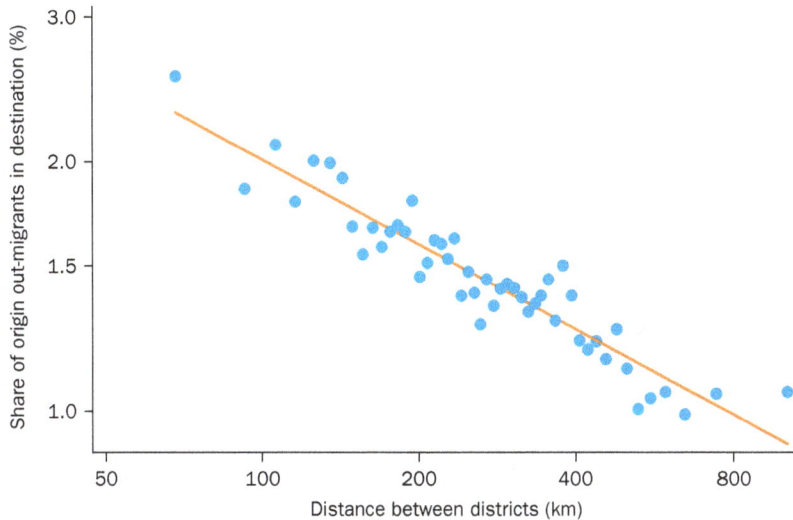

Sources: Data from the 2001 Census of India and the 1999/2000 National Sample Survey (55th round).

Note: Figure plots the residuals from regressions of the x- and y-axis variables on a set of controls. Controls include origin fixed effects, (log) average wage differences, contiguity, linguistic similarity, and (log) destination population. Dots represent averages over 100 equally sized bins. Sample includes males ages 14–65 and district-pair corridors with internal migrant stocks greater than 250.

This same negative relationship is found in India. Figure 2.14 plots Indian internal out-migration shares against distance. A clear and tight negative relationship exists between distance and internal migration.

Distance matters for refugee location decisions even more so than for migrants. Figure 2.15 shows the cumulative distribution of refugees and low- and high-skilled economic migrants by distance. The overall pattern shows that high-skilled economic migrants travel farther than low-skilled economic migrants, who in turn travel farther than refugees.

Contiguity is particularly critical for refugees. Over 80 percent of refugees end up in neighboring countries. Refugees from the Syrian Arab Republic flee primarily to Turkey, Lebanon, and Jordan; Afghans to Pakistan and the Islamic Republic of Iran; and Somalis to Ethiopia, Kenya, and the Republic of Yemen (across the Gulf of Aden). This pattern holds for practically all refugee flows. In addition to contiguity, distance continues to play a prominent role for refugees' destination choices, as shown in figure 2.16. Distant countries are significantly less likely to host refugees from a source country whereas nearer—often poorer—countries host the vast majority of refugees.

Figure 2.15   **Cumulative distribution of world migration, by distance**

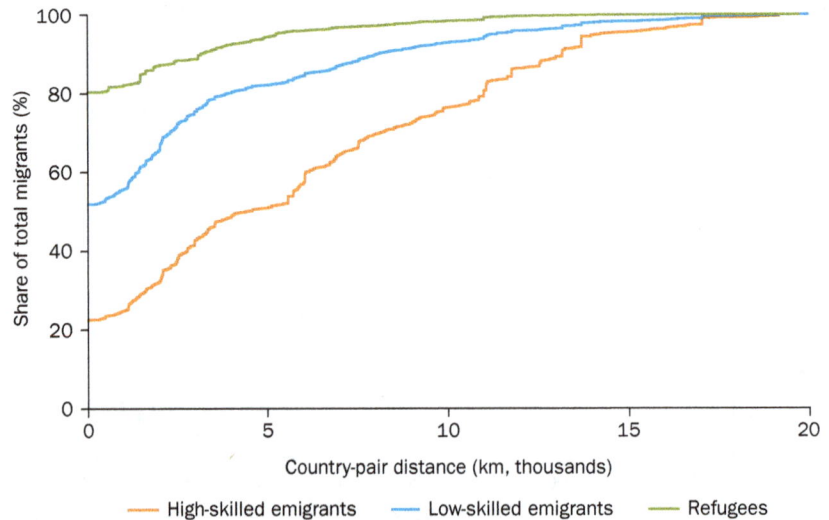

Sources: Figure uses year 2000 migrant stocks from the World Bank Global Bilateral Migration Database (1960–2000) and 2015 refugee stocks from UNHCR Population Statistics Database. Distance and contiguity data derive from the CEPII GeoDist database.

Note: Distance is defined as distance between two most populous cities, and contiguous countries are treated as zero distance. The cumulative distribution function plots the share of all international migrants who reside in a country less than or equal to a given distance from their home country. UNHCR = United Nations High Commissioner for Refugees.

Figure 2.16   **Distance and refugee location**

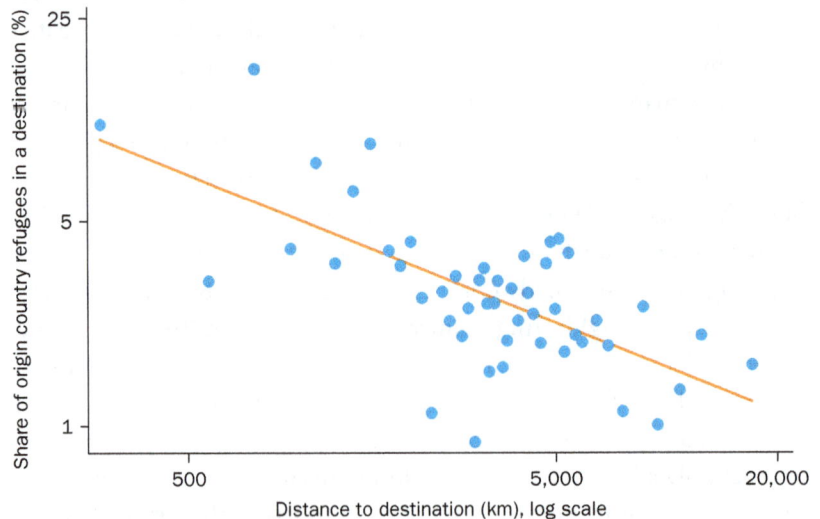

Source: Data from UNHCR Population Statistics Database.

Note: "Refugees" defined as the sum of both refugees (and those in refugee-like situations) and asylum seekers in 2015. Figure plots the residuals from regressions of the x- and y-axis variables on a set of origin country fixed effects. Dots represent averages over 50 equally sized bins. Sample restricted to all corridors with refugee stocks greater than 500 with available data. UNHCR = United Nations High Commissioner for Refugees.

Migrant networks

A major cost of migration is having to settle in a new location. Migrants must find jobs and housing. They want a social life, need to overcome legal hurdles, and must familiarize themselves with cultural norms. As a preexisting network of co-nationals, their diaspora is among the most useful tools in all of these endeavors. Furthermore, social networks and diaspora links make migration flows highly persistent over time: past and current migrant stocks are an excellent predictor of future flows.[7] Figure 2.17 plots the stock of migrants from a source in a specific destination country in 1980 against that in 1990 (panel a) and against that in 2000 (panel b).[8] Each figure also depicts the linear best fit and a 45-degree line.

Figure 2.17 suggests three patterns. First, a very close relationship exists between past and current migrant stocks. Second, the relationship between historic and current migrant stocks is less than proportional—that is, in figure 2.17 the slope of the linear best-fit line (orange) is less than the 45-degree line (black dashed). The implication is that existing migration patterns do not reinforce themselves but rather that there is a process of diffusion over time. Historically popular migrant destinations for the citizens of a specific source country continue to attract many migrants but at a lower rate than in the past. Third, this process of

Figure 2.17 Network effects and emigrant shares

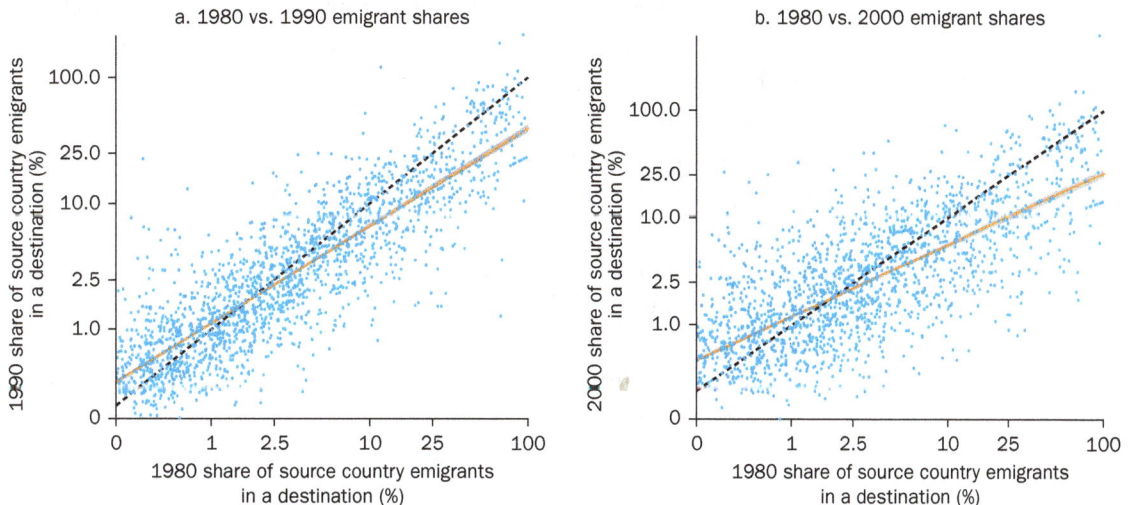

a. 1980 vs. 1990 emigrant shares

b. 1980 vs. 2000 emigrant shares

Source: Data from the World Bank Global Bilateral Migration Database (1960–2000).

Note: Graphs plot the residuals from regressions of the x- and y-axis variables on a set of controls. Controls include origin fixed effects, (log) distance, and contiguity. Dots represent averages over 100 equally sized bins. Sample restricted to all migration corridors with migrant stocks greater than 1,000 with available data. In each panel, the dashed line is the 45-degree line, and the orange line shows linear best fit.

Figure 2.18 Network effects and refugee location

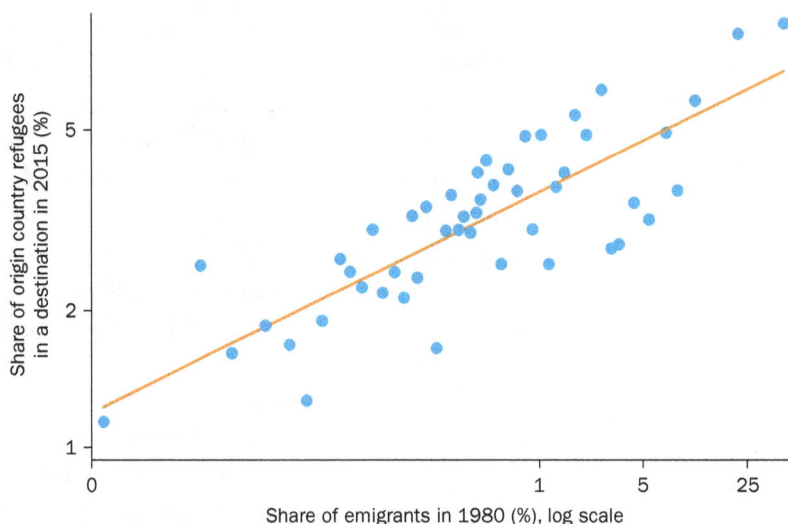

Sources: Data from UNHCR Population Statistics Database and the World Bank Global Bilateral Migration Database (1960–2000).

Note: "Refugees" defined as the sum of both refugees (and those in refugee-like situations) and asylum seekers in 2015. Figure plots the residuals from regressions of the x- and y-axis variables on a set of origin country fixed effects, (log) distance, and contiguity. Dots represent averages over 50 equally sized bins. Sample restricted to all corridors with refugee stocks greater than 500 with available data. UNHCR = United Nations High Commissioner for Refugees.

migrant diffusion across destination countries has continued over time. The best-fit line comparing 1980 and 2000 migrant stocks (panel b) is flatter, with an elasticity of 0.51, which is a weaker relationship than the one between the 1980 and 1990 stocks (panel a).

Diaspora networks affect refugee flows as strongly as they do flows of economic migrants. Figure 2.18 shows a strong positive relationship between the historic (in the year 1980) proportion of a country's emigrants in a destination country and the subsequent (in the year 2015) distribution of refugees from that source country. Specifically, a 10 percent larger network of co-nationals in a certain destination country increases by 1.6 percent the probability that a refugee chooses that country. That relationship is about one-third the magnitude of the relationship for economic migrants but is still strong, especially given that the figure controls for distance and contiguity.

Language

Fluency in the language of the destination country or region plays an important role in immigrants' success in the destination country's labor market, in establishing a social life, and in integration more generally (see, for example, Bleakley and Chin 2004, 2010; Chiswick and Miller 1995, 2002; Dustmann 1994; Dustmann and Fabbri 2003; Dustmann and van Soest 2001; Kossoudji 1988). This suggests that the ability to learn and speak a foreign language quickly may be a factor in the potential migrants' choices of locations. Several studies show that global bilateral migration patterns are significantly influenced by linguistic similarity.[9] However, the relationship is less clear than for most of the other factors discussed in this chapter.

In figure 2.19, emigration probabilities are plotted against an index of linguistic similarity.[10] The correlation is positive and significant. It implies that the probability of emigration to a country with the same native language is double that of emigration to a country with no linguistic similarity (for example, with native languages such as English or Korean).

The positive relationship between linguistic similarity and migration probabilities also holds for internal migration in India, which has significant linguistic heterogeneity (see figure 2.20).[11] The correlation suggests that a 10 percentage point increase in linguistic similarity increases

Figure 2.19   Linguistic similarity and emigrant shares

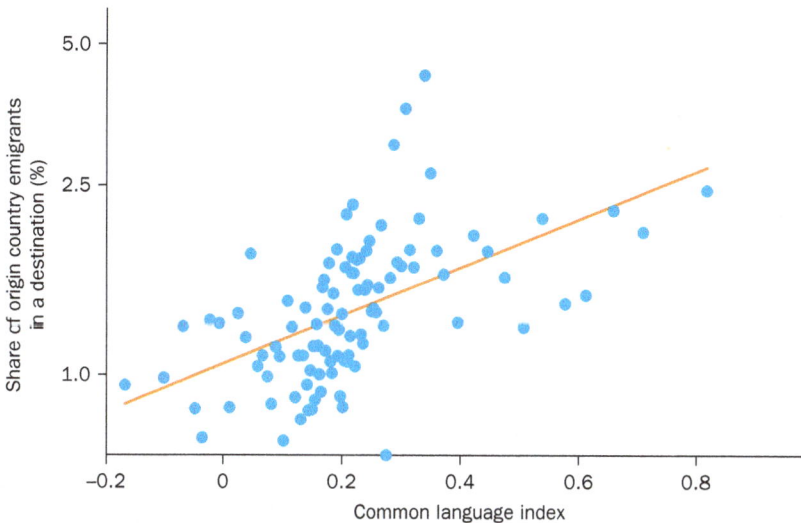

Sources: Data from the World Bank Global Bilateral Migration Database (1960–2000), the 2010/2011 OECD Database on Immigrants in OECD and Non-OECD Countries (DIOC-E), and language data from the CEPII GeoDist database.

Note: Figure plots the residuals from regressions of the x- and y-axis variables on a set of controls. Controls include origin fixed effects, (log) distance, and contiguity. Dots represent averages of 100 equally sized bins. Sample restricted to all migration corridors with migrant stocks greater than 1,000 with available data. OECD = Organisation for Economic Co-operation and Development.

Figure 2.20   **Linguistic similarity and Indian internal migration**

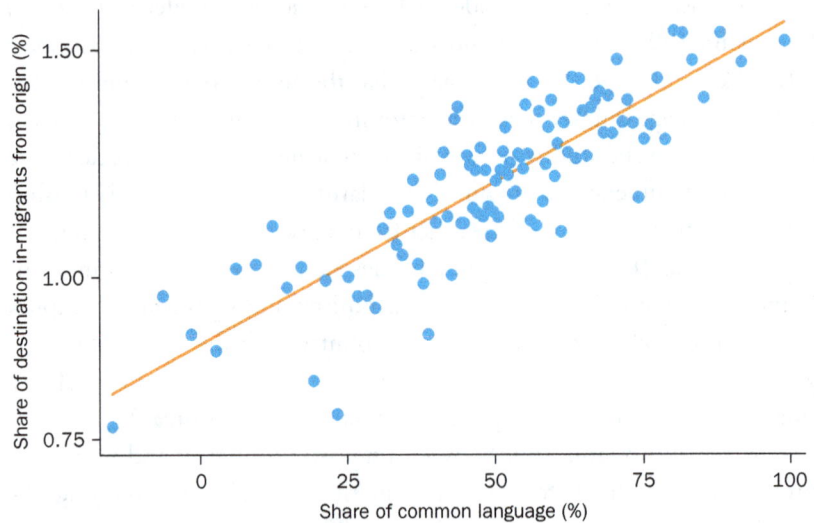

Sources: Data from the 2001 Census of India and the 1999/2000 National Sample Survey (55th round).

Note: Figure plots the residuals from regressions of the x- and y-axis variables on a set of controls. Controls include destination district fixed effects, (log) average wage differences, and contiguity. Dots represent averages over 100 equally sized bins. Sample includes males ages 14–65 and district-pair corridors with internal migrant stocks greater than 250 (see Kone et al. 2017 for details).

migration flows to a particular district by 5 percent. Refugee flows, in contrast, do not seem to be significantly correlated with linguistic similarity, once we control for contiguity and distance.

Migration policies

At the heart of debates on the impact of immigration are destination countries' immigration policies. Destination countries use immigration policy to alter the magnitude and skill composition of immigration flows and, at times, to address the humanitarian needs of those migrating.

A central challenge of understanding the impact of immigration policies is the sheer complexity of immigration pathways. For both historical and policy reasons, the scale and nature of international migration movements differ from country to country. Countries have dozens of different immigrant categories of varying importance. The complex ways these interact, together with undocumented migration, make assessing their impact very difficult. Figure 2.21 provides a sense of this variability across Organisation for Economic Co-operation and Development (OECD) countries in 2013. It shows both the relative importance of permanent migration and the

Figure 2.21 Permanent immigration, by category of entry to select OECD countries, 2013

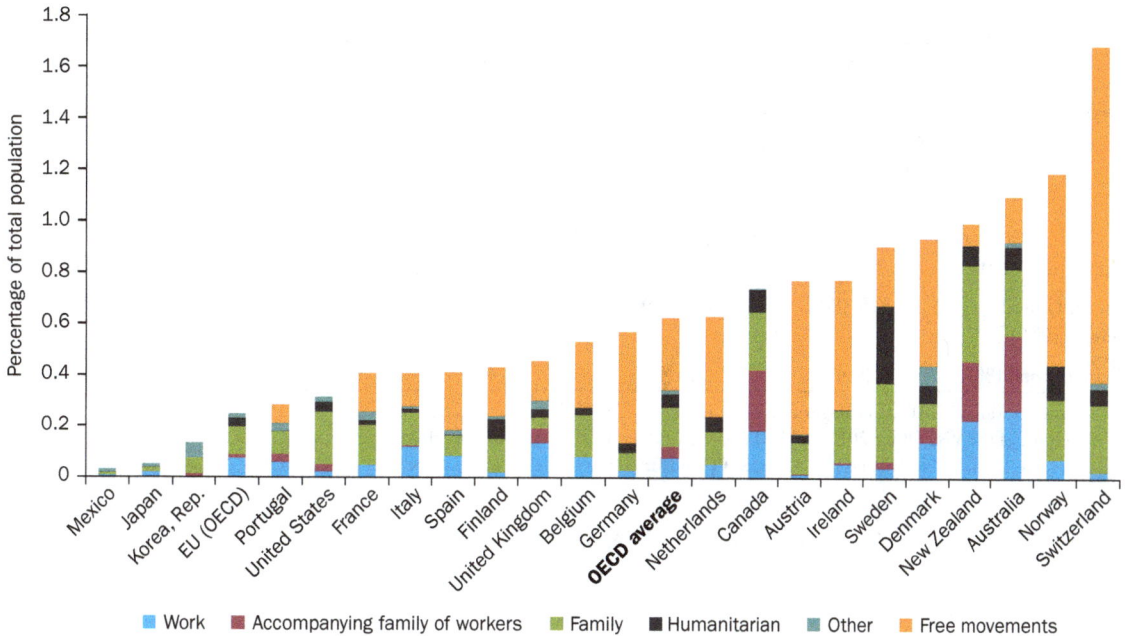

Source: Data from OECD 2015, figure 1.3.

Note: EU = European Union; OECD = Organisation for Economic Co-operation and Development.

distribution by category of entry. Free circulation has become an important category of entry for many European countries, although it was less so prior to the enlargement of the European Union (EU) in 2004. Labor migration (excluding free-circulation movements) tends to be a minority phenomenon in almost all countries, and the number of people entering under this category is generally smaller than those entering for family reasons.

Researchers have lately had an impetus to increase the quantity and quality of data on immigration policies to assess those policies' impact on migration patterns and outcomes. A recent high-profile contribution is the International Migration Policy and Law Analysis (IMPALA) database. The IMPALA project categorizes immigration policies by type of entry path: economic, family, humanitarian, student, or citizenship.[12] Each category involves many tracks, or visa categories (see table 2.1), which differ in importance across countries. For example, in the United States, 30 percent of visas are issued to economic migrants and 30 percent to students, 16 percent are family based, 23 percent are for citizenship, and only 3 percent are for humanitarian immigrants.

Table 2.1   International Migration Policy and Law Analysis (IMPALA) entry path categories and U.S. immigration

	IMPALA entry path category				
	Economic	Family	Humanitarian	Student	Citizenship
Migration group	Workers, investors, entrepreneurs	Partners, children, parents, and extended family members	Asylum seekers, refugees, subsidiary protection, violence, human trafficking, etc.	University, school, exchange, vocational, and language students	All: acquisition and modes of loss of naturalization
Tracks per country	15–64	16–46	6–43	4–10	13–28
No. in United States (2015)	925,884	487,849	106,432	895,053	729,995
Share of total (%)	29.4	15.5	3.4	28.5	23.2

Sources: Description of IMPALA categories is from Beine et al. 2015. U.S. immigration totals are calculated from U.S. Department of State, "Report of the Visa Office 2016," table II and table XVIa; U.S. Department of Homeland Security, *2015 Yearbook of Immigration Statistics*, table 13 and table 16; and U.S. Citizenship and Immigration Services, "Naturalization Fact Sheet" (August 12, 2016).

An additional level of complexity emerges with the degree of stringency in implementation in each category. Figures 2.22 and 2.23 compare stringency patterns across countries and immigrant groups. In general, immigration is easiest for high-skilled migrants, more difficult for low-skilled migrants, and most complicated for asylum seekers. Stringency varies, however, across countries and immigrant groups. For example, the United States makes it particularly easy for high-skilled immigrants but has relatively more stringent rules for low-skilled immigrants and asylum seekers. Meanwhile, Switzerland is generally stringent toward all three groups. Australia makes it easier for economic immigrants but particularly hard for asylum seekers.

Immigration policies have changed substantially over time. The Determinants of International Migration (DEMIG) Policy database has tracked policy changes for a set of 45 countries over more than 100 years.[13] Figure 2.24 shows changes in policy restrictiveness over time across all 45 countries. Several conclusions emerge. First, increasing restrictiveness of migration policies in the first half of the 20th century coincided with the Great Depression and the Second World War. Second, beginning around the end of the Second World War, policies become less restrictive, with a dramatic shift toward liberalization from the late 1940s to the early 1990s. Finally, more recently, migration policy has continued its trend toward more liberalization, although at a slower rate than in the previous generation.

Figure 2.22 Regulatory stringency of immigration tracks for skilled and unskilled migrants, by country, 1999 and 2008

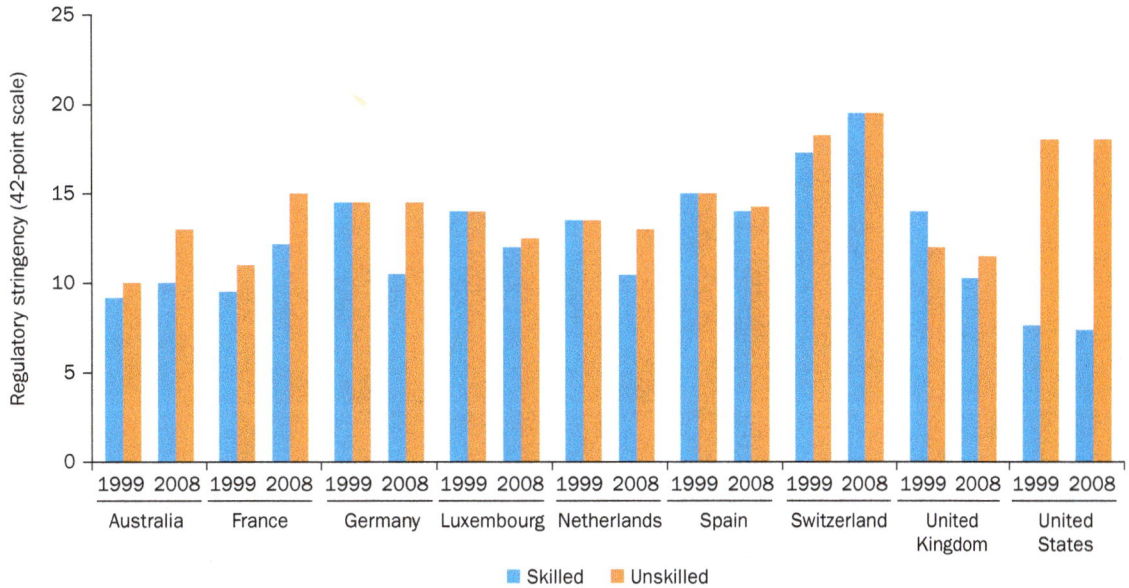

Source: Reproduced from Beine et al. 2015, figure IV. Reproduced with permission; further permission required for reuse.

Note: The researchers determine stringency by asking a series of questions regarding countries' immigration policies and assigning a score on the basis of the answers. The higher the score, the more stringent the immigration rules.

Figure 2.23 Regulatory stringency of asylum track, by country, 1999 and 2008

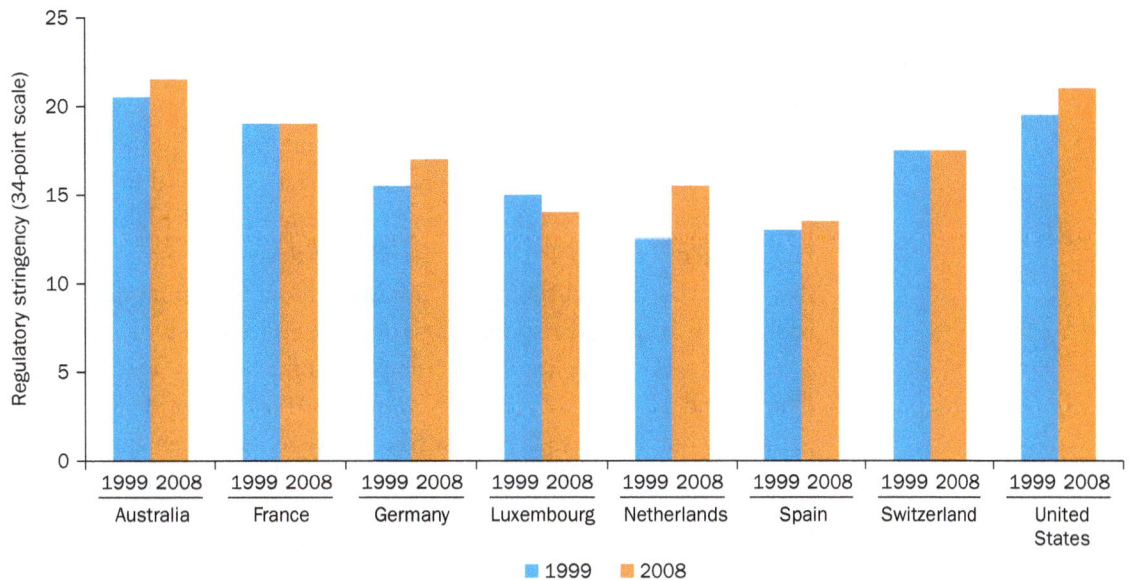

Source: Beine et al. 2015, figure VIII. Reproduced with permission; further permission required for reuse.

Note: The researchers determine stringency by asking a series of questions regarding countries' immigration policies and assigning a score on the basis of the answers. The higher the score, the more stringent the immigration rules.

109

Figure 2.24 Changes in immigration policy restrictiveness, 1900–2015

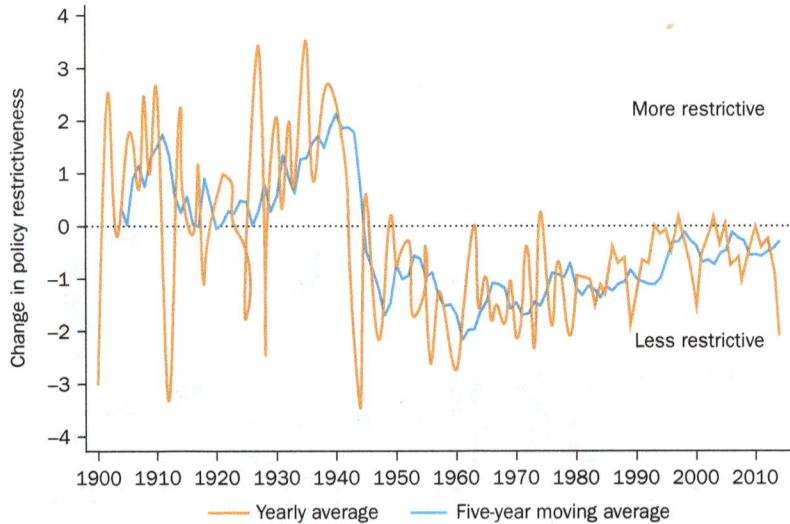

Source: de Haas, Natter, and Vezzoli 2016. Reproduced with permission; further permission required for reuse.

Note: Values derived from taking the weighted sum of all policy changes in each year; weights are defined by the "policy level" variable in the Determinants of International Migration (DEMIG) Policy database. DEMIG tracks policy changes for a set of 45 countries.

Recent work that uses policy indexes to measure the effect of policies suggests a substantial impact on migration flows and stocks. Mayda (2010) finds that lowering policy restrictions has a larger positive effect on immigration flows for destinations with stronger pull factors (with high GDP per capita the most important). Ortega and Peri (2012) find that more-restrictive country policies decrease migration into European countries but increase migration between EU countries, plausibly as tighter external immigration policies are correlated with policies to facilitate internal EU migration. Czaika and de Haas (2016) look at the effect of travel visa policies and show that restrictive visa policies reduce inflows and outflows from destination countries, reducing the responsiveness of migrants to the business cycle.[14]

Asylum seekers' application decisions are influenced by asylum policy. Hatton and Moloney (2015) and Hatton (2016) analyze three types of policies: those related to (1) access (the ability to submit an application), (2) processing (the likelihood applicants receive recognition), and (3) welfare (after a successful application). They find that stricter policies on access and processing have a strong negative effect on asylum applications, but more generous welfare policies have a slightly positive effect on asylum applications.

Internal migration, too, is affected by policy choices. An interesting example is the introduction of a new national ID card (*shenfen zheng*) in China in 1984. Although urban residents received IDs in 1984, residents of most rural counties did not receive them immediately, and cards were distributed sporadically over the next several years. IDs were not necessary for migration, and large numbers of migrants live in cities without legal temporary residence cards. However, migrants with temporary residence cards have a more secure position in the destination community, hold better jobs, and thus make up part of a longer-term network in migrant destinations. Figure 2.25, replicated from de Brauw and Giles (2016), shows the share of the village labor force working as migrants as a function of the years since cards were issued. There is a clear positive relationship, suggesting that ID cards increased internal migration rates in China.

Migration policy has been instrumental in shaping one of the world's largest migration flows—from Mexico to the United States. A particular feature of this flow is that about half of Mexicans in the United States are unauthorized. More important, illegal Mexican migration to the United States started with a policy decision—the end of the Bracero Program. The Bracero Program, originally established in 1942 and effectively ended in 1965, was an important contributor to circular migration of temporary agricultural workers between Mexico and the United States.

Figure 2.25 **Share of Chinese internal migrants, by village, in years since identification cards were issued**

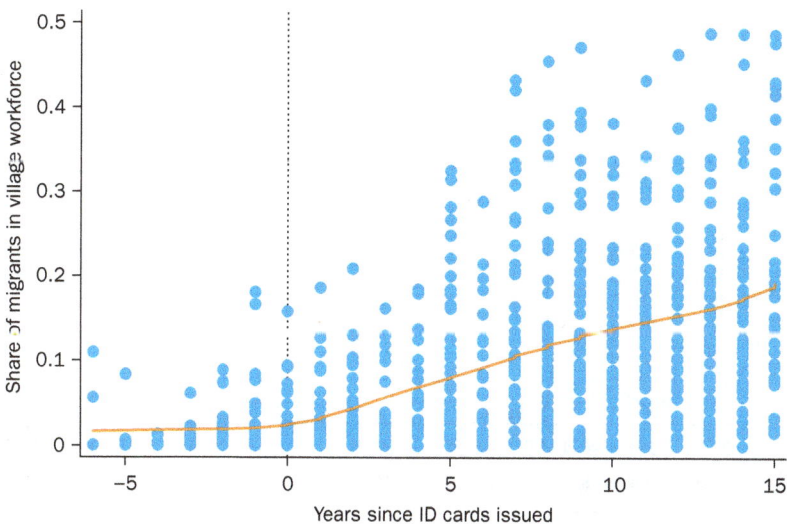

Source: De Brauw and Giles 2016. Reproduced with permission; further permission required for reuse.

With the end of the Bracero Program, the Mexico–United States migration situation changed drastically. From an annual access of about 450,000 guest worker visas and a large number of resident visas in the United States (averaging about 50,000 per year), the new regime led to a situation with no guest worker visas and just 20,000 resident visas annually (see Massey and Pren 2012). The effect is illustrated in figure 2.26, which shows Mexican entries into the United States in three categories by legal status for the period 1955–95: (1) temporary migrants (orange line—Braceros before 1965 and H-visa holders thereafter), (2) documented immigrants (blue line—those entering with permanent resident visas), and (3) undocumented immigrants (green line).[15] As clearly seen, with the end of the Bracero Program, undocumented migrants replaced temporary migrants, almost one for one. Because the labor market demand for Mexican workers still existed, the only way to meet that demand was through illegal entries. The markets prevailed.

One interesting case study of the impact of policy on migration is to assess the effects of enforcement on the United States' southwest border. The United States has pursued both external border enforcement and internal enforcement to discourage undocumented immigrants from Mexico since the end of the Bracero Program and the subsequent increase in illegal migration. This policy shift is likely to have reduced illegal border crossings and discouraged unauthorized immigrants significantly.

Figure 2.26 **Mexican migration to the United States, 1955–95**

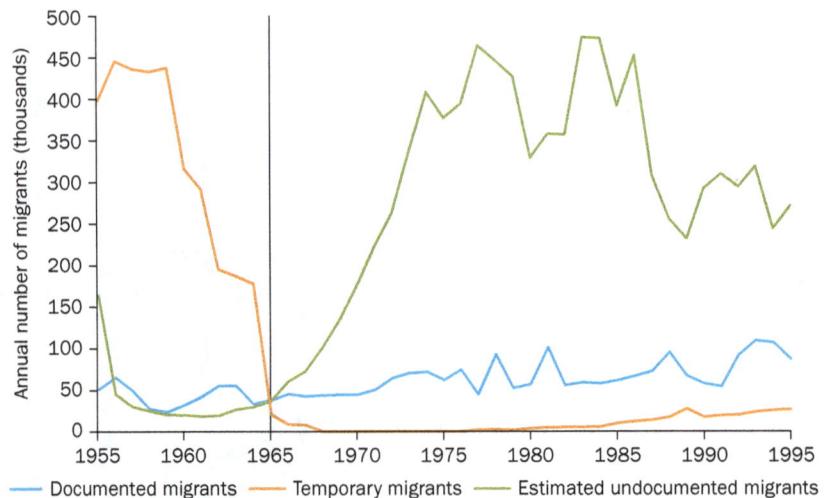

Source: Massey and Pren 2012. Reproduced with permission; further permission required for reuse.

Note: The vertical line (1965) represents the termination of the Bracero Program, which provided a legal framework for the circular migration of temporary agricultural workers.

Figure 2.27 shows border patrol staffing and the average payment to human smugglers (known as "coyotes") over time. The number of U.S. Border Patrol agents assigned to the southwest border rose from 4,139 in 1992 to a high of 21,444 in 2011 and has since stabilized. At the same time, and in significant part due to the increase in border enforcement,[16] the average payment to smugglers for help crossing the border rose from $495 in 1990 to $3,218 in 2013 (in 2014 U.S. dollars). The sixfold increase in the cost of illegally crossing the border is correlated with a rapid decline in the number of border crossings. The best evidence on border crossings comes from apprehension data because those data broadly reflect the number of people crossing the border. The probability of apprehension has been trending upward to about one-third of those crossing the border; however, the number of apprehensions has fallen from a peak of about 1.6 million in 2000 to about 400,000 in 2016 (see figure 2.28).

The increase in the cost of illegal crossings is only part of the explanation for the dramatic decrease in border crossings. The fall in employment opportunities in the United States is likely to be more important: apprehensions declined sharply after 2007 with the onset of the financial crisis and the collapse of the construction sector, which employed a large number of migrant workers.

Figure 2.27 **Mexico–United States illegal border-crossing costs and U.S. Border Patrol staffing, 1990–2016**

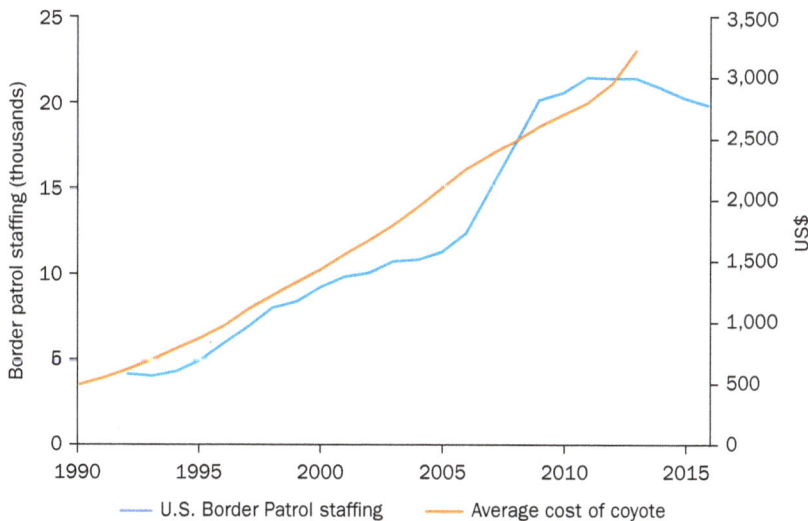

Sources: Data from U.S. Border Patrol Fiscal Year Staffing Statistics (FY1992–FY2016; https://www.cbp .gov/newsroom/media-resources/stats) and the Mexican Migration Project (MMP 161; http://mmp.opr .princeton.edu/). A "coyote" is someone who helps smuggle immigrants into the United States.

Figure 2.28 Mexico–United States illegal border-crossing costs and border apprehensions, 1980–2016

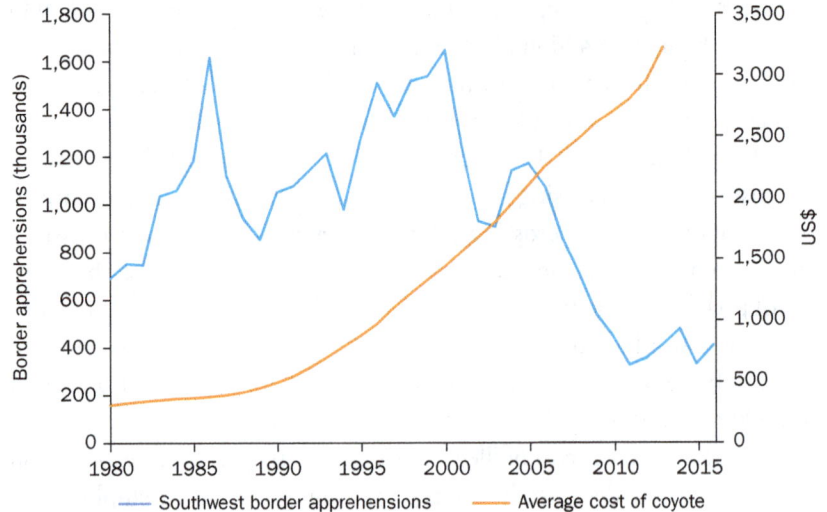

Sources: Data from the U.S. Department of Homeland Security, U.S. Customs and Border Protection "Stats and Summaries" (https://www.cbp.gov/newsroom/media-resources/stats), and the Mexican Migration Project (MMP 161; http://mmp.opr.princeton.edu/). A "coyote" is someone who helps smuggle immigrants into the United States.

Migrants' adaptive behavior can reduce the efficacy of deterrence measures, which will have larger effects if substitute routes are readily available. For example, large, localized ramp-ups in border enforcement in the United States—such as Operation Hold the Line in El Paso in 1993 and Operation Gatekeeper in San Diego in 1994—led, on the one hand, to steep declines in migrant apprehensions in those specific locations. On the other hand, these efforts also led to increased apprehensions in other locations along the border, such as in Tucson. In other words, instead of crossing through urban areas in West Texas and Southern California, migrants simply went through the deserts of Arizona (Gathmann 2008).[17] This shift, of course, is primarily true for localized efforts; as border enforcement has increased along the entire border, migrants have fewer ways to avoid apprehension. Costs—as with all migration decisions—play an important role. For example, one set of estimates suggests that a 10 percent increase in border patrol linewatch hours reduces illegal inflows by 4–8 percent (Angelucci 2012).

Two important limitations hinder the efficacy of border enforcement in deterring unauthorized immigrants. First, not all unauthorized immigrants cross the border illegally. Some 25–40 percent of unauthorized immigrants in the United States are believed to have entered legally and either overstayed their visa or otherwise violated its terms, such as working on a tourist visa (National Research Council 2013).

Second, enforcement efforts have also dramatically reduced the number of immigrants who are in the United States only temporarily. Mexican migrants in the United States used to be overwhelmingly on temporary work permits (figure 2.26). Even after the termination of the Bracero Program in the late 1960s, over 50 percent of unauthorized immigrants would return to Mexico within a year. As enforcement made reentry costlier, undocumented migrants already in the United States decided it would simply be easier to stay. As a consequence, temporary migration has become rare and return migration rates (within a year) have dropped to 10 percent. It is estimated that about two-thirds of unauthorized immigrants have been in the United States for over 10 years, up from about one-third in 1995 (Passel and Cohn 2016).

The limitations of border enforcement have resulted in a large-scale increase in internal enforcement. Figure 2.29 shows criminal and noncriminal deportation data from the U.S. Department of Homeland Security. Deportations have increased from 188,000 in 2000 to a high of 434,000 in 2013. These deportations target unauthorized immigrants who have committed crimes, but over half are noncriminal deportations.

Figure 2.29   Immigrant deportations from the United States, 2000–2015

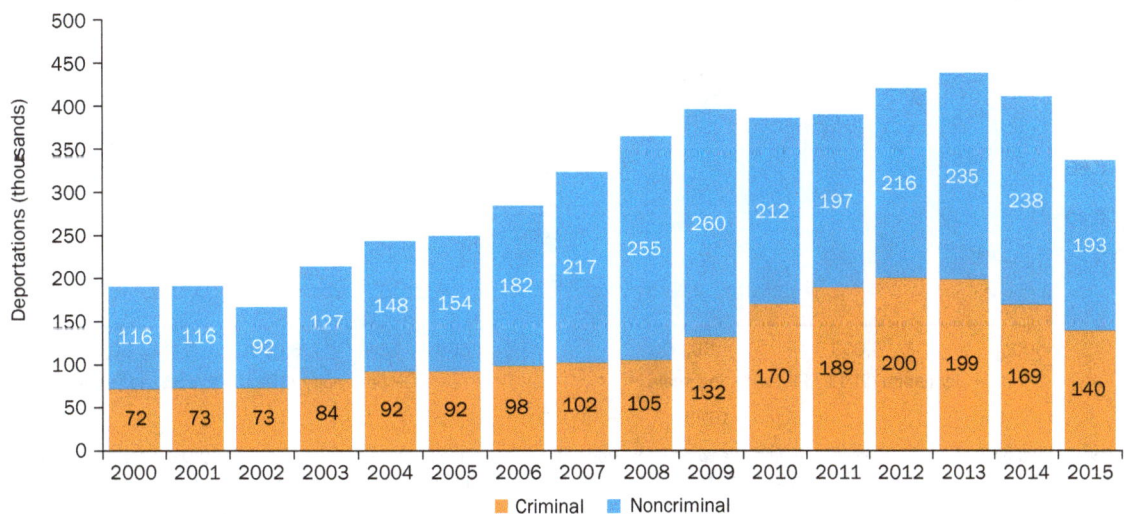

Sources: DHS 2010, 2016b, table 41.

Why migrate? A cost-benefit analysis

Migration decisions are made by weighing the costs and benefits of migrating against each other. As the previous two sections demonstrate, both costs and benefits play an important role in determining the key patterns—size and composition—of global and internal migration, as well as the destination choices. This section will now discuss and explain how it all adds up.

Do people migrate from poor to rich countries?

The data presented so far suggest that the poorest countries should be sending the largest share or number of migrants. Recent analysis finds evidence that is somewhat different. Figure 2.30, panel a, constructed using the methodology from Clemens (2014), shows the relationship between the emigration rate and the GDP per capita of origin countries. We observe an inverse-U-shaped relationship where emigration rises with economic development, at least until countries reach the upper-middle-income level. Only thereafter, as countries become even richer, do emigration rates typically fall.[18] The likely reason behind this emigration pattern

Figure 2.30 **GDP per capita and migration rates, 1990, 2000, and 2010**

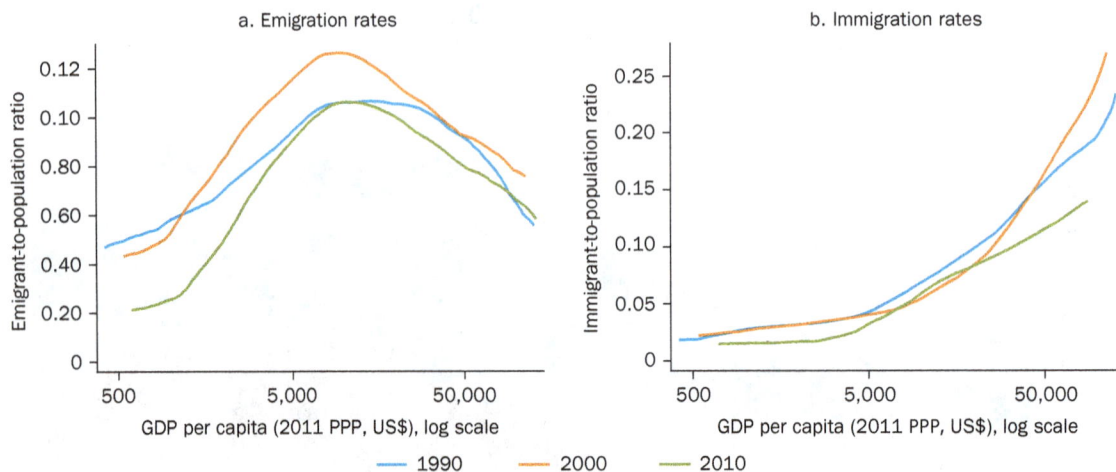

Sources: Based on Clemens 2014, using data from the World Bank Global Bilateral Migration Database, 2010/2011 OECD Database on Immigrants in OECD and Non-OECD Countries (DIOC-E), World Bank DataBank, Penn World Tables, and United Nations World Population Prospects.

Note: Graphs plot the relationship between country-level emigration and immigration rates estimated as Nadaraya-Watson kernel-weighted local mean (bandwidth = 0.7 log points, kernel: Epanechnikov). OECD = Organisation for Economic Co-operation and Development; PPP = purchasing power parity.

is the existence of substantial moving costs. It is simply too expensive for the poorest to migrate. They lack the resources and borrowing ability to finance migration. It is the interaction of these costs and benefits that determines the overall emigration patterns. Figure 2.30, panel b, plots country-level immigration rates against per capita GDP. Here, an entirely different picture emerges. Immigration is heavily concentrated among a few rich countries. Most low-income countries experience very little immigration. Then, at a per capita GDP of about $8,000, immigration rates start to increase rapidly.

The interplay between costs and benefits leads to the different patterns across origin and destination countries. From the origin country perspective, middle-income countries send the most emigrants in relative terms. Emigrants from these countries have both the financial means to migrate and the economic potential to realize significant benefits. From the destination country perspective, it is the richest countries that receive the most immigrants. Regardless of the origin of the migrant, the largest economic gains (through wages and employment) tend to be found in the richest countries. Figure 2.30 presents the overall pattern emphasized in the first chapter: whereas emigrants come from a wide array of countries, immigrants are concentrated in a few rich destinations.

The natural question to ask is whether the same patterns hold for internal migration within a country. Do people systematically leave poorer regions of a country to move to wealthier regions? Internal out-migration rates (blue line) are plotted against average income in figure 2.31 for China and in figure 2.32 for India. In both cases, no clear relationship exists between emigration rates and income in origin regions, showing that high economic benefits for migrants from the poorest regions do not translate into higher migration rates from those regions.

Figures 2.31 and 2.32 also show the relationship between internal in-migration rates (orange line) and average incomes in destination regions. People tend to migrate to wealthier regions in both China and India. As was the case with international migration, this results in a strong positive relationship between a region's GDP per capita and the fraction of the population who are (internal) immigrants. In the case of India, the data indicate that the share of immigrants in a destination district rises from about 2 percent in the poorest districts to over 6 percent in the wealthiest districts. Immigration rates are, however, nowhere near as concentrated as they are for international migration.

Figure 2.31   Income and Chinese internal migration rates

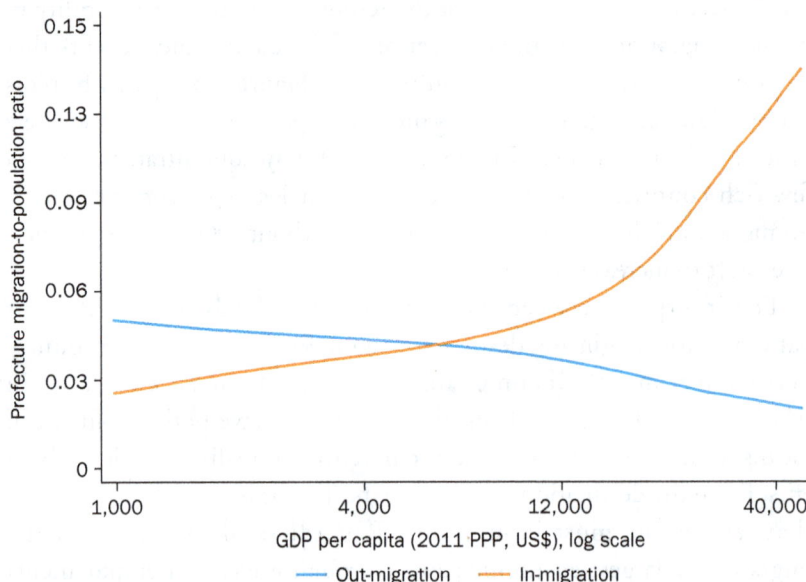

Prefecture migration-to-population ratio

GDP per capita (2011 PPP, US$), log scale

——— Out-migration   ——— In-migration

Sources: Data from the Fifth National Population Census 2000, *China City Statistical Yearbook 2001*, and *China Statistical Yearbook 2001*.

Note: Trend line estimated as Nadaraya-Watson kernel-weighted local mean (bandwidth = 1 natural log point, kernel: Epanechnikov). Only between-prefecture migration used. PPP = purchasing power parity.

Figure 2.32   Income and Indian internal migration rates

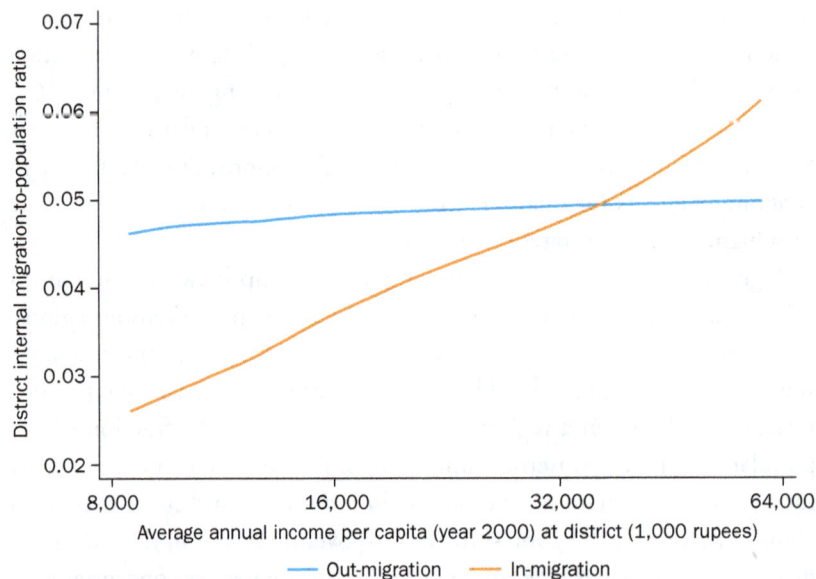

District internal migration-to-population ratio

Average annual income per capita (year 2000) at district (1,000 rupees)

——— Out-migration   ——— In-migration

Sources: Data from the 2001 Census of India and the 1999/2000 National Sample Survey (55th round).

Note: Trend line estimated as Nadaraya-Watson kernel-weighted local mean (bandwidth = 0.5 natural log points, kernel: Epanechnikov). Sample includes males ages 14–65.

Do refugees flee poor for wealthier countries?

Although refugees and economic migrants consider many of the same costs and benefits in deciding *where* to move, the reasons for *why* they move are often entirely different. Civil war, genocide, and other forms of violence are the causes of the humanitarian crises that result in refugee flows. Figure 2.33 plots war deaths in Syria against refugee outflows during the recent crisis. As one would expect, there is a very clear and strong correlation between violence and subsequent out-migration in Syria. The relationship between violence and migration (both internal and cross-country) has been documented in numerous studies. Violence against civilians, human rights abuses, and different forms of war and conflict have all been shown to correlate with refugee flights and internal displacement.[19] Schmeidl (1997) looks closely at different forms of violence and finds civil wars and genocides to be the strongest predictors of refugee crises.

Some of the complexities of the decisions faced by the refugees are illustrated in figure 2.34, which documents the migration patterns of the Syrian conflict. Currently, over 50 percent of the Syrian population has been displaced. The civilians of war-torn Syria have several potential outcomes: they could be internally displaced, move to a neighboring country, travel to distant (typically developed) countries, or remain in their homes.

Figure 2.33 **War deaths in the Syrian Arab Republic and migrant outflows, 2011–16**

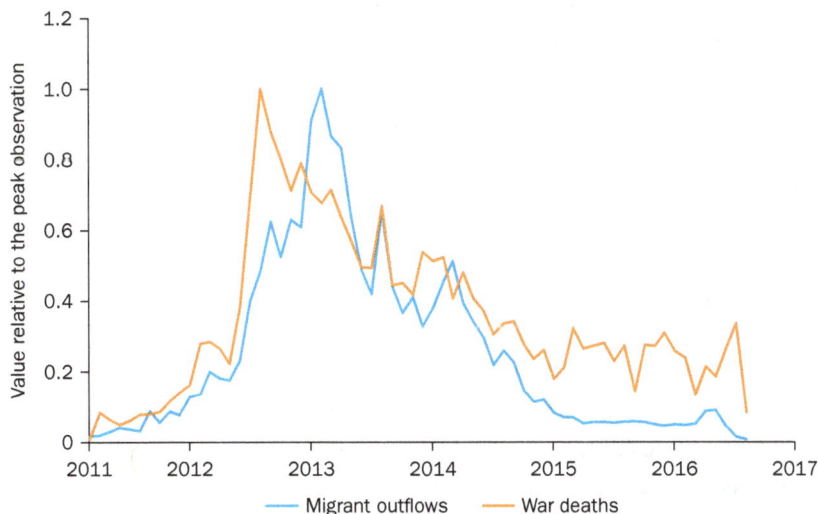

Source: World Bank 2018.

Figure 2.34 **The complexity of the Syrian Arab Republic refugee crisis as of 2015**

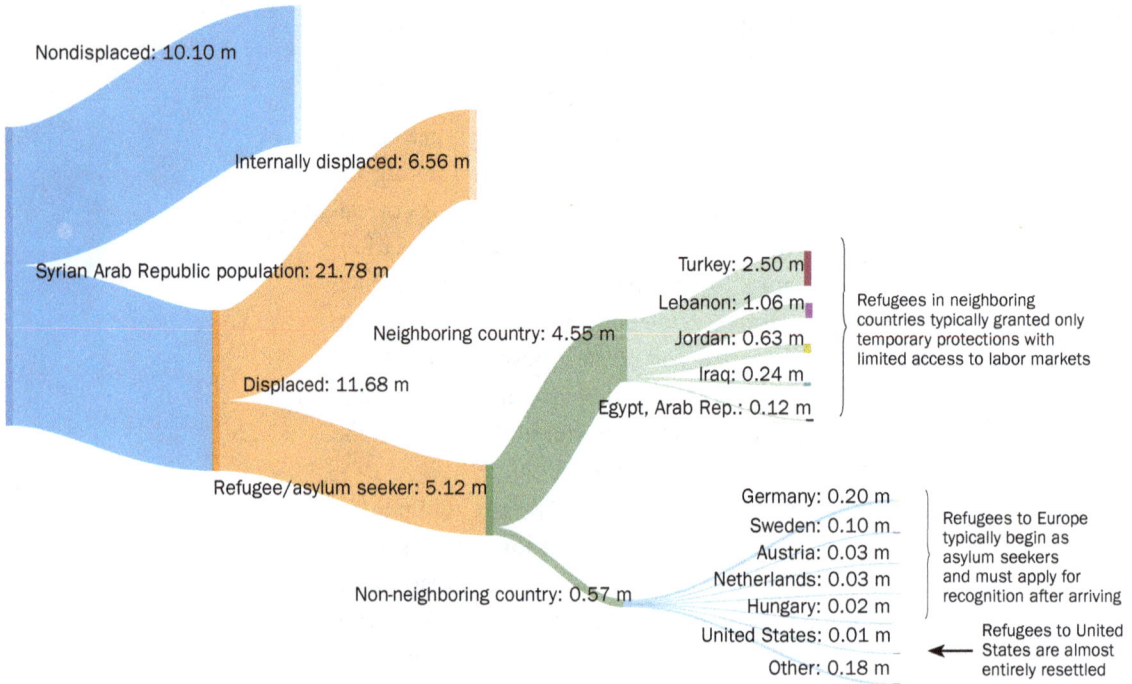

Nondisplaced: 10.10 m

Internally displaced: 6.56 m

Syrian Arab Republic population: 21.78 m

Neighboring country: 4.55 m

Displaced: 11.68 m

Turkey: 2.50 m
Lebanon: 1.06 m
Jordan: 0.63 m
Iraq: 0.24 m
Egypt, Arab Rep.: 0.12 m

Refugees in neighboring countries typically granted only temporary protections with limited access to labor markets

Refugee/asylum seeker: 5.12 m

Germany: 0.20 m
Sweden: 0.10 m
Austria: 0.03 m
Netherlands: 0.03 m
Hungary: 0.02 m
United States: 0.01 m
Other: 0.18 m

Refugees to Europe typically begin as asylum seekers and must apply for recognition after arriving

Refugees to United States are almost entirely resettled

Non-neighboring country: 0.57 m

Sources: Data from UNHCR Population Statistics Database and United Nations World Population Prospects.

Note: m = million; UNHCR = United Nations High Commissioner for Refugees.

Whether victims of systemic violence stay or flee their homes depends on the strategies of the aggressors, the political context of the conflict, economic resources, and future prospects. If a conflict is directed toward a specific political or ethnic group, it is typically members of that group who face the biggest risks of displacement. Those from other groups who stay may face lower rates of victimization. And those from the targeted group who decide to stay may take other strategic actions to protect their well-being, for example, by joining the armed group or remaining neutral and negotiating protections.[20]

Economic considerations also matter for those fleeing conflict. In some instances it has been primarily land owners and wealthier individuals who end up leaving (Adhikari 2013; Engel and Ibáñez 2007; Ibáñez and Vélez 2008; Verwimp 2005). They are often the targets of violence because of attempts to seize assets and property by military force. They also are most likely to have the financial resources readily available to make an unplanned and possibly expensive move. Highly educated individuals may also have more transferrable skills and face a lower opportunity cost of adjusting to a new environment. In certain cases, however, it has been found that, in the face of violence, wealthier individuals have a lower probability of migration. Property, livestock, and other productive assets may increase the opportunity cost of moving and thus reduce the incentive (see Ibáñez 2014; Ibáñez and Moya 2016).

Unlike economic migrants, most refugees are from poorer countries and are not more likely to relocate to high-income OECD ones. Figure 2.35 shows that the vast majority of refugee flows originate from low- and middle-income countries, at an average rate of about 1 percent for the poorest countries and decreasing as income levels increase. There are rare examples of refugees coming from wealthier countries; however, because poor countries are more likely to experience political and civil chaos, the vast majority of refugees come from poorer countries like Afghanistan, the Central African Republic, the Democratic Republic of Congo, Eritrea, Myanmar, Somalia, South Sudan, Sudan, and Syria. Figure 2.35 also indicates that, unlike economic migrants, refugees do not disproportionately relocate to wealthier countries. Over 80 percent of refugees are hosted by developing countries, as highlighted in chapter 1.

Figure 2.35 **GDP per capita and refugees**

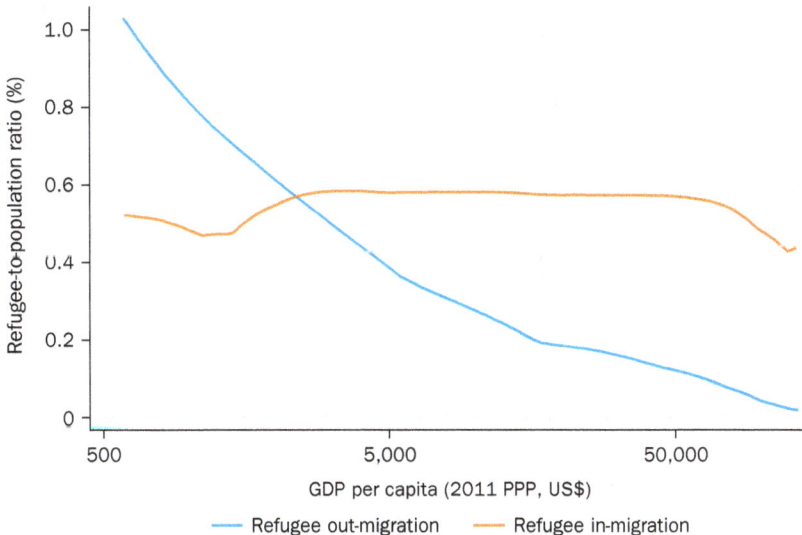

Sources: Data from UNHCR Population Statistics Database, United Nations World Population Prospects, World Bank DataBank, and Penn World Tables.

Note: Trend line estimated as Nadaraya-Watson kernel-weighted local mean (bandwidth = 1 natural log point, kernel: Epanechnikov). PPP = purchasing power parity; UNHCR = United Nations High Commissioner for Refugees.

This pattern is maintained despite the fact that refugees do systematically move to higher-wage countries over time (see the "Why migrate? The benefits of migrating" section of this chapter).

So why do more refugees not go to high-income countries? One reason is the importance of migration costs. Refugees, who are disproportionately from poor origin countries, often flee to neighboring countries that also tend to have lower income levels. Moreover, policy barriers of high-income countries make it difficult to migrate to them. For example, the United States currently hosts less than 2 percent of the world's refugees, in part because of restrictive policies and burdensome qualification processes.

Empirical analysis

The evidence in this chapter so far identifies several factors that determine how and why people move across international borders or within countries. The impact of these factors on both benefits and costs of mobility are qualitatively similar for economic migrants or refugees, although with significant quantitative differences. The next question is how these varied factors fit together to determine global migration flows.

The previous sections showed that we have to account for both the costs and the benefits of migration to obtain a clear understanding of the determinants of migration patterns. The standard approach is to use gravity-type models to describe the factors that affect multicountry migration flows.[21] Table 2.2 presents determinants of 2010 migrant stocks (column 1) and 2015 refugee stocks (column 2). Each specification includes (log) wage differentials between source and destination country, (log) distance, dummies for contiguity and a colonial relationship, a common language index, a measure of the migrant network (the log number of migrants in 1980), and three destination country characteristics, (log) population, (log) GDP per capita, and (log) population density, as explanatory variables. All specifications include origin fixed effects, which control for all factors that are common to a migrant source country. Importantly, the fixed effects control for the dependency of migration costs on economic conditions at the origin.[22] The results address the question of where people choose to emigrate, given that they are emigrating, and not necessarily why some countries have higher emigration or immigration rates than others.[23] See annex 2A for further details on our empirical specifications.

Table 2.2   Correlates of global migrant and refugee stocks

	Migrant stocks (2010)	Refugee stocks (2015)
Difference in mean log wages (destination – source)	0.638***	0.382**
	(0.215)	(0.152)
Diaspora network (1980 stocks)	0.318***	0.0882**
	(0.0268)	(0.0362)
Log distance	−0.292***	−0.794***
	(0.0765)	(0.212)
Contiguous countries	0.564***	0.644
	(0.171)	(0.394)
Common language index	0.553*	0.0835
	(0.299)	(0.528)
Countries have colonial ties	0.850***	−0.205
	(0.179)	(0.362)
Log destination population	0.383***	0.455***
	(0.0509)	(0.0725)
Log destination GDP per capita (PPP)	0.00143	0.0943
	(0.190)	(0.218)
Log destination population density	−0.0303	−0.0827
	(0.0418)	(0.0716)
Observations	1,563	295

Note: Sample is all migration corridors with a migrant stock of over 1,000 (500 in the case of refugees) and country pairs in which no variables are missing. Standard errors in parentheses. GDP = gross domestic product; PPP = purchasing power parity.
Significance level: * = 10 percent, ** = 5 percent, *** = 1 percent.

Determinants of migrant stocks

Wages. Migrant stocks are highly responsive to differences in (log) wages, with an elasticity of 0.64. This means that a destination country with 10 percent higher mean wages will tend to attract 6.4 percent more migrants from the average source country. Interestingly, GDP per capita—which is what the literature tends to use to proxy for average incomes in a country—is not statistically significant, with a coefficient close to zero, once the wage differences and other factors are considered.[24] Even though GDP per capita and mean wages are highly correlated across the world, it is higher wages that are a key driver of global migration flows, rather than the desire to live in a wealthier country for reasons other than high wages.

Diaspora networks. Historic (1980) bilateral migration stocks, the measure of the extent of the diaspora networks, are also strong predictors of subsequent migration patterns, with an elasticity of 0.32.[25]

Contiguity and distance. Contiguity is an important determinant of migration flows, with countries receiving 56 percent more immigrants from neighboring countries than from non-neighboring countries, holding other characteristics constant. Beyond contiguity, migration decreases with distance, with an elasticity of –0.29.

Common language and shared colonial history. The common language index is also positively correlated with bilateral migrant stocks, suggesting that countries with a common language or similar languages see larger bilateral flows. The relationship is, however, only marginally significant. Colonial history matters: migration is 85 percent higher between countries with a shared colonial history.

Destination country characteristics. As expected, larger countries receive more migrants even though the estimated elasticity of 0.38 is significantly lower than 1, implying that the impact of country size is less than proportional. In other words, more-populous countries receive more immigrants, but the immigrant-to-population ratio declines with the population of a country. Finally, neither GDP per capita nor population density is significantly correlated with migrant flows. These variables are meant to proxy for other characteristics of wealthy and spacious destination countries—such as amenities, public infrastructure, and house prices—that may attract inward migration.

Determinants of refugee stocks

One of the main takeaways from this chapter is that the distribution of refugees across the world is influenced by the same set of factors that matter for economic migrants. What is different is the relative importance of these factors: the empirical analysis shows that, for refugees, geographic factors matter a lot more and economic factors less.

Wage differentials matter significantly for refugee location decisions. The elasticity of 0.38, however, is smaller than that of the overall migrant stocks. Everyone wants to live in countries with higher wages, and refugees are no exception. Refugee decisions are also not influenced by the amenities provided by higher GDP per capita (conditional on wages).

For refugees, distance from the country they are fleeing is possibly the most important determinant of their location decision. The elasticity of the refugee stock with respect to distance is almost triple that of the general migrant stock. Contiguity matters (recall that about 80 percent of refugees are located in neighboring countries) (see figure 2.15); however, given the small sample, the impact of contiguity is no longer statistically significant once we control for (log) distance.

Common language and a colonial history are not important determinants of refugee patterns once geographic factors are included. Finally, refugees are more likely to flee to larger countries, with the same elasticity as economic migrants. Because that elasticity is below 1, smaller populous countries face disproportionately large refugee inflows.

Who chooses to migrate? Skill composition and the selection of migrants

The skill or educational composition of migration flows is as important as their size. The economic impact of migration on source and destination countries or regions depends on who migrates. Are migrants the "best and brightest" or the "huddled masses"? This section presents evidence on the determinants of the skill composition of migration, both for global migration, and in specific country case studies.

The Roy model of migration

The foundation of the economic perspective to address the question of who migrates is the idea, employed in the previous section, that observed patterns of migration reflect individual choices responding to (economic) incentives (that is, costs and benefits). The most prominent formulation of this view of migration is George Borjas's adaptation of the Roy model in "Self-Selection and the Earnings of Immigrants" (1987). The article outlines a simple yet powerful framework for understanding migration decisions and composition.

Figure 2.36 depicts the simplest version of the Roy model and its empirical predictions. Wages and skill levels are measured on the y- and x-axes, respectively. For each given skill level of potential migrants, the figures depict the wages that people with that skill level can earn in (1) the source country, for example, Mexico (black line), and (2) the host country, for example, the United States (orange line). Although wages increase with skill level in both countries, the slope of the lines represents the returns to skill for a given country. A steeper line indicates a higher skill premium.

Figure 2.36 The Roy model of migration

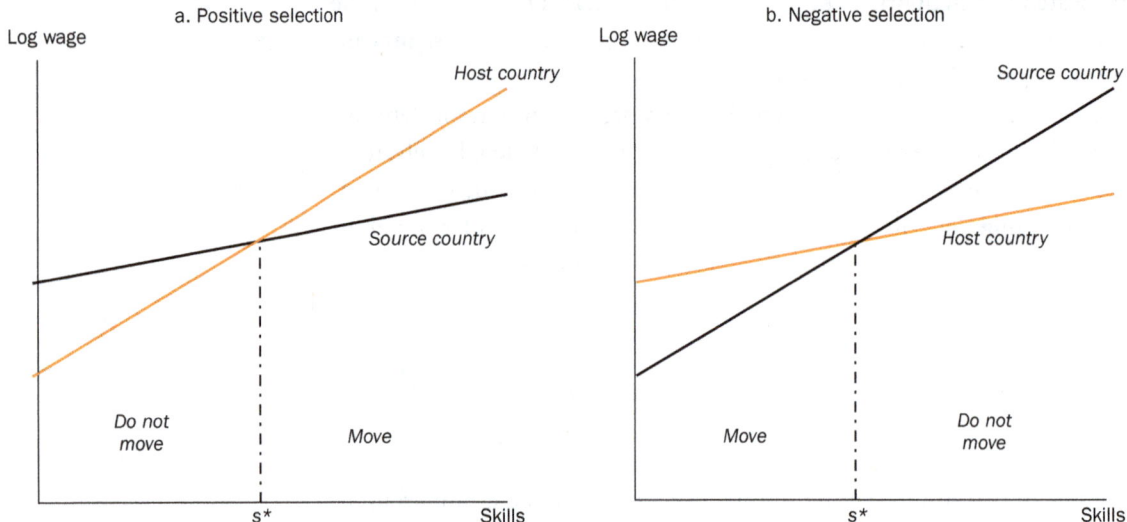

Note: Panel B depicts the scenario where the wage rates are increasing more slowly with the skill level in the host country relative to the source country. Hence, those with skills below s* will choose to migrate, whereas those with skills above s* will stay home. This corresponds to the case of the low-skilled migrant, which the literature calls *negative selection*. Note that this framework is readily extended to allow for multiple possible destinations for each potential migrant.

Panel a of figure 2.36 depicts the scenario where the returns to skill are increasing faster with the skill level in the host than the source country. Visually, this corresponds to a situation where the relationship between skills (s) and the (log) wage is steeper in the host country than in the source country. Potential migrants will choose to migrate if their expected income is higher in a destination country. Those with skills below s^* earn more in the source than the host country. As a consequence, this group will choose not to migrate. Those with skills above s^* earn more in the host than the source country; hence, they will want to migrate. In this scenario, it is the "best and brightest" who choose to migrate, which the literature calls *positive selection*. Panel b depicts the opposite scenario, where the skill premium is higher in the origin country, and we end up with *negative selection*.

The skill composition of global migration flows

Skill premiums

The Roy model is intuitively appealing, but do the observed international migration patterns support the implications of the model? Do more skilled migrants, compared to low-skilled migrants, disproportionately go to destinations with higher skill premiums?

Figure 2.37 **Wage premium and emigrant skill intensity**

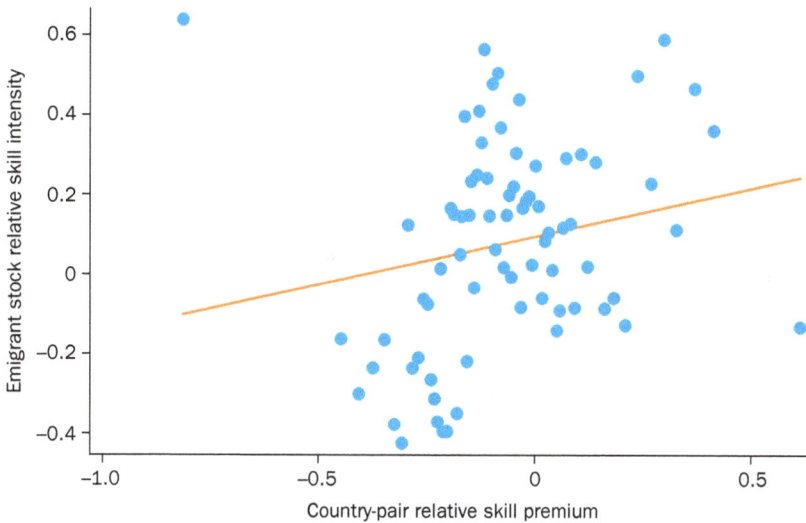

Sources: Data from the 2010/2011 OECD Database on Immigrants in OECD and Non-OECD Countries (DIOC-E) and World Bank International Income Distribution Data (I2D2).

Note: Figure plots the residuals from regressions of the x- and y-axis variables on a set of controls. Controls include origin fixed effects, (log) distance, contiguity, linguistic similarity, (log) average wages, and (log) destination population. Dots represent averages over 100 equally sized bins. Sample restricted to all migration corridors with migrant stocks greater than 1,000 with available data. See annex 2A for a detailed description of the variables. OECD = Organisation for Economic Co-operation and Development.

Figure 2.37 plots the (log) skill ratio of migrant flows (the ratio of high- to low-skilled emigrants) divided by the skill ratio among all emigrants from that country,[26] against the relative skill premium between source and destination country.[27] There is a clear positive relationship between the relative skill intensity of emigration flows and the relative skill premium across destination countries. The slope of the fitted line indicates that emigrant stocks from a given source country include 3.6 percent more high-skilled people in destination countries with a 10 percent higher skill premium.

The flip side of analyzing the relative skill content of emigration from a specific source country is exploring the skill content of immigration to a specific destination. Figure 2.38, taken from Borjas (2014), tests the Roy model from this angle. In the absence of skill premium estimates, the study considers income inequality (Gini coefficient) in the source country or economy as a measure of the returns to skills, and the weekly wage in a host country of immigrants as a measure of the level of skills of those immigrants. According to the Roy model, higher-skill-premium origin countries will send lower-skilled migrants (as in panel b of figure 2.36). The relationship

Figure 2.38 Immigrant earnings in the United States and origin economy Gini coefficients

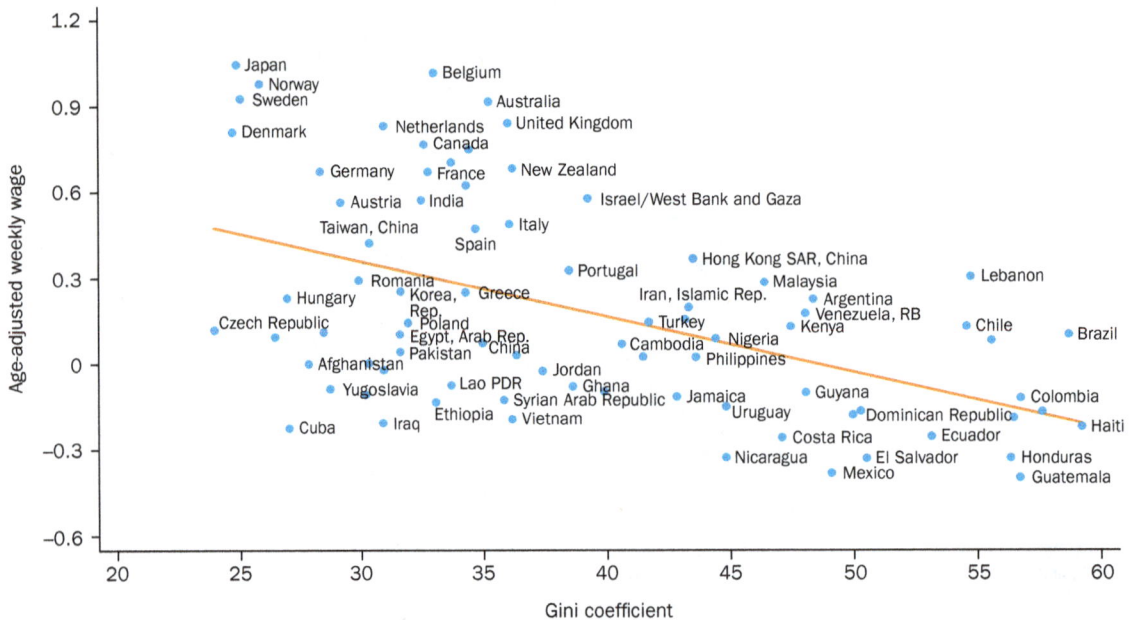

Source: Borjas 2014. Reproduced with permission; further permission required for reuse.

Note: The y-axis gives the age-adjusted average log weekly wage of immigrants who entered the United States between 1995 and 1999, by source economy. The x-axis gives the average Gini coefficient in that economy between 1978 and 2012.

between these two variables is negative in the United States. An increase in the Gini coefficient from 36 to 49 (or the difference between the United Kingdom and Mexico) lowers earnings by about 16 percent. This negative correlation between earnings and the Gini coefficient is consistent with the Roy model prediction that immigrants are more likely to be negatively selected if they originate in countries with higher rates of return to skills.

The role of costs

The importance and the magnitude of the costs associated with migration vary across education groups. The factors that influence mobility costs—such as distance, contiguity, diaspora networks, and policy variables—have a different impact on migrants with different education and skill levels.

Distance, for example, is much less a barrier to migration to high-skilled workers for several reasons. First, skilled workers may have more savings or better access to credit to finance a distant migration. Figure 2.15, in the "Distance" section of this chapter, depicts the cumulative distribution function of bilateral migrant stocks by distance. About 20 percent of high-skilled workers move to a neighboring country. That fraction is above 50 percent for low-skilled workers and is 80 percent for refugees. Only 20 percent of low-skilled migrants move more than 4,000 kilometers whereas over 50 percent of high-skilled migrants do. Additionally, more highly skilled people might more easily adapt and assimilate to the destination country. Possibly, and most important, high-skilled migrants face lower policy barriers from destination countries (see figure 2.22).

Regression results

How do the costs and benefits of migration interact with education to influence the skill composition of migration stocks? To address this question, we use an empirical specification that closely resembles the gravity estimation (presented in the section titled "Do refugees flee poor for wealthier countries?"). The results are presented in table 2.3. The outcome variable of interest is the (log) high-skilled ratio of bilateral migrant stocks. The explanatory variables are the (log) skill premium differentials between source and destination country, (log) distance, dummies for contiguity and a colonial relationship, a common language index, a measure of the migrant network (the log number of migrants in 1980), and three destination country characteristics: log population, log GDP per capita, and log population density. Origin fixed effects control for the skill composition of natives in each source country and the differential propensity of low- and high-skilled people to emigrate from that country. See annex 2A for a detailed discussion of our empirical specifications.

The most salient variable in explaining the skill composition of migration is the difference in the skill premiums between origin and destination countries. The elasticity of the high-to-low skill ratio with respect to the relative skill premium is 0.86. This implies that, if the skill premium is 10 percent higher in a destination country relative to the origin country, the immigrant stock in that corridor will be 8.6 percent more high-skilled relative to low-skilled.

Among the other explanatory variables, the GDP per capita at destination also matters for the skill composition of immigrants. Wealthier countries receive more skilled immigrants, and the elasticity of skill composition to GDP per capita is 0.61. This implies that immigrant skill ratios are also responsive to absolute wage differences because, holding relative wage premiums constant, increased GDP leads to increased absolute wage differences. These results are consistent with the recent debate about whether absolute or relative wage differentials matter for the skill

Table 2.3 **Correlates of the skill composition of global migrant stocks**

	Skill composition
Difference in log skill premium (destination – source)	0.862***
	(0.316)
Diaspora network (1980 stocks)	–0.0633**
	(0.0273)
Log distance	0.0354
	(0.0714)
Contiguous countries	–0.647***
	(0.158)
Common language index	0.508*
	(0.280)
Countries have colonial ties	0.212
	(0.157)
Log destination population	0.166***
	(0.0452)
Log destination GDP per capita (PPP)	0.611***
	(0.105)
Log destination population density	–0.177**
	(0.0882)
Observations	1,395

Note: The dependent variable is the log share of high-skilled (education beyond high school) workers in a bilateral migration stock. Sample is all migration corridors with a migrant stock of over 1,000 and country pairs in which no variables are missing. Standard errors in parentheses. GDP = gross domestic product; PPP = purchasing power parity.
Significance level: * = 10 percent, ** = 5 percent, *** = 1 percent.

composition of migration flows (see Belot and Hatton 2012; Borjas 2014; Grogger and Hanson 2011). Our results suggest that both matter. Migrant stocks between neighboring countries are far less skilled than average; they have about a 65 percent lower skill ratio than otherwise identical bilateral corridors. This difference is related to the idea that migration costs may matter more for low-skilled individuals even though distance per se is uncorrelated with the skill composition of migrants. Common language seems to matter more for high-skilled migrants, skewing the migrant composition. High-skilled migrants may select into jobs that require more communication skills, and, thus, knowledge of the local language increases the value of other accumulated human capital. Colonial links and, perhaps surprisingly, distance do not affect the skill composition of immigrants. Finally, more-populous countries have larger numbers of high-skilled immigrants, plausibly because these countries provide thicker high-skilled labor markets where productivity spillovers are more prevalent.

Country-specific evidence

Research on particular migration corridors, as opposed to global stocks, yields additional insights about the factors that influence the selection of migrants. We highlight insights from work on Mexico–United States migration, Italy, India, and the Age of Mass Migration.

Mexico–United States migration

The largest bilateral migration flow of the past three decades has been between Mexico and the United States, with 11.8 million migrants as of 2010. It is also, by some margin, the most extensively studied. Numerous papers and books have investigated the skill composition of Mexican immigrants and how it matches up with the predictions of the Roy model.

Chiquiar and Hanson (2005) use data from Mexican population censuses and data on Mexican immigrants in U.S. population censuses to examine who in Mexico migrates and how their earnings and observable skills compare to those who remain at home. To evaluate the selection of Mexican immigrants in terms of observable skills (education and experience), Chiquiar and Hanson compare actual wage densities for residents of Mexico with counterfactual wage densities that workers would have obtained if the Mexican immigrants were paid according to skill prices in Mexico. They find that, if Mexican immigrants in the United States were paid according to Mexican skill prices, they would fall disproportionately in the middle and upper portions of Mexico's wage distribution. This result is quite at odds with the predictions of Borjas's Roy model, which predicts that Mexican immigrants would hail primarily from the lower end of the skill distribution, representing negative selection.

In a follow-up study, Fernández-Huertas Moraga (2011) (see figure 2.39), uses a nationally representative Mexican survey (the Quarterly National Labor Survey) that follows households for five quarters. This allows researchers to recover the wage income and other characteristics (such as education) of both documented and undocumented Mexican emigrants

Figure 2.39 Distribution function of Mexican migrant and non-migrant wages

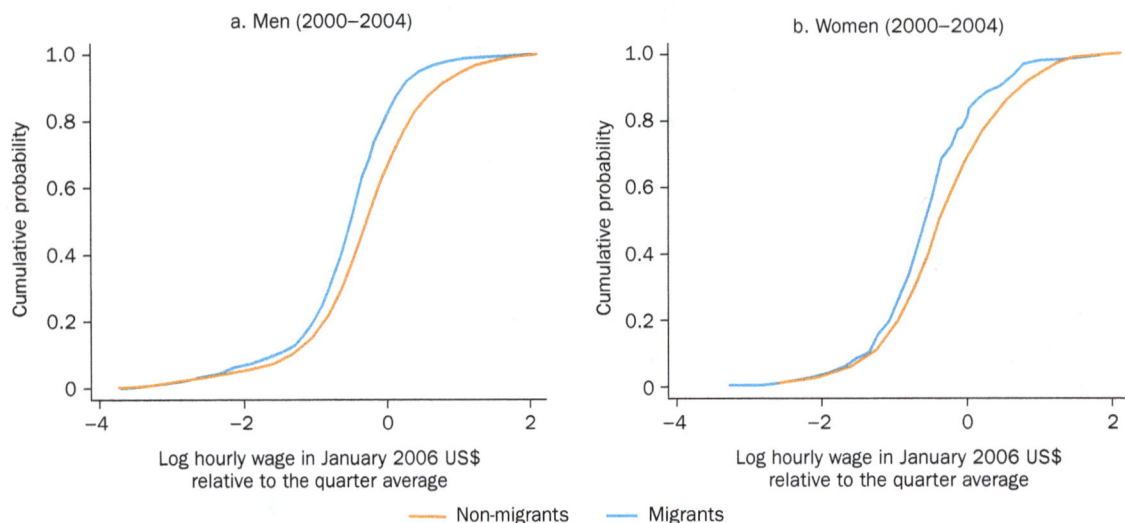

a. Men (2000–2004)

b. Women (2000–2004)

— Non-migrants — Migrants

Source: From Fernández-Huertas Moraga 2011, figure 5.

Note: Empirical distributions of the (log) hourly wage relative to the quarter average.

during the quarter prior to their emigration. The data allow comparison of the wage densities for migrants and non-migrants based on a direct observation of their wages. This study, however, finds evidence of negative selection consistent with the Roy model. In terms of skills, measured as wages before migration, Mexican immigrants fall below their non-migrant counterparts.

The role of hard-to-measure skills in Italy

A conclusion emerging from the recent work on Mexico–United States migration patterns is that returns to skills and selection patterns may differ "dramatically between observed and unobserved skills" (Borjas 2014, 34).[28] Using Italian administrative panel data on migrants between poor southern Italy and wealthy northern Italy, Bartolucci, Villosio, and Wagner (2018) provide evidence on this issue. The study highlights two conclusions. First, migrants are negatively selected on unobserved worker characteristics that contribute to productivity (typically called "ability"). Second, selection is far more pronounced (negative) when accounting for differences in employment propensities and not just wages.

Figure 2.40 graphically depicts these results on the selection of migrants. The figure depicts the estimated density of ability using a model in which the outcome of interest is the (log) weekly wage (in panel a) and log weekly

Figure 2.40 Selection of migrants (from south to north of Italy) on ability

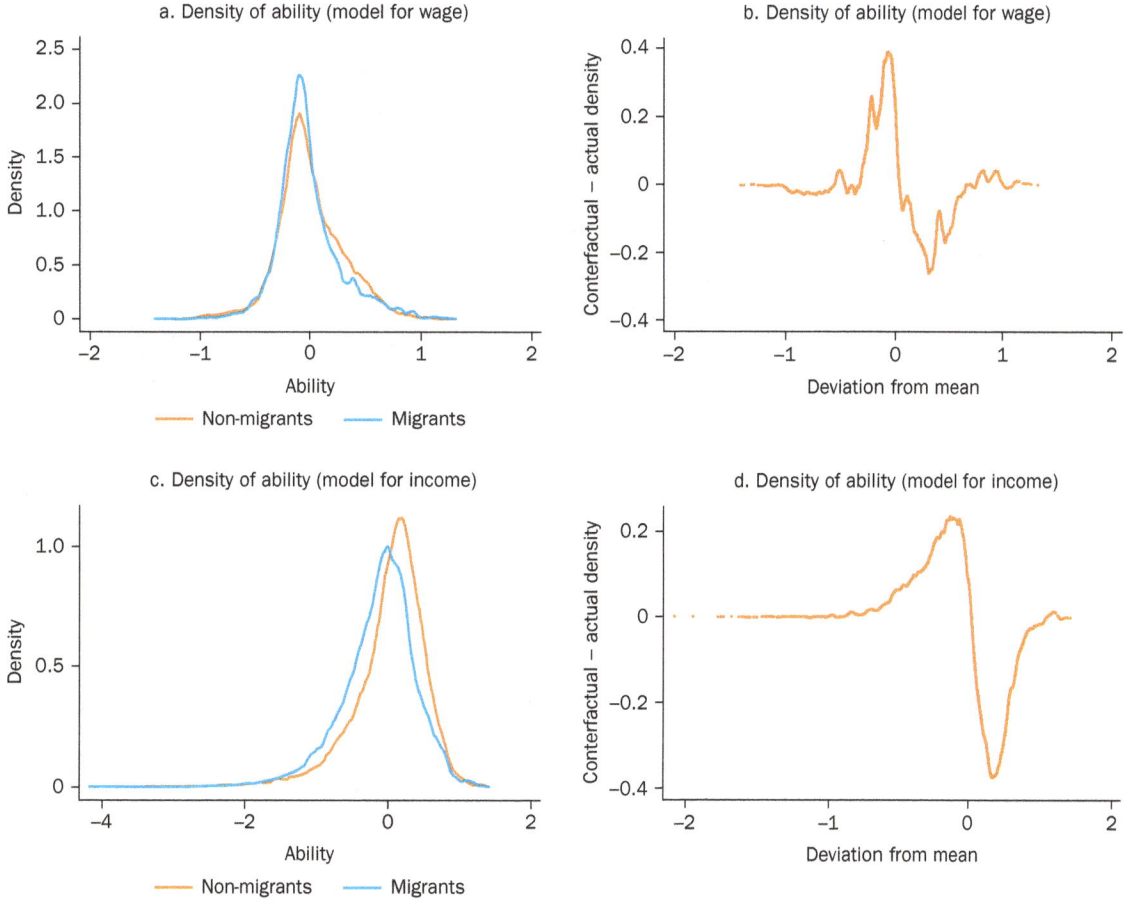

Source: Bartolucci, Villosio, and Wagner 2018, figure 5.

income, the weekly wage times the weeks worked divided by 52 (in panel c).[29] The difference in the wage densities between migrants and non-migrants, providing a clearer depiction of the type of selection, is depicted in panel b for log wages and in panel d for log income.

Migrants are clearly disproportionately drawn from the lower half of the ability distribution. The degree of negative selection is much more pronounced in terms of income, highlighting the importance of both ability and employment opportunities in characterizing the selection of migrants. Median ability as measured by income is 22 log points lower for migrants than for non-migrants, but only 3 log points lower when measured in wages. This suggests that most negative selection is driven by workers with low labor market attachment in the south of Italy, who presumably migrate to find more stable employment.

Selection of migrants in India

There are also pronounced selection patterns for internal migrants in India. Figure 2.41 provides a comparison of the actual income distribution of non-migrants in their origin state and the counterfactual income distribution for migrants. Panel a of figure 2.41 shows those from rural areas whereas panel B shows those from urban origins.[30] Selection patterns differ dramatically for migrants from urban and rural areas.[31] Migrants from rural areas moving to both urban and rural areas are strongly positively selected (see panel a). Migrants from urban areas show a different pattern: those who travel to other urban areas are slightly positively selected whereas those who travel to rural areas are strongly negatively selected (see panel b). Overall urban-to-rural migration makes up a very small share of total internal migration, and the resulting selection is strongly positive with mean incomes at origin roughly 50 percent higher for migrants than for non-migrants.

Figure 2.41   Wage distribution for migrants and non-migrants in India

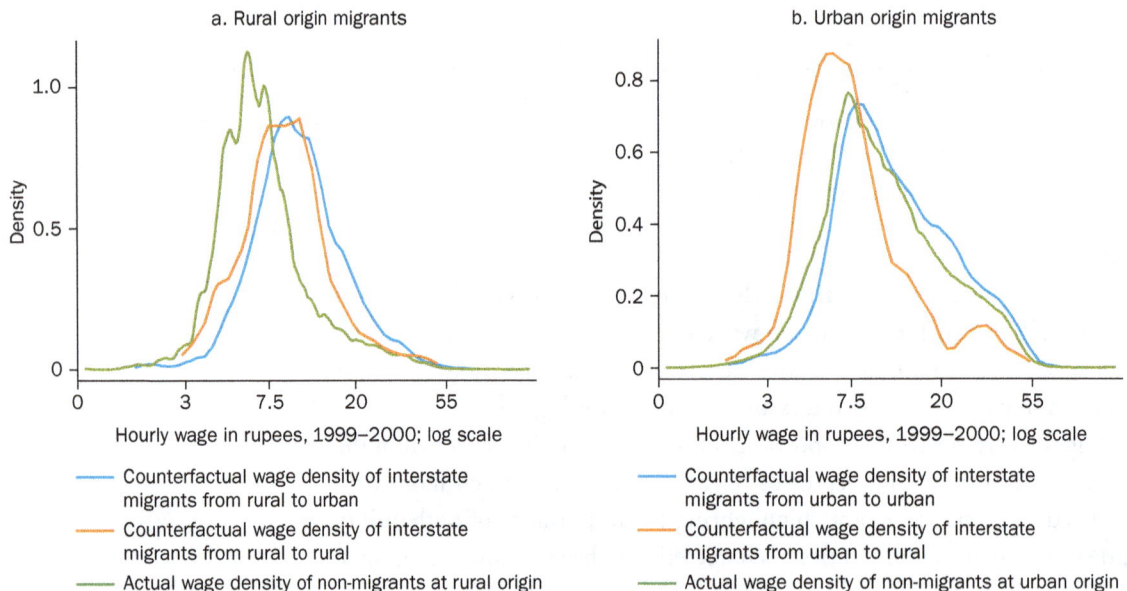

a. Rural origin migrants

b. Urban origin migrants

Hourly wage in rupees, 1999–2000; log scale

Hourly wage in rupees, 1999–2000; log scale

— Counterfactual wage density of interstate migrants from rural to urban
— Counterfactual wage density of interstate migrants from rural to rural
— Actual wage density of non-migrants at rural origin

— Counterfactual wage density of interstate migrants from urban to urban
— Counterfactual wage density of interstate migrants from urban to rural
— Actual wage density of non-migrants at urban origin

Sources: Data from the 2001 Census of India and 1999/2000 National Sample Survey (55th round).

Note: Sample includes male wage earners ages 14–65.

The Age of Mass Migration

Recent work has tackled the same set of questions from the Age of Mass Migration from Europe to the New World. In one of the largest migration episodes in human history, between 1850 and 1913, the United States absorbed nearly 30 million European immigrants. Abramitzky, Boustan, and Eriksson (2012) combine the 1865 and 1890 Norwegian censuses with genealogical records from the United States censuses of the time. They match men by name and age from their birth families in Norway in 1865 to the labor markets in either Norway or the United States in 1900. The study then assigns individuals the mean earnings for their occupation in either Norway or the United States (in real PPP-adjusted 1900 U.S. dollars).

Comparing the earnings of migrants to the earnings of their brother(s) who remained in Europe the study finds a 70 percent return to migration. More important, the study finds that migrants from Norway to the United States are negatively selected on occupations, consistent with evidence that Norway offered a higher return to skills than did the United States at that time. Comparing the earnings distributions in the United States and Norway in 1900, the study also finds that American workers below the 50th percentile of the earnings distribution out-earned similar Norwegians, whereas Norwegians above the 90th percentile commanded higher earnings than their U.S. counterparts—more evidence of negative selection consistent with the Roy model.

ANNEX 2A   Gravity models

Gravity regressions and bilateral migration scatterplots

Economists have for decades used gravity models to study international phenomena such as trade and capital flows. Recently, with the improvement of bilateral migration data, these methods have been applied to study the determinants of both international and internal migration patterns.[32]

Throughout chapter 2 we evaluate the importance of available measures of the costs and benefits of migration by presenting regressions on bilateral migration stocks. We use these regressions to evaluate the relationships between migration and different variables of interest (such as distance, wages, or population) while holding other factors constant. In our model specifications, unless stated otherwise, we evaluate relationships using the natural log of each variable. This allows us to interpret the results as the effects of proportional changes in a variable.

To isolate various migration determinants, we use fixed effects models. Specifically, to evaluate the dyadic and destination characteristics, we estimate a model with origin fixed effects. This helps us isolate "pull" factors of migration and focus specifically on how emigrants decide *where* to migrate, while remaining agnostic on what determines the magnitude of emigration flows from each country. The emigration regression specification is as follows:

$$\ln(m_{i,j}) = \alpha_i + X_{i,j}\beta + Z_j\theta + \varepsilon_{i,j}, \tag{2A.1}$$

where i and j represent origin and destination countries, respectively; $m_{i,j}$ is the migrant stock from origin i in destination j; $X_{i,j}$ and Z_j are dyadic and destination-specific variables, respectively; and α_i is the origin country fixed effect. The origin fixed effect controls in equation 2A.1 for any origin-specific characteristics that determine migrant stocks—that is, it will control for any of the "push" factors in the migration decision. The evidence on why people leave their countries of origin is much weaker than the evidence on where they choose to go, hence our choice of fixed effects.

For ease of interpretation, when displaying these relationships in a scatterplot, as in figures 2.1 and 2.2, we divide the dependent variable by the origin (destination) country's entire emigrant (immigrant) stock and refer to these values as emigrant (immigrant) shares. Although this transformation will not affect the estimated relationship, it allows for an easier interpretation because of the large variation in the size of migrant stocks across corridors.

In our regressions of equation (2A.1), we limit our sample to migration corridors with over 1,000 individuals (500 in the case of refugees). There are two main reasons for this choice, as opposed to including all possible corridors. First, eliminating small corridors reduces measurement error. In a log-log specification, the difference between one and two migrants in a corridor is the same as between one and two million; however, the former small flows are very unlikely to be measured with any degree of accuracy. Second, the widespread prevalence of empty migration corridors is likely simply a function of the highly skewed population size of countries. Many very small countries have naturally very few people migrating to them, and migrants from them are unlikely to be sampled in host country population surveys. Because there are many such countries, our estimates would be heavily weighted toward these uninformative empty corridors. Qualitatively, all the main results are robust to running regressions that include all possible bilateral migration corridors.

Skill composition regressions

In assessing the relationship between wage premiums and migrant skill selection, we apply the same gravity-type model to measuring the skill intensity of migration flows. Specifically, we estimate the following regression:

$$\ln\left(\frac{m_{i,j}^h/m_{i,j}^l}{m_i^h/m_i^l}\right) = \alpha_i + \gamma\left(\ln\frac{w_j^h}{w_j^l} - \ln\frac{w_i^h}{w_i^l}\right) + X_{i,j}\beta + Z_j\theta + \varepsilon_{i,j}. \quad (2A.2)$$

The dependent variable in equation (2A.2) is the log of the ratio of high- to low-skilled migrants from country i in country j normalized to the skill ratio of an origin's entire emigrant stock. The independent variable of interest is the bilateral difference in wage premiums $\left(\ln\frac{w_j^h}{w_j^l} - \ln\frac{w_i^h}{w_i^l}\right)$, and we are interested in estimating γ. The coefficient γ can be interpreted as the elasticity of the migrant skill composition with respect to skill premium. Specifically, a 100 percent increase in the skill premium at destination results in a γ percent increase in skill composition of the migrant stock. $X_{i,j}$ is a set of bilateral variables (such as distance, contiguity, and migrant networks), and Z_j is a set of destination-specific variables (such as GDP per capita and population at destination). Origin country fixed effects, α_i, allow us to identify γ on the basis of variation in destination country wage premiums.

Notes

1. All wages are in purchasing power parity (PPP) terms and 2011 U.S. dollars.
2. To reduce the role of measurement error, we focus only on bilateral migration stocks of at least 1,000 people.
3. See Kone et al. (2017) for a detailed description of the data and a broad overview of migration patterns in India.
4. Evidence suggests that the scope of displacement depends on a number of parameters, including the nature of the conflict and the geographic spread of violence, as well as its intensity. See, for example, Schmeidl (1997); Davenport, Moore, and Poe (2003); and Moore and Shellman (2004).
5. This includes principals, spouses, and children. We have limited the sample to those ages 20 and above. Included visa categories are CW1, CW2, E1 to E3, H1B, H1B1, H1C, H2A, H2B, H2R, H3, H4, I1, L1, L2, O1 to O3, P1 to P4, Q1, R1, R2, TD, and TN.
6. These figures exclude students who account for 25 percent of Green Card recipients, retirees (1 percent), and those with unknown occupation (28 percent).

7. The literature on the economic impact of immigration (see chapter 3) relies on this observation by frequently predicting contemporaneous flows to locations in a country using the historical distribution of immigrants across these locations.

8. Note that the plots adjust for log distance and contiguity, so that those factors are not what drive the relationship.

9. See Adserà and Pytliková (2016) for a detailed investigation of the role of linguistic similarity in determining internal migration patterns.

10. As a measurement of linguistic similarity we use the common language index developed by Melitz and Toubal (2014). The index is a combination of three separate measures of linguistic similarity: common native language, common official language, and linguistic proximity. Common native language is an index that measures the share of language overlap between two countries' native languages. Common official language is a binary indicator indicating whether a pair of countries shares a common official language. Linguistic proximity measures the similarity between a given pair of languages by comparing 40 commonly used words; the measure is then applied to the set of native languages assigned to each country.

11. For India the common language used is calculated as follows. Let s_i^l and s_j^l be the share of individuals speaking mother tongue l in districts i and j, respectively. Then $s_i^l * s_j^l$ is the probability that an individual from i can speak to an individual from j in language l. Summing over all possible mother tongues, *Common Language* measures the likelihood of any two individuals able to communicate to each other in a common language. Specifically,

$$Common\ Language_{ij} = \sum_l s_i^l * s_j^l.$$

12. The database, developed in collaboration with research across multiple disciplines and research institutions, captures trends in immigration selection, naturalization (citizenship), illegal immigration, and humanitarian policies across 20 OECD countries and over time. Currently, pilot data cover 9 immigrant-receiving countries over 10 years. See http://www.impaladatabase .org for further description.

13. The DEMIG Policy database documents policy by country and year. Measures are coded by policy area, the migration group targeted, and the direction and magnitude of the policy change. See https://www.imi.ox.ac.uk/data/demig-data.

14. Other work finds that signatories of the Schengen Agreement experience larger bilateral migration flows (Grogger and Hanson 2011; Beine, Bourgeon, and Bricongne 2013). Visa waivers can also facilitate bilateral flows by allowing for the legal entry of migrants (Bertoli and Fernández-Huertas Moraga 2013; Beine and Parsons 2015).

15. Former illegal migrants adjusting under the 1986 Immigration Reform and Control Act have been removed from the series on legal immigrants because they are already accounted for in the series on illegal immigrants.

16. The U.S. Border Patrol budget rose more than fourfold over this period. The Border Patrol also invested in advanced technology, including double fences, watchtowers, ground sensors, remote video monitoring, and aerial and marine surveillance. By 2012 about one-third of the southwest border was fenced (Hollifield, Martin, and Orrenius 2014).

17. Another good example comes from Hoekstra and Orozco-Aleman (2017), who document the effects of anti-immigration bill Arizona SB 1070. They find the bill reduced the flows of Mexican immigrants into Arizona by 30–70 percent.

18. It is worth noting that this relationship between emigration rates and GDP per capita is entirely driven by low-skilled emigrants; there is no relationship if we focus only on high-skilled emigrants.

19. See Ibáñez (2014) for a review of the literature.

20. See recent literature reviews by Ibáñez (2014) and Ibáñez and Moya (2016). Kalyvas and Kocher (2007), Korf (2004), and Steele (2009) also document the strategies taken by natives in conflict areas.

21. See Beine, Bertoli, and Fernández-Huertas Moraga (2016) for an overview.

22. The importance of controlling for credit constraints is emphasized by Vogler and Rotte (2000); Clark, Hatton, and Williamson (2007); Pedersen, Pytlikova, and Smith (2008); and Belot and Hatton (2012).

23. Recall that, as throughout this chapter, we consider only bilateral migration flows that include at least 1,000 people. This helps deal with poor measurement of small flows, and, importantly, makes the constant elasticity assumption (all variables are in natural logs) more plausible. The results reflect the choices migrants make across existing migration corridors, and do not address the question of why most potential migration corridors are effectively empty. The standard errors in all specifications are clustered by origin country and by destination country.

24. Studies looking at the relationships between incomes—as measured by GDP per capita—and migration include Mayda (2010); Bertoli and Fernández-Huertas Moraga (2013); Ortega and Peri (2013); and McKenzie, Theoharides, and Yang (2014).

25. The consensus in the literature is that this will result in a 4 percent increase in the bilateral migration flow over the next 10 years; see Beine, Docquier, and Özden (2011); Beine and Parsons (2015); and Bertoli and Fernández-Huertas Moraga (2015).

26. Mathematically this is written as $\ln\left(\dfrac{m_{i,j}^{h} / m_{i,j}^{l}}{m_{i}^{h} / m_{i}^{l}} \right)$, where $m_{i,j}^{s}$ refers to the bilateral migrant stock for a given skill group s, and m_{i}^{s} refers to all emigrants from a given skill group and origin country i (see annex 2A for more details).

27. Mathematically written as $\left[\ln\left(w_{j}^{h} / w_{j}^{l} \right) - \ln\left(w_{i}^{h} / w_{i}^{l} \right) \right]$, where w_{k}^{s} refers to the wage of skill group s in country k (see annex 2A for more details).

28. Economists use the term *unobserved skills* to refer to worker characteristics that are typically unobservable to the researcher but that contribute to a worker's productive capacity.

29. The ability term is the estimated individual-level fixed effect in a Mincer-type wage equation where the authors correct for selection bias on ability due to migration.

30. Methodologically we, like Chiquiar and Hanson (2005), follow DiNardo, Fortin, and Lemieux (1996). We match migrants and non-migrants on polynomials of education, age, origin state, and their interactions.

31. This is also true for Mexico–United States migration. Fernández-Huertas Moraga (2013) finds negative selection for urban Mexican migrants to the United States but positive selection in emigration out of rural Mexico.
32. For a more in-depth analysis of gravity models and their use in migration research, see Beine, Bertoli, and Fernández-Huertas Moraga (2016) and Ramos (2016).

References

Abramitzky, R., L. P. Boustan, and K. Eriksson. 2012. "Europe's Tired, Poor, Huddled Masses: Self-Selection and Economic Outcomes in the Age of Mass Migration." *American Economic Review* 102 (5): 1832–56.

Adhikari, P. 2013. "Conflict-Induced Displacement, Understanding the Causes of Flight." *American Journal of Political Science* 57 (1): 82–89.

Adserà, A., and M. Pytliková. 2016. "Language and Migration." In *The Palgrave Handbook of Economics and Language*, edited by V. Ginsburgh and S. Weber, 342–72. Basingstoke, U.K.: Palgrave Macmillan.

Angelucci, M. 2012. "US Border Enforcement and the Net Flow of Mexican Illegal Migration." *Economic Development and Cultural Change* 60 (2): 311–57.

Ashenfelter, O. 2012. "Comparing Real Wage Rates." *American Economic Review* 102 (2): 617–42.

Bartolucci, C., C. Villosio, and M. Wagner. 2018. "Who Migrates and Why? Evidence from Italian Administrative Data." *Journal of Labor Economics* 36 (2): 551–88.

Beine, M., S. Bertoli, and J. Fernández-Huertas Moraga. 2016. "A Practitioners' Guide to Gravity Models of International Migration." *World Economy* 39 (4): 496–512.

Beine, M., A. Boucher, B. Burgoon, M. Crock, J. Gest, M. Hiscox, P. McGovern, H. Rapoport, J. Schaper, and E. Thielemann. 2015. "Comparing Immigration Policies: An Overview from the IMPALA Database." *International Migration Review* 50 (4): 827–63.

Beine, M., P. Bourgeon, and J. C. Bricongne. 2013. "Aggregate Fluctuations and International Migration." CESifo Working Paper No. 4379, Center for Economic Studies and Ifo Institute, Munich.

Beine, M., F. Docquier, and Ç. Özden. 2011. "Diasporas." *Journal of Development Economics* 95 (1): 30–41.

Beine, M., and C. Parsons. 2015. "Climatic Factors as Determinants of International Migration." *Scandinavian Journal of Economics* 117 (2): 723–67.

Belot, M. V., and T. J. Hatton. 2012. "Immigrant Selection in the OECD." *Scandinavian Journal of Economics* 114 (4): 1105–128.

Bertoli, S., and J. Fernández-Huertas Moraga. 2013. "Multilateral Resistance to Migration." *Journal of Development Economics* 102: 79–100.

———. 2015. "The Size of the Cliff at the Border." *Regional Science and Urban Economics* 51: 1–6.

Bleakley, H., and A. Chin. 2004. "Language Skills and Earnings: Evidence from Childhood Immigrants." *Review of Economics and Statistics* 86 (2): 481–96.

———. 2010. "Age at Arrival, English Proficiency, and Social Assimilation among U.S. Immigrants." *American Economic Journal. Applied Economics* 2 (1): 165.

Borjas, G. J. 1987. "Self-Selection and the Earnings of Immigrants." *American Economic Review* 77 (4): 531–53.

———. 2014. *Immigration Economics*. Cambridge, MA: Harvard University Press.

China National Bureau of Statistics. *China City Statistical Yearbook 2001 [Zhongguo Chengshi Tongji Nianjian 2001]*. 2001. Beijing: China Statistics Press.

———. *China Statistical Yearbook 2001 [Zhongguo Tongji Nianjian 2001]*. 2001. Beijing: China Statistics Press.

Chiquiar, D., and G. H. Hanson. 2005. "International Migration, Self-Selection, and the Distribution of Wages: Evidence from Mexico and the United States." *Journal of Political Economy* 113 (2): 239–81.

Chiswick, B. R., and P. W. Miller. 1995. "The Endogeneity between Language and Earnings: International Analyses." *Journal of Labor Economics* 13 (2): 246–88.

———. 2002. "Immigrant Earnings: Language Skills, Linguistic Concentrations and the Business Cycle." *Journal of Population Economics* 15 (1): 31–57.

Clark, X., T. J. Hatton, and J. G. Williamson. 2007. "Explaining U.S. Immigration, 1971–1998." *Review of Economics and Statistics* 89 (2): 359–73.

Clemens, M. A. 2014. "Does Development Reduce Migration?" *International Handbook on Migration and Economic Development*, edited by R. E. B. Lucas, 152–85. Cheltenham, U.K.: Edward Elgar.

Clemens, M. A., C. E. Montenegro, and L. Pritchett. 2016. "Bounding the Price Equivalent of Migration Barriers." IZA Discussion Paper 9789, Institute for the Study of Labor, Bonn.

Czaika, M., and H. de Haas. 2016. "The Effect of Visas on Migration Processes." *International Migration Review*. https://doi.org/10.1111/imre.12261.

Davenport, C., W. Moore, and S. Poe. 2003. "Sometimes You Just Have to Leave: Domestic Threats and Forced Migration, 1964–1989." *International Interactions* 29 (1): 27–55.

de Brauw, A., and J. Giles. 2016. "Migrant Opportunity and the Educational Attainment of Youth in Rural China." *Journal of Human Resources* 53 (2): 272–311.

de Haas, H., K. Natter, and S. Vezzoli. 2016. "Growing Restrictiveness or Changing Selection? The Nature and Evolution of Migration Policies." *International Migration Review* Fall: 1–44.

DHS (U.S. Department of Homeland Security). 2010. *Yearbook of Immigration Statistics: 2009*. Washington, DC: U.S. Department of Homeland Security, Office of Immigration Statistics.

———. 2016a. *Yearbook of Immigration Statistics: 2014*. Washington, DC: U.S. Department of Homeland Security, Office of Immigration Statistics.

———. 2016b. *Yearbook of Immigration Statistics: 2015*. Washington, DC: U.S. Department of Homeland Security, Office of Immigration Statistics.

DiNardo, J., N. M. Fortin, and T. Lemieux. 1996. "Labor Market Institutions and the Distribution of Wages, 1973–1992: A Semiparametric Approach." *Econometrica* 64 (5): 1001–44.

Dustmann, C. 1994. "Speaking Fluency, Writing Fluency and Earnings of Migrants." *Journal of Population Economics* 7 (2): 133–56.

Dustmann, C., and F. Fabbri. 2003. "Language Proficiency and Labour Market Performance of Immigrants in the U.K." *Economic Journal* 113 (489): 695–717.

Dustmann, C., and A. van Soest. 2001. "Language Fluency and Earnings: Estimation with Misclassified Language Indicators." *Review of Economics and Statistics* 83 (4): 663–74.

Engel, S., and A. M. Ibáñez. 2007. "Displacement Due to Violence in Colombia: A Household-Level Analysis." *Economic Development and Cultural Change* 55 (2): 335–65.

Fernández-Huertas Moraga, J. 2011. "New Evidence on Emigrant Selection." *Review of Economics and Statistics* 93 (1): 72–96.

———. 2013. "Understanding Different Migrant Selection Patterns in Rural and Urban Mexico." *Journal of Development Economics* 103: 182–201.

Fulford, S. L. 2015. "Marriage Migration in India: Vast, Varied, and Misunderstood." Working Paper 820, Boston College. http://fmwww.bc.edu/EC-P/wp820.pdf.

Gathmann, C. 2008. "Effects of Enforcement on Illegal Markets: Evidence from Migrant Smuggling along the Southwestern Border." *Journal of Public Economics* 92 (10): 1926–41.

Gibson, J., D. McKenzie, H. Rohorua, and S. Stillman. 2018. "The Long-Term Impacts of International Migration: Evidence from a Lottery." *World Bank Economic Review* 32 (1): 127–47.

Grogger, J., and G. H. Hanson. 2011. "Income Maximization and the Selection and Sorting of International Migrants." *Journal of Development Economics* 95 (1): 42–57.

Hatton, T. J. 2016. "Refugees and Asylum Seekers, the Crisis in Europe and the Future of Policy." *Economic Policy* 32 (91): 447–96.

Hatton, T. J., and J. Moloney. 2015. "Applications for Asylum in the Developed World: Modelling Asylum Claims by Origin and Destination." CEPR Discussion Paper No. 10678, Centre for Economic Policy Research, London.

Hoekstra, M., and S. Orozco-Aleman. 2017. "Illegal Immigration, State Law, and Deterrence." *American Economic Journal: Economic Policy* 9 (2): 228.

Hollifield, J., P. L. Martin, and P. Orrenius, eds. 2014. *Controlling Immigration: A Global Perspective*. Palo Alto, CA: Stanford University Press.

Ibáñez, A. M. 2014. "The Growth of Forced Displacement: Cross-Country, Subnational and Household Evidence on Potential Determinants." In *International Handbook on Migration and Economic Development*, edited by Robert Lucas, Jr., 350–87. Cheltenham, U.K.: Edward Elgar.

Ibáñez, A. M., and A. Moya. 2016. "Who Stays and Who Leaves During Mass Atrocities?" In *Economic Aspects of Genocides, Other Mass Atrocities, and Their Prevention*, edited by C. H. Anderton and J. Brauer, 251–73. New York: Oxford University Press.

Ibáñez, A. M., and C. E. Vélez. 2008. "Civil Conflict and Forced Migration: The Micro Determinants and Welfare Losses of Displacement in Colombia." *World Development* 36 (4): 659–76.

Kalyvas, S. N., and M. A. Kocher. 2007. "How 'Free' Is Free Riding in Civil Wars? Violence, Insurgency, and the Collective Action Problem." *World Politics* 59 (02): 177–216.

Kone, Z., M. Liu, A. Mattoo, Ç. Özden, and S. Sharma. 2017. "Internal Borders and Migration in India." Policy Research Working Paper 8244, World Bank, Washington, DC.

Korf, B. 2004. "War, Livelihoods and Vulnerability in Sri Lanka." *Development and Change* 35 (2): 275–95.

Kossoudji, S. A. 1988. "English Language Ability and the Labor Market Opportunities of Hispanic and East Asian Immigrant Men." *Journal of Labor Economics* 6 (2): 205–28.

Massey, D. S., and K. A. Pren. 2012. "Unintended Consequences of U.S. Immigration Policy: Explaining the Post-1965 Surge from Latin America." *Population and Development Review* 38 (1): 1–29.

Mayda, A. M. 2010. "International Migration: A Panel Data Analysis of the Determinants of Bilateral Flows." *Journal of Population Economics* 23 (4): 1249–74.

McKenzie, D., S. Stillman, and J. Gibson. 2010. "How Important Is Selection? Experimental vs. Non-experimental Measures of the Income Gains from Migration." *Journal of the European Economic Association* 8 (4): 913–45.

McKenzie, D., C. Theoharides, and D. Yang. 2014. "Distortions in the International Migrant Labor Market: Evidence from Filipino Migration and Wage Responses to Destination Country Economic Shocks." *American Economic Journal: Applied Economics* 6 (2): 49–75.

Melitz, J., and F. Toubal. 2014. "Native Language, Spoken Language, Translation and Trade." *Journal of International Economics* 93 (2): 351–63.

Mian, A. R., and A. Sufi. 2012. "What Explains High Unemployment? The Aggregate Demand Channel." NBER Working Paper 17830, National Bureau of Economic Research, Cambridge, MA.

Molloy, R., C. L. Smith, and A. Wozniak. 2011. "Internal Migration in the United States." *Journal of Economic Perspectives* 25 (3): 173–96.

Monras, J. 2015. "Economic Shocks and Internal Migration." IZA Discussion Paper 8840, Institute for the Study of Labor, Bonn.

Moore, W. H., and S. M. Shellman. 2004. "Fear of Persecution: Forced Migration, 1952–1995." *Journal of Conflict Resolution* 48 (5): 723–45.

Morten, M., and J. Oliveira. 2016. "The Effects of Roads on Trade and Migration: Evidence from a Planned Capital City." Working paper.

National Research Council. 2013. *Options for Estimating Illegal Entries at the US–Mexico Border.* Washington, DC: National Academies Press.

OECD (Organisation for Economic Co-operation and Development). 2015. *International Migration Outlook 2015.* Paris: OECD Publishing.

Ortega, F., and G. Peri. 2012. "The Role of Income and Immigration Policies in Attracting International Migrants." IZA Discussion Paper 6655, Institute for the Study of Labor, Bonn.

———. 2013. "The Effect of Income and Immigration Policies on International Migration." *Migration Studies* 1 (1): 47–74.

Passel, J. S., and D. Cohn. 2016. "Overall Number of U.S. Unauthorized Immigrants Holds Steady since 2009." *Pew Research Center Hispanic Trends*, September 30.

Pedersen, P. J., M. Pytlikova, and N. Smith. 2008. "Selection and Network Effects—Migration Flows into OECD Countries 1990–2000." *European Economic Review* 52 (7): 1160–186.

Ramos, R. 2016. "Gravity Models: A Tool for Migration Analysis." *IZA World of Labor*, article no. 239. https://wol.iza.org/articles/gravity-models -tool-for-migration-analysis.

Ransom, T. 2016. "The Effect of Business Cycle Fluctuations on Migration Decisions." Available at SSRN: https://papers.ssrn.com/sol3/papers .cfm?abstract_id=2741117.

Saks, R. E., and A. Wozniak. 2011. "Labor Reallocation over the Business Cycle: New Evidence from Internal Migration." *Journal of Labor Economics* 29 (4): 697–739.

Schmeidl, S. 1997. "Exploring the Causes of Forced Migration: A Pooled Time-Series Analysis, 1971–1990." *Social Science Quarterly* 78 (2): 284–308.

Steele, A. 2009. "Seeking Safety: Avoiding Displacement and Choosing Destinations in Civil Wars." *Journal of Peace Research* 46 (3): 419–29.

Verwimp, P. 2005. "An Economic Profile of Peasant Perpetrators of Genocide: Micro-Level Evidence from Rwanda." *Journal of Development Economics* 77 (2): 297–323.

Vogler, M., and R. Rotte. 2000. "The Effects of Development on Migration: Theoretical Issues and New Empirical Evidence." *Journal of Population Economics* 13 (3): 485–508.

World Bank. 2018. *Syrian Refugees and Their Hosts: Lives, Livelihoods, and Local Impacts in Jordan, Lebanon, and Kurdish Region of Iraq*. Washington, DC: World Bank.

CHAPTER THREE

The Wage and Employment Impacts of Migration

Recent decades have seen dramatic changes in labor markets as the result of the confluence of rapid technological change, unprecedented increases in international trade, and large-scale migration from poor to rich countries. The resulting structural changes in patterns of employment and wage inequality have given rise to a highly politicized debate about the merits of trade and immigration. Immigrants are frequently blamed for many of the economic woes of native-born workers and accused of displacing them, resulting in unemployment and lower wages. This chapter seeks to assess these claims and to consider the evidence on the impact of immigrants on labor market outcomes of native-born workers.

The literature on this subject is large and varied and has not yet reached a definitive consensus. This chapter does not seek to provide an exhaustive review of that vast literature on this subject.[1] Rather, it will provide a broad framework for thinking about the topic, highlight why it is difficult to reach a consensus on this question, and outline the main conclusions.

Three stylized facts emerge from studies that rely on large and sudden inflows of immigrant or refugee labor. First, immigration results in large displacement effects among groups of native-born workers that most directly compete with the immigrant labor. Second, groups of native-born workers who do not directly compete with the immigrants frequently experience significant gains. Third, short-run average wage effects tend to be small as compared to the employment and displacement effects of immigration.

The fact that these studies frequently find short-run displacement effects due to an inflow of refugees provides a seeming contrast to much of the voluntary immigration literature, which typically finds small average impacts on wages (positive and negative).[2] The findings are, however, entirely compatible. Evidence from labor supply shocks finds significant dislocation and native-born worker adjustment in certain geographic areas, sectors, or occupations in the presence of inflows of immigrants. The native-born worker adjustments seem, in practice, sufficiently large that there are only small relative wage effects in these local labor markets. The literature on voluntary migration flows has tended to focus on those average wage effects and concluded that, for most groups of native workers, immigration has little impact. In most cases, the overall effect is positive, especially when long-term spillovers are taken into account. However, even if relative wage effects are small, the dislocation experienced because of immigration can be costly and can explain, in part, some of the opposition many native-born workers exhibit toward immigrants.

In sum, it is likely true that immigration impacts certain groups of native-born workers adversely, yet its overall wage effects remain small.

Conceptual issues: The factor proportions approach

The most common approach to conceptualize the impact of immigration, which we will refer to as the *factor proportions approach*, underpins most studies in this literature. The key insight of the factor proportions approach is that immigrants change the *relative* abundance of different skill groups in the economy. For example, the standard argument in many destination countries is that immigrants are less skilled than native-born workers and therefore their arrival will increase the relative abundance of lower-skilled workers in the labor force. That, in turn, will change the relative wages across skill groups. Specifically, an increase in the quantity of lower-skilled labor is likely to depress low-skilled wages, and thereby increase inequality.

The factor proportions approach is not the only way to conceptualize the labor market implications of immigration. For example, immigration may affect wages and employment outcomes by stimulating innovation and the ability to produce new products. It could also transform the quality of institutions in a country. These long-term dynamic issues will be discussed in subsequent chapters. In this chapter, as in most of the academic and policy literature, immigration is thought of as a change in labor supply, thereby changing relative wages and employment in destination countries.

The seminal work of Katz and Murphy (1992) on inequality forms the basis of the factor proportions approach. Their paper's main concern is how the skill premium in the United States—that is, the relative wages of high- and low-education workers—changed over time.[3] The key economic determinant of changes in skill premium is the elasticity of substitution between skill groups, which determines how responsive *relative* wages are to changes in the *relative* skill composition of the labor force. In other words, they want to find out how substitutable or complementary different skill groups are.

The factor proportions approach is appealing, and has been used extensively in the migration literature, because it allows researchers to estimate the impact of immigration on wages using only the observed characteristics of immigrants and native-born workers and the average wages by skill group.[4] It requires estimating only the elasticities of substitution between skill groups, making it a parsimonious way to tackle a complex issue.[5]

Figure 3.1 depicts, theoretically, the dynamics of the factor proportions approach for a simple scenario consisting of only low- and high-skilled labor (the case analyzed by Katz and Murphy 1992). The y-axis of the figure depicts the (log) relative wage of low-skilled workers compared to

Figure 3.1 Theoretical impact of an inflow of low-skilled immigrants in a labor market

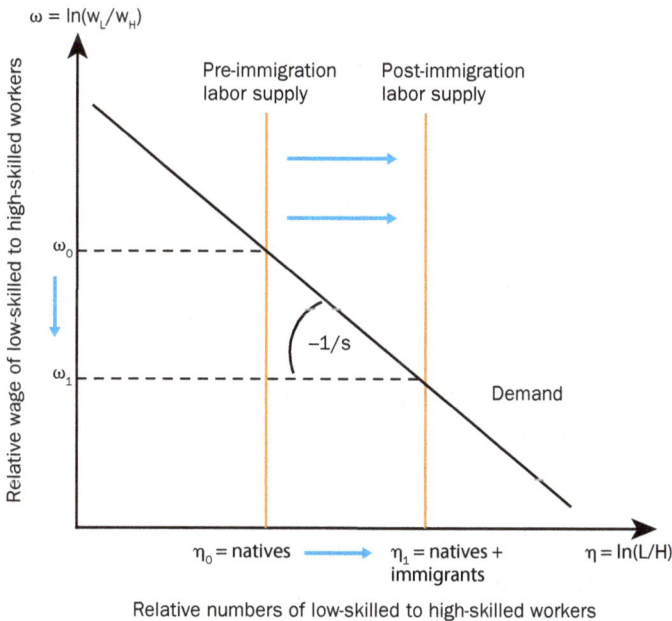

Relative numbers of low-skilled to high-skilled workers

Note: Pre-immigration and post-immigration low-skilled wage are $_0$ and $_1$, respectively; $_L$ and $_H$ are the low-skilled and high-skilled wage, respectively; L and H are the quantity of low-skilled and high-skilled workers, respectively; and s is the elasticity of substitution in production between low- and high-skilled labor.

high-skilled workers, and the x-axis depicts the (log) relative quantity of workers for each type of labor. The relative demand for each type of labor is depicted by the downward sloping labor demand curve. The relative supply of these factors is considered exogenous and is depicted by the vertical line labeled "Pre-immigration labor supply."

Using this model, we can study the impact of an inflow of low-skilled immigrants. The pre-immigration relative low-skilled wage is ω_0. When low-skilled immigration inflow shifts the labor supply curve out, the relative amount of low-skilled labor increases from η_0 to η_1, and the relative low-skilled wage decreases to ω_1, accordingly.

The slope of the demand curve is given by $-1/s$, which is the inverse of the elasticity of substitution, denoted by s. It can be calculated, or estimated using a simple linear regression, as

$$s = -\frac{\eta_1 - \eta_0}{\omega_1 - \omega_0}, \tag{3.1}$$

that is, using just the pre- and post-immigration wage and employment numbers. The single most important variable in this model, the elasticity of substitution, is the relationship between the skill composition of labor demand and the relative wage ratios. Specifically, an elasticity of s tells us that a 1 percent increase in the ratio of low- to high-skilled labor, due to immigration, will decrease the ratio of low- to high-skilled wages by $1/s$ percent.

One of the strengths of the factor proportions approach is its flexibility in how the relevant labor factors are defined.[6] We can distinguish between workers according to their education, age, gender, or immigration status (native-born versus immigrant), or any other relatively exogenous labor market characteristic that we think is salient. However, the approach imposes certain restrictions in important ways that are elaborated in annex 3A.

Understanding the simple theoretical underpinnings of the factor proportions approach also helps build intuition for what we might expect to be the impact of immigration.[7] The elasticity of substitution between these types of workers in the United States has been estimated to be about 1.7. Now consider, for example, the case where immigration to the United States increases the ratio of low- to high-skilled workers by 5 percent. In that case, immigration increases income inequality, as measured by the log ratio of wages, between low- and high-skilled workers by 3 percent. That is a substantial, but not enormous, impact. Typically, as we show in the next section, changes in labor factor proportions due to immigration simply are not large enough to result in very large changes in relative wages.

Empirical challenges: Immigrants and natives choose where to live and work

In an ideal world (for the sake of economic analysis), immigrants would show up at random in a labor market, native-born workers would not change jobs or move at all, and then we could observe the wage impact of immigration. This is exactly the scenario depicted in figure 3.1, where the labor demand is downward sloping and the (native-born) labor supply is completely unresponsive to wage changes (inelastic).

Unfortunately for economists and policy makers, the world is not as simple. Specifically, two main complications arise. First, immigrants do not simply show up in a labor market by accident, but rather as the result of a deliberate (economic) decision. The determinants of these decisions, especially those related to underlying labor market conditions, were discussed in great detail in the previous chapter. Second, some native-born workers will respond to immigration by changing sectors or moving to a new labor market. They can change jobs, occupations, sectors, or cities or exit the labor market altogether. Ignoring these complications leads to errors in identifying the size and direction of the impact of immigration.

The endogeneity of immigrant location decisions

Economic conditions are a key determinant of migration patterns, as documented extensively in chapter 2. On the one hand, places that experience wage gains—for example, because of productivity growth or improved economic prospects such as discovery of natural resources—will see rapid increases in immigration flows. On the other hand, places in relative economic decline will see the arrival of fewer immigrants or even departures.

The factor proportions model indicates that immigrants will decrease wages in the destination labor markets by shifting the labor supply curve. If immigrants systematically target high-wage growth markets, it may look as though the opposite is occurring. Simple estimates of the relationship will be misleading, and we will observe simultaneously increasing wages and immigration levels. It is the presence of a third factor—for example, productivity growth, which will cause both immigration and wage growth—that shifts labor demand (see figure 3.2).[8]

Figure 3.2   An increase in low-skilled labor demand causing both immigration and wage growth

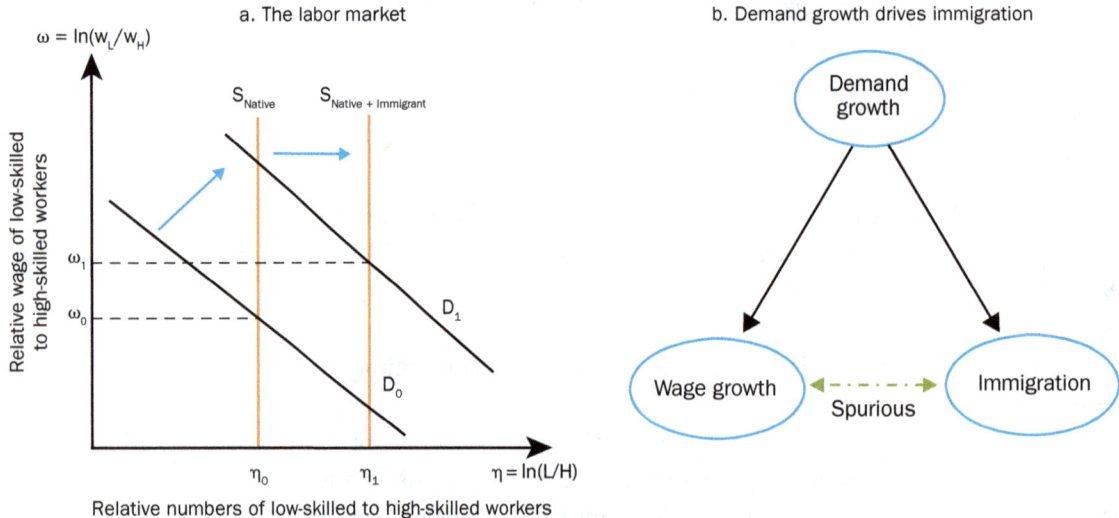

a. The labor market

b. Demand growth drives immigration

$\omega = \ln(w_L/w_H)$

Relative wage of low-skilled to high-skilled workers

S_{Native} $S_{Native + Immigrant}$

ω_1

ω_0

D_1

D_0

η_0 η_1 $\eta = \ln(L/H)$

Relative numbers of low-skilled to high-skilled workers

Demand growth

Wage growth   ← - - - - → Immigration

Spurious

Note: w_L and w_H are the low-skilled and high-skilled wage, respectively; L and H are the quantity of low-skilled and high-skilled workers, respectively. S is the relative supply of low-skilled workers; D_0 and D_1 are relative demands for low-skilled labor before and after growth in productivity; and ω_0 and ω_1 are relative low-skilled wages before and after growth in productivity.

Figure 3.2 depicts the impact of an increase in the (relative) demand for low-skilled labor. The outward shift in the (relative) demand curve from D_0 to D_1 is due to reasons other than immigration and puts upward pressure on wages. That, in turn, results in an inflow of immigrants and a shift in the labor supply curve from S_{Native} to $S_{Native + Immigrant}$. The increase in labor supply now puts downward pressure on relative wages but does not necessarily fully offset the initial increase. The end result, depicted in the figure, may well be lower wage inequality and higher low-skilled employment. However, the critical issue is that an underlying increase in relative labor demand—not the inflow of low-skilled immigrants—causes both of these effects.

The endogeneity of native location (and employment) decisions

Native-born workers, just like immigrants, respond to changing labor market conditions. In our original figure 3.1, we had ruled out that possibility by making native labor supply completely unresponsive to wages (perfectly vertical or inelastic). In practice, however, native-born workers

Figure 3.3 The impact of low-skilled immigration when native labor supply is elastic

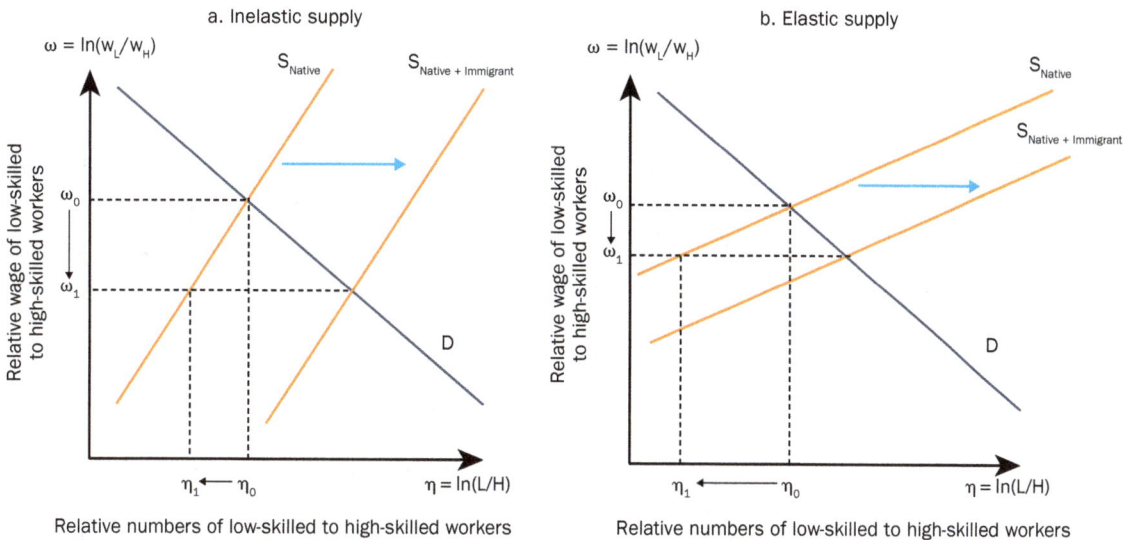

a. Inelastic supply

b. Elastic supply

Note: w_L and w_H are the low-skilled and high-skilled wage, respectively; L and H are the quantity of low-skilled and high-skilled workers, respectively. S and D are the relative supply and demand of low-skilled workers. ω_0 (η_0) and ω_1 (η_1) are relative low-skilled wages (employment) before and after a shift in relative labor supply.

may relocate within a country, relocate across sectors, or switch in or out of the labor force, to name a few possible responses.

In figure 3.3, panels a and b, native labor supply is now responsive to the wage changes, that is, it has become more elastic. Consider again the inflow of low-skilled immigrants as a shift in (relative) labor supply from S_{Native} to $S_{\text{Native + Immigrant}}$. This shift puts a downward pressure on low-skilled wages, which also encourages some low-skilled natives to leave this market (native labor supply is upward sloping).

The degree to which the immigration affects native wages or employment depends on the slope of the labor supply curve. If native labor supply is relatively unresponsive to wage changes, relatively vertical as in panel a, then the immigration effect will show up primarily in wages, and native employment will not decrease much. If, in contrast, native labor supply is very elastic as in panel b, then the impact of immigration will significantly affect native employment with a small decline in wages.

The empirical consequence of both of these challenges is significant. We cannot simply study the correlation between immigration and native wages and employment levels (pre- and post-immigration) to determine the causal impact of immigration.

Measurement challenges: Skill "downgrading" and the undocumented

Skill "downgrading"

A critical assumption of the factor proportions approach is that immigrants and natives can be assigned to comparable skill groups on the basis of their observed educational characteristics. This assumption is problematic for two reasons. (Please see the appendix for further discussion on how these issues of educational characteristics are addressed in global migration databases.)

First, observed characteristics capture only a fraction of the variation in earnings across individuals. Many characteristics that affect wages and employment outcomes cannot be directly observed or collected in surveys, which typically contain information only on education, age, and sometimes work experience.

Second, the evidence suggests that immigrants typically "downgrade" their occupation or human capital upon arrival.[9] Local employers often discount the value and human capital content of degrees from foreign institutions, and poor language skills prevent many new immigrants from realizing the benefits of the higher education they arrive with (Mattoo, Neagu, and Ozden 2008). A nuclear physicist driving a taxi in New York is the most commonly given example of this phenomenon. Immigrants may compete with native-born workers at parts of the skill or education distribution different from where their observed characteristics would place them.

Figure 3.4, from Dustmann, Schönberg, and Stuhler (2016), depicts the actual and predicted position of recent immigrants in the native wage distribution in several Organisation for Economic Co-operation and Development (OECD) destination countries. Recent immigrants are defined as those who arrived over the last two years. Panel a shows evidence for the United States, panel b for the United Kingdom, and panel c for Germany. The orange lines denote immigrants' actual wage position, based on their observed earnings. The blue lines denote the position they would occupy in the native wage distribution if immigrants were to receive the same returns to observable characteristics (such as age and education) as the native-born workers. The figures show that immigrants are actually placed at different parts of the wage distribution compared to where their observable characteristics would have predicted. In particular, they are overrepresented at the lower end of the wage distribution, as clear evidence of immigrant skill downgrading.

Figure 3.4 **Immigrant skill downgrading in the wage distribution**

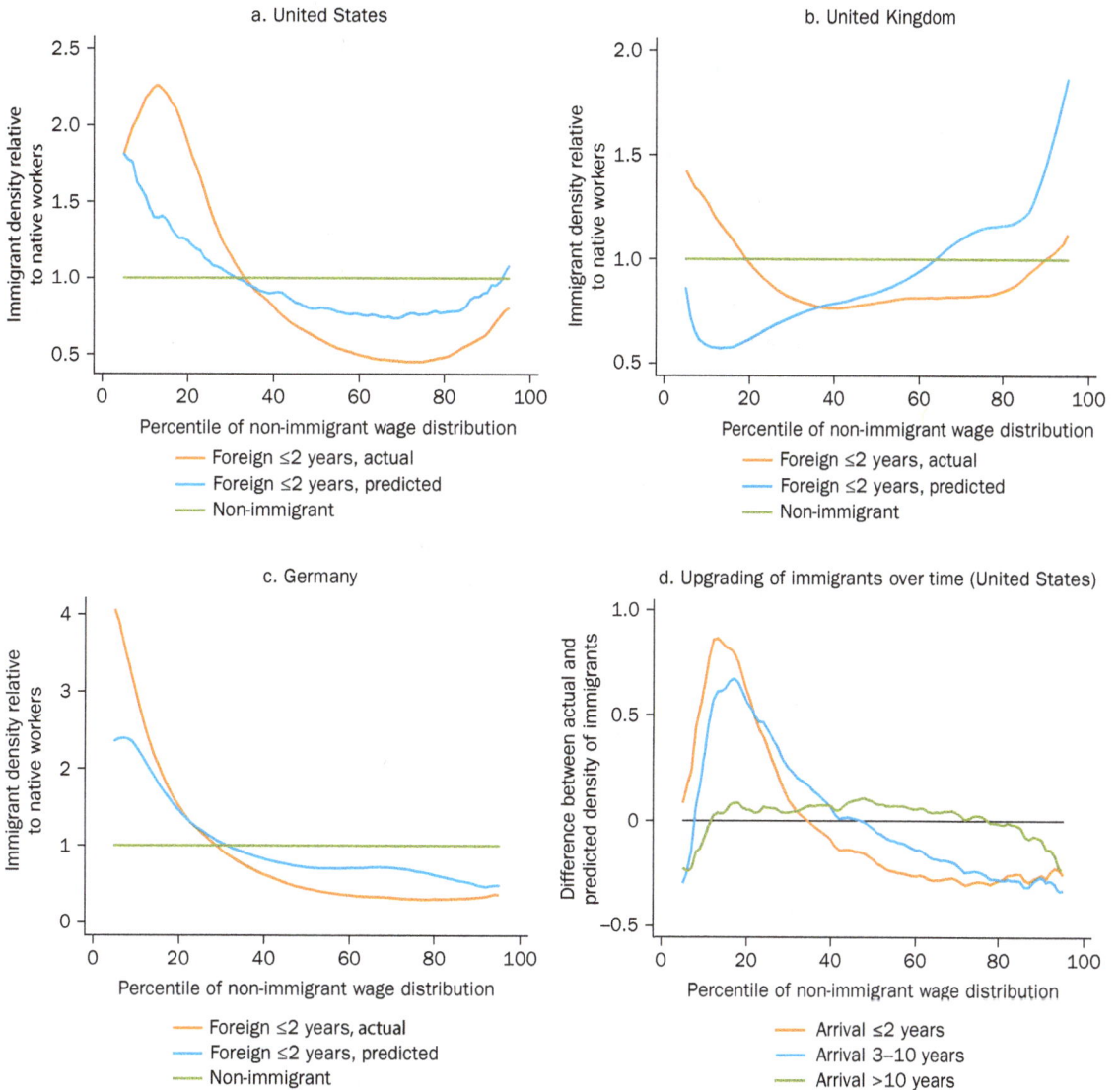

a. United States

b. United Kingdom

c. Germany

d. Upgrading of immigrants over time (United States)

Foreign ≤2 years, actual
Foreign ≤2 years, predicted
Non-immigrant

Arrival ≤2 years
Arrival 3–10 years
Arrival >10 years

Sources: Dustmann, Schönberg, and Stuhler 2016. Data from the U.S. Census 2000; U.K. Labour Force Survey 1995–2005; and Integrierten Arbeitsmarktbiografien Sample, 2% sample 2000.

Note: The figure shows kernel estimates of the actual and predicted density of immigrants in the native wage distribution. The horizontal lines represent the native wage distribution. Estimates above the horizontal line show immigrants more concentrated than natives; estimates below the solid line show immigrants less concentrated. Panel d shows the difference between the actual and predicted density of immigrants at different points along the non-immigrant wage distribution.

153

Panel d of figure 3.4 depicts actual wages for different groups of immigrants, depending on the number of years they have been in the United States, together with the predicted wages based on their observables. The figure shows that, as immigrants spend more time in the United States, their actual wages converge to their predicted wages. The implication is that, after arrival, immigrants may move along the distribution of native wages through "upgrading" or "assimilation" as they accumulate the necessary and complementary human capital and as they transfer their existing skills to the needs of the host country labor market.

Evidence of immigrant skill downgrading at arrival, and subsequent gradual upgrading, is a serious problem for the factor proportions approaches because it suggests that observable characteristics may not be reliable indicators of immigrant human capital, skills, and wages in the host country. Dustmann and Preston (2012) discuss the implications of these measurement issues. They show how downgrading may bias estimates of imperfect substitutability within education and age cells, with the bias being dependent on the degree of downgrading, the pace of subsequent upgrading, and the length of the interval between two observations.

Undocumented immigrants

The high prevalence of undocumented immigrants in destination labor markets creates issues in accurately measuring the number of immigrants, their characteristics, and their impact. Surveys, such as labor force surveys, typically expend considerable effort to obtain a representative sample of a country's population, including undocumented immigrants in the labor force. Nevertheless, there is likely to be serious undercounting or miscounting of undocumented immigrants in many countries.

Figure 3.5 depicts the fraction of undocumented, or irregular, immigrants in several European countries. The fraction varies greatly—from 2.4 and 2.9 percent in Germany and Austria, respectively, to 16.0 and 14.9 percent in Greece and Italy, respectively. That fraction will also vary over time.

Figure 3.6 depicts the fraction of unauthorized immigrants in the United States for the period 2000–14. Note that far more undocumented immigrants reside in the United States than in Europe. Moreover, that fraction varies—from 27 to 32 percent over 15 years.

Different empirical strategies have different ways of dealing with this type of measurement error. It should be noted, however, that the issue is

Figure 3.5   Fraction of undocumented immigrants, by European country, various years

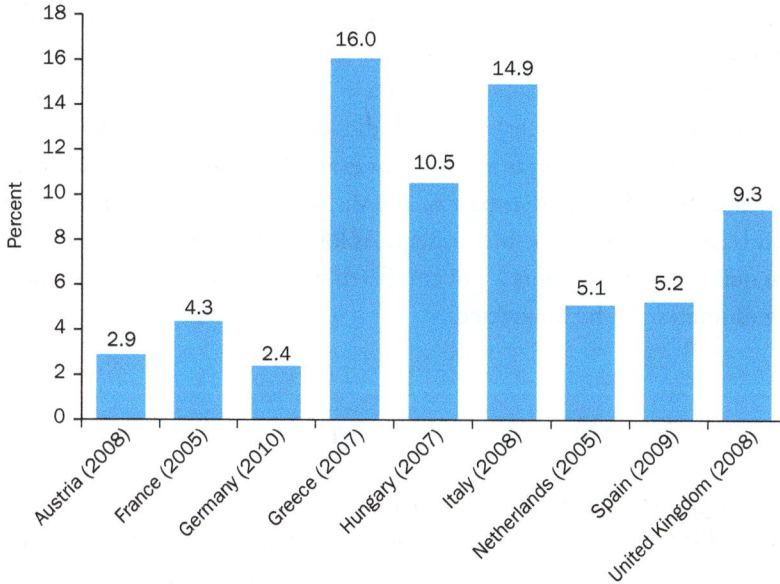

Estimated share of immigrants classified as irregular

Sources: Irregular immigration data are from the CLANDESTINO Project (http://clandestino.eliamep.gr /project-results/), data on total foreign-born population from the Organisation for Economic Co-operation and Development (https://data.oecd.org/migration/foreign-born-population.htm), and data on Greece from the United Nations (http://www.un.org/en/development/desa/population/migration/data/).

Figure 3.6   Fraction of undocumented immigrants in the United States, 2000–14

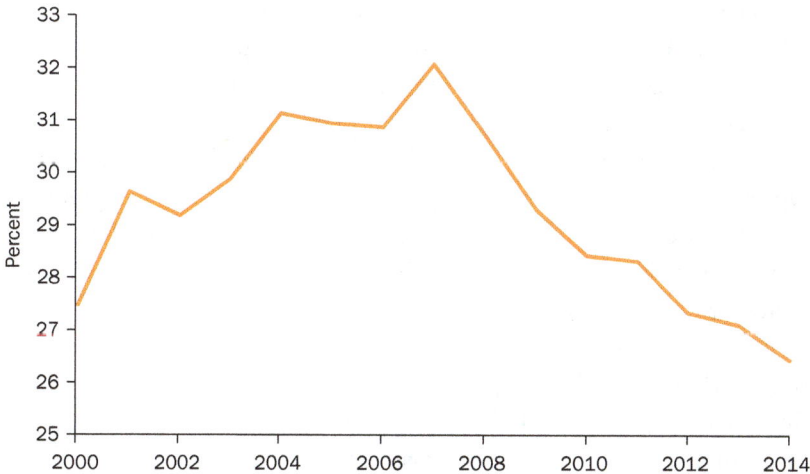

Source: Data from Pew Research, with estimates based on the Current Population Survey (2000–2004) and American Community Survey (2005–14; http://www.pewresearch.org/data-trend/society-and -demographics/immigrants/).

likely not as dramatic as it might seem at first glance. Most empirical strategies include a large number of time fixed effects, and these will typically pick up many of the measurement errors in variables. Further, empirical strategies that rely on instrumental variable estimates of immigration's impact need worry less about measurement error (see also the "Instruments" section later in this chapter). These studies do not rely on the full variation in the number of immigrants across, for example, regions or labor markets. Instead, they use only that part of the variation in immigration numbers that is correlated with the instrument. As long as the measurement error in the number of immigrants is not correlated with the instrument, the resulting estimates will be unaffected.

Empirical strategy I: The national skill cell approach

The migration literature tackles the described empirical challenges in several different ways. One influential strand of literature considers a whole country as the unit of analysis.[10] The appeal of this approach is that considering relatively fixed and exogenous characteristics (such as age, gender, education levels, and citizenship status) within a national market makes more plausible the assumption that the supply of native-born labor does not respond to immigration.

The *national skill cell approach* hews closely to the basic methodology described earlier in the section on the factor proportions approach. The skill cell approach categorizes native-born workers and immigrants into different skill groups.[11] Instead of just two skill groups, papers in this literature try to capture the complex interaction between workers of different characteristics. Then elasticities of substitution across skill groups are estimated using variation over time at the national level. Finally, these papers typically compare the actual supply of workers in particular skill groups to those that would have prevailed in the absence of immigration. The papers simulate the change in wages of native-born workers on the basis of estimates for the elasticity of substitution between skill groups.[12]

Figure 3.7, taken from Borjas (2014), graphically depicts the variation used by the skill cell approach to identify the impact of immigration on wages in the United States. It compares the change in the share of immigrants and log weekly wages by skill cell in the United States for the period 1960–2010. The negative slope implies that cells that experience increases in immigrant shares also experience corresponding decreases in wages.

Figure 3.7 Relationship between wages and employment across skill groups for the United States, 1960–2010

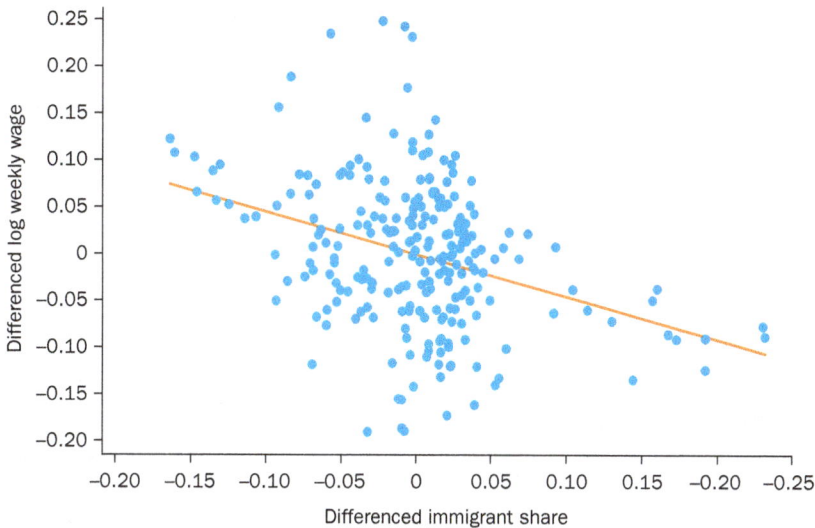

Source: Borjas 2014, figure 5-2.

Note: Each point in the scatter gives a differenced measure of log weekly wages and a differenced measure of the immigrant share for a particular skill group at a point in time (where each statistic is differenced from the sample mean for the respective skill group over the entire period). The scatter removes decade effects from the differenced data. Wages are calculated using male wage earners.

The national skill cell approach relies on correlations rather than estimates of causal effects to identify the impact of immigration, which gives the approach all the advantages associated with ordinary least squares (OLS) estimates, including far greater precision of estimates and a very clear identification strategy. One disadvantage of the approach is that it requires the researcher to assume that the characteristics of immigrants are exogenous with respect to relative wages for different skill groups in that country. We will return to this endogeneity issue shortly.

Evidence from the United States

Table 3.1, taken from a 2017 National Academies of Sciences, Engineering, and Medicine report, *The Economic and Fiscal Consequences of Immigration*, neatly summarizes the findings for the United States. The table considers the impact of immigration for five education groups (the first five columns) and the overall impact across all education groups (the last column). The first row describes the percentage labor supply increase for each education

Table 3.1 Simulated percentage wage impacts of 1990–2010 immigrant supply shock in the United States

	High school dropouts	High school graduates	Some college	College graduates	Post-college	All education groups
Percentage supply shift	25.9	8.4	6.1	10.9	15.0	10.6
Wage impacts						
Scenario 1: Native and foreign workers perfect substitutes ($\sigma_{MN} = \infty$)						
All workers	–3.1	0.4	0.9	–0.1	–0.9	0.0
Scenario 2: Native and foreign workers imperfect substitutes ($\sigma_{MN} = 20.0$)						
Native workers	–1.7	0.9	1.2	0.5	–0.1	0.6
Foreign workers	–5.3	–3.4	–2.7	–4.9	–5.3	–4.4
All workers	–3.1	0.4	0.9	–0.1	–0.9	0.0

Source: National Academies of Sciences, Engineering, and Medicine 2017, table 5-1. Reproduced with permission; further permission required for reuse.

Note: Results come from simulations using nested constant elasticity of substitution framework, set $\sigma_E = 5.0$, using a Cobb–Douglas aggregate production function, with $\sigma_{KL} = 1.0$.

group due to immigration over the period 1990–2010. Scenario 1 considers a situation in which immigrants and native-born workers within the same skill group are perfect substitutes. Scenario 2 allows for imperfect substitutability between otherwise observably identical immigrants and native-born workers (with an elasticity of substitution of 20).[13]

Three features of these results are worth highlighting. First, by assumption, the *average* impact of immigration across *all* workers (native and immigrant) is zero. This of course need not be the case, and evidence by Ozden and Wagner (2014) suggests that it is not; we return to this issue in annex 3A.

Second, whether the wage impact is positive or negative in Scenario 1 simply depends on whether the supply shift for a specific education group is larger or smaller than the average supply shift (10.6 percent). Immigrants over this period disproportionately came from the extremes of the skill distribution: they were either high school dropouts or had a post-college degree. Correspondingly, the simulation shows that natives in those groups experienced wage losses due to immigration. In contrast, immigrants from the middle of the skill distribution (high school graduates and those with some college education) are relatively underrepresented. As a consequence, those native groups experience wage gains due to immigration.

Third, in Scenario 2, immigration decreases wages of existing immigrants without exception because labor demand is downward sloping.

The assumption that the average wage impact across all workers is zero implies that, on average, native wages have to increase. It is worth emphasizing that this is a simple function of the assumptions that underlie the estimation, not an empirical result. The relative wage changes across education groups for native-born workers follow the same pattern as in Scenario 1.

So what do we learn from the national skill cell approach about the wage impact of immigration? George Borjas (2014, 127), in his book *Immigration Economics*, concludes that "the nested CES [constant elasticity of substitution] structural approach seems far too sensitive to the imposition of unverifiable (but necessary) assumptions to be of much use in giving a robust and convincing answer" about the impacts of immigrant inflows. Borjas puts a lot of weight on the extensive caveats, some of which are discussed earlier in this chapter and in annex 3A, that plague the results in this literature.

Card and Peri (2016) provide a different perspective. In their recent review of Borjas's book, they conclude that the simulated effects of immigrant arrivals on native wages are quite small, under a variety of specific assumptions used in the simulations. Immigration flows simply do not result in sufficiently large changes in the relative size of skill groups to have a very large impact on relative wages.

Cross-country evidence

The key information required to make use of the national skill cell approach is the skill content of immigration flows. In recent years, tremendous progress has been made in measuring the factor content of international migration stocks. Internationally comparable data are now available for a number of decades as discussed in detail in chapters 1 and 2. (Please note that global migration databases rely on national censuses that are generally conducted every ten years. This frequency can lead to difficulties in tracking changes in global patterns. See the appendix for further discussion.)

Migrants are more educated than native-born individuals in many destination countries. In figure 3.8 we present 2010 data on the high-skilled share in the immigrant and native-born populations in many countries. The graph contains a (dashed) 45-degree line; observations above the line suggest that native-born individuals are more skilled, and observations below the line suggest that they are less skilled than the immigrant stock. The figure shows that observations are predominantly below the 45-degree

Figure 3.8 The skilled share among immigrants and natives, 2010

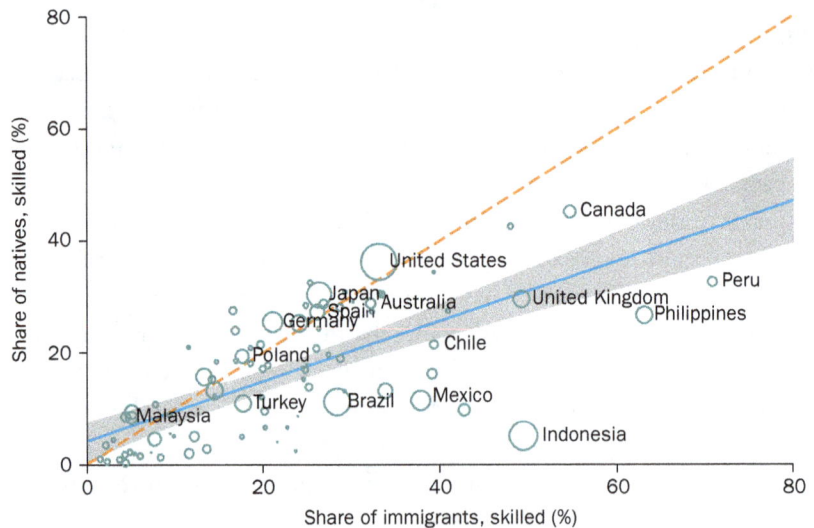

Sources: Migration data from the 2010/2011 OECD Database on Immigrants in OECD and Non-OECD Countries (DIOC-E). Skilled population data from Barro and Lee 2013.

Note: "Skilled" defined as the population with completed tertiary education; shares represent the skilled population divided by the overall population of interest. For the 88 destination countries included in the DIOC-E 2010/2011 dataset, natives' skill rates are calculated from the native-born population; for all other countries skill rates are calculated from the entire population using Barro and Lee 2013 data. Size of circles are scaled by (log) country population. The dashed line is the 45-degree line, and the blue line shows linear best fit. OECD = Organisation for Economic Co-operation and Development.

line; immigrant stocks are on average more highly skilled than the native population. Note also that the graph includes a linear best-fit line, and the slope of that line is less than 45 degrees, suggesting that the degree of skill bias in the immigrant stock becomes more pronounced as destination countries become more high skilled. For example, in 2010, immigration changed the fraction of the population that is high skilled in Germany from 25.5 to 24.8 percent, in the United Kingdom from 29.5 to 32.3 percent, in the United States from 36.2 to 35.7 percent, and in France from 25.2 to 25 percent.

Docquier, Ozden, and Peri (2014) use this information to simulate the impact of immigration across a wide array of OECD countries. Because, for most countries, including OECD members, immigrants are actually more educated than natives, immigration results in an increase in the relative abundance of skilled people in the host countries. As a result, the authors conclude that immigration tends to increase the relative wage of low-skilled native-born workers and reduce inequality. And the increase is larger in countries where the skill gap between immigrants and native-born workers is the largest. Furthermore, emigrants are also more skilled than those native-born workers who decide to stay at home. As a result, emigration leads to a decline in relative abundance of high-skilled people, including in many OECD source countries. Docquier, Ozden, and Peri (2014) conclude that skill-biased emigration patterns end up hurting low-skilled workers more in OECD countries.

Empirical strategy II: The local labor market approach

The *local labor market approach*, often called the spatial approach, uses the geographic variation in immigration flows within a country to identify the local impact of immigration. The inflow of immigrants to a local labor market, such as in Miami, changes the factor proportions in that labor market. That, in turn, changes the relative wages in the labor market.[14] Again, we emphasize that this is quite different from the national skill cell approach, which treats the whole country as a single labor market.

Instruments

A major advantage of the local labor market approach is that it is straight-forward to use an instrument to predict for immigration flows. We use instruments because the correlation between immigrant inflows and the outcome of interest (employment and wages) does likely not reflect the causal relationship arising from the presence of, for example, demand shocks (see "Empirical challenges: Immigrants and natives choose where to live and work" earlier in this chapter). A valid instrument induces changes in immigrant flows but has no direct effect on native wages and employment. This then allows a researcher to uncover the causal effect of immigration.

In practice, studies typically predict the current distribution of immigration flows by using the historical distribution of immigrants across local labor markets. Those predicted immigrant values, which now depend solely on the past distribution of immigrants and not on contemporaneous demand shocks, are then used to estimate the impact of immigration.[15]

Past immigrant settlement patterns are excellent for predicting future immigration flows, as discussed in chapter 2. Figure 3.9 depicts such a correlation between the actual immigration flows into a U.S. metropolitan statistical area (MSA) between 2000 and 2011 and the predicted inflows.

Figure 3.9 Actual and predicted immigration flows, by U.S. metropolitan statistical area, 2011

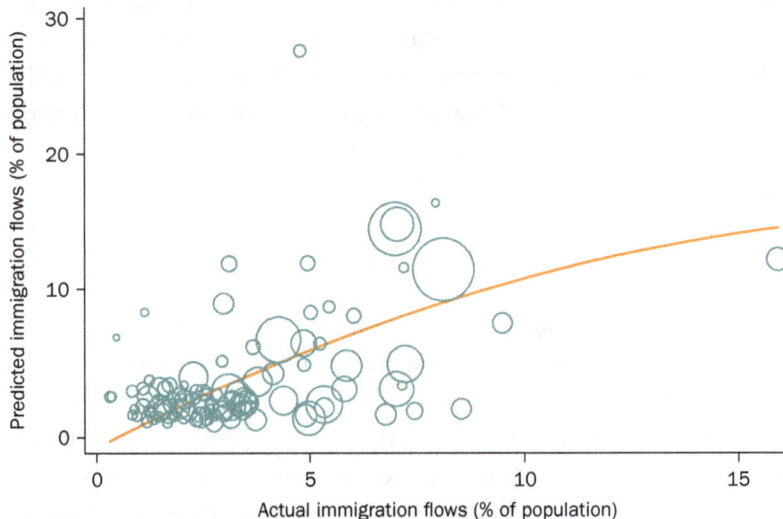

Source: Data from IPUMS (Integrated Public Use Microdata Series) using the 2011 ACS (American Community Survey) and the 1970 1% census sample (Ruggles et al. 2017).

Note: The figure shows predicted immigrant inflows to the U.S. metropolitan statistical areas (MSAs) in 2011 using the 1970 distribution of immigrants as a predictor and compares them to the actual flows. Size of circles are scaled by (log) MSA population.

These predictions are based on the historic distribution of immigrants across these MSAs in 1970, and the correlation coefficient is 0.62.

Researchers have further attempted to refine this instrument. Pugatch and Yang (2011), for example, use rainfall shocks in Mexico as a component of an instrument for Mexican flows to the United States. Ozden and Wagner (2014), in a study of the impact of immigration in Malaysia, use the age structure of the population of sending countries, primarily Indonesia and the Philippines, in the instrument, with the idea that migration tends to be concentrated in relatively younger age groups.[16]

Evidence from the local labor market approach

The local labor market approach also has the advantage that, although immigration shocks have a relatively small effect nationally on skill composition (as seen in figure 3.8), immigrants can potentially have a much larger impact at the local level. Measuring this local effect should help with providing precise estimates of the impact of immigration. However, using the local labor market approach offers mixed evidence on the impact of economic migrants. No clear consensus exists among the most prominent studies—especially those for the United States—on whether immigration results in substantial—positive or negative—wage or employment effects for native workers.

It is worth noting that this literature has been almost entirely focused on OECD countries, and primarily the United States.[17] An exception is Facchini, Mayda, and Mendola (2013), who study relatively high-skilled migration to South Africa. They find that a 10 percent increase in the labor supply of a skill group through immigration leads to a 6.7 percent decrease in native total employment without any significant effect on earnings. The negative employment effects are concentrated among the more-skilled South Africans who are presumably the direct competitors in the labor market.

In contrast, in a second paper on a non-OECD country, Ozden and Wagner (2014) focus on the inflow of very low-skilled immigrants from neighboring countries to Malaysia. They find that immigrants displace native-born workers who have at most primary education, while benefitting those with some secondary schooling and barely affecting the outcomes for the college educated.

Similar methodologies are employed in exploring the impact of internal migration. Meng and Zhang (2011) show that rural migrants in urban China have modest positive effects on the average employment and an insignificant impact on the earnings of urban workers. Figure 3.10, panels a

Figure 3.10   Correlation between internal migration and labor market outcomes, urban China, 1990 vs. 2000

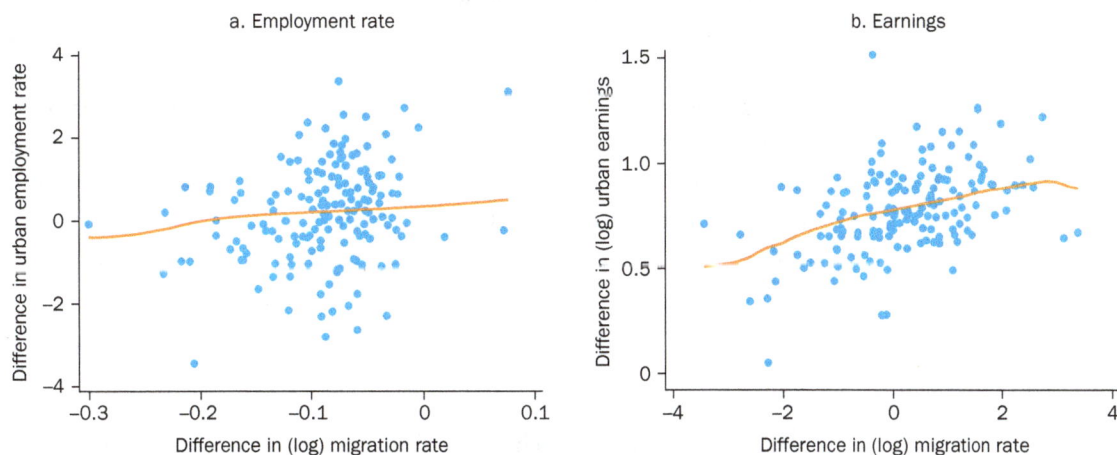

a. Employment rate

b. Earnings

Source: Meng and Zhang 2011.

and b, plot changes in the urban employment rates and (log) urban earnings, respectively, against (log) migrant ratios across Chinese cities. Both panels show either no relationship or a slightly positive relationship, and instrumental estimates reinforce these findings.

Native responses to immigration

One reason for the lack of clear conclusions from the local labor market approach is that it, like most empirical approaches, has some disadvantages (Borjas 2003, 2006; Borjas, Freeman, and Katz 1996). Notably, the main argument is that these studies typically fail to take account of offsetting capital and native labor mobility patterns across local labor markets. If not properly accounted for, these will tend to attenuate the wage effects of immigration (see also the discussion in "The endogeneity of native location (and employment) decisions" earlier in this chapter).

At the heart of that discussion is the following example. Consider comparing wage changes in cities that experience large increases in immigration levels versus in those cities that do not. If we find little impact on native wages, as does Card (2001) in his seminal work on Cuban migration to Miami, we have two possible interpretations. First, immigrants to the United States have little effect on wages. Or, second, native-born workers may be highly mobile across U.S. cities: their movement in response to the presence of immigrants rapidly equalizes wages across cities, making it appear as though immigration has no relative impact when, in reality, all cities experience negative wage effects due to native mobility.

The degree to which immigration shocks show up in wages or employment data depends, in general, on how responsive native labor is to these wage changes (as discussed in "Empirical challenges: Immigrants and natives choose where to live and work" earlier in this chapter). For example, Morten and Oliveira (2016) present evidence from Brazil on how migration generates heterogeneity in regional responses to economic shocks. They find that a region in Brazil that is 10 percent more connected to the rest of Brazil will have a 5.6 percentage point higher population elasticity to wage shocks.

Empirical strategy III: Natural experiments

A third empirical approach takes advantage of quasi-natural experiments in economics and relies on relatively sudden, relatively unanticipated, and

Figure 3.11   Natural experiments in immigration

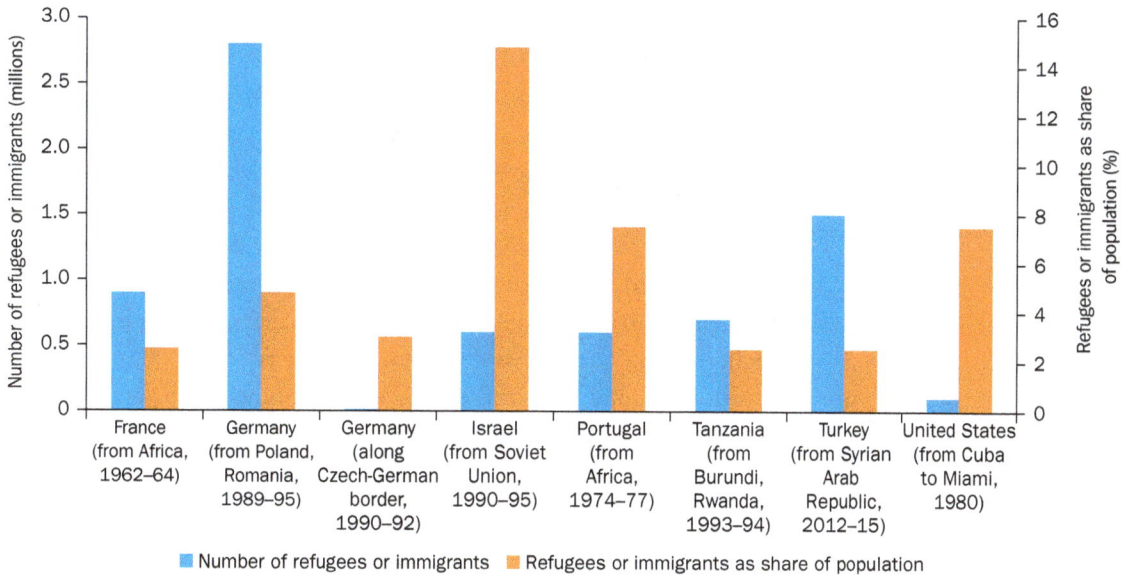

Legend: ■ Number of refugees or immigrants   ■ Refugees or immigrants as share of population

large immigration flows. The major advantage of papers using this approach is that these immigration shocks are both large and typically not driven by the availability of jobs but rather by supply or push factors. These factors can be natural disasters, sudden changes in the political environment (such as a crisis), or random selection of migrants through lotteries. Figure 3.11 provides examples of such natural experiments.

The studies discussed in this section share many methodological commonalities and face common challenges. The first challenge is that—although a refugee crisis or similar labor supply shock may generate exogenous emigration flows—the location and occupations chosen by the refugees may very well be endogenous and depend on the economic opportunities available in the receiving country. Hence, defining a credible unbiased comparison group may still be difficult. A second challenge is obtaining proper and meaningful inference with a small number of "treatment" observations. This challenge is particularly significant for studies taking the difference-in-differences approach, where the comparison can effectively be between a single treatment and control group before and after an immigration shock.[18] In the following sections, we discuss these methodological issues and the conclusions from this strand of the literature in the context of specific examples.[19]

The Mariel Boatlift

The natural experiment approach was pioneered in Card's (1990) study of the effects of the Mariel Boatlift, the influx of about 125,000 Cuban refugees in 1980, on Miami, the largest location in which they settled. Figure 3.12 shows the number of Cuban immigrants in Miami over time.

The approach used to analyze the impact of the Mariel Boatlift is essentially a difference-in-differences approach. Changes over time in Miami are compared to those in comparable other cities that did not experience an influx of Cuban refugees. Recent work by Abadie, Diamond, and Hainmueller (2010) provides a more sophisticated version of this approach, providing a technique to allow for a more systematic search for an appropriate control group. Their synthetic control technique uses data-intensive techniques to construct a matched comparison group and also allows inference by placing the estimates in a distribution of similar structured "placebo" regressions.

Evidence from Card (1990) and Peri and Yasenov (2017) suggest that the boatlift did not have a significant impact on Miami's labor market. Average wages in Miami were broadly unaffected. However, as Borjas (2017) finds, wages decreased significantly for the native groups most likely to be in direct competition with the Cuban refugees, specifically high school dropouts. Figure 3.13, using data from Borjas (2017), depicts (log) wages for high school dropouts in Miami and a control group over time.

Figure 3.12   Inflow of Cubans to Miami, 1955–2010

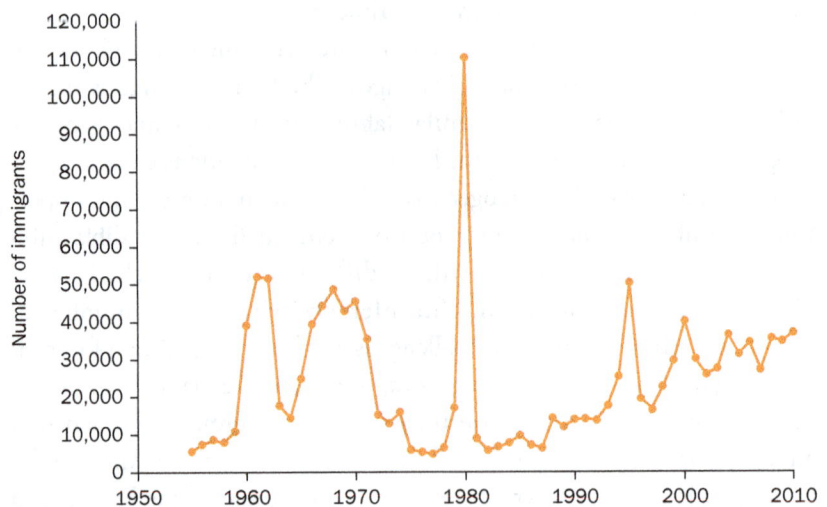

Source: Borjas 2017, figure 1.

Figure 3.13 Log wage of high school dropouts in Miami, 1972–2004

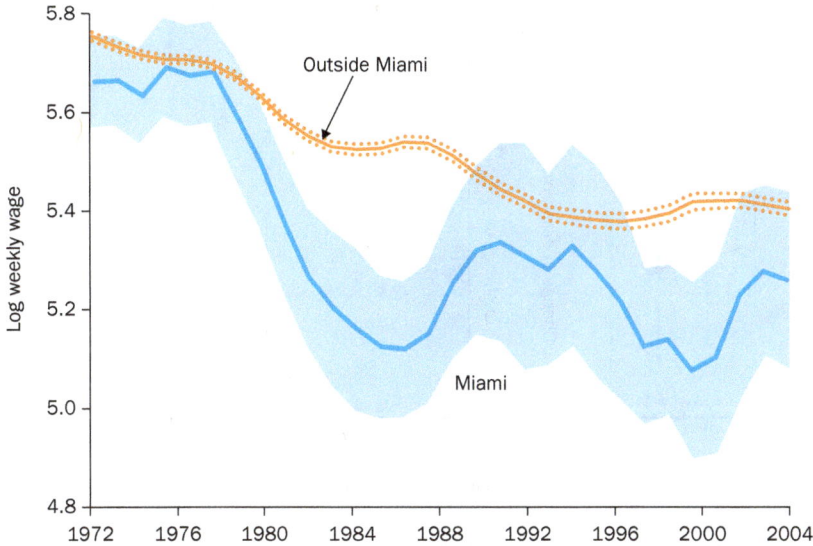

Source: Borjas 2017, figure 1.

Interestingly, the impact in Miami is temporary. After an initial decline, wages in Miami catch up with the outside wages after about eight years. The likely explanation is that native labor mobility, as well as adjustments to the capital stock and number of firms, eliminated wage differentials between Miami and comparable outside cities during this time. The substantial inflow of refugees in the mid-1990s shows up in high school dropout wages in Miami in the graph.

The end of the Cold War

The end of the Cold War was accompanied by large flows of people across national borders. Among the main studies that focus on this period, several papers investigate the effects of over 600,000 immigrants from the former Soviet Union moving to Israel (Friedberg 2001; Lach 2007; Paserman 2013). Aydemir and Kirdar (2013) explore the impact of the arrival of ethnic Turks from Bulgaria in 1989.

In an innovative study, Glitz (2012) analyzes the inflow of 3 million ethnic Germans moving from Eastern Europe and the Soviet Union to Germany. Importantly, from a methodological perspective, Germany instituted a dispersal policy for these immigrants, placing them quasi-randomly across Germany. The results indicate a displacement effect of

Figure 3.14   Wage and employment effects of Czech commuters in Germany, 1986–95

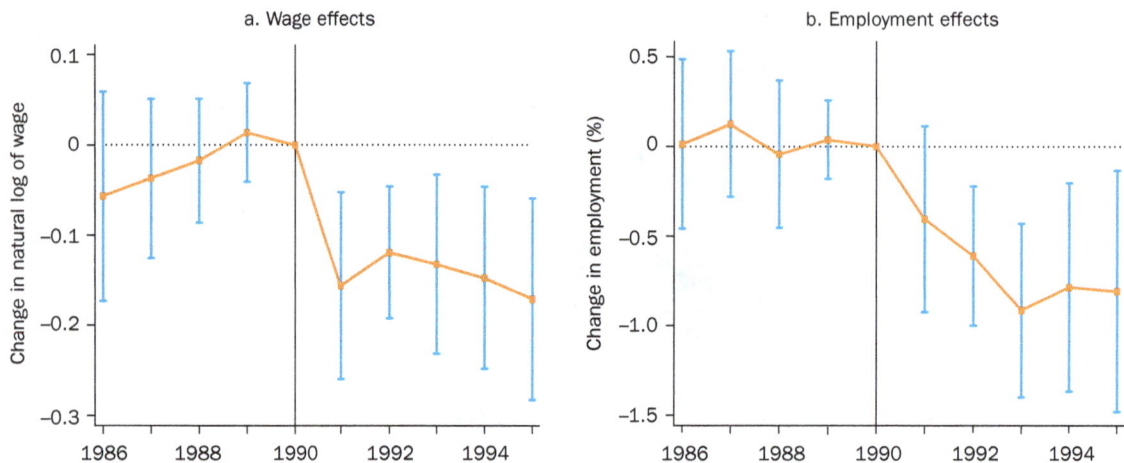

a. Wage effects

b. Employment effects

Note: The vertical black lines represent the implementation of the policy in 1990 that allowed Czech workers in Germany. The blue lines are the confidence intervals.

3.1 unemployed workers for every 10 immigrants who found a job in a given region in Germany, but indicate no effect on relative wages.[20]

Dustmann, Schönberg, and Stuhler (2017) analyze a post-1989 policy that allowed workers from the Czech Republic to seek employment, but not residence rights, in eligible German border municipalities. The study first finds appropriate control regions throughout Germany, akin to the synthetic control approach, but then also provides instrumental variable estimates based on each region's distance from the Czech Republic border. Figure 3.14 depicts the difference between wage and employment rates in treatment and control regions over time. By 1993, a 1 percentage point increase in the inflow of Czech workers relative to native employment had led to about a 0.13 percent decrease in native wages, and a 0.93 percent (almost one-to-one) decrease in native local employment.

Wars of independence

Several studies have looked at the return of expatriates from former colonies after these colonies became independent. Hunt (1992) examines repatriates from Algeria to France, and Carrington and De Lima (1996) look at African repatriates to Portugal. Borjas and Monras (2016) reanalyze the impact of Algerians and repatriates moving to France during the Algerian war of independence. Their results show that both the repatriates and the Algerian refugee inflows had a significant impact on employment and unemployment rates of French natives. For example, a 10 percent increase in the number of French repatriates increased the unemployment rate by about 1 percent.

Refugees

Evidence on the impact of refugee inflows on labor market conditions is still scant, but is rapidly increasing.[21] Existing work includes studies on the impact of the refugee flows from the breakup of Yugoslavia (Angrist and Kugler 2003), of displaced people in the West Bank (Mansour 2010), and of expelled ethnic Germans after World War II (Braun and Mahmoud 2014).[22]

The second-largest population of internally displaced people worldwide is in Colombia (after the Syrian Arab Republic). Calderón-Mejía and Ibáñez (2015) argue that these displaced people compete primarily in the informal sector in host communities. Figure 3.15 shows the wage distribution of formal workers, informal workers, and the internally displaced in Colombia.

Figure 3.15 Wage distributions of formal workers, informal workers, and the internally displaced, Colombia

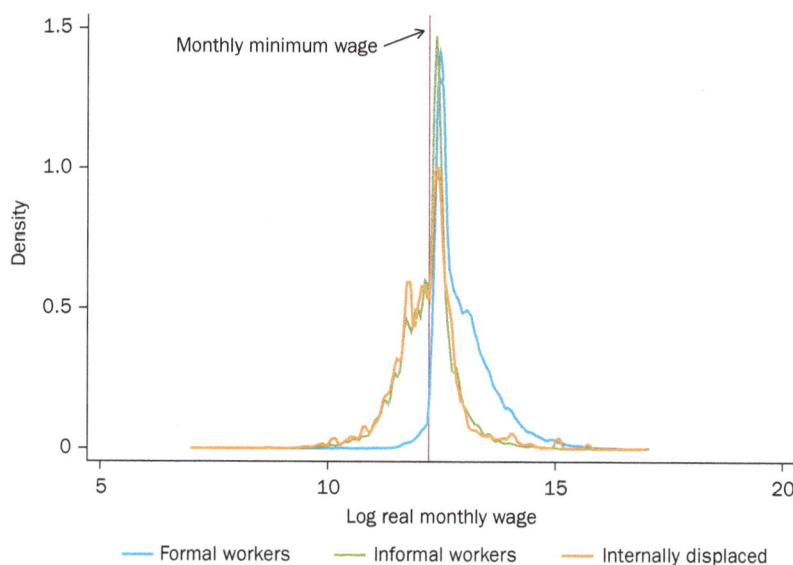

Source: Calderón-Mejía and Ibáñez 2015, figure 2. Reproduced with permission; further permission required for reuse.

The estimates suggest that these internal migrations substantially reduce wages for urban unskilled workers who compete with forced migrants for jobs in the informal sector.

Several studies make a similar observation on the impact in Turkey of the recent refugee crisis caused by war in Syria (see Ceritoglu et al. [2017] and del Carpio and Wagner [2016]). An important aspect of this refugee shock is that Turkey has not issued work permits to Syrian refugees. Because these refugees are, therefore, overwhelmingly employed informally in Turkey's large informal sector, their arrival is a well-defined supply shock to informal labor, with clear predictions about what we should expect to see.

One approach, common to the refugee literature, is to compare labor market outcomes in regions close to the border with those in regions farther away (possibly chosen using the synthetic control method). Del Carpio and Wagner (2016) take this approach to study the impact of Syrian refugees in Turkey. Their comparison of treatment and control regions (see figure 3.16, based on a similar study) suggests that immigration displaced Turkish natives from informal employment but increased the demand for Turks in formal employment.

An alternative to this simple comparison is to use travel distances to instrument for refugee flows. The dangers faced by refugees make travel

Figure 3.16 Turkish native employment rates by sector, 2005–14

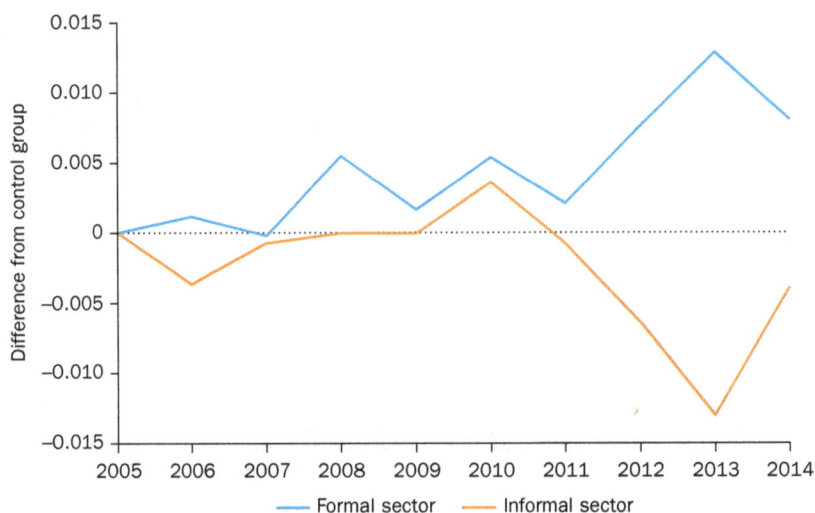

Source: Del Carpio and Wagner 2016.

Note: Figure shows difference in share of population employed, by sector, between treatment and control groups.

distance a particularly good predictor of their destination decisions.[23] The most serious potential shortfall of this instrument, as well as of the simple comparison of treatment and control regions, is that distance from the border may also capture other differences between communities. Specifically, places close to the border will feel the effects of war in a neighboring country for many reasons other than the inflow of refugees. Del Carpio and Wagner (2016) deal with that issue by relying on the fact that refugees from different Syrian governorates will use different border crossings (among the six main crossings) to reach different parts of Turkey. Figure 3.17 shows actual and predicted refugee flows of Syrian refugees based on travel distances from Syrian governorates to Turkish subregions.

Their instrumental variable estimates suggest large-scale displacement of natives in the informal sector. At the same time, consistent with occupational upgrading, they find increases in formal employment for the Turks, although only for men who have not completed high school. The low educated and women experience net displacement from the labor market and, like those in the informal sector, declining earning opportunities.

Over 20 percent of refugees live in camps, and this ratio is higher if the host is a neighboring low-income country. There is an active policy debate and research on the impact of these camps on the host countries, especially their labor markets and local economies. Box 3.1 discusses some of the important findings.

Figure 3.17 Actual and predicted (based on travel distances) refugee-to-working-age-population ratio in Turkey, 2014

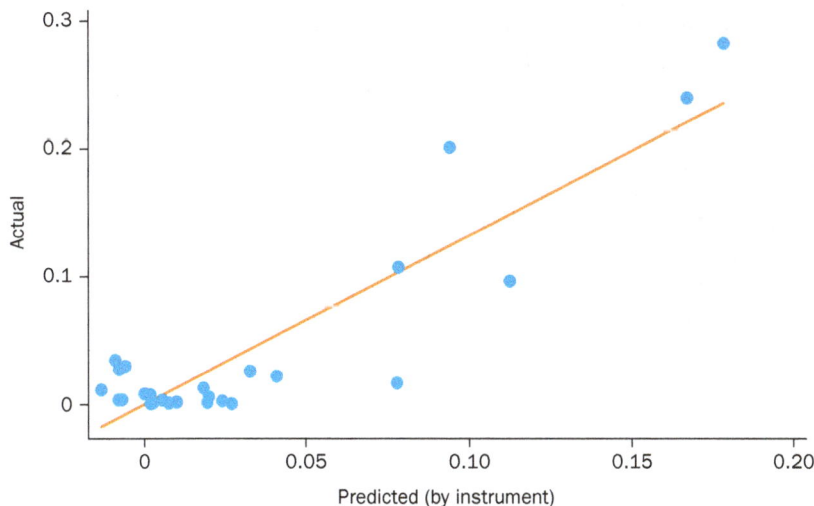

Source: Del Carpio and Wagner 2016.

Box 3.1 Refugee camps and their impact on host countries

A substantial fraction of the world's refugees are housed in camps—an estimated 21 percent in 2015 (UNHCR 2016). The existence of these camps substantially complicates our understanding of the impact of refugee flows on destination countries and their labor markets.

Relief agencies and government agencies invest significant resources for the construction and maintenance of these camps. For example, local authorities in Gaziantep, Turkey, informed the United Nations High Commissioner for Refugees (UNHCR) that the cost (in Turkish liras, or TL) of the Syrian refugees in the camps in Turkey is between TL 6.8 and TL 15.5 per person per day (UNHCR 2014). Median labor income in Turkey is only about TL 23 per day and is substantially lower for unskilled workers in the border regions where the camps are located.

Refugee camps develop their own economic ecosystems for several reasons. First, temporary situations end up lasting a long time in many cases, resulting in what UNHCR calls the problem of protracted refugee situations (Crisp 2003; Slaughter and Crisp 2009). Despite their traumatic experiences and poor health conditions, refugees have productive capacities as well as assets (human capital, livestock, and so on). And they use networks to gain access to such assets (Perouse de Montclos and Kagwanja 2000; Werker 2007). Therefore, refugees are likely to exercise important economic functions and have a significant impact on their hosts' livelihoods. City-sized refugee camps have often mushroomed in very poor areas where native-born inhabitants struggle to make a living.

Assessing the impact of camps is complicated (see Alix-Garcia, Artuc, and Onder 2017).

Camps offer mixed consequences for the host population through price increases, wage competition, and competition for natural resources. The more well-off and more-visible hosts most likely gain from the presence of refugees and refugee programs, whereas poor hosts tend to lose because of competition for food, work, services, and common property resources. Alix-Garcia, Artuc, and Onder (2017) point to these vulnerable hosts as the hidden losers.

Maystadt and Verwimp (2014) identify how the local population in the region of Kagera in northwestern Tanzania has been affected by the refugee inflows from Burundi in 1993 and Rwanda in 1994. On average, they find that doubling the number of refugees increases real consumption (in per adult equivalents) by about 8 percent. These benefits are not equally distributed: those initially working as agricultural workers or self-employed in nonagricultural activities gain 3–4 percentage points less than the rest of the population. The authors argue that the relative loss of the agricultural workers can be explained by the fiercer competition encountered in labor markets.

The special nature of refugee camps even generates plausible long-term effects on the local economy. Maystadt and Duranton (2014) exploit a 1991–2010 Tanzanian household panel to assess the effects of the temporary refugee inflows originating from Burundi (in 1993) and Rwanda (in 1994). The study finds that the refugee presence has had a persistent and positive impact on the welfare of the local population. The authors argue that the most likely explanation is the reduction in transportation costs arising from the construction of major roads to supply the refugee camps.

Emigration and labor markets

This chapter offers extensive discussion of how migration affects labor market outcomes in receiving countries and how these effects can be empirically identified. The flip side of those questions is what impact migration has on sending countries. Even though empirical evidence is much scarcer, there is a broad consensus that, consistent with theory, emigration increases wages in the sending countries—but only for non-emigrants with substitutable skills similar to those of emigrants. Non-emigrants with different or complementary skills tend to lose.[24]

Historical evidence

Economic historians have collected impressive amounts of data on migration in the 19th and early 20th centuries, when large numbers of Europeans left for the New World. These data are mostly based on passenger lists and national statistical yearbooks. Knowing whether emigration increased wages in sending countries is central to understanding why living standards in Europe caught up rapidly to those in North America. Europe was labor abundant, with most workers earning very low wages, whereas North America had too few workers who were paid very high wages. Mass emigration increased the wages in Europe while decreasing wages in North America. Economic historians estimated the impact of emigration on wages in the most important sending countries and quantified the role of emigration in closing the income gap between Europe and North America. Figure 3.18 shows the clear positive relationship between the share of emigrants and wages.

The mass emigration from Ireland, triggered by the famine of the mid-19th century, provides a salient example of the importance of emigration for wage levels and, ultimately, living standards. Emigration reduced the Irish population from 8.1 million in 1841 to 4.4 million in 1914. Several economic historians have estimated that Irish wages would have been 20–40 percent lower without emigration. To put it differently, emigration accounted for half the wage growth in Ireland in the second half of the 19th century and a third of the wage convergence between Ireland and the United States. Similarly, Swedish emigration during the same period increased wages at home by about 12 percent, which also accounted for a third of the wage convergence between Sweden and the United States (O'Rourke and Williamson 1999).

Figure 3.18 Emigration and wages by country, 1870–1910

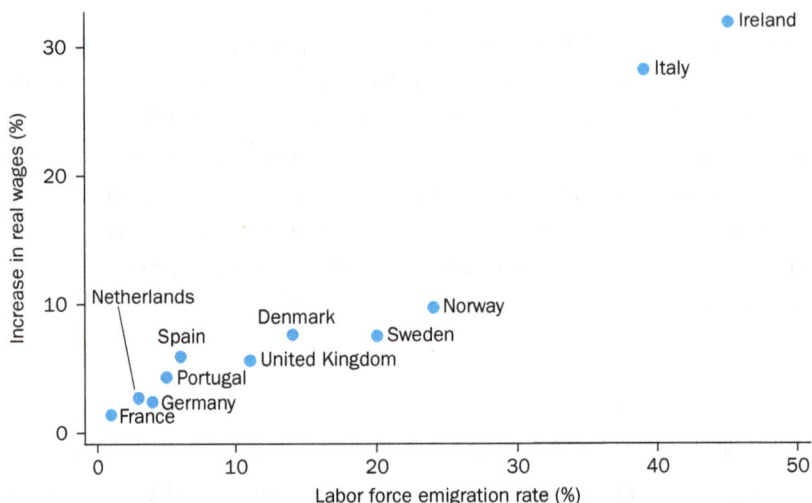

Source: Created using data from O'Rourke and Williamson 1999.

Evidence from Latin America

When looking at today's most important origin countries, we find Mexico at the center of attention because of its rich history of emigration to the United States. Despite severe entry barriers, about 10 percent of the Mexican population currently lives in the United States. Several studies have examined the impact of various emigration waves on wages in the Mexican labor market.

One fact often exploited in estimating the effects of migration is that migration today begets migration tomorrow. Emigrants from a particular sending region who moved in previous decades make it easier for today's emigrants to move, mostly to the same destination areas in the United States. Hanson (2007) exploits these migration links by comparing current wages in Mexican regions that had high and low shares of emigrants in 1950. The study finds that regions with a higher share of emigrants relative to other regions in 1950 had substantially higher wages 50 years later.

Other studies consider emigration and wages at the national level, comparing groups of workers with high and low emigration rates at multiple points in time (Aydemir and Borjas 2007; Mishra 2007). Young workers, for example, were more likely to emigrate than old workers, and medium- and high-skilled workers were more likely to emigrate than low-skilled workers. Groups with a higher emigration rate had significantly larger wage increases.

The impact on the wage distribution is as important as the impact on wages. By no means do all non-emigrants gain as a result of emigration by others; some groups may even lose. For example, emigration from Mexico may have lowered the wages of low-skilled non-emigrants while increasing the wages of medium- and high-skilled non-emigrants (Aydemir and Borjas 2007).

Lessons from European Union enlargement

An important recent migration episode was due to the enlargement of the European Union (EU) in 2004 and 2007, which, overnight, allowed citizens from 10 Central European countries to move to work in Ireland, Sweden, and the United Kingdom and subsequently in the rest of the EU. The lifting of these internal EU migration restrictions triggered a large and sudden emigration wave from the new member countries, which had significantly lower wage levels.

Two examples of emigration received particular attention in the economic literature. These are Lithuania, from which 9 percent of the workforce emigrated to Ireland and the United Kingdom, and Poland, which had an emigration rate of about 5 percent (Dustmann, Frattini, and Rosso 2015; Elsner 2013a, 2013b). In Lithuania, most emigrant workers were aged 20–30, and the shares of high-skilled and low-skilled workers were similar among emigrants and non-emigrants. As predicted by a simple labor market model, this emigration wave led to wage increases for groups that had many emigrants, but it had a small negative effect for groups with few emigrants, such as old workers. In Poland, where medium-educated workers dominated emigration flows, the pattern was similar. The wages of medium-skilled workers (workers with skills similar to those of most emigrants) rose significantly, whereas the wage change for high-skilled workers was close to zero, and low-skilled workers faced declining wages.

ANNEX 3A   Methodological challenges in the immigration literature

In this annex, we highlight two additional difficulties with the methodological approaches in the immigration literature.

The constant elasticity of substitution nesting structure

The approaches in much of the literature on the impact of immigration are structural, in the sense that they use a model to guide the empirics and then, in the case of the national-level time series approach, use simulation to obtain estimates. The ease with which this can be done has made these approaches very popular. That ease, as always, comes at a price. Specifically, the results can be sensitive to the particular assumptions made.

In particular, the factor proportions approach requires assumptions about the production technology representing the labor demand side of the economy. This problem is made tractable by the choice of a nested, often three-level CES production technology. See figure 3A.1, from Ottaviano and Peri (2012), for examples of this nesting structure.

The imposed structure is clearly restrictive, typically relying on estimating as few as three or four elasticities of substitutions between groups of (labor) inputs. There are no easy answers on how to make the necessary modeling decisions.[25] Researchers often deal with this issue by estimating ever more complicated nesting structures. This leads to two important debates.

First, there is an active discussion among researchers about whether immigrants and native-born workers with the same observables are imperfect substitutes. The answer to that question depends on the exact way in which people are categorized into skill groups, but it has important consequences for the results.[26] One can also easily see how the issue of immigrant downgrading can skew potential results.

Figure 3A.1   The nested constant elasticity of substitution production function

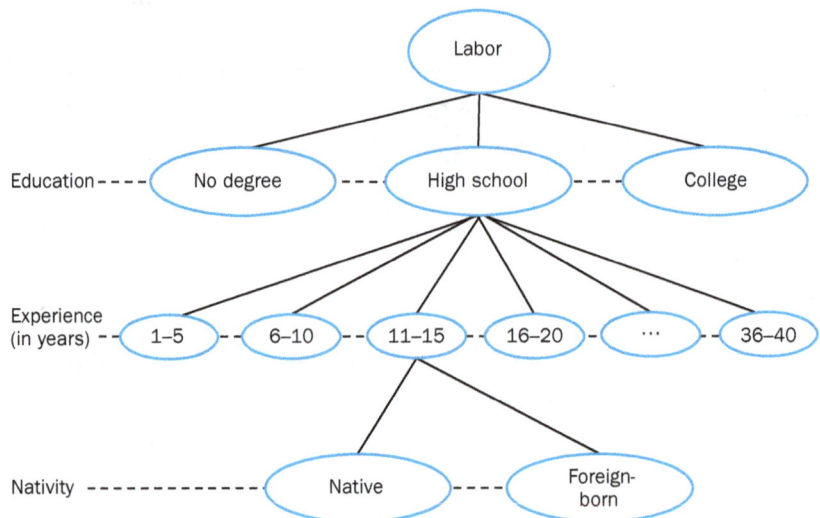

Source: Ottaviano and Peri 2012. Reproduced with permission; further permission required for reuse.

Figure 3A.2 Impact of immigration along the wage distribution

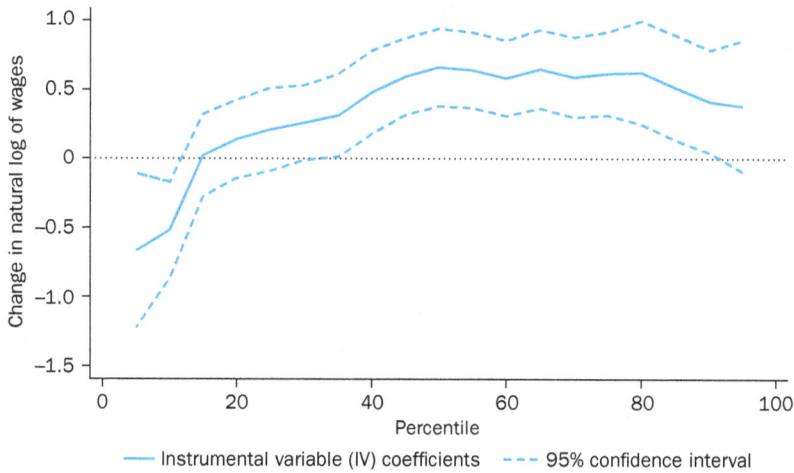

Source: Dustmann, Frattini, and Preston 2012.

Note: Figure shows estimated effects of immigration along the wage distribution.

Second, the literature typically assumes that the farther away in skill-space the immigration shock and native characteristics are, the more positive the impact has to be. This means that low-skilled immigration has to increase high-skilled native wages more than it does medium-skilled native wages. This assumption of the model does not result from the data and may not hold in practice.[27]

Reducing the restrictiveness of the assumptions employed is an important avenue for further research. In an interesting innovation, Dustmann, Frattini, and Preston (2012) propose a methodology that does not rely on preassignment of immigrants to skill groups. Instead, the paper estimates the impact of overall immigration along the distribution of wages. The authors demonstrate an association between the location of measured effects and the actual location of immigrants in the native wage distribution. They then estimate the impact of immigration across the full wage distribution (see figure 3A.2). Immigration decreases the wage of individuals at the bottom end of the age distribution, and has an increasingly positive impact for those higher up the wage distribution.

The impact of immigration on relative wages and wage levels

Studies in the literature on immigration frequently refer to the "wage effect" of immigration. Most studies, however, do not estimate the impact on wage levels but rather on relative wage effects. We illustrated this issue earlier in the chapter when discussing the basic intuition of the empirical strategies employed. The result is that, as Card (2009, 3) points out in his Ely Lecture, "most of the existing research on immigration has focused on between-group inequality." That distinction is often not made when discussing the impact of immigration on wages.

In general, two factors determine the effect of immigration on native labor demand. First, for a given level of output, firms will substitute immigrant for native labor. That is the standard substitution effect analyzed extensively in the literature. Second, for a given relative wage, firms will employ more native workers as the reduction in the cost of production results in an increased demand for all types of labor—the scale effect. The relative magnitude of these two effects determines the net effect of immigration on the demand for native labor.

The impact of low-skilled immigration on employers' hiring decisions is depicted in figure 3A.3, which considers the simple case with only two types of labor—low-skilled (L) and high-skilled (H). Firms choose a combination of low- and high-skilled labor given their relative cost, w_L/w_H (given by the isocost line C) and their relative marginal products (given by the isoquant I).[28] Panel a depicts the total effect of a decrease in the wage of low-skilled labor due to immigration (from isocost line C_0 to C_1).

Figure 3A.3 **Impact of immigration on hiring decisions along the wage distribution**

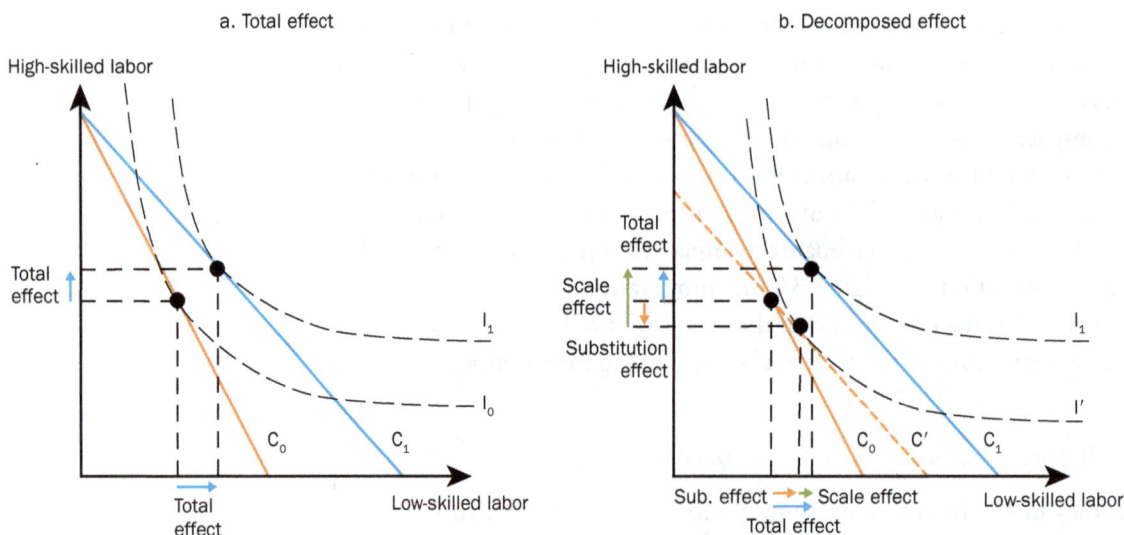

As low-skilled labor becomes less expensive, firms intuitively demand more workers, which is how the low-skilled immigrants are absorbed in the labor market.

Figure 3A.3 also depicts an increase in the demand for high-skilled labor, even though that input has become relatively more expensive. How is that possible? Panel b provides the answer to that question. First, consider the case where only the relative wage changes, that is, where we go from isocost line C_1 to C'. In that case, the demand for high-skilled labor would have to decrease because it has become relatively more expensive—the substitution effect. However, immigration decreases the absolute cost of low-skilled labor, not just the relative cost. Firms can now produce more output at the same cost. This change is reflected in the parallel shift of the isocost line from C' to C_1, which results in an increase in the demand for both labor inputs—the scale effect.

If the scale effect is larger than the substitution effect, low-skilled immigration increases the demand for high-skilled labor. If the substitution effect is greater than the scale effect, low-skilled immigration decreases the demand for high-skilled labor. The literature has invested a great deal of effort in estimating elasticities of substitution—the substitution effect—but has paid much less attention to the scale effect.

The local labor markets approach has typically included fixed effects to control for the scale effect. For example, Card (2001) emphasizes how city fixed effects control for the average city effect of immigration. Hence, the identification of the effect of immigration comes from changes in relative wages. When we discuss the wage effect of immigration, we implicitly assume that average wages are unaffected.

The national time-series approach, in contrast, has made assumptions about the magnitude of the scale effect and simulated the effects of immigration. The magnitude of the scale effect depends on assumptions about the elasticity of supply of capital and the elasticity of product demand.

Recent work has simulated the impact of immigration assuming perfectly inelastic and perfectly elastic supply of capital, corresponding to the short-term and long-term effects of immigration (for example, Borjas 2014; Manacorda, Manning, and Wadsworth 2012; Ottaviano and Peri 2012). The long-term effect will always be more positive because capital inflows will accompany immigration, raising the marginal product of labor.

There is also a second assumption implicit in these simulations. The product demand is assumed to be perfectly elastic, which—together with perfectly elastic supply of capital—implies that "the average wage does not depend on labor supply" (Ottaviano and Peri 2012, 157–58). In other words, by assumption, immigration does not affect the *average* wage rate in an economy and has only distributional consequences. The idea is that the economy can always fully adjust to an increase in labor supply due to immigration. There is simply a replication of existing firms, and output can be expanded without any loss of efficiency.

However, the product demand elasticities used in other literature are always imperfectly elastic (see Broda, Greenfield, and Weinstein 2006). Di Giovanni, Levchenko, and Ortega (2015), in a calibrated model of the world economy, emphasize the importance of downward-sloping product demand curves in a heterogeneous firm model for understanding the global impact of immigration. Allowing for downward-sloping product demand also allows for immigration to decrease the price of goods and services (see, for example, Cortes 2008).

Ozden and Wagner (2014) treat the elasticity of labor demand as a parameter to estimate, allowing the data to tell us whether an immigrant labor supply shock has an impact on average wages. Their estimates of the elasticity of product demand are significantly below infinite, with the consequence that an immigration-induced increase in labor supply decreases wages, averaged across natives and immigrants, in an economy.

Notes

1. Recent literature reviews include Dustmann, Glitz, and Frattini (2008); Card (2009); Borjas (2014); Lewis and Peri (2014); Blau and Kahn (2012); and Dustmann, Schönberg, and Stuhler (2016).
2. It is worth recalling that the two findings are not entirely comparable because the labor supply shocks studied are relatively sudden and not driven by the availability of jobs in the host country. Hence, it is unsurprising that—at least in the short run—the impact is more negative than is the case for host countries of voluntary migrants.
3. The paper shows that considering only two factors can explain important patterns. These are (1) the relative number of college graduates and non-college workers in the labor force and (2) skill-biased technological change. Increased college attainment in the labor force will tend to decrease the relative wage of college-educated workers, while skill-biased technological change increases that wage.
4. The definition of a skill group varies widely, and includes occupations (Card 2001; Friedberg 2001), education/experience (Borjas 2003, 2006), education/immigrant-native (Docquier, Ozden, and Peri 2014), education/experience/native-immigrant (Manacorda, Manning, and Wadsworth 2012; Ottaviano

and Peri 2012), and immigrant/native (Chiswick, Chiswick, and Miller 1985; Cortes 2008; Grossman 1982; LaLonde and Topel 1991).

5. Note that this methodology allows researchers to estimate only the relative wage impact of immigration on different groups of natives and cannot, without additional assumptions, speak to the impact on wage levels. We return to this issue in annex 3A.

6. Card and Lemieux (2001) provide a key extension to that framework, by allowing workers to differ not only by education but also by experience. Crucially, they show how a nested constant elasticity of substitution (CES) framework can accommodate modeling of any number of skill groups.

7. Borjas (2013, 2014) makes this point in great detail.

8. This is not the only possible way in which immigrant location decisions might be affected by labor market conditions in a destination. For example, Friedberg (2001) and Ozden and Wagner (2014) find evidence consistent with the idea that immigrants actually locate in regions, of Israel and Malaysia, respectively, that are in relative decline. One possible explanation is that firms in those regions make a particular effort to recruit immigrants and cut labor costs so as to avoid bankruptcy.

9. This downgrading is illustrated in papers by Mattoo, Neagu, and Ozden (2008); Dustmann, Frattini, and Preston (2012); Dustmann and Preston (2012); and Dustmann, Schönberg, and Stuhler (2016).

10. Methodologically, these most closely resemble the work on inequality. Early examples include Borjas, Freeman, and Katz (1996) and Borjas (2003).

11. These skill groups are then embedded into a CES model, which further simplifies the estimation.

12. Subsequent work (see Manacorda, Manning, and Wadsworth 2012; Ottaviano and Peri 2012) extends this framework by allowing immigrants and natives to be imperfect substitutes within experience and education cells. This final simulation step is often described as a "structural approach."

13. The simulations reproduced in table 3.1 assume that the supply of capital adjusts perfectly to accommodate the arrival of immigrants. In the extreme case where there is no adjustment of capital, all the estimates in the table should be reduced by 3.2 percentage points.

14. The definition of local labor markets varies by paper. Most commonly these are geographic localities (cities and regions). Alternatively, some papers use variation across industries (for example, Altonji and Card 1991; Ottaviano, Peri, and Wright 2013) or variation across both industries and regions (for example, Del Carpio et al. 2015; Ozden and Wagner 2014).

15. The approach was pioneered by Altonji and Card (1991) and Card (2001).

16. The variation induced by the demographic changes in source countries is similar to the instrument constructed by Hanson and McIntosh (2010).

17. See the recent literature reviews for details. Prominent examples are Dustmann, Glitz, and Frattini (2008); Card (2009); Borjas (2014); Lewis and Peri (2014); National Academies of Sciences, Engineering, and Medicine (2017); and Dustmann, Schönberg, and Stuhler (2016).

18. This is the classic difference-in-difference scenario for which Bertrand, Duflo, and Mullainathan (2004) discuss standard errors. See also Donald and Lang (2007).

19. The studies discussed in these sections largely involve immigrants who flow into the lower end of the labor market. At the high end of the skill distribution, Borjas and Doran (2012) study an influx of Soviet mathematicians to the United States; Moser, Voena, and Waldinger (2014) look at the impact of Jewish émigrés from Nazi Germany. We will discuss these and other papers on the impact of high-skilled migration in chapter 5.
20. See also Damm (2009), who uses a Danish dispersal policy implemented through the provision of public housing to study the impact of immigration.
21. Two recent survey articles, Ruiz and Vargas-Silva (2013) and Mabiso et al. (2014), emphasize the lack of evidence.
22. See also Foged and Peri (2016), who use identification related to refugee flows to Denmark, and Kugler and Yuksel (2008), for example, on flows resulting from natural disasters.
23. The use of distance as an instrument goes back to at least Card (1995).
24. See Elsner (2015) for a recent overview.
25. This is illustrated nicely by Ottaviano and Peri (2012), who present results for several different nesting structures.
26. See Ottaviano and Peri (2012) and Borjas, Grogger, and Hanson (2008). It also depends on even more subtle issues, such as whether researchers use log average wages or average log wages in their estimation.
27. For example, Ozden and Wagner (2014) find that low-skilled immigrants to Malaysia decrease the wages of low-skilled Malaysians, increase those of the medium-skilled, and leave high-skilled wages unaffected. To deal with this issue, the paper relies on a nonsymmetric nesting structure based on Krusell et al. (2000).
28. The optimal choice is found where the isoquant and isocost lines are tangent.

References

Abadie, A., A. Diamond, and J. Hainmueller. 2010. "Synthetic Control Methods for Comparative Case Studies: Estimating the Effect of California's Tobacco Control Program." *Journal of the American Statistical Association* 105 (490): 493–505.

Alix-Garcia, J., E. Artuc, and H. Onder. 2017. "The Economics of Hosting Refugees." Report No. 113183, World Bank, Washington, DC.

Altonji, J. G., and D. Card. 1991. "The Effects of Immigration on the Labor Market Outcomes of Less-Skilled Natives." In *Immigration, Trade, and the Labor Market*, edited by John M. Abowd and Richard B. Freeman, 201–34. Chicago: University of Chicago Press.

Angrist, J. D., and A. D. Kugler. 2003. "Protective or Counter-Productive? Labour Market Institutions and the Effect of Immigration on EU Natives." *Economic Journal* 113 (488): F302–F331.

Aydemir, A., and G. J. Borjas. 2007. "Cross-Country Variation in the Impact of International Migration: Canada, Mexico, and the United States." *Journal of the European Economic Association* 5 (4): 663–708.

Aydemir, A., and M. G. Kirdar. 2013. "Quasi-Experimental Impact Estimates of Immigrant Labor Supply Shocks: The Role of Treatment and Comparison Group Matching and Relative Skill Composition." IZA Discussion Paper 7161, Institute for the Study of Labor, Bonn.

Barro, R. J., and J. W. Lee. 2013. "A New Data Set of Educational Attainment in the World, 1950–2010." *Journal of Development Economics* 104 (C): 184–98.

Bertrand, M., E. Duflo, and S. Mullainathan. 2004. "How Much Should We Trust Differences-in-Differences Estimates?" *Quarterly Journal of Economics* 119 (1): 249–75.

Blau, F. D., and L. M. Kahn. 2012. "Immigration and the Distribution of Incomes." NBER Working Paper 18515, National Bureau of Economic Research, Cambridge, MA.

Borjas, G. J. 2003. "The Labor Demand Curve Is Downward Sloping: Reexamining the Impact of Immigration on the Labor Market." *Quarterly Journal of Economics* 118 (4): 1335–74.

———. 2006. "Native Internal Migration and the Labor Market Impact of Immigration." *Journal of Human Resources* 41 (2): 221–58.

———. 2013. "The Analytics of the Wage Effect of Immigration." *IZA Journal of Migration* 2 (1): 22.

———. 2014. *Immigration Economics.* Cambridge, MA: Harvard University Press.

———. 2016. "The Wage Impact of the Marielitos: Additional Evidence." NBER Working Paper 21850, National Bureau of Economic Research, Cambridge, MA.

———. 2017. "The Wage Impact of the Marielitos: A Reappraisal." *Industrial and Labor Relations Review* 70 (5): 1077–1110.

Borjas, G. J., and K. B. Doran. 2012. "The Collapse of the Soviet Union and the Productivity of American Mathematicians." *Quarterly Journal of Economics* 127 (3): 1143–203.

Borjas, G. J., R. B. Freeman, and L. Katz. 1996. "Searching for the Effect of Immigration on the Labor Market." *American Economic Review* 86 (2): 246–51.

Borjas, G. J., J. Grogger, and G. H. Hanson. 2008. "Imperfect Substitution between Immigrants and Natives: A Reappraisal." NBER Working Paper 13887, National Bureau of Economic Research, Cambridge, MA.

Borjas, G. J., and J. Monras. 2016. "The Labor Market Consequences of Refugee Supply Shocks." NBER Working Paper 22656, National Bureau of Economic Research, Cambridge, MA.

Braun, S., and T. O. Mahmoud. 2014. "The Employment Effects of Immigration: Evidence from the Mass Arrival of German Expellees in Postwar Germany." *Journal of Economic History* 74 (1): 69–108.

Broda, C., J. Greenfield, and D. Weinstein. 2006. "From Groundnuts to Globalization: A Structural Estimate of Trade and Growth." NBER Working Paper 12512, National Bureau of Economic Research, Cambridge, MA.

Calderón-Mejía, V., and A. M. Ibáñez. 2015. "Labour Market Effects of Migration-Related Supply Shocks: Evidence from Internal Refugees in Colombia." *Journal of Economic Geography* 16 (3): 695–713.

Card, D. 1990. "The Impact of the Mariel Boatlift on the Miami Labor Market." *Industrial and Labor Relations Review* 43 (2): 245–57.

———. 1995. *Using Geographical Variation in College Proximity to Estimate the Return to Schooling.* Aspects of Labor Market Behavior: Essays in Honor of John Vanderkamp. Toronto: University of Toronto Press.

———. 2001. "Immigrant Inflows, Native Outflows, and the Local Labor Market Impacts of Higher Immigration." *Journal of Labor Economics* 19 (1): 22–64.

———. 2009. "Immigration and Inequality." NBER Working Paper 14683, National Bureau of Economic Research, Cambridge, MA.

Card, D., and T. Lemieux. 2001. "Can Falling Supply Explain the Rising Return to College for Younger Men? A Cohort-Based Analysis." *Quarterly Journal of Economics* 116 (2): 705–46.

Card, D., and G. Peri. 2016. "*Immigration Economics* by George J. Borjas: A Review Essay." *Journal of Economic Literature* 54 (4): 1333–49.

Carrington, W. J., and P. J. De Lima. 1996. "The Impact of 1970s Repatriates from Africa on the Portuguese Labor Market." *ILR Review* 49 (2): 330–47.

Ceritoglu, E., H. B. G. Yunculer, H. Torun, and S. Tumen. 2017. "The Impact of Syrian Refugees on Natives' Labor Market Outcomes in Turkey: Evidence from a Quasi-Experimental Design." *IZA Journal of Labor Policy* 6 (1): 5.

Chiswick, B. R., C. U. Chiswick, and P. W. Miller. 1985. "Are Immigrants and Natives Perfect Substitutes in Production?" *International Migration Review* 19 (4): 674–85.

Cortes, P. 2008. "The Effect of Low-Skilled Immigration on U.S. Prices: Evidence from CPI Data." *Journal of Political Economy* 116 (3): 381–422.

Crisp, J. 2003. "Refugees and the Global Politics of Asylum." *Political Quarterly* 74 (Suppl 1): 75–87.

Damm, A. P. 2009. "Determinants of Recent Immigrants' Location Choices: Quasi-Experimental Evidence." *Journal of Population Economics* 22 (1): 145–74.

Del Carpio, X., C. Ozden, M. Testaverde, and M. Wagner. 2015. "Local Labor Supply Responses to Immigration." *Scandinavian Journal of Economics* 117 (2): 493–521.

Del Carpio, X. V., and M. Wagner. 2016. "The Impact of Syrian Refugees on the Turkish Labor Market." Policy Research Working Paper WPS7402, World Bank, Washington, DC.

Di Giovanni, J., A. A. Levchenko, and F. Ortega. 2015. "A Global View of Cross-Border Migration." *Journal of the European Economic Association* 13 (1): 168–202.

Docquier, F., C. Ozden, and G. Peri. 2014. "The Labour Market Effects of Immigration and Emigration in OECD Countries." *Economic Journal* 124 (579): 1106–145.

Donald, S. G., and K. Lang. 2007. "Inference with Difference-in-Differences and Other Panel Data." *Review of Economics and Statistics* 89 (2): 221–33.

Dustmann, C., T. Frattini, and I. P. Preston. 2012. "The Effect of Immigration along the Distribution of Wages." *Review of Economic Studies* 80 (1): 145–73.

Dustmann, C., T. Frattini, and A. Rosso. 2015. "The Effect of Emigration from Poland on Polish Wages." *Scandinavian Journal of Economics* 117 (2): 522–64.

Dustmann, C., A. Glitz, and T. Frattini. 2008. "The Labour Market Impact of Immigration." *Oxford Review of Economic Policy* 24 (3): 477–94.

Dustmann, C., and I. Preston. 2012. "Comment: Estimating the Effect of Immigration on Wages." *Journal of the European Economic Association* 10 (1): 216–23.

Dustmann, C., U. Schönberg, and J. Stuhler. 2016. "The Impact of Immigration: Why Do Studies Reach Such Different Results?" *Journal of Economic Perspectives* 30 (4): 31–56.

———. 2017. "Labor Supply Shocks, Native Wages, and the Adjustment of Local Employment." *Quarterly Journal of Economics* 132 (1): 435–83.

Elsner, B. 2013a. "Emigration and Wages: The EU Enlargement Experiment." *Journal of International Economics* 91 (1): 154–63.

———. 2013b. "Does Emigration Benefit the Stayers? Evidence from EU Enlargement." *Journal of Population Economics* 26 (2): 531–53.

———. 2015. "Does Emigration Increase the Wages of Non-emigrants in Sending Countries?" *IZA World of Labor*, November. https://wol.iza.org /articles/does-emigration-increase-wages-of-non-emigrants-in-sending-coun tries/long.

Facchini, G., A. M. Mayda, and M. Mendola. 2013. "South-South Migration and the Labor Market: Evidence from South Africa." IZA Discussion Paper 7362, Institute for the Study of Labor, Bonn.

Foged, M., and G. Peri. 2016. "Immigrants' Effect on Native Workers: New Analysis on Longitudinal Data." *American Economic Journal: Applied Economics* 8 (2): 1–34.

Friedberg, R. M. 2001. "The Impact of Mass Migration on the Israeli Labor Market." *Quarterly Journal of Economics* 116 (4): 1373–408.

Glitz, A. 2012. "The Labor Market Impact of Immigration: A Quasi-Experiment Exploiting Immigrant Location Rules in Germany." *Journal of Labor Economics* 30 (1): 175–213.

Grossman, J. B. 1982. "The Substitutability of Natives and Immigrants in Production." *Review of Economics and Statistics* 64 (4): 596–603.

Hanson, G. H. 2007. "Globalization, Labor Income, and Poverty in Mexico." In *Globalization and Poverty*, edited by Ann Harrison, 417–56. Chicago: University of Chicago Press.

Hanson, G. H., and C. McIntosh. 2010. "The Great Mexican Emigration." *Review of Economics and Statistics* 92 (4): 798–810.

Hunt, J. 1992. "The Impact of the 1962 Repatriates from Algeria on the French Labor Market." *ILR Review* 45 (3): 556–72.

Katz, L. F., and K. M. Murphy. 1992. "Changes in Relative Wages, 1963–1987: Supply and Demand Factors." *Quarterly Journal of Economics* 107 (1): 35–78.

Krusell, P., L. E. Ohanian, J. V. Ríos-Rull, and G. L. Violante. 2000. "Capital-Skill Complementarity and Inequality: A Macroeconomic Analysis." *Econometrica* 68 (5): 1029–53.

Kugler, A., and M. Yuksel. 2008. "Effects of Low-Skilled Immigration on U.S. Natives: Evidence from Hurricane Mitch." NBER Working Paper 14293, National Bureau of Economic Research, Cambridge, MA.

Lach, S. 2007. "Immigration and Prices." *Journal of Political Economy* 115 (4): 548–87.

LaLonde, R. J., and R. H. Topel. 1991. "Labor Market Adjustments to Increased Immigration." In *Immigration, Trade, and the Labor Market*, edited by John M. Abowd and Richard B. Freeman, 167–99. Chicago: University of Chicago Press.

Lewis, E., and G. Peri. 2014. "Immigration and the Economy of Cities and Regions." NBER Working Paper 20428, National Bureau of Economic Research, Cambridge, MA.

Mabiso, A., J. F. Maystadt, J. Vandercasteelen, and K. Hirvonen. 2014. *Refugees, Food Security, and Resilience in Host Communities: Transitioning from Humanitarian Assistance to Development in Protracted Refugee Situations*, vol. 2. Washington, DC: International Food Policy Research Institute.

Manacorda, M., A. Manning, and J. Wadsworth. 2012. "The Impact of Immigration on the Structure of Wages: Theory and Evidence from Britain." *Journal of the European Economic Association* 10 (1): 120–51.

Mansour, H. 2010. "The Effects of Labor Supply Shocks on Labor Market Outcomes: Evidence from the Israeli–Palestinian Conflict." *Labour Economics* 17 (6): 930–39.

Mattoo, A., I. C. Neagu, and C. Ozden. 2008. "Brain Waste? Educated Immigrants in the U.S. Labor Market." *Journal of Development Economics* 87 (2): 255–69.

Maystadt, J. F., and G. Duranton. 2014. "The Development Push of Refugees: Evidence from Tanzania." IFPRI Discussion Paper 1377, International Food Policy Research Institute, Washington, DC.

Maystadt, J. F., and P. Verwimp. 2014. "Winners and Losers among a Refugee-Hosting Population." *Economic Development and Cultural Change* 62 (4): 769–809.

Meng, X., and D. Zhang. 2011. "Labour Market Impact of Large-Scale Internal Migration on Chinese Urban Native Workers." IZA Discussion Paper 5208, Institute for the Study of Labor, Bonn.

Mishra, P. 2007. "Emigration and Wages in Source Countries: Evidence from Mexico." *Journal of Development Economics* 82 (1): 180–99.

Morten, M., and J. Oliveira. 2016. "The Effects of Roads on Trade and Migration: Evidence from a Planned Capital City." NBER Working Paper 22158, National Bureau of Economic Research, Cambridge, MA.

Moser, P., A. Voena, and F. Waldinger. 2014. "German Jewish Émigrés and U.S. Invention." *American Economic Review* 104 (10): 3222–55.

National Academies of Sciences, Engineering, and Medicine. 2017. *The Economic and Fiscal Consequences of Immigration*. Washington, DC: National Academies Press. https://doi.org/10.17226/23550.

O'Rourke, K. H., and J. G. Williamson. 1999. *Globalization and History: The Evolution of a Nineteenth-Century Atlantic Economy.* Cambridge, MA: MIT Press.

Ottaviano, G. I., and G. Peri. 2012. "Rethinking the Effect of Immigration on Wages." *Journal of the European Economic Association* 10 (1): 152–97.

Ottaviano, G. I., G. Peri, and G. C. Wright. 2013. "Immigration, Offshoring, and American Jobs." *American Economic Review* 103 (5): 1925–59.

Ozden, C., and M. Wagner. 2014. "Immigrant versus Natives? Displacement and Job Creation." Policy Research Working Paper 6900, World Bank, Washington, DC.

Paserman, M. D. 2013. "Do High-Skill Immigrants Raise Productivity? Evidence from Israeli Manufacturing Firms, 1990–1999." *IZA Journal of Migration* 2 (1): 6.

Peri, G., and V. Yasenov. 2017. "The Labor Market Effects of a Refugee Wave: Synthetic Control Method Meets the Mariel Boatlift." NBER Working Paper 21801, National Bureau of Economic Research, Cambridge, MA.

Perouse de Montclos, M. A., and P. M. Kagwanja. 2000. "Refugee Camps or Cities? The Socio-economic Dynamics of the Dadaab and Kakuma Camps in Northern Kenya." *Journal of Refugee Studies* 13 (2): 205–22.

Pugatch, T., and D. Yang. 2011. "The Impact of Mexican Immigration on U.S. Labor Markets: Evidence from Migrant Flows Driven by Rainfall Shocks." University of Michigan, Ann Arbor.

Ruggles, S., K. Genadek, R. Goeken, J. Grover, and M. Sobek. 2017. *Integrated Public Use Microdata Series: Version 7.0* [dataset]. Minneapolis: University of Minnesota. https://doi.org/10.18128/D010.V7.0.

Ruiz, I., and C. Vargas-Silva. 2013. "The Economics of Forced Migration." *Journal of Development Studies* 49 (6): 772–84.

Slaughter, A., and J. Crisp. 2009. "A Surrogate State? The Role of UNHCR in Protracted Refugee Situations." New Issues in Refugee Research, Research Paper 168, United Nations High Commissioner for Refugees, Policy Development and Evaluation Service, Geneva.

UNHCR (United Nations High Commissioner for Refugees). 2014. "UNHCR Turkey Syrian Refugee Daily Sitrep." Reliefweb, June 23. https://relief web.int/sites/reliefweb.int/files/resources/UNHCRTurkeySyriaSitrep23June 2014.pdf.

———. 2016. *Global Trends: Forced Displacement in 2015.* http://www.unhcr.org /statistics/unhcrstats/5943e8a34/global-trends-forced-displacement-2016 .html.

Werker, E. 2007. "Refugee Camp Economies." *Journal of Refugee Studies* 20 (3): 461–80.

CHAPTER FOUR

Longer-Term Dynamics: Immigrant Economic Adjustment and Native Responses

After immigrants and refugees have arrived and settled in a country, they experience a period of economic integration and assimilation. They must adjust to a new language, new social norms, and unfamiliar bureaucratic hurdles. Native-born workers must also adjust to their new neighbors, but in several different ways. As a changing workforce alters the demand for skills and occupations in the labor market, represented by changing wage and employment opportunities, native-born workers respond by altering their education and professional decisions accordingly. This chapter addresses these issues. Specifically, we discuss the economic and labor market integration of immigrants and refugees in a host country. Then, we look at how frequently and why immigrants decide to emigrate again, through either onward migration to other countries or returning to their country of origin. Finally, the chapter discusses the various ways in which native-born individuals respond to immigration, including decisions about education, occupation, fertility, and labor supply. A few key lessons are worth highlighting.

Upon arriving in a new country, immigrants and refugees are at a severe economic disadvantage—as measured by their employment patterns, wage levels, and occupational distribution—compared to natives. This disadvantage amounts to a wage gap of roughly 20 percent in the United States and over 40 percent in other Organisation for Economic Co-operation and Development (OECD) countries and many other non-OECD destination countries. Through a process of economic integration over time, immigrants and refugees catch up with natives in terms of wages and employment. This process takes about 10–20 years, on average.

Language acquisition aids immigrants in the integration and assimilation process. Local language skills complement other dimensions of accumulated human capital and allow immigrants to take advantage of specialized skills. Increased occupational and residential segregation of immigrants, however, is problematic because evidence suggests it may reduce their incentives to learn a host country's common language and to integrate both economically and culturally.

Return and onward migration rates are very high, especially in Europe, where on average about 50 percent of an arrival cohort has left the destination country within 10 years. Return and onward migration can be due to an unsuccessful migration experience, in terms of low wages and weak labor market attachment, or can be part of a (human or financial) capital acquisition strategy. Additionally, destination country policy may mandate temporary migration by granting only temporary work visas.

Return migration also plays an important role in understanding the assimilation process of immigrant cohorts. Less successful immigrants, those with below-average wages, are more likely to return migrate. This selection process, as lower-wage immigrants leave, makes it appear that immigrant wages in a cohort are rising more rapidly than is actually the case.

Native-born workers respond and adjust to immigration in different ways. Importantly, they change their occupations in response to immigration as we see in many destination countries ranging from high-income OECD countries to other key destinations like Malaysia, Saudi Arabia, and Singapore. This switch is generally away from occupations requiring manual skills toward those that require more interpersonal, technical, and cognitive skills (see World Bank 2017b). Native-born workers also invest more in education as immigration increases the returns to education. If immigration depresses wages for low-skilled migrants, returns to education become higher and, thus, further incentivize human capital accumulation.

Women in destination countries are particularly affected by low-skilled immigration. Immigrant labor decreases the cost, and increases the quality, of household services. This, in turn, allows native-born women—especially the high skilled—to increase their supply of labor and plausibly change their fertility decisions as well.

Economic integration of immigrants and refugees

On arrival, immigrants tend not to earn as much as comparable natives (even though on average they experience large wage gains upon migrating). The usual explanation for the observed immigrant–native wage and employment gaps is that the human and social capital of immigrants are not fully portable. Productivity and wages depend on many factors: education, work experience, social capital and networks, cultural norms, and language ability, to name a few. Many of these factors have place-specific components, putting newly arrived immigrants at a disadvantage compared with the locals. There may also be less benign explanations for observed gaps. Immigrants may have poor bargaining power, allowing firms to pay them below their marginal product—that is, to exploit them. This tends to be the case especially in non-OECD destination countries where the enforcement (or even presence) of labor laws is weak and most immigrants are low skilled. Numerous factors put immigrants at a disadvantage. Work permits are typically, at least initially, tied to an employer, preventing immigrants from seeking other job opportunities and removing a key form of leverage in employer-employee wage bargaining. Immigrants may also face discrimination, be less aware of job opportunities, and have less access to high-paying jobs through social networks. These factors give employers considerable power over their immigrant employees, plausibly resulting in below-productivity wages or otherwise poor working conditions. As time goes by, however, immigrants may overcome their initial disadvantages and economically integrate. This section outlines the evidence on immigrant and refugee economic assimilation and integration in host country labor markets.[1]

Employment and wage gaps

Employment gaps

Recent studies using the European Union Labour Force Survey (EULFS) also allow us to differentiate between economic migrants and refugees.[2] Figure 4.1 graphs unconditional and conditional (controlling for age, gender, and educational attainment) employment rate differentials between native workers and EU15 economic immigrants, non-EU15 economic immigrants, and refugees.[3] The employment gaps are larger for non-EU15 immigrants than for EU15 immigrants, roughly 7 versus 3 percentage points, respectively, unconditional on socioeconomic

Figure 4.1 Immigrant–native employment gaps in the European Union

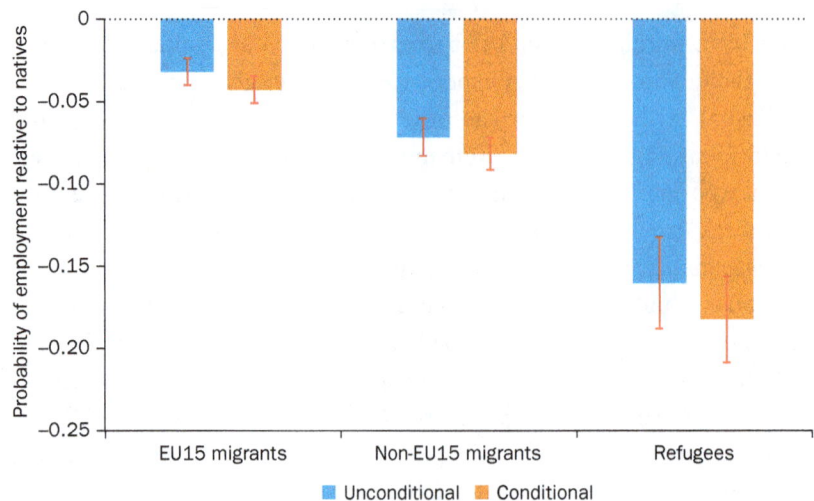

Source: Dustmann et al. 2016. Reproduced with permission; further permission required for reuse.

Note: The figure shows the unconditional and conditional differences in employment probabilities between EU15 and non-EU15 economic immigrants and natives, as well as between refugees and natives, obtained using linear probability models. All regressions include host country fixed effects. Conditional employment gaps control for gender, age (dummy variables for five-year age groups), and education (dummy variables for lower-secondary and tertiary education). The sample includes all individuals ages 25–64 not in full-time education or military service. The reported 90 percent confidence intervals are based on robust standard errors. EU15 = the original 15 European Union countries: Austria, Belgium, Denmark, Finland, France, Germany, Greece, Ireland, Italy, Luxembourg, the Netherlands, Portugal, Spain, Sweden, and the United Kingdom.

characteristics; for refugees, the gaps increase to 16 percentage points. Employment gaps are even larger when we control for demographic and educational characteristics, reflecting the fact that refugees are disproportionately male and young, both of which are positively associated with a likelihood of employment.

The described employment gaps aggregate over people who have lived in their host country for different lengths of time but do not address what happens with regard to immigrants over time. Figure 4.2 speaks directly to the issue of economic assimilation by plotting the (again conditional on age, gender, and educational attainment) refugee–native and immigrant–native employment rate differentials against years since arrival. The employment probabilities of both refugees and economic immigrants relative to native-born workers increase with years in the country. Refugees start with much lower initial employment rates but subsequently experience much more rapid increases. During the first three years after arrival, refugees are 50 percentage points less likely to be employed than

Figure 4.2 Immigrant and refugee employment gaps, by years since arrival

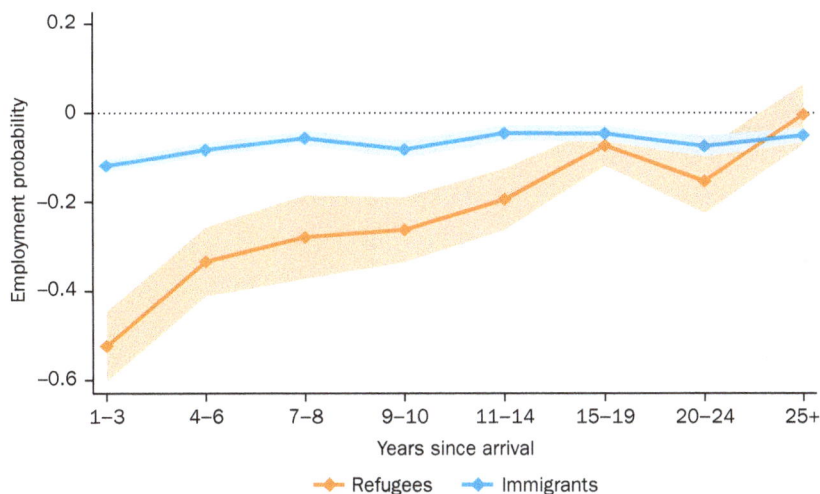

Source: Dustmann et al. 2016 based on 2008 European Union Labour Force Survey data. Reproduced with permission; further permission required for reuse.

Note: The figure displays gaps (together with 90 percent confidence intervals) in the employment probabilities of economic immigrants versus natives, and refugees versus natives, by years since arrival obtained from linear probability models that condition on gender, age (dummy variables for five-year age groups), education (dummy variables for lower-secondary and tertiary education), and host country fixed effects. The sample includes individuals ages 25-64 not in full-time education or military service.

native-born workers. Some of this gap may be due to legal restrictions on labor market participation during the application-processing period. This refugee–native employment gap declines by about half 7–10 years after arrival, and is no longer statistically significant at 15–19 years after arrival. On arrival, economic immigrants are only 10 percentage points less likely to be employed than native-born individuals, but subsequent convergence is much slower and uneven.

Women and men have distinctive immigration experiences. For example, consider the employment rates in the United States by gender for native-born individuals and immigrants depicted in figure 4.3, based on data in a National Academies of Sciences, Engineering, and Medicine report (2017). The figure offers a few key takeaways. First, men have consistently higher employment rates than women in the United States; this is true for both native-born workers and immigrants, although male employment rates have been trending downward whereas female employment rates have been trending upward. Until 2005 male immigrants' employment probability was consistently 2–4 percentage points lower than that of native-born men.

Figure 4.3 **Native and immigrant employment rates in the United States, by gender, 1970–2012**

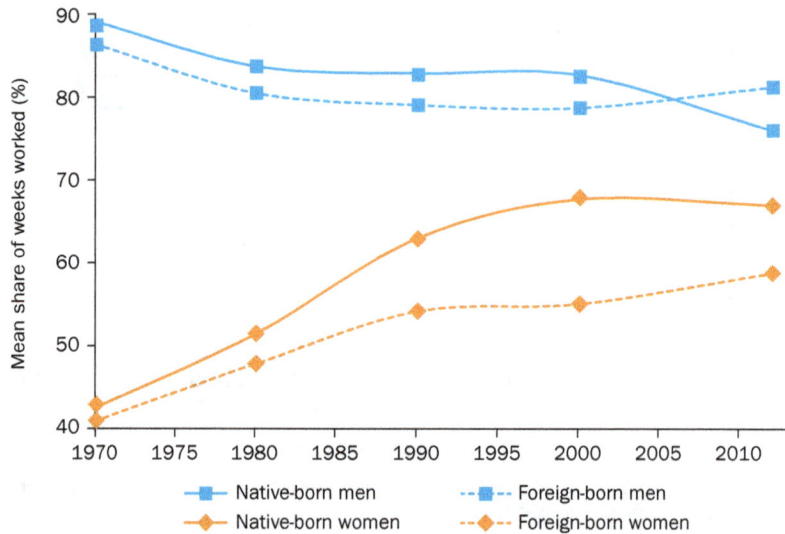

Source: Created using data from tables 3-4 and 3-5 in National Academies of Sciences, Engineering, and Medicine 2017.

Note: Underlying data are for population ages 25–64 using U.S. Decennial Census Public Use Microdata Series, 1970, 1980, 1990, 2000, and ACS (American Community Survey) Public Use Microdata Series, 2010–12.

During the Great Recession, after the financial crisis of 2007–08, this pattern very rapidly reversed, and by 2012 the employment rate for foreign-born men was 5 percentage points higher.

For women, in contrast, employment rates diverged until about 2000, with immigrant women steadily losing ground to native-born women. The female immigrant–native employment rate gap increased from about 2 to 12 percentage points between 1970 and 2000. By 2012 that gap had shrunk back to 8 percentage points, again likely in part a consequence of the Great Recession. The upward-trending employment rates of women, as well as the widening immigrant–native gap, can be explained by changing gender roles in the United States. As American women increasingly entered the labor force, the trend among immigrant women was not quite as fast. The cultural changes that increased female labor supply for American women may have occurred more slowly for immigrants. For example, Blau (2015) finds that female labor participation in their origin country strongly influences the behavior of female immigrants in the United States.

Wage gaps

The dynamics of the immigrant–native wage gap provide more insight into immigrant economic assimilation. Across many OECD countries, studies have found that immigrant wages start well below those of comparable native-born workers and then converge within 10–20 years. Specifically, on arrival in the United States, immigrants earn about 15 percent less than native-born workers; for a sample of 15 OECD countries, the gap is about 40 percent (see figure 4.4). For immigrants to the United States who arrived in the 1960s and 1970s, convergence took about 10 years, and subsequently average immigrant wages actually exceeded those of native-born workers. Starting for immigrants arriving in the 1980s, the rate of immigrant wage assimilation has slowed; even after 20 years, wages had not yet reached parity. These slower economic assimilation rates are comparable to those in other OECD countries, where, for cohorts arriving from

Figure 4.4   Immigrant wage gaps, by years since arrival, for the United States (by arrival cohort) and for OECD countries

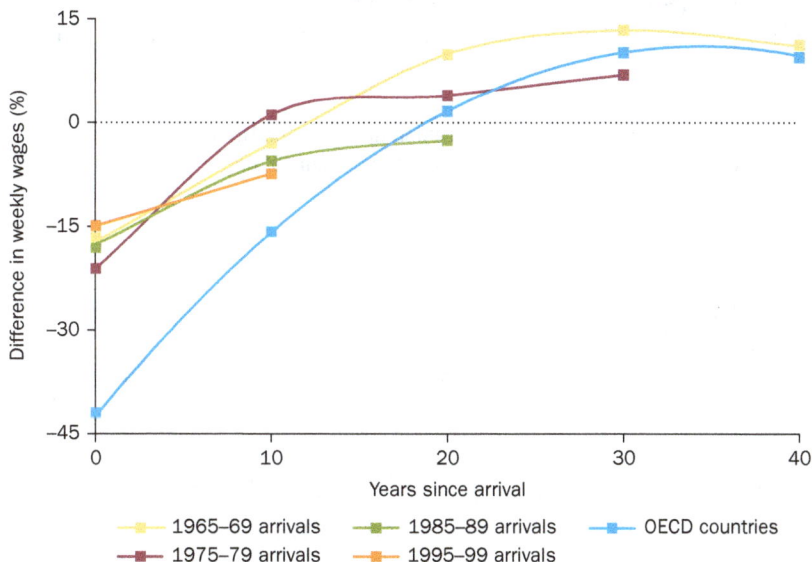

Sources: Created using data from table 3-12 in National Academies of Sciences, Engineering, and Medicine 2017 for U.S. wage gaps and table 8, column 1, from Adsera and Chiswick 2007 for OECD wage gaps.

Note: The U.S. wage gaps are a result of a regression of (log) wages on age (cubic), education, and years since migration, which were binned into groups (0-4, 10-14, 20-24, 30-34, and 40-44 years). Sample is of men, ages 25-64, using U.S. Decennial Census Public Use Microdata Series, 1970, 1980, 1990, and 2000, and ACS (American Community Survey) Public Use Microdata Series, 2010-12. OECD wage gaps are the result of a regression of (log) earnings on immigrant status, years since migration, squared years since migration, and a set of controls using the 1994-2000 European Community Household Panel. OECD = Organisation for Economic Co-operation and Development.

1994 to 2000, on average convergence takes a little under 20 years. We return to the topic of the speed of wage assimilation later in the chapter.

Occupational quality

A further indicator of economic performance is the quality of immigrants' occupations. First, we look at occupational quality of newly arrived immigrants.[4] Looking across origin countries, there is quite a bit of variation in occupational standing. In the United States, migrants from developed countries (such as Australia and Canada) attain the highest level of performance, whereas we see the lowest indexes among immigrants from Latin American countries (such as Mexico). The progress within the 10 years closest to migration is presented in figure 4.5, where we plot the change in occupational placement between years 1990 and 2000 against the original occupational placement in 1990. The fact that all countries (except for the Netherlands) are above zero indicates significant improvement over time in the occupational placement levels for skilled immigrants coming from different countries. Additionally, the negative correlation (that is, the lowest-placed countries experience the largest gains) suggests the existence of a convergence effect such that the differences in performance levels among various

Figure 4.5 Occupational placement upon arrival in the United States and the change over the next 10 years, by country or economy of origin

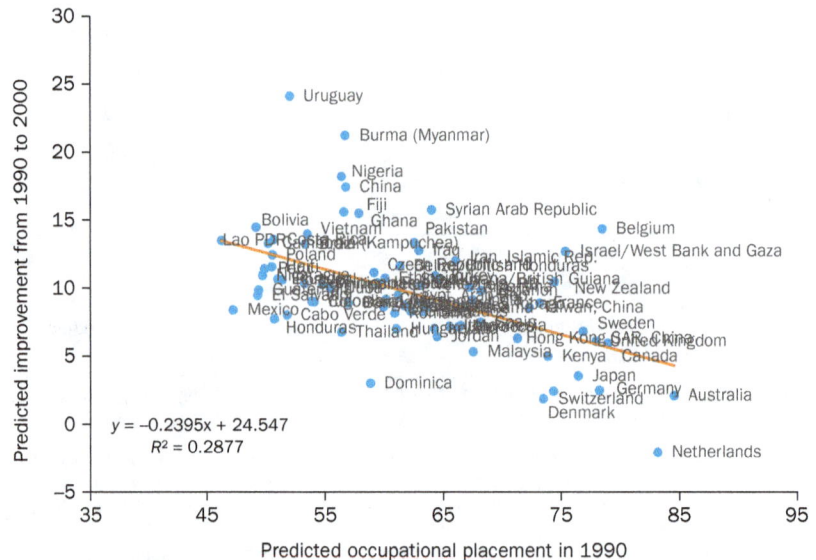

$$y = -0.2395x + 24.547$$
$$R^2 = 0.2877$$

Source: Mattoo, Neagu, and Ozden 2012. Reproduced with permission; further permission required for reuse.

countries decline. The results show convergence among immigrant groups; economic integration proceeds fastest for those groups that find themselves initially at the greatest disadvantage.

A broad consensus exists across many countries and studies, although definitely in the case of OECD destination countries, that immigrant and refugee assimilation does tend to occur and is fairly rapid.[5] The next sections discuss some important difficulties in correctly assessing the speed of economic assimilation, and evidence on the factors that encourage integration.

The changing characteristics of immigrants and measuring integration

A great deal of empirical research has attempted to measure the extent of economic assimilation. Much of that literature has focused on solving methodological issues in order to properly measure changes in immigrant earnings with time spent in the host country.

The initial studies in this literature used cross-sectional datasets, that is, data where individuals are observed at the same point in time, to assess the age-earnings profiles of immigrants and native-born workers. These studies typically found a very rapid rate of wage convergence (notably Chiswick 1978). However, there are two important reasons why a declining earnings gap between immigrants and native-born workers with time spent in the host country may not (solely) reflect immigrants' earnings growth.

First, declining skill levels of immigrants across arrival cohorts may drive the apparent assimilation of immigrants. When we look only at a single cross-section, any decline over time we observe in wage gaps could be caused by older cohorts having higher human capital rather than by assimilation. Second, there may be negative selection of return migrants, that is, those immigrants who eventually leave the host country could be, on average, less skilled than those who remain. Therefore, the wage assimilation observed could actually reflect the fact that the older cohort is only a positively selected group of the original arrivals. For both of those reasons it may appear as though immigrants are integrating well—after all, those who have been longer in a country do better—even when no wage convergence is taking place.

By following immigrant arrival cohorts across U.S. Census waves—that is, repeated cross-sections—in a very influential study, Borjas (1985) documents the importance of the changing skill composition of immigrant arrival cohorts. He finds that in the United States about half of the convergence observed in a single cross-section can be attributed to declining skills across arrival cohorts. The fact that immigrants who have been in the United States for a long time do very well economically compared to new entrants is in large part because those older cohorts were more skilled even upon arrival.

Measuring wage convergence, even within a cohort, is still problematic because it does not account for the changing composition within the cohort. As described above, the composition of an immigrant cohort changes primarily as immigrants migrate again—back home or to another country (see the section titled "Why is migration frequently temporary?" later in the chapter). The changing composition will either exaggerate or attenuate the measured assimilation depending on whether the return migrants are negatively or positively selected. Researchers address this issue by using panel datasets that follow individual immigrants over time. Lubotsky (2007) does this for the United States and is thus able to assess the importance of selective return migration. Figure 4.6 compares

Figure 4.6 **Immigrant–native earnings gaps in longitudinal and repeated cross-sectional data, 1970–79 arrivals in the United States**

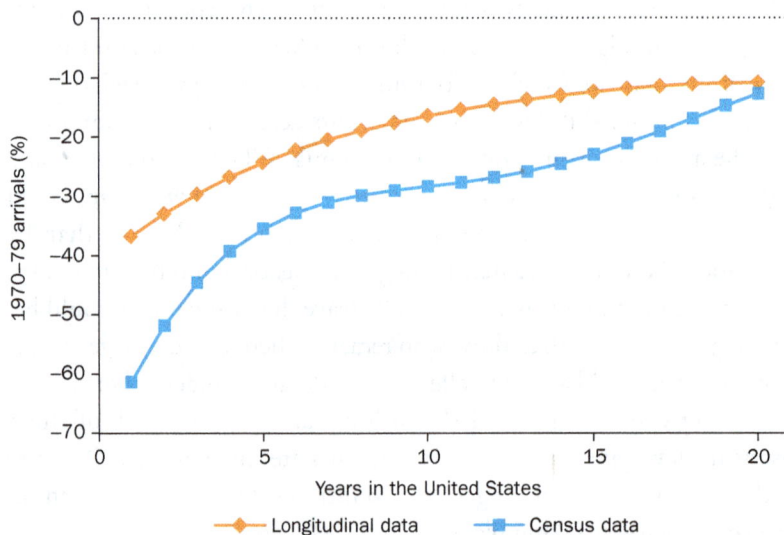

Source: Lubotsky 2007. Reproduced with permission; further permission required for reuse.

Note: Each line represents the predicted median earnings of immigrants relative to native-born workers; the orange line represents results from the longitudinal data, while the blue line represents repeated cross-sections. The cohorts in the longitudinal data are defined by the earlier of an immigrant's reported date of entry and his or her first year of earnings. The level of earnings pertains to immigrants who arrived in the United States with five years of potential experience.

immigrant–native earnings gaps for the 1970s arrival cohort in the repeated cross-sectional census data and the longitudinal data.

The earnings gap among the 1970s arrivals closes by around 40 percentage points according to the repeated cross-sectional data, but by only 20 percentage points according to the longitudinal data. The implication is that return migrants from the United States are negatively selected—that is, immigrants with below-average wages are more likely to migrate again. This negative selection results in overestimates of the wage progress of immigrants who remain.[6]

The Age of Mass Migration (1850–1914), the voluntary migration of European laborers to the United States, accounted for about 40 percent of overall population growth in the United States. Abramitzky, Boustan, and Eriksson (2014) use panel data to study the economic assimilation of these migrants and come to the same conclusions. Figure 4.7 depicts the immigrant–native wage gap, based on occupational information, for arrival cohorts 1900, 1910, and 1920 in the United States.

Figure 4.7 Immigrant–native wage gaps in the United States after the Age of Mass Migration, by years since arrival

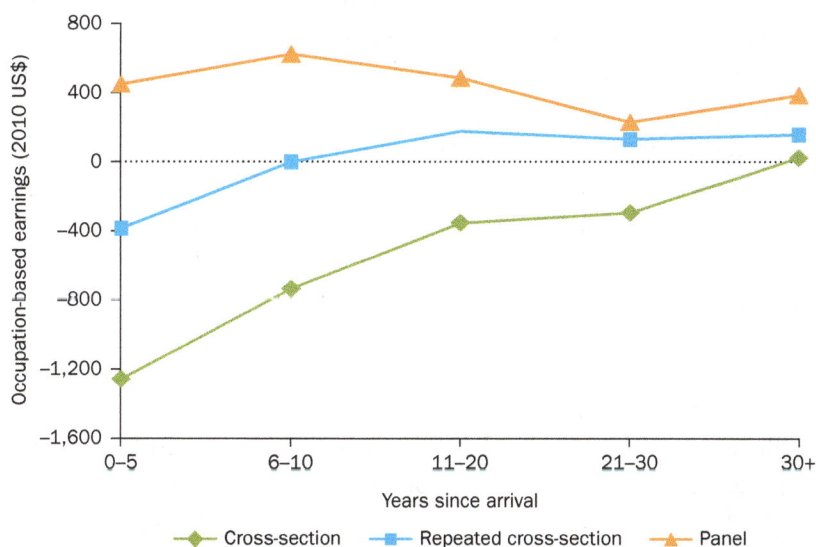

Source: Re-created from figure 2 in Abramitzky, Boustan, and Eriksson 2014. Reproduced with permission; further permission required for reuse.

Note: Data for cross-section and repeated cross-section are taken from 1900, 1910, and 1920 IPUMS (Integrated Public Use Microdata Series) samples; panel data from a subset of IPUMS samples for which authors could match individuals across samples.

199

On the basis of the simple cross-section estimates in figure 4.7, immigrants appear to face a very large wage penalty relative to native-born workers upon first arrival, but they are able to erase this gap over time. In contrast, the estimates based on repeated cross-sections of data show a much smaller initial gap but slower wage assimilation. The main reason is that later immigrant arrival cohorts are engaged in lower-paying occupations, mainly because of lower human capital levels.

In addition, temporary migrants who eventually return to Europe have lower than average wages. This accounts for the differences between the repeated cross-section and the panel data estimates in figure 4.7. Panel data on permanent immigrants show that they hold slightly higher-paying occupations than native-born workers, even upon first arrival, and retain this advantage over time. Both changing cohort quality and return migration make it appear that assimilation is rapid, when in fact changing immigrant cohort composition and selective return migration drive many of the patterns observed in a single cross-section of data.

Economic integration across generations

Differences between immigrants and the native born can persist across generations. Persistence arises as children inherit ability or skills from their parents (whether through nature or nurture) as well as financial assets. There are also environmental sources of persistence, notably the impact of the broader ethnic environment. Given the results with respect to first-generation immigrants, we would expect immigrant–native economic gaps to also diminish across generations. In the United States, for example, the image of the "melting pot" is part of the national myth. Even if the American Dream does not come true for first-generation immigrants, the hope is that it will for their children.

The evidence suggests that lack of economic assimilation during the Age of Mass Migration, discussed above, persisted over generations. Immigrant advantage (or disadvantage) relative to native-born individuals is a strong predictor of future generations. If first-generation immigrants from a sending country outperformed native-born workers—as did immigrants from England or Russia—so too would the second generation. Whereas, if the first generation held lower-paid occupations than native-born workers—as did immigrants from Norway or Portugal—the second generation would as well (Abramitzky, Boustan, and Eriksson 2014).

Figure 4.8 Multigenerational persistence in immigrant–native wage gaps in the United States, by country of origin

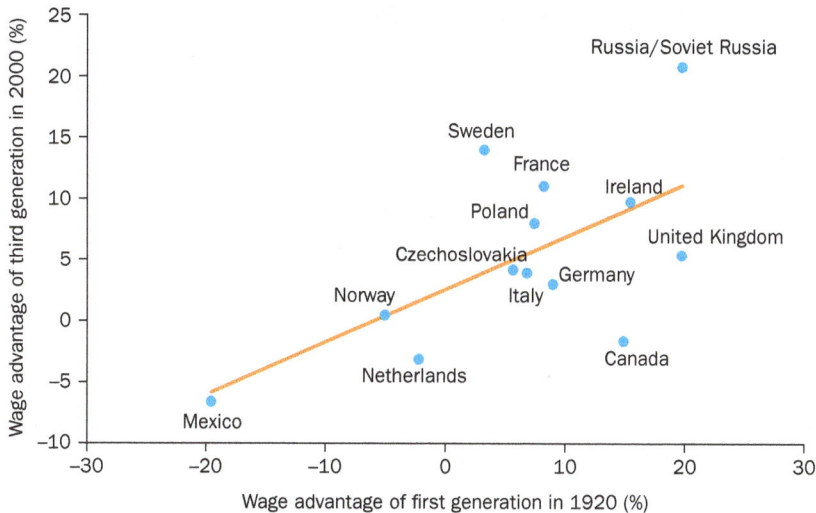

Source: Borjas 2014. Reproduced with permission; further permission required for reuse.

Note: Data from pooled 1910–20 decennial censuses and pooled 1972–2010 General Social Surveys.

Figure 4.8, from Borjas (2014), illustrates the strength of these correlations even across three generations using data from the United States. The figure shows the correlation between the immigrant–native-born worker wage gap in 1920 and 2000 for different countries of origin. There is a surprisingly strong relationship, suggesting an enduring role for ethnic and national social capital.

Factors facilitating labor market assimilation

The speed at which immigrants are able to integrate into host country labor markets depends on many factors. In this section, we focus on three: language, ethnic enclaves, and policy (with discussions of both domestic labor market regulations and legalization issues).

Language

A key determinant of immigrant economic integration is language acquisition. Knowledge of the local language is vital in finding employment and maximizing the value of one's skills. One way to address the role of language in the assimilation process in the United States is to compare immigrants from English- and non-English-speaking countries who arrived at different ages. Using this approach, Bleakley and Chin (2004, 2010) find large economic returns to knowing English, both in the labor market and along other dimensions of assimilation (including marriage and fertility). However, English is not equally important for everyone. Rather, the returns to knowing English are occupation-specific. Compared to occupations that require more interpersonal and cognitive skills, those that require mostly manual skills experience lower returns to English proficiency (Chiswick and Miller 2010).

Given the importance of language for integration and assimilation, it is concerning that, at least in the United States, language acquisition of new immigrants has slowed; see figure 4.9. The cohorts that entered the country in the 1970s typically experienced a 12 percentage point increase in their fluency rate during their first decade, whereas the cohorts that entered the country after the 1980s show only a 4 percentage point increase.

Figure 4.9 English language proficiency of immigrants in the United States, by gender and years since arrival

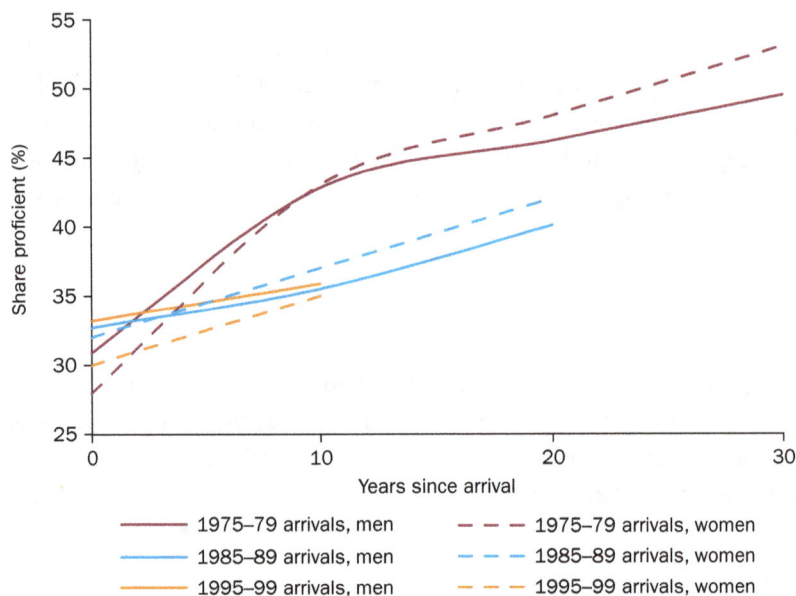

Source: Created using data from figures 3-6 and 3-7 in National Academies of Sciences, Engineering, and Medicine 2017.

Note: Wage-earning immigrants using U.S. Decennial Census Public Use Microdata Series, 1970, 1980, 1990, 2000, and ACS (American Community Survey) Public Use Microdata Series, 2010–12. Estimates from regressions adjusted for age (cubic).

Language is clearly important to the successful economic assimilation of immigrants. An obvious public policy response is to provide language programs; interestingly, however, the evidence on the success of such programs is mixed. The broad lesson seems to be that these programs improve the employability of workers but not wage assimilation. This is true for government-sponsored language programs for immigrants in both Norway and Denmark (see Hayfron 2001 and Liebig 2007, respectively). These programs improved immigrants' language proficiency and increased the probability of being employed, but wage assimilation was unaffected. An OECD report (Liebig 2007) concludes that language education is more effective if coordinated with employment or focused on job-related communication rather than general fluency.

Ethnic enclaves

Networks of diaspora are an important determinant of migrant location decisions, as discussed in chapter 2, and also affect how well immigrants assimilate in a new country. Upon first arrival, many immigrants settle in ethnic enclaves. It is often their network of compatriots that provides information on housing and job opportunities. The degree of immigrant segregation in the United States has varied considerably over time. Figure 4.10, using data from Cutler, Glaeser, and Vigdor (2008), depicts a measure of

Figure 4.10 **Immigrant stock and segregation in the United States, 1910–2000**

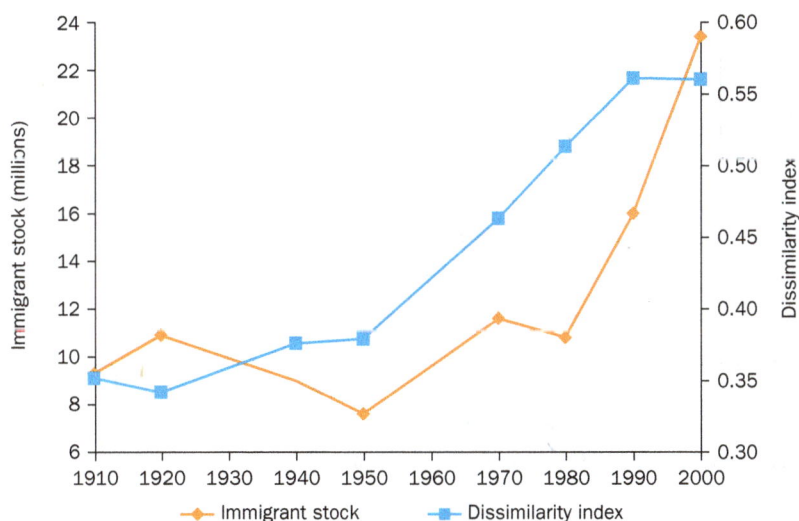

Source: Created using data from table 1 in Cutler, Glaeser, and Vigdor 2008.

immigrant segregation, the index of dissimilarity for immigrants, and overall immigration levels in the United States.[7] Immigrant segregation was stable in the early part of the 20th century, then rose steadily, and is currently at a historic high. This pattern mirrors trends in the overall size of the immigrant population; having a large number of immigrants makes it easier to segregate.

Living in ethnic enclaves is likely to have both positive and negative effects for new immigrants. It enhances employment opportunities if immigrants receive job referrals or other assistance from their compatriots (see, for example, Lafortune and Tessada 2014; Munshi 2003). However, immigrant neighborhoods could also limit employment opportunities if they isolate residents from information about the broader labor market or if they restrict local language acquisition. Moreover, members of an ethnic network face a trade-off: although network members may provide job referrals to new arrivals, they also may compete for employment in an occupational niche. Since the 1970s, the United States has seen a rapid increase in the degree of occupational segregation (figure 4.11), which is particularly pronounced for immigrant women, who are increasingly concentrated in a few service sector occupations.

Figure 4.11 Immigrant occupational segregation in the United States, 1970–2014

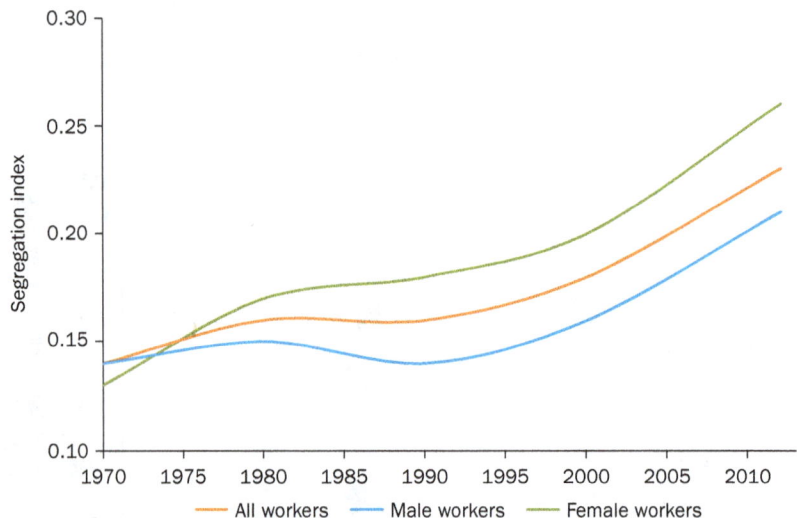

Source: National Academies of Sciences, Engineering, and Medicine 2017.

Note: The segregation index can be interpreted as the minimum proportion for each type of worker whose occupation would have to be reassigned in order to achieve equal representation among foreign-born workers across all occupations.

Evidence on the net effect of ethnic enclaves comes from Sweden and Denmark (see Edin, Fredriksson, and Åslund 2003 and Damm 2009, respectively). The papers rely on quasi-random assignment of immigrants and refugees to publicly subsidized housing. They conclude that immigrants who choose to live in immigrant neighborhoods have lower earnings but that, correcting for this selection, living in an enclave can improve labor market performance.

Recent evidence for the United States is suggestive of a less benign dynamic (Borjas 2016). Large-scale immigration from a few source countries, especially Mexico and Central American countries, has resulted in increased segregation. Evidence suggests that both the rate of increase in English language proficiency and the rate of economic assimilation are significantly slower for larger national origin groups. The strong negative correlation between the size of an immigrant group and the improvements in English fluency for that group (over a decade) neatly makes this point (see figure 4.12).

Figure 4.12   **English fluency and the size of ethnic enclaves in the United States**

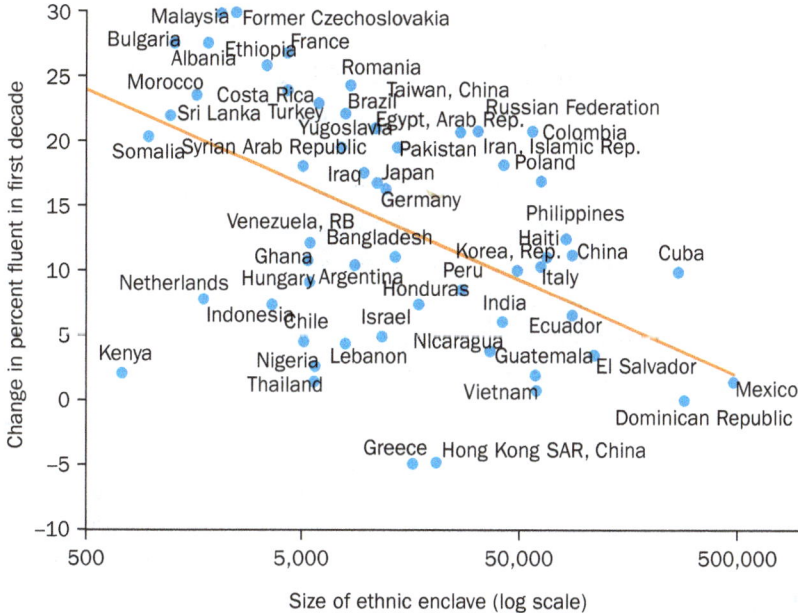

Source: Borjas 2016.

Note: The size of an ethnic enclave is measured by how many compatriots a new immigrant would have to find if he or she settled in the same metropolitan area as the average member of that group. Data from 2000 decennial census and the pooled 2009–11 ACS (American Community Survey).

Labor market regulations

Labor market regulations and credentialing restrictions are important obstacles to immigrants' ability to access host country labor markets.

These restrictions are most prominent for refugees, more than half of whom live in countries where they have no route to obtaining access to formal labor markets.[8] Even in countries where such a route exists, asylum applications have to be processed and accepted before work permits are issued, which typically takes at least several months. Even legal economic migrants, however, face numerous obstacles.

Comparing the wages and employment of immigrants in Australia, Canada, and the United States, Antecol, Kuhn, and Trejo (2006) find that assimilation in total earnings is largely due to employment assimilation in Australia and Canada and to wage assimilation in the United States. The authors argue that this is because wages are more flexible in the United States, allowing immigrants easier access to labor markets but at lower wages. In contrast, in Australia and Canada, the main hurdle is entering the labor market, but wages on successful entry are more comparable to those of native-born workers.

Active labor market policies (ALMPs) are direct means to encourage immigrant and refugee assimilation. However, a recent review of ALMPs in OECD countries found little evidence on their effectiveness for immigrant employment assimilation (see OECD 2014). ALMP programs include training, wage subsidies for private sector jobs, public employment, services (counseling, job training), sanctions, and so on. Wage subsidy programs, like Denmark's "step model," were the only ones with a significant impact on employment. The idea behind these programs is that a subsidized wage gives employers an incentive to hire immigrant workers who do not have local work experience. Then, as the immigrant workers acquire local knowledge—or assimilate—they become more productive and the subsidy is no longer required.

An area in which cross-border cooperation is required is professional credentialing. In most professions, credentials do not readily transfer across borders (or even across states within the same country). Even when credentials do transfer, employers have difficulty judging the qualifications and work experience of immigrants. Reforms in this area help ensure that regulatory burdens do not cause the loss of immigrants' human capital. Much progress has been made (see OECD 2014), especially within the European Union but also more broadly. For example, the "Bologna Process" is an attempt to assure higher education quality and recognition of foreign degrees by 47 signatory countries.

Legal immigrant status

Undocumented immigrants face some of the largest barriers to assimilation. In the United States, undocumented immigrants account for over a quarter of all immigrants and, historically, that share reached almost a third. Some European countries also have high rates of undocumented immigration; in Italy and Greece, for example, 15 percent and 16 percent, respectively, of immigrants are undocumented (see figures 3.5 and 3.6 in chapter 3). Undocumented immigrants are barred from participating in the formal labor market as well as from receiving public benefits. The lives of undocumented immigrants are often characterized by lower wages and higher poverty rates than their documented counterparts (please see the appendix for a discussion on proper data collection on undocumented immigration).

In the United States, the wage and employment profiles of undocumented immigrants look much different than those of both immigrants residing legally and native-born workers. Borjas (2017a, 2017b) investigates the employment and wage profiles of undocumented immigrants. He finds that undocumented immigrants work significantly more and earn significantly less than both native-born workers and other immigrants, although the documented–undocumented wage gap has shrunk over time. More astonishingly, however, is that undocumented immigrants face nearly no wage growth and experience an almost completely flat age-earnings profile after age thirty. This is a stark difference from native-born workers and documented immigrants, who experience earnings growth into their forties (see figure 4.13).

To the extent that these differences are due, causally, to legal status is a critical policy question and one that has been studied extensively. Undocumented immigrants cannot enter the formal labor market and thus face limited employment options that offer lower returns to human capital and wage growth. Rivera-Batiz (1999) finds that documented immigrants make 15–30 percent more than their undocumented counterparts and that observable characteristics explain less than half of that gain. Additionally, the lack of better alternatives through the formal labor market may increase the probability that undocumented immigrants resort to crime to support themselves and their families. Legal status will also affect the investment decisions of migrants; decreasing uncertainty by removing the risk of deportation will encourage investments into location-specific human capital (such as language skills) that will potentially facilitate long-term wage growth.

The most compelling research on the causal relationship between labor market outcomes and legal status comes from large-scale policy changes

Figure 4.13 Age-earnings profiles of immigrants and native-born workers in the United States, by legal status

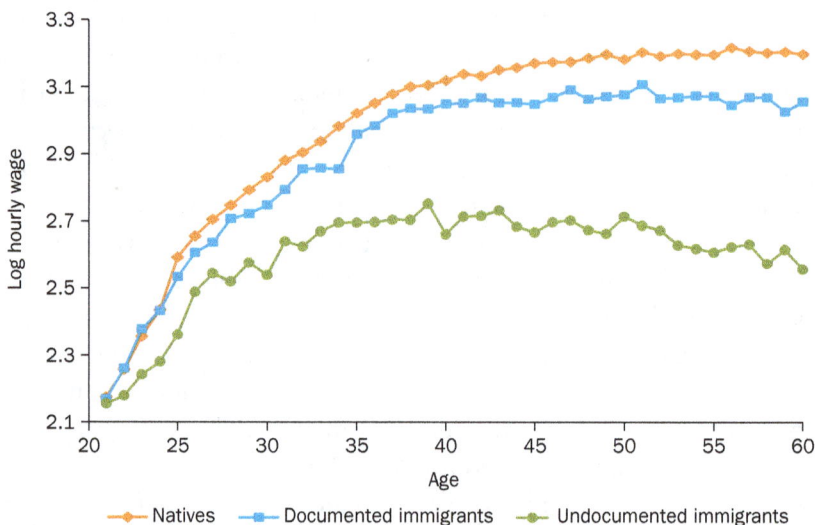

Source: Borjas 2017a.

that provide legal status to undocumented immigrants. By comparing outcomes before and after the policy change, researchers can identify the causal impact of gaining legal status. In the United States, the two largest of such policy changes are the Immigration Reform and Control Act (IRCA) of 1986 and the Deferred Action for Childhood Arrivals (DACA) policy of 2012.[9]

Studying the effects of IRCA, researchers have found that the wage growth of legalized immigrants increased significantly after legalization (Kossoudji and Cobb-Clark 2002; Rivera-Batiz 1999). Amuedo-Dorantes and Bansak (2011) also find increased wage growth as well as decreased employment and increased unemployment rates. They attribute the combination of decreased employment rates and faster wage growth to improved job market efficiency through increased job mobility that leads to better-quality job matches. Research has also found that IRCA led to increased educational attainment and lower crime rates (Baker 2015; Cortes 2013).

Evidence from DACA has been mixed. On the one hand, Amuedo-Dorantes and Antman (2017) find that DACA resulted in increased employment and decreased school attendance for eligible immigrants and found no effects on wages. Pope (2016), on the other hand, finds that DACA resulted in increased employment and wages for eligible immigrants and found no effect on school attendance. The most promising result, however, is that of Amuedo-Dorantes and Antman (2016), who find that poverty rates of households headed by DACA-eligible individuals decrease by 38 percent as compared to their ineligible counterparts.

In Italy, undocumented immigrants commit serious crimes at four times the rate of documented immigrants (Pinotti 2017). This stark difference likely results both from inherent differences in the migrant populations (education, income, age, and so on) and causally, specifically because of their legal status. Undocumented immigrants' lack of labor market opportunities increases the economic incentive to participate in criminal activity. Mastrobuoni and Pinotti (2015) and Pinotti (2017) study the causal impact of legal status on criminal activity. Taking advantage of two natural experiments, they find that attaining legal status significantly decreases the probability of committing a crime. Mastrobuoni and Pinotti (2015) find that legal status decreases the crime rates of economically motivated offenses—with the largest effects concentrated in areas that provide better labor market opportunities. Pinotti (2017) finds that the probability of committing a crime drops by over half after immigrants gain legal recognition.

Return and onward migration

A continuing theme in this chapter is that migration decisions are not necessarily permanent. Length of stay in a country affects our interpretation of the economic impacts of migration. From the standpoint of migrants, understanding the implications of assimilation depends heavily on whether and when immigrants return to their home country, and whether they had planned to return. From the point of view of native-born workers, the fiscal impacts of immigration depend on the length of stay of the migrants, at what stage in their life they migrate, and whether or not their children are educated in the host country. This section will document the magnitude of return and onward migration rates. It will also discuss the reason immigrants emigrate again: their failed or successful migration experiences.

How permanent is the migration decision?

We illustrate the impermanence of migration in figure 4.14. The figure, taken from Dustmann and Görlach (2016), plots the fraction of immigrants who leave the host country against the time since immigration, where each data point is a separate result from a wide array of studies. The figure also shows best-fit lines for two groups of destination countries: (1) Australia, Canada, New Zealand, and the United States and (2) European countries. The graph reveals three interesting details. First, immigrant outmigration rates are substantial and larger from European destination countries than from the more traditional immigration countries. Second, 10 years after arrival, close to 50 percent of the original arrival cohort has left the destination country in the case of Europe and 20 percent in the case of Australia, Canada, New Zealand, and the United States. Third, outmigration rates are highest during the first decade and then level out.

The same stylized facts do not hold for refugees, for whom return rates have varied considerably over time. Figure 4.15 shows the number of refugees worldwide and their return rate by year. Return rates fluctuate wildly between 0 and 20 percent per year, and are currently at a historic low. In general, the migration decision of refugees is far more permanent than that of the typical economic migrant.

Figure 4.14 **Outmigration rates by host region**

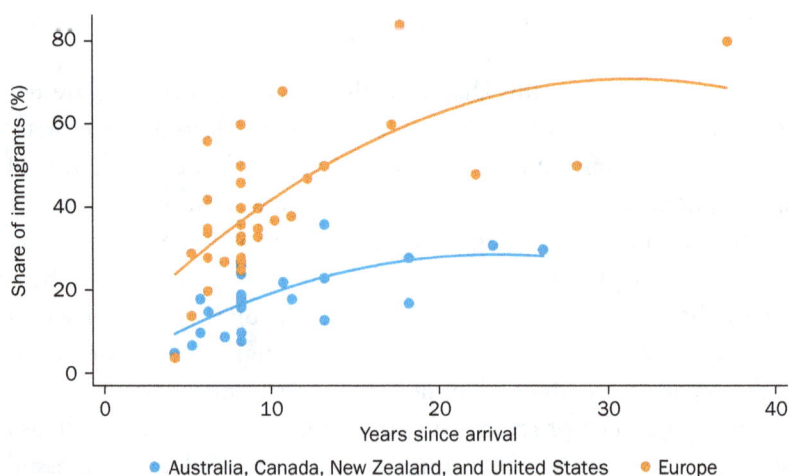

Source: Dustmann and Görlach 2016. Reproduced with permission; further permission required for reuse.

Note: Each data point is a separate result from a wide array of studies.

Figure 4.15   Refugees and returnees worldwide, 1975–2015

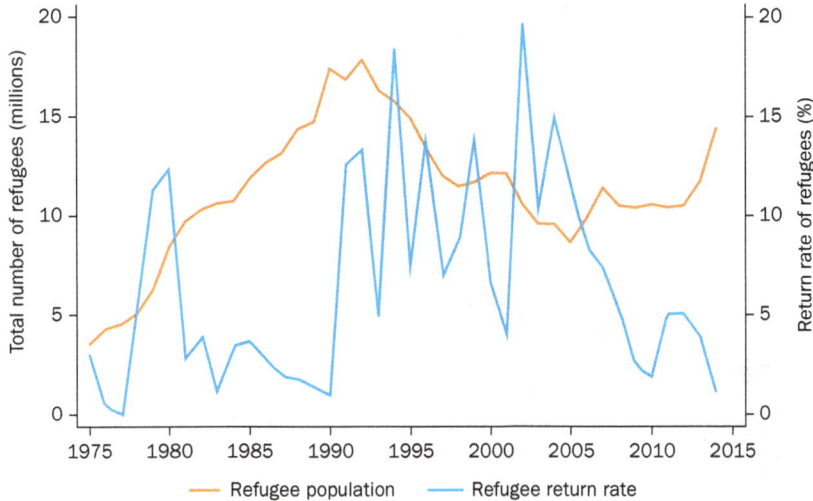

Source: Created using data from the UNHCR Population Statistics Database.

Note: Return rate calculated as the total number of returned refugees divided by the previous year's global refugee stock. UNHCR = United Nations High Commissioner for Refugees.

The remigration decision is far more complicated than a choice between staying in a host country and returning home. The paths of many migrants include multiple destinations and transit routes, as illustrated in map 4.1 (from Artuc and Ozden, forthcoming). Panel a shows the percentage of immigrants born in a country who resided in a different country before migrating to the United States. For example, 7 percent of Canadian-born migrants came to the United States from a country other than Canada. The same ratio is only 1 percent for Mexican migrants but is over 20 percent for migrants born in many European countries like Italy, the Russian Federation, and the United Kingdom. Transit migration is higher among migrants born in Africa and the Middle East and lower for those born in Latin America because geographic proximity and diaspora links give migrants from the latter region more direct access to the United States.

Panel b of map 4.1 presents the percentage of immigrants coming from a given location who were born somewhere else. The data indicate that transit migration to the United States is quite high among the migrants who were living in higher-income OECD countries. For example, 30 percent of migrants coming from Canada to the United States were actually born in another country; for migrants from the United Kingdom, that ratio is

Map 4.1   Transit migration to the United States

a. By birthplace

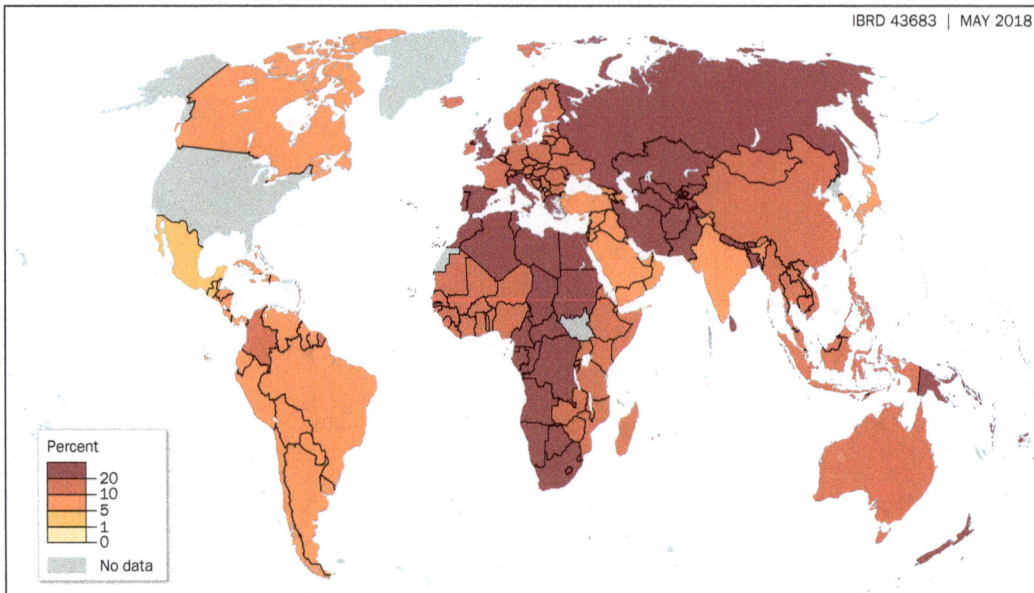

IBRD 43683 | MAY 2018

Percent
- 20
- 10
- 5
- 1
- 0
- No data

b. By country of last residence

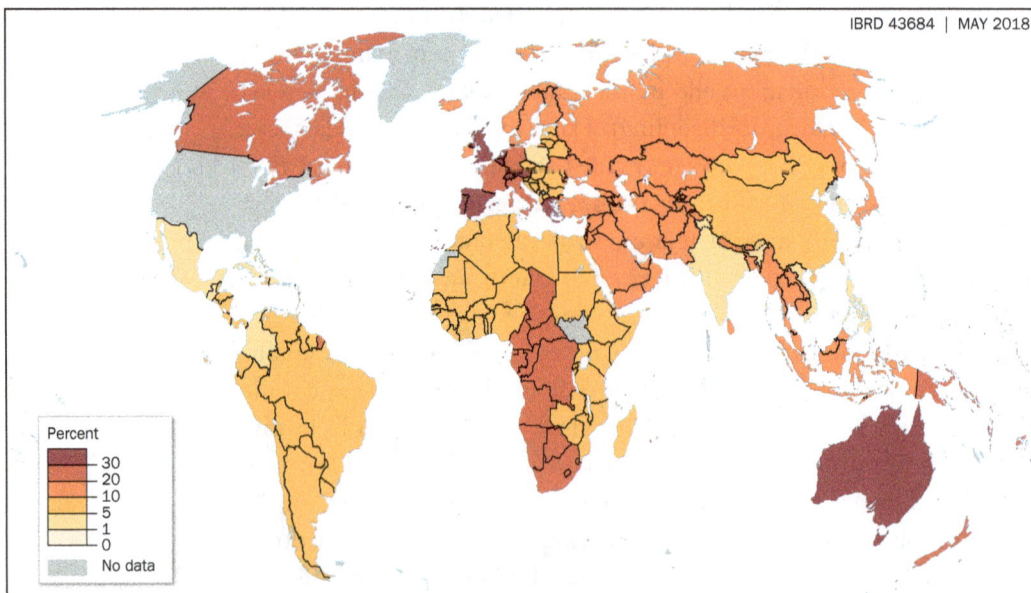

IBRD 43684 | MAY 2018

Percent
- 30
- 20
- 10
- 5
- 1
- 0
- No data

Source: Artuc and Ozden, forthcoming. Reproduced with permission; further permission required for reuse.

Note: Panel a shows the percentage of immigrants born in the location shown who resided in a different country before migrating to the United States. Panel b shows the percentage of immigrants coming from the location shown who were born somewhere else.

37 percent. These patterns highlight the importance of transit migration routes to high-income countries like the United States and lead us to several conclusions. First, transit migration is actually higher among the high-skilled (14 percent versus 7 percent for low-skilled migrants). Second, it takes place mostly through other high-income OECD countries. Third, unilateral migration policies, for example blocking migration from low-income countries to the United States, might have unintended consequences on other countries and might even be ineffective in the presence of these dynamic paths. All of this evidence indicates that many commonly held misperceptions, however, do not seem to be correct and that we need further in-depth analysis to unearth actual migration patterns.

Why is migration frequently temporary?

There are two main explanations for temporary migration. One view is that returns are not planned. Potential migrants are uncertain about the economic conditions they will face after migration. Those migrants who do not achieve the success they anticipated—perhaps because they become unemployed or face a high cost of living in the host country—might return home if they cannot meet their target savings or skills acquisition. Personal, family, or political crises can also drive migrants to return. In short, workers who experience worse-than-expected outcomes in the receiving country may wish to return home.

Alternatively, return and onward migration may be part of a human capital acquisition strategy. Migrants may move temporarily to accumulate savings and to acquire skills and knowledge to use in their home country.[10] People return migrate because they prefer living at home with friends and family, the purchasing power of their savings is often far higher at home, and the returns to human capital accumulated abroad may be high. Policy plays an important role in encouraging this form of planned temporary migration. Work permits are typically time-limited, and the transition to a permanent work permit is typically onerous and in many countries practically impossible.

If migrants return as part of a successful migration strategy, these returnees may be highly successful (a theme we also address in chapter 5). If, in contrast, immigrants emigrate again because of failed migration experiences, we can use the Roy model to describe the type of selection that characterizes the return migrants (Borjas and Bratsberg 1996). The two panels in figure 4.16 illustrate the nature of selection in this model. If the immigrant pool was initially positively selected, the return migrants are the

Figure 4.16   Selection in a Roy model with return migration

a. Positively selected immigrants   b. Negatively selected immigrants

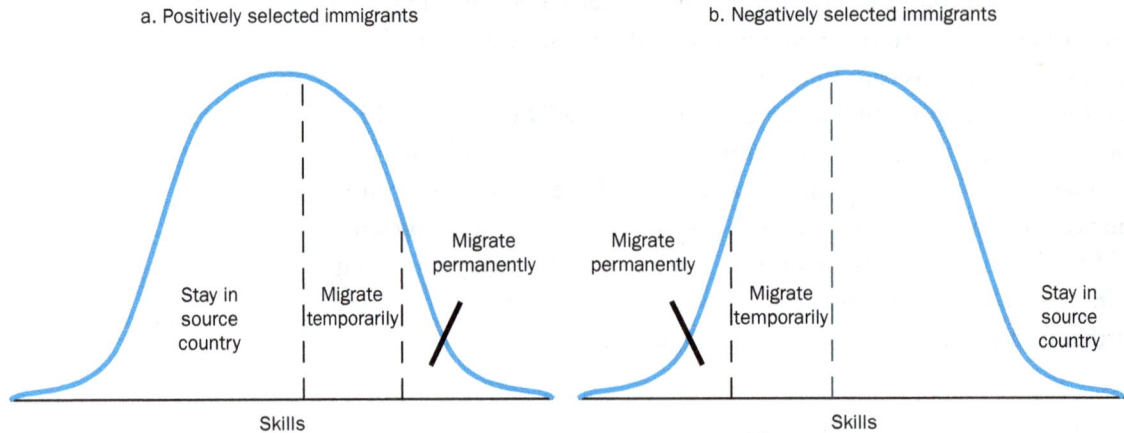

Source: Borjas 2014, 22. Reproduced with permission; further permission required for reuse.

Note: The figure shows the migration decisions of a country's population with respect to skill level. Each panel shows the skill density of a (hypothetical) country's population and the expected migration decisions based on a simple model of skill selection.

least-skilled workers from the initial high-skill flow. In contrast, if the immigrant pool was initially negatively selected, the return migrants are the most-skilled workers from the low-skill group.

The intuition for these results is straightforward. Suppose, for example, that the immigrants were positively selected (panel a). The most-skilled migrant workers experience, on average, very large gains to migration. As a result, they will wish to remain in the host country even if they end up with lower wages than expected. In contrast, the marginal immigrant in this self-selected sample is the least skilled of the high-skill flow. Those marginal migrants are much more likely to return because they barely had an incentive to migrate in the first place, and earnings below their expectations will motivate them to return to their source country. The same logic applies if immigrants are negatively selected (panel b). In short, the return migration decision reinforces the original selection pattern. It is the marginal immigrants who are most likely to become return migrants, and therefore the stayers are the "best of the best" if there is positive selection and the "worst of the worst" if there is negative selection.

Dustmann, Fadlon, and Weiss (2011) provide empirical evidence of planned temporary migration. Their study demonstrates that return migration can be induced by migration to "learning centers," countries in which migrants can more quickly accumulate human capital that has a high value in the home country. Additionally, some migrants plan to use their savings to set up a business when they return because of the higher rate of return on entrepreneurial activities in their home country (Mesnard 2004; Wahba and Zenou 2012).

A few studies have focused on the relationship between immigrant earnings and return migration, where earnings are used as a measure of success. Looking again at the Age of Mass Migration, Abramitzky, Boustan, and Eriksson (2016) find that return migrants were somewhat negatively selected from the migrant pool. Norwegian immigrants who returned to Norway held slightly lower-paid occupations than Norwegian immigrants who stayed in the United States. This is evidence for return migration as the consequence of a failed migration experience. However, upon returning to Norway, these return migrants held higher-paid occupations than Norwegians who never moved, despite hailing from poorer backgrounds before migration. They were also more likely to get married after return. These patterns suggest that, despite being negatively selected, return migrants were able to accumulate savings and improve their economic circumstances once they returned home.

Recent evidence for the Netherlands suggests a U-shaped relationship, with both low- and high-income immigrants returning but with the low-income immigrants returning faster (Bijwaard and Wahba 2014). This pattern supports the empirical evidence that unemployment pushes immigrants to leave their host country. Thus, unsuccessful immigrants are more likely to leave their host country than the average immigrant and are also more likely to do so early in the migration cycle because of failure. Successful immigrants are also more likely to leave than the average immigrant, but they leave because they have achieved their target savings.

Native responses to immigration

Native workers adjust to immigration in important ways. Chapter 3 discussed at length the labor market response (through employment and wages) due to the arrival of immigrants or refugees. In this section, we will discuss in more detail the longer-term nature of the response, focusing on changes in the occupation and educational attainment of native-born individuals. We will also look at the effect of immigration on the female labor market. An increase in low-skilled labor will decrease the price of childcare and housekeeping, altering the incentives women face regarding labor supply and fertility decisions. In addition to these labor market–oriented changes, our main focus, there are numerous additional responses, such as decisions on investment, trade, and flows of foreign direct investment. We review some of these effects in the next chapter, in the context of the global links created by high-skilled diasporas.

Native educational attainment and occupational choice

Possible mechanisms

There are a number of mechanisms by which immigration changes the educational attainment of natives and affects occupational choice.

First, immigration changes the skill composition of a country's population (as discussed throughout this book). This, in turn, changes the relative returns to education and occupations for native-born workers, affecting their investment in different types of human capital. For example, the employment of immigrants predominantly in lower-paid occupations would increase the returns for native-born workers to acquire more education and choose more skill-intensive occupations.

In Malaysia, for example, close to 90 percent of immigrants have, at most, primary education. Their arrival increased the estimated returns to secondary education, relative to primary education, for native-born Malaysians (see Ozden and Wagner 2014). This in turn may explain some of the correlation between immigration rates and secondary school attendance in Malaysia (see figure 4.17).

The impact of immigration on human capital acquisition by native-born individuals extends beyond changes in labor market returns. In particular, the process might be different when migrants are highly skilled. On one hand, native-born workers with directly competing skills might see their wages decline, and we might observe fewer native-born workers entering these fields. On the other hand, high-skilled sectors and occupations, such as those in research and technology (and even sports), are characterized by productivity spillovers. The arrival of highly skilled migrants might increase the productivity, and so the market wages, of native-born workers leading to further entry into these areas. We return to this important mechanism in chapter 5.

Finally, there is the direct impact of having more immigrant children in school. Immigrant students represent a large fraction of school children in a wide array of countries. Figure 4.18 shows the share of 15-year-old students who have an immigrant background. The blue bars represent the percentage of first-generation students, and the orange bars represent

Figure 4.17 Secondary school attendance and immigration in Malaysia, 1990–2010

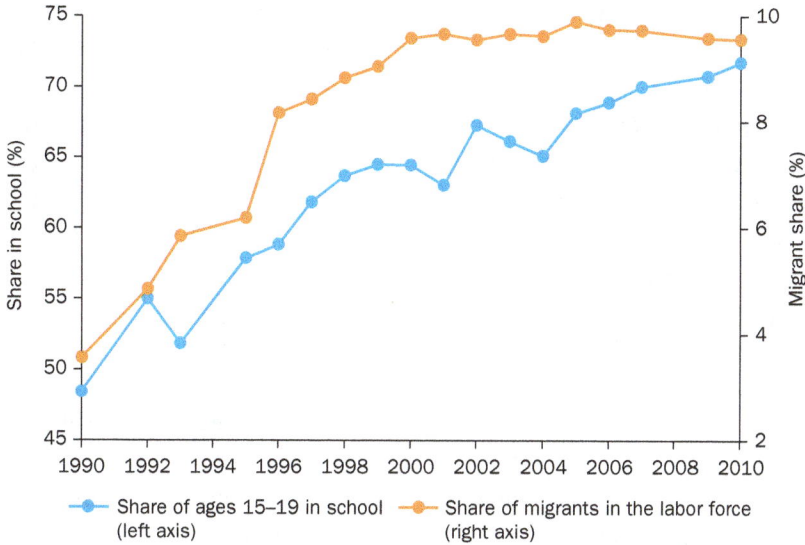

Source: Based on data from Ozden and Wagner 2014.

Figure 4.18 Share of students with an immigrant background, by economy

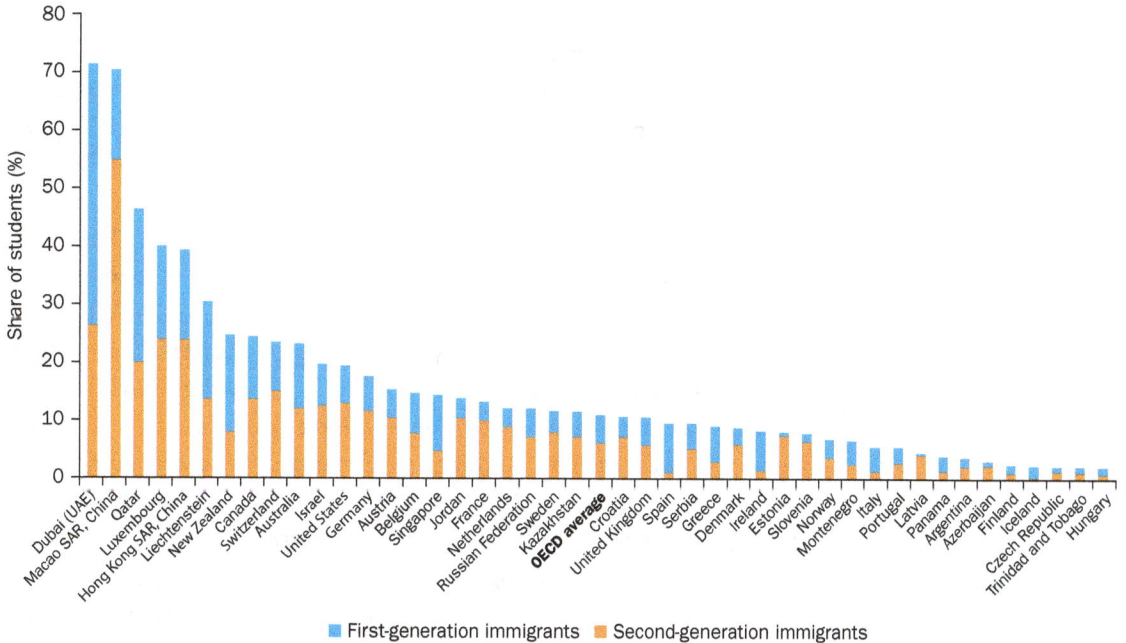

Source: OECD 2012. Reproduced with permission; further permission required for reuse.

Note: OECD = Organisation for Economic Co-operation and Development; UAE = United Arab Emirates.

the percentage of second-generation students. Across OECD countries, 10 percent of the students assessed by the Programme for International Student Assessment (PISA) are first- or second-generation immigrants. This group represents about 70 percent of the student population in Dubai (United Arab Emirates), 40 percent and more in Hong Kong SAR, China and Qatar, and over 25 percent of students in Canada, New Zealand, and Switzerland. In Australia, Austria, Germany, Israel, and the United States, immigrant students make up over 15 percent of the student population; in Belgium, Croatia, France, Jordan, Kazakhstan, the Netherlands, Russia, Singapore, Sweden, and the United Kingdom, they make up more than 10 percent.

Immigrant children may have limited knowledge of the local language, they are often of different religion and ethnicity than native-born children, and many of their parents are relatively poorly educated. These challenges have raised concerns among politicians and parents that sending native-born children to schools that have a high share of immigrant children may harm the native-born children's educational performance.

Evidence on native-born workers' occupational choice

It is often argued that immigrants do jobs that native-born workers do not want to do (at the low end of the occupational distribution) or cannot do (at the high end of the occupational distribution). This intrinsically problematic claim dodges the question: At what wage? Many native-born workers would likely perform jobs taken by migrants given a higher market wage. Precisely because immigrants change wage levels in the labor market, native-born workers have a clear incentive to change industry and occupation.

Of the numerous ways to measure what workers do, one is to look at the task content of the work they perform. Using individual data on the task intensity of occupations across U.S. states from 1960 to 2000, Peri and Sparber (2009) show that foreign-born workers specialize in occupations that require manual tasks, such as cleaning, cooking, and building. Immigration then causes native-born workers to pursue jobs requiring interactive tasks such as coordinating, organizing, and communicating, presumably because of native-born workers' comparative advantage in language skills and familiarity with social norms. Similarly, Cattaneo, Fiorio, and Peri (2015), using a sample of native-born European residents, find native-born European workers are more likely to move to occupations associated with higher skills and status when a larger number of immigrants enters their labor market.

Figure 4.19   Impact of refugees on occupational choice of low-skilled Danish natives, by years since exposure

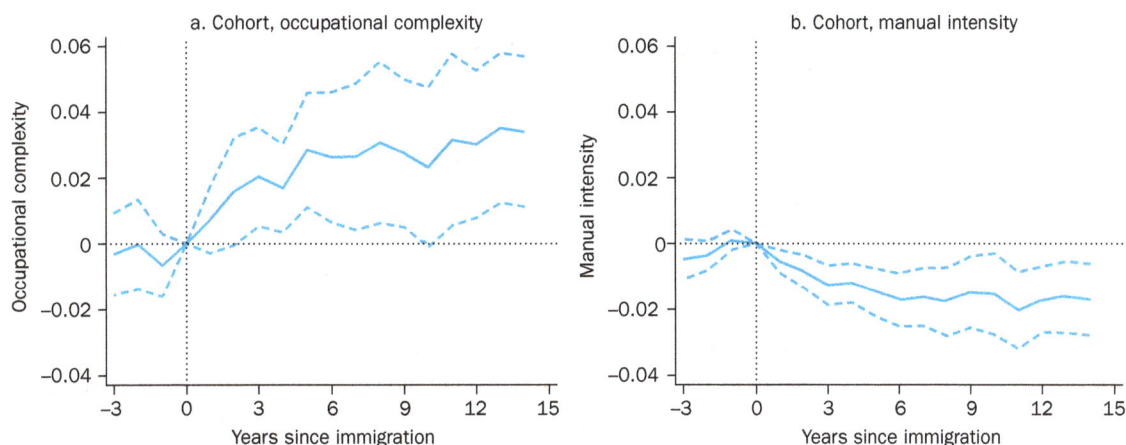

a. Cohort, occupational complexity

b. Cohort, manual intensity

Source: Foged and Peri 2016, figure 4. Reproduced with permission; further permission required for reuse.

Note: Values represent results from difference-in-differences regressions controlling for industry-by-year, region-by-year, education-by-year, occupation-by-year, and municipality fixed effects. Solid lines indicate parameter estimates, and dashed lines indicate 95 percent confidence intervals.

The panels in figure 4.19 depict the estimated impact of refugees—dispersed across Denmark by a refugee dispersal policy—on a measure of occupational complexity (panel a) and manual intensity (panel b) of the occupations engaged in by Danish natives.[11]

The reported estimates show the difference in outcomes of less-skilled native-born workers between municipalities exposed to refugees and less-exposed municipalities. The figures allow us to see how the adjustments and effects of immigrants on native-born workers unfolded over time. An increase of the supply of low-skilled refugees pushes less-educated native-born workers (especially the young and low-tenured) to pursue fewer manual-intensive occupations and more occupations with a higher degree of complexity. The impact is remarkably stable across time, suggesting that these changes are permanent.

In related evidence on the impact in Turkey of refugees from the Syrian Arab Republic, Del Carpio and Wagner (2016) find that the arrival of Syrian refugees—almost all informally employed—pushes native Turks to switch from the informal to formal sector. The evidence clearly suggests that the arrival of immigrants and refugees results in important changes in the composition of native employment in a country. An inflow of migrants forces native-born workers to make changes; although they often profit from the increase in the value to their country-specific skills, native-born workers must nevertheless adjust.

Much of the findings presented in this section can be thought of as the result of changing returns to different types of skills. Immigrants, who work in physically and manually intensive jobs, will increase the productivity of complementary work, typically jobs that require more communication and management skills. Native-born workers will adjust to these changing returns by moving into occupations where they are most productive. These adjustments do not, as discussed in chapter 3, represent an unambiguously positive or negative experience for native-born workers; such a calculation will depend on the effect of immigrants on wages as well as the costs of adjustment (see discussion in World Bank 2017b, on the experience of many East Asian destination countries).

Policy makers can maximize the benefits of immigrants by making it easier for native-born workers to take advantage of the new opportunities created by migrant labor. This could be done by decreasing the costs of adjustment and making it easier for natives to move across different sectors of the labor force. Unfortunately, many well-intentioned policies end up working against this goal. Research by Angrist and Kugler (2003) and D'Amuri and Peri (2014) looks at the relationship between labor market protections in Europe and the effect of immigrants on the labor force. They find that employment protection legislation, which aims to protect employees from being fired, will make it more difficult for native-born workers to change jobs in order to benefit from the presence of immigrant workers. This is borne out in the research of D'Amuri and Peri (2014), who find that the reallocation of native-born workers into more complex jobs in response to immigration was slowest in countries that have more strict labor market policies.

Evidence on native-born workers' educational attainment

In most countries, the raw data show a negative correlation between the shares of immigrant children in schools and school performance by native-born children (OECD 2012). This relationship is, however, not primarily causal. Immigrants often live in ethnically concentrated and low-income neighborhoods. The characteristics of native-born children enrolled in such schools are not representative of the native population as a whole; such children tend to come from lower-education households. Hence, the naïve correlation of immigrants and native school performance will tend to exaggerate any negative impact of immigrant children in schools. (See also box 4.1 for a discussion of immigration's effect on education in source countries.)

Box 4.1   Migration's impact on the education of children left behind

The impact of migration on educational attainment is not limited to the impact in host countries. Emigration also affects the education of those left behind.[a]

Emigration of a parent affects children who have been left behind through two main channels. Parents migrate primarily to increase their earning power and remit much of the additional funds back home to their family. On the one hand, the availability of remittances should have a positive impact on the education and health of children left behind. On the other hand, absent parents can no longer provide direct inputs, in terms of care and attention, into their children's welfare, likely having negative impacts on the welfare of those left behind.

Assessing the empirical relevance of these two channels is difficult. Researchers, as usual in the migration literature, must deal with the self-selection of migrants. In particular, if migration is costly, families with higher socioeconomic standing may be better able to afford its costs for one of their members. Thus, although it may appear that migration of a family member has improved the situation of the family remaining behind, rather it is the more well-off families that send someone abroad. If, on the other hand, family members from lower socioeconomic backgrounds migrate, then it will incorrectly appear that migration is to blame for the poor outcomes of those left behind.[b] The growing literature in this field uses various methodologies to deal with this selection issue, including the use of panel data, instrumental variables based on source country push factors and destination country pull factors, and even data from migration lotteries.

The consensus in the literature is that remittances do improve the outcomes of children left behind, but that parental absence also has negative consequences. The literature finds positive impacts of remittances in El Salvador, Mexico, and the Philippines (see Acosta 2011; Alcaraz, Chiquiar, and Salcedo 2012; Edwards and Ureta 2003; Yang 2008). Evidence on the net impact of remittances and parental absence is more mixed, but a general theme of the literature is that girls benefit more than boys.

For Mexico, McKenzie and Rapoport (2011) find a negative impact of migration on the schooling of older children, which they attribute to increased housework for girls and migration for boys. In contrast, Hanson and Woodruff (2003) and Antman (2012) find a positive impact on girls' educational attainment and no impact on boys', and Hildebrandt et al. (2005) find a positive impact on child health.

Much of the work focuses on paternal migration; Cortes (2015), looking at evidence from the Philippines, finds that maternal absence is more detrimental than paternal absence. An interesting observation is that migration also changes bargaining power in the families left behind—with the mother playing a much bigger role in household spending—which tends to benefit the girls in a family (see Antman 2011).[c]

a. See Antman (2013) and Démurger (2015) for recent literature reviews.

b. In this instance, the selection problems can get very complicated; see Gibson, McKenzie, and Stillman (2013).

c. A final channel through which migration affects children's outcomes is that the very prospect of migration changes the incentives to invest in education. For example, De Brauw and Giles (2016) find a negative relationship between internal migration opportunities and high school enrollment in China. See Gibson and McKenzie (2011) for a literature review of this phenomenon.

The evidence does, however, broadly suggest that immigrant children in schools have either no impact or a negative impact on native test scores and high school completion rates. Evidence from Denmark, Israel, Italy, Norway, and the United States suggests a negative impact of immigration on native schooling, as measured by test scores and school completion rates (Jensen and Rasmussen 2011; Gould, Lavy, and Paserman 2009; Ballatore, Fort, and Ichino 2015; Hunt 2016). In contrast, studies for the Netherlands and England find no negative impact (and the estimates are fairly precise) (Geay, McNally, and Telhaj 2013; Ohinata and van Ours 2013). No clear evidence exists about the circumstances in which immigrants do and do not harm the human capital acquisition of native-born school children. What is clear is that governments frequently devote insufficient public resources to mitigating negative spillovers from the presence of immigrants in schools.

There is another mechanism, however, by which immigrants can alter the educational attainment of native-born individuals. In the United States, high school–aged youth are often the demographic most in competition with low-skilled immigrant labor. Low-skilled immigration can incentivize youth to stay in school for two reasons. First, the increased labor supply will push down wages for currently available jobs. And, second, the decreased wages increase the relative benefit of accumulating human capital (by staying in school).

Smith (2012) investigates the decline of youth employment and its relationship to low-skilled immigration. He finds that low-skilled (less than high school) immigration decreases youth employment by three times as much as it decreases employment of similarly skilled adults. Additionally, the decline is strongest for those employed while in school.

Female labor force participation

A recurring theme in this book is that, although the impact of immigration on average wages is likely small, certain industries can see substantial impacts. Two such industries are childcare and housekeeping. Immigrant labor decreases the cost, and increases the quality, of household services. These changes, in turn, free up native-born women—especially the high-skilled—to increase their supply of labor and plausibly change their fertility decisions as well.

Suggestive evidence for Italy, Spain, and the United States shows that an increase in low-skilled female immigrants in a region decreases the cost of childcare (Barone and Mocetti 2011; Farré, González, and Ortega 2011; Furtado 2016). To illustrate these results, figure 4.20, from Furtado (2015), shows the relationship between changes in the share of low-skilled immigrants and changes in log median wages for childcare workers in metropolitan areas of the United States. A clear negative relationship exists: cities receiving more immigrants also had the smallest increases in median childcare wages. Note that this correlation persists despite the fact that immigrants tend to migrate to U.S. cities that experience wage growth.

The arrival of immigrants increases purchases of household services in the United States and reduces the time that women at the top of the wage distribution spend on household chores (Cortes and Tessada 2011). Similarly, in Australia, Germany, Italy, Spain, Switzerland, and the United Kingdom, more immigration results in an increase in the labor supply of high-skilled women (Barone and Mocetti 2011; Farré, González, and Ortega 2011; Forlani, Lodigiani, and Mendolicchio 2015). Focusing specifically on the role of foreign-born domestic workers, Cortes and Pan (2013) analyze a policy that rapidly increased the availability of visas for domestic workers in Hong Kong SAR, China, in the late 1970s. They find that this policy substantially increased labor supply among medium- and high-skilled native-born female workers.[12]

Figure 4.20   Low-skilled immigration and changing childcare costs, by U.S. city

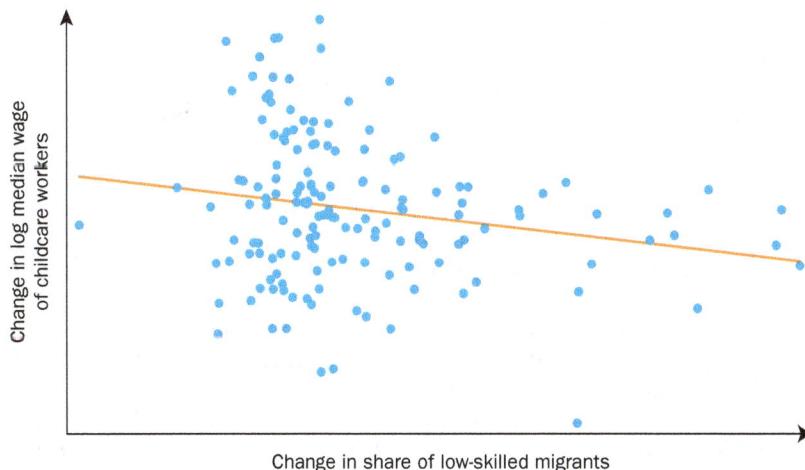

Source: Furtado 2015. Reproduced with permission; further permission required for reuse.

Note: Each dot represents a U.S. metropolitan area.

In practice, reduced childcare costs, due to the arrival of immigrants engaged in household services, increase female native labor supply. In principle, this need not be the case. One reason female labor supply may actually fall—labor market causes apart—is that native-born women may decide to have more children as it becomes cheaper to do so. Not much evidence exists on the plausibility of this mechanism; however, Furtado (2016) does find that college-educated women in the United States increasingly bear children in response to immigration flows.

Notes

1. Recent surveys include Borjas (2014), Anderson (2015), and Abramitzky and Boustan (2016).
2. See Dustmann et al. (2016), who focus on individuals of working age (between 26 and 64 years old) not in full education or military service. The authors define refugees as those migrants who report "international protection" as the reason for migration.
3. The EU15 are the countries in the European Union prior to the accession of ten candidate countries on May 1, 2004. The 15 are Austria, Belgium, Denmark, Finland, France, Germany, Greece, Ireland, Italy, Luxembourg, the Netherlands, Portugal, Spain, Sweden, and the United Kingdom.
4. Here we use educational content as the measure of occupational quality: the share of individuals who have undergraduate and graduate degrees in an occupation.
5. The extensive literature on earnings trends within and across immigrant cohorts in the United States includes Douglas (1919) and Abramitzky, Boustan, and Eriksson (2014) using evidence from the Age of Mass Migration; for later periods it includes LaLonde and Topel (1992), Baker and Benjamin (1994), Schoeni (1997), and Borjas (2015). Multicountry evidence comes from Antecol, Kuhn, and Trejo (2006). On refugees, see also Cortes (2004), who focuses on the particularly successful integration of Indo-Chinese refugees in the United States; Bevelander and Pendakur (2014) for Canada; and Luik, Emilsson, and Bevelander (2016) for Sweden. A striking example of the lack of refugee assimilation comes from Bratsberg, Raaum, and Røed (2014), who highlight that refugees in Norway become increasingly dependent on social insurance transfers.
6. Other studies using panel data to understand immigrant assimilation in different countries include Hu (2000); Edin, Lalonde, and Åslund (2000); Constant and Massey (2003); and Eckstein and Weiss (2004).
7. The dissimilarity index can be interpreted as the share of immigrant households that would need to move such that each neighborhood would reflect the overall immigrant share in the population. In the context of racial segregation, a dissimilarity index of 35 is considered low, whereas an index value of 55 is considered moderate (Abramitzky and Boustan 2016).

8. Countries in which refugees have, in practice, no route to formal labor market access include Bangladesh, Ethiopia, India, Jordan, Kenya, Lebanon, Sudan, Thailand, Turkey, República Bolivariana de Venezuela, and Zambia. Countries that have a clear route to formal labor market access include Australia, Canada, Ecuador, the Islamic Republic of Iran, Iraq, Pakistan, South Africa, Uganda, the United States, and all Western European countries (World Bank 2017a).

9. IRCA granted full legal status (amnesty) to undocumented immigrants who had arrived before 1982 and had resided within the United States continuously, as well as to certain undocumented seasonal agricultural workers. DACA, in contrast, provided temporary but renewable legal status (including work permits) for undocumented immigrants who arrived before their 16th birthday and prior to June 2007; are either currently in school, high school graduates, or honorably discharged from the military; are under the age of 31 as of June 15, 2012; and have not been convicted of a felony, significant misdemeanor, or three other misdemeanors, or otherwise pose a threat to national security.

10. A number of studies—including (Dustmann 1996, 1997, 2003); Dustmann and Weiss (2007); Thom (2010); Adda, Dustmann, and Görlach (2016); and Görlach (2016)—develop models of temporary migration in which migrants working abroad acquire additional skills that are rewarded in the home country. Reinhold and Thom (2013); De Coulon and Piracha (2005); Co, Gang, and Yun (2000); and Barrett and Goggin (2010) find that Mexican, Albanian, Hungarian, and Irish return migrants, respectively, command a wage premium. Lacuesta (2006) attributes the gains to Mexican return migrants to selection.

11. The complexity index is increasing in communication and cognitive content and decreasing in manual content of occupations.

12. Similarly, Suen (1994) and Chan (2006) for Hong Kong SAR, China, and Tan and Gibson (2013) for Malaysia find that the increased availability of household workers increases female labor force participation.

References

Abramitzky, R., and L. P. Boustan. 2016. "Immigration in American Economic History." NBER Working Paper 21882, National Bureau of Economic Research, Cambridge, MA.

Abramitzky, R., L. P. Boustan, and K. Eriksson. 2014. "A Nation of Immigrants: Assimilation and Economic Outcomes in the Age of Mass Migration." *Journal of Political Economy* 122 (3): 467–506.

———. 2016. "To the New World and Back Again: Return Migrants in the Age of Mass Migration." NBER Working Paper 22659, National Bureau of Economic Research, Cambridge, MA.

Acosta, P. 2011. "School Attendance, Child Labour, and Remittances from International Migration in El Salvador." *Journal of Development Studies* 47 (6): 913–36.

Adda, J., C. Dustmann, and J. S. Görlach. 2016. "The Dynamics of Return Migration, Human Capital Accumulation, and Wage Assimilation." Unpublished manuscript.

Adsera, A., and B. R. Chiswick. 2007. "Are There Gender and Country of Origin Differences in Immigrant Labor Market Outcomes across European Destinations?" *Journal of Population Economics* 20 (3): 495.

Alcaraz, C., D. Chiquiar, and A. Salcedo. 2012. "Remittances, Schooling, and Child Labor in Mexico." *Journal of Development Economics* 97 (1): 156–65.

Amuedo-Dorantes, C., and F. Antman. 2016. "Can Authorization Reduce Poverty among Undocumented Immigrants? Evidence from the Deferred Action for Childhood Arrivals Program." *Economics Letters* 147: 1–4.

———. 2017. "Schooling and Labor Market Effects of Temporary Authorization: Evidence from DACA." *Journal of Population Economics* 30 (1): 339–73.

Amuedo-Dorantes, C., and C. Bansak. 2011. "The Impact of Amnesty on Labor Market Outcomes: A Panel Study Using the Legalized Population Survey." *Industrial Relations: A Journal of Economy and Society* 50 (3): 443–71.

Anderson, K. H. 2015. "Can Immigrants Ever Earn as Much as Native Workers?" IZA World of Labor, article no. 159. https://wol.iza.org/articles/can-immigrants-ever-earn-as-much-as-native-workers/long.

Angrist, J. D., and A. D. Kugler. 2003. "Protective or Counter-Productive? Labour Market Institutions and the Effect of Immigration on EU Natives." *Economic Journal* 113 (488): F302–F331.

Antecol, H., P. Kuhn, and S. J. Trejo. 2006. "Assimilation via Prices or Quantities? Sources of Immigrant Earnings Growth in Australia, Canada, and the United States." *Journal of Human Resources* 41 (4): 821–40.

Antman, F. 2011. "International Migration and Gender Discrimination among Children Left Behind." *American Economic Review* 101 (3): 645–49.

Antman, F. M. 2012. "Gender, Educational Attainment, and the Impact of Parental Migration on Children Left Behind." *Journal of Population Economics* 25 (4): 1187–214.

———. 2013. "The Impact of Migration on Family Left Behind." In *International Handbook on the Economics of Migration*, edited by Amelie F. Constant and Klaus F. Zimmerman, 293–308. Cheltenham, U.K.: Edward Elgar Publishing.

Artuc, E., and C. Ozden. Forthcoming. "Transit Migration: All Roads Lead to America." *Economic Journal.*

Baker, M., and D. Benjamin. 1994. "The Performance of Immigrants in the Canadian Labor Market." *Journal of Labor Economics* 12 (3): 369–405.

Baker, S. R. 2015. "Effects of Immigrant Legalization on Crime." *American Economic Review* 105 (5): 210–13.

Ballatore, R. M., M. Fort, and A. Ichino. 2015. "The Tower of Babel in the Classroom: Immigrants and Natives in Italian Schools." CEPR Discussion Paper 10341, Centre for Economic Policy Research, London.

Barone, G., and S. Mocetti. 2011. "With a Little Help from Abroad: The Effect of Low-Skilled Immigration on the Female Labour Supply." *Labour Economics* 18 (5): 664–75.

Barrett, A., and J. Goggin. 2010. "Returning to the Question of a Wage Premium for Returning Migrants." *National Institute Economic Review* 213 (1): R43–R51.

Bevelander, P., and R. Pendakur. 2014. "The Labour Market Integration of Refugee and Family Reunion Immigrants: A Comparison of Outcomes in Canada and Sweden." *Journal of Ethnic and Migration Studies* 40 (5): 689–709.

Bijwaard, G. E., and J. Wahba. 2014. "Do High-Income or Low-Income Immigrants Leave Faster?" *Journal of Development Economics* 108: 54–68.

Blau, F. D. 2015. "Immigrants and Gender Roles: Assimilation vs. Culture." *IZA Journal of Migration* 4 (1): 23.

Bleakley, H., and A. Chin. 2004. "Language Skills and Earnings: Evidence from Childhood Immigrants." *Review of Economics and Statistics* 86 (2): 481–96.

———. 2010. "Age at Arrival, English Proficiency, and Social Assimilation among U.S. Immigrants." *American Economic Journal. Applied Economics* 2 (1): 165.

Borjas, G. J. 1985. "Assimilation, Changes in Cohort Quality, and the Earnings of Immigrants." *Journal of Labor Economics* 3 (4): 463–89.

———. 2014. *Immigration Economics*. Cambridge, MA: Harvard University Press.

———. 2015. "The Slowdown in the Economic Assimilation of Immigrants: Aging and Cohort Effects Revisited Again." *Journal of Human Capital* 9 (4): 483–517.

———. 2016. *We Wanted Workers: Unraveling the Immigration Narrative.* New York: W.W. Norton.

———. 2017a. "The Earnings of Undocumented Immigrants." NBER Working Paper 23236, National Bureau of Economic Research, Cambridge, MA.

———. 2017b. "The Labor Supply of Undocumented Immigrants." *Labour Economics* 46: 1–13.

Borjas, G., and B. Bratsberg. 1996. "Who Leaves? The Outmigration of the Foreign-Born." *Review of Economics and Statistics* 78 (1): 165–76.

Bratsberg, B., O. Raaum, and K. Røed. 2014. "Immigrants, Labour Market Performance and Social Insurance." *Economic Journal* 124 (580): F644–F683.

Cattaneo, C., C. V. Fiorio, and G. Peri. 2015. "What Happens to the Careers of European Workers When Immigrants 'Take Their Jobs'?" *Journal of Human Resources* 50 (3): 655–93.

Chan, A. H. N. 2006. "The Effects of Full-Time Domestic Workers on Married Women's Economic Activity Status in Hong Kong, 1981–2001." *International Sociology* 21 (1): 133–59.

Chiswick, B. R. 1978. "The Effect of Americanization on the Earnings of Foreign-Born Men." *Journal of Political Economy* 86 (5): 897–921.

Chiswick, B. R., and P. W. Miller. 2010. "Occupational Language Requirements and the Value of English in the U.S. Labor Market." *Journal of Population Economics* 23 (1): 353–72.

Co, C. Y., I. N. Gang, and M. S. Yun. 2000. "Returns to Returning." *Journal of Population Economics* 13 (1): 57–79.

Constant, A., and D. S. Massey. 2003. "Self-Selection, Earnings, and Out-Migration: A Longitudinal Study of Immigrants to Germany." *Journal of Population Economics* 16 (4): 631–53.

Cortes, K. E. 2004. "Are Refugees Different from Economic Immigrants? Some Empirical Evidence on the Heterogeneity of Immigrant Groups in the United States." *Review of Economics and Statistics* 86 (2): 465–80.

Cortes, K. E. 2013. "Achieving the DREAM: The Effect of IRCA on Immigrant Youth Postsecondary Educational Access." *American Economic Review* 103 (3): 428–32.

———. 2015. "The Feminization of International Migration and Its Effects on the Children Left Behind: Evidence from the Philippines." *World Development* 65: 62–78.

Cortes, P., and J. Pan. 2013. "Outsourcing Household Production: Foreign Domestic Workers and Native Labor Supply in Hong Kong." *Journal of Labor Economics* 31 (2): 327–71.

Cortes, P., and J. Tessada. 2011. "Low-Skilled Immigration and the Labor Supply of Highly Skilled Women." *American Economic Journal: Applied Economics* 3 (3): 88–123.

Cutler, D. M., E. L. Glaeser, and J. L. Vigdor. 2008. "Is the Melting Pot Still Hot? Explaining the Resurgence of Immigrant Segregation." *Review of Economics and Statistics* 90 (3): 478–97.

D'Amuri, F., and G. Peri. 2014. "Immigration, Jobs, and Employment Protection: Evidence from Europe before and during the Great Recession." *Journal of the European Economic Association* 12 (2): 432–64.

Damm, A. P. 2009. "Ethnic Enclaves and Immigrant Labor Market Outcomes: Quasi-Experimental Evidence." *Journal of Labor Economics* 27 (2): 281–314.

De Brauw, A., and J. Giles. 2016. "Migrant Opportunity and the Educational Attainment of Youth in Rural China." *Journal of Human Resources* 52 (1): 272–311.

De Coulon, A., and M. Piracha. 2005. "Self-Selection and the Performance of Return Migrants: The Source Country Perspective." *Journal of Population Economics* 18 (4): 779–807.

Del Carpio, X. V., and M. C. Wagner. 2016. "The Impact of Syrian Refugees on the Turkish Labor Market." Policy Research Working Paper 7402, World Bank, Washington, DC.

Démurger, S. 2015. "Migration and Families Left Behind." IZA World of Labor, article no. 144. https://wol.iza.org/articles/migration-and-families-left-behind/long.

Douglas, P. H. 1919. "Is the New Immigration More Unskilled than the Old?" *Quarterly Publications of the American Statistical Association* 16 (126): 393–403.

Dustmann, C. 1996. "Return Migration: The European Experience." *Economic Policy* 11 (22): 213–50.

———. 1997. "Return Migration, Uncertainty and Precautionary Savings." *Journal of Development Economics* 52 (2): 295–316.

———. 2003. "Return Migration, Wage Differentials, and the Optimal Migration Duration." *European Economic Review* 47 (2): 353–69.

Dustmann, C., I. Fadlon, and Y. Weiss. 2011. "Return Migration, Human Capital Accumulation and the Brain Drain." *Journal of Development Economics* 95 (1): 58–67.

Dustmann, C., F. Fasani, T. Frattini, L. Minale, and U. Schönberg. 2016. "The Economics and Politics of Refugee Migration." CESifo Working Paper Series No. 6111, CESifo Group, Munich.

Dustmann, C., and J. S. Görlach. 2016. "The Economics of Temporary Migrations." *Journal of Economic Literature* 54 (1): 98–136.

Dustmann, C., and Y. Weiss. 2007. "Return Migration: Theory and Empirical Evidence from the UK." *British Journal of Industrial Relations* 45 (2): 236–56.

Eckstein, Z., and Y. Weiss. 2004. "On the Wage Growth of Immigrants: Israel, 1990–2000." *Journal of the European Economic Association* 2 (4): 665–95.

Edin, P. A., P. Fredriksson, and O. Åslund. 2003. "Ethnic Enclaves and the Economic Success of Immigrants—Evidence from a Natural Experiment." *Quarterly Journal of Economics* 118 (1): 329–57.

Edin, P. A., R. J. LaLonde, and O. Åslund. 2000. "Emigration of Immigrants and Measures of Immigrant Assimilation: Evidence from Sweden." Working Paper 2000:13, Uppsala University, Department of Economics, Uppsala, Sweden.

Edwards, A. C., and M. Ureta. 2003. "International Migration, Remittances, and Schooling: Evidence from El Salvador." *Journal of Development Economics* 72 (2): 429–61.

Farré, L., L. González, and F. Ortega. 2011. "Immigration, Family Responsibilities and the Labor Supply of Skilled Native Women." *BE Journal of Economic Analysis & Policy* 11 (1): 1–48.

Foged, M., and G. Peri. 2016. "Immigrants' Effect on Native Workers: New Analysis on Longitudinal Data." *American Economic Journal: Applied Economics* 8 (2): 1–34.

Forlani, E., E. Lodigiani, and C. Mendolicchio. 2015. "Impact of Low-Skilled Immigration on Female Labour Supply." *Scandinavian Journal of Economics* 117 (2): 452–92.

Furtado, D. 2015. "Immigrant Labor and Work-Family Decisions of Native-Born Women." IZA World of Labor, article no. 139. https://wol.iza.org/articles/immigrant-labor-and-work-family-decisions-of-native-born-women/long.

———. 2016. "Fertility Responses of High-Skilled Native Women to Immigrant Inflows." *Demography* 53 (1): 27–53.

Geay, C., S. McNally, and S. Telhaj. 2013. "Non-native Speakers of English in the Classroom: What Are the Effects on Pupil Performance?" *Economic Journal* 123 (570): F281–F307.

Gibson, J., and D. McKenzie. 2011. "Eight Questions about Brain Drain." *Journal of Economic Perspectives* 25 (3): 107–28.

Gibson, J., D. McKenzie, and S. Stillman. 2013. "Accounting for Selectivity and Duration-Dependent Heterogeneity when Estimating the Impact of Emigration on Incomes and Poverty in Sending Areas." *Economic Development and Cultural Change* 61 (2): 247–80.

Görlach, J. S. 2016. "Borrowing Constraints, Migrant Selection, and the Dynamics of Return and Repeat Migration." Working paper. http://www.ucl.ac.uk/~uctpjgo/GorlachJobMarketPaper.pdf.

Gould, E. D., V. Lavy, and M. Daniele Paserman. 2009. "Does Immigration Affect the Long-Term Educational Outcomes of Natives? Quasi-Experimental Evidence." *Economic Journal* 119 (540): 1243–69.

Hanson, G. H., and C. Woodruff. 2003. "Emigration and Educational Attainment in Mexico." Preliminary working paper, University of California at San Diego.

Hayfron, J. E. 2001. "Language Training, Language Proficiency, and Earnings of Immigrants in Norway." *Applied Economics* 33 (15): 1971–79.

Hildebrandt, N., D. J. McKenzie, G. Esquivel, and E. Schargrodsky. 2005. "The Effects of Migration on Child Health in Mexico [with comments]." *Economia* 6 (1): 257–89.

Hu, W.-Y. 2000, "Immigrant Earnings Assimilation: Estimates from Longitudinal Data." *American Economic Review* 90 (2): 368–72.

Hunt, J. 2016. "The Impact of Immigration on the Educational Attainment of Natives." *Journal of Human Resources*, September 2, 0115-6913R1.

Jensen, P., and A. W. Rasmussen. 2011. "The Effect of Immigrant Concentration in Schools on Native and Immigrant Children's Reading and Math Skills." *Economics of Education Review* 30 (6): 1503–15.

Kossoudji, S. A., and D. A. Cobb-Clark. 2002. "Coming Out of the Shadows: Learning about Legal Status and Wages from the Legalized Population." *Journal of Labor Economics* 20 (3): 598–628.

Lacuesta, A. 2006. "Emigration and Human Capital: Who Leaves, Who Comes Back and What Difference Does It Make?" Banco de España Research Paper No. WP-0620, Banco de España, Madrid, August 30.

Lafortune, J., and J. Tessada. 2014. "Smooth(er) Landing? The Dynamic Role of Networks in the Location and Occupational Choice of Immigrants." ClioLab Working Paper 14, EH Clio Lab, Instituto de Economía, Pontificia Universidad Católica de Chile.

LaLonde, R. J., and R. H. Topel. 1992. "The Assimilation of Immigrants in the U.S. Labor Market." In *Immigration and the Workforce: Economic Consequences for the United States and Source Areas*, edited by George J. Borjas and Richard B. Freeman, 67–92. Chicago: University of Chicago Press.

Liebig, T. 2007. "The Labour Market Integration of Immigrants in Denmark." OECD Social, Employment, and Migration Working Paper 50, OECD Publishing, Paris. http://dx.doi.org/10.1787/233783261534.

Lubotsky, D. 2007. "Chutes or Ladders? A Longitudinal Analysis of Immigrant Earnings." *Journal of Political Economy* 115 (5): 820–67.

Luik, M. A., H. Emilsson, and P. Bevelander. 2016. "Explaining the Male Native–Immigrant Employment Gap in Sweden: The Role of Human Capital and Migrant Categories." IZA Discussion Paper 9943, Institute for the Study of Labor, Bonn.

Mastrobuoni, G., and P. Pinotti. 2015. "Legal Status and the Criminal Activity of Immigrants." *American Economic Journal: Applied Economics* 7 (2): 175–206.

Mattoo, A., I. C. Neagu, and Ç. Ozden. 2012. "Performance of Skilled Migrants in the U.S.: A Dynamic Approach." *Regional Science and Urban Economics* 42 (5): 829–43.

McKenzie, D., and H. Rapoport. 2011. "Can Migration Reduce Educational Attainment? Evidence from Mexico." *Journal of Population Economics* 24 (4): 1331–58.

Mesnard, A. 2004. "Temporary Migration and Capital Market Imperfections." *Oxford Economic Papers* 56 (2): 242–62.

Munshi, K. 2003. "Networks in the Modern Economy: Mexican Migrants in the U.S. Labor Market." *Quarterly Journal of Economics* 118 (2): 549–99.

National Academies of Sciences, Engineering, and Medicine. 2017. *The Economic and Fiscal Consequences of Immigration*. Washington, DC: National Academies Press. https://doi.org/10.17226/23550.

OECD (Organisation for Economic Co-operation and Development). 2012. *Untapped Skills: Realising the Potential of Immigrant Students*. Paris: OECD Publishing.

———. 2014. *International Migration Outlook 2014.* Paris: OECD Publishing.

Ohinata, A., and J. C. van Ours. 2013. "How Immigrant Children Affect the Academic Achievement of Native Dutch Children." *Economic Journal* 123 (570): F308–F331.

Ozden, Ç., and M. C. Wagner. 2014. "Immigrant versus Natives? Displacement and Job Creation." Policy Research Working Paper 6900, World Bank, Washington, DC.

Peri, G., and C. Sparber. 2009. "Task Specialization, Immigration, and Wages." *American Economic Journal: Applied Economics* 1 (3): 135–69.

Pinotti, P. 2017. "Clicking on Heaven's Door: The Effect of Immigrant Legalization on Crime." *American Economic Review* 107 (1): 138–68.

Pope, N. G. 2016. "The Effects of DACAmentation: The Impact of Deferred Action for Childhood Arrivals on Unauthorized Immigrants." *Journal of Public Economics* 143 (November): 98–114.

Reinhold, S., and K. Thom. 2013. "Migration Experience and Earnings in the Mexican Labor Market." *Journal of Human Resources* 48 (3): 768–820.

Rivera-Batiz, F. L. 1999. "Undocumented Workers in the Labor Market: An Analysis of the Earnings of Legal and Illegal Mexican Immigrants in the United States." *Journal of Population Economics* 12 (1): 91–116.

Schoeni, R. F. 1997. "New Evidence on the Economic Progress of Foreign-Born Men in the 1970s and 1980s." *Journal of Human Resources* 32 (4): 683–740.

Smith, C. L. 2012. "The Impact of Low-Skilled Immigration on the Youth Labor Market." *Journal of Labor Economics* 30 (1): 55–89.

Suen, W. 1994. "Market-Procured Housework: The Demand for Domestic Servants and Female Labor Supply." *Labour Economics* 1 (3): 289–302.

Tan, P. L., and J. Gibson. 2013. "Impact of Foreign Maids on Female Labor Force Participation in Malaysia." *Asian Economic Journal* 27 (2): 163–83.

Thom, K. 2010. "Repeated Circular Migration: Theory and Evidence from Undocumented Migrants." Working paper, New York University.

Wahba, J., and Y. Zenou. 2012. "Out of Sight, Out of Mind: Migration, Entrepreneurship and Social Capital." *Regional Science and Urban Economics* 42 (5): 890–903.

World Bank. 2017a. *Forcibly Displaced: Toward a Development Approach Supporting Refugees, the Internally Displaced, and Their Hosts.* Washington, DC: World Bank.

———. 2017b. *Migrating to Opportunity: Overcoming Barriers to Labor Mobility in Southeast Asia.* Washington, DC: World Bank.

Yang, D. 2008. "International Migration, Remittances and Household Investment: Evidence from Philippine Migrants' Exchange Rate Shocks." *Economic Journal* 118 (528): 591–630.

CHAPTER FIVE

High-Skilled Migration

High-skilled migration occupies a special and sometimes controversial place in the policy debate and academic literature on migration. High-skilled workers play a unique role in today's economy. They are innovators, entrepreneurs, scientists, and teachers. They lead, coordinate, and manage activities of other high-skilled people in complex organizations—from multinational corporations to research centers to governments. They are also highly mobile, moving between jobs and geographic locations. High-income destination countries depend on foreign talent to create and sustain many of their leading economic sectors, including many of those that are at the forefront of knowledge creation and economic growth. Low-income countries, which already suffer from human capital shortages, fear the impact of high-skilled emigration, often referred to as "brain drain," on their economic growth and productivity, public finances, and delivery of key services such as health care and education. It is not surprising that the global mobility of talent is a major policy concern entangled with the gains from globalization as well as its pitfalls.

This chapter has three main goals. First, we present the key patterns of skilled migration observed over time and across a range of origin and destination countries. Second, we discuss the labor market causes and implications of these patterns. More specifically, we present some of the key insights on their implications for economic welfare in both source and destination countries. Finally, we compare various policies implemented by source and destination countries as they try to influence these patterns to attract talent in global labor markets.

Several key patterns emerge immediately when we analyze high-skilled migration. The first and most obvious pattern is the speed with which skilled migration has been growing, especially relative to the pace of overall migration. This is due to both increased demand for skills and increased supply of young tertiary-educated professionals across the world. Second, a significant share of these migrants end up in just four countries—Australia, Canada, the United Kingdom, and the United States—even though they come from a broad base of origin countries. Third, emigration of highly skilled women is increasing faster than that of men.

Many of these patterns are unique to the highly skilled. The significant concentration of skills in just a few countries—actually in certain geographic areas within these countries—cannot be fully explained by simple demand and supply models. Productivity spillovers and agglomeration effects, unique to high-skilled occupations and sectors, are likely to be driving these processes as many studies attest.

The impact of high-skilled migration on origin and destination countries is also the source of intense academic and political debate. Yet these debates are not based on compelling evidence; this is one area where there is clear need for extensive and more detailed research. Although the economic losses associated with high-skilled emigration can potentially be damaging for low-income origin countries, these countries can also benefit from several compensating mechanisms. Remittances sent by emigrants or diaspora externalities via increased global integration in product and capital markets can be significant. Migrants returning home with professional expertise, technical knowledge, and financial capital can create new jobs, wealth, and economic growth for their communities. Whether the gains of high-skilled emigration outweigh the costs depends on many factors and may depend on the origin country.

The main beneficiaries of skilled migration, along with the migrants themselves, are the destination countries. In addition to meeting supply shortages in labor markets for high-skilled occupations, destination countries enjoy the positive spillovers created by a more educated and skilled labor force. The potential still exists, of course, for many high-skilled native-born workers to be squeezed out of their jobs with the arrival of migrants, especially in sectors where the employment capacity or output demand is rigid. However, from information technology to finance, from entertainment and professional sports to education, the evidence on this issue is quite compelling. Many sectors at the knowledge frontier, including many high-tech sectors, would simply not exist in their current form without high-skilled migrants.

Despite these perceptions, however, many questions on the issues surrounding high-skilled migration, from its extent to its impact to appropriate policy responses, remain unanswered. Many destination countries aim to design their policies to attract and retain high-skilled workers, but the evidence is also thin on their effectiveness. In addition to the difficulties associated with quantifying policies for empirical analysis, governments tend not to share certain data, on various security and confidentiality grounds, making rigorous analysis almost impossible.

Defining a high-skilled migrant

Before discussing the determinants and impact of high-skilled immigration, the actual definition of a high-skilled immigrant deserves more careful attention. The discussion in this book so far assumes that high skilled and tertiary educated are synonymous. An extensive labor economics literature discusses what constitutes "skills" and how various measures of human capital differ from formal education in the labor markets context (see, for example, Acemoglu and Autor 2011). Most studies equate education to skills, mainly because of data availability. And these studies generally classify a high-skilled immigrant as someone with tertiary-level education and living in a country other than his or her place of birth. Most of the available cross-country data are compiled and disseminated according to this classification (Docquier and Rapoport 2012). Approaching this question from a policy perspective, Parsons et al. (2015) argue that there is a discord over how statistical offices, policy makers, and academics view and differentiate high-skilled migrants. They compare several common definitions used in the academic sphere with those based on occupational attainment levels and income level (two measures especially prevalent in the policy context). Taking the United States as an example, they illustrate that, of the 12 million migrants with some tertiary education in the country, only slightly more than a million would be considered high-skilled if a *combined* measure based on educational attainment, occupational attainment, and income levels was used.

The occupational distribution of tertiary-educated immigrants in major Organisation for Economic Co-operation and Development (OECD) destination countries is reported in table 5.1. The first two data columns of the table listing the educational distribution of immigrants for each occupation identify the discordance put forth by Parsons et al. (2015). The last column shows that very few tertiary-educated native-born individuals work in occupations considered "unskilled," such as craft and related

Table 5.1   Occupational distribution of immigrant and native-born workers, by education, 2010

Occupation	Immigrants		Natives	
	Nontertiary (%)	Tertiary (%)	Nontertiary (%)	Tertiary (%)
Managers	4.9	11.1	5.6	11.2
Professionals	2.8	36.0	4.0	44.0
Technicians and associate professionals	8.3	16.9	13.9	21.8
Clerical support workers	8.0	8.6	13.2	8.6
Services and sales workers	20.7	11.0	20.3	6.9
Skilled agriculture, forestry, and fishery	1.6	0.5	4.0	1.0
Craft and related trades	17.5	4.7	16.2	2.6
Plant and machine operators	10.5	3.4	9.4	1.4
Elementary occupations	24.7	6.9	11.9	1.5
Armed forces and unknown occupations	1.1	1.0	1.6	1.1

Source: Organisation for Economic Co-operation and Development (OECD) Database on Immigrants in OECD and Non-OECD Countries (DIOC-E) 2010/2011 Dataset.

Note: Figures do not add up to 100 percent; the remaining share represents those with an unknown educational attainment level. Data not available for Japan, New Zealand, and the United States. Other countries excluded are Chile, the Czech Republic, Estonia, Mexico, the Slovak Republic, and Slovenia. Data include workers aged 15 years and older.

trades, plant and machine operators, and elementary occupations. In contrast, almost 15 percent of tertiary-educated migrants are in these occupations (second data column), which relates closely to the issue of brain waste, highlighted by Mattoo, Neagu, and Ozden (2008). Another useful comparison is in occupations for which a tertiary education is likely to be a requirement, such as managerial, professional, and associate professional occupations. Note that a large number of non-tertiary-educated migrants and native-born individuals actually work in these occupations. Clearly, using alternative measures of "high skilled" would likely lead to a more nuanced picture than the one portrayed by focusing only on education levels.

Another potential distortion to high-skilled migration data is caused by an important data constraint—the location of education of immigrants. Most migration datasets do not contain information on where the migrant was educated because their original sources—censuses and labor force surveys—do not collect such data (please see the appendix on the sources and construction of such migration datasets). If we were to compare education to international trade, this would be akin to not knowing where different components of a car are manufactured. However, in modern production chains, engines, tires, and electronic systems are manufactured in different locations, on the basis of comparative advantage. The location of the car's final assembly is not necessarily the place where most value added occurs or the product is consumed. Understanding the economic implications of international trade requires a clearer picture of the production chain. The same logic applies to acquisition of education and high-skilled immigration. Many people obtain different "components" of their education in different locations and then are employed in a completely different country. Effective policy design requires a clear picture of educational location decisions of migrants.

The most important complication in data collection and analysis arises with people who are born in one country and who then migrate with their parents to another country as children and subsequently complete their education in that destination country. Even though they appear as high-skilled migrants in migration statistics, their human capital will be acquired in the country where they live and work. Many additional people migrate for educational purposes, mostly completing the final stages of their education in high-income countries. These types of high-skilled emigrants need to be differentiated from those who complete their education in their birth countries and then emigrate. The economic and fiscal impact of these different types of emigration will also be different. Such differences not only create important biases in skilled migration numbers but also have important implications for policy design.

Ozden and Phillips (2015) consider the example of African doctors to illustrate the importance of the distinction between place of birth and place of education. They show that only 60 percent of African-born doctors were actually educated in Africa. The rest were educated in OECD countries, after arriving there as children or students. About 10 percent of African-educated doctors were not even born in Africa, but moved there for medical training. To complicate matters, significant variation exists across African countries with respect to these shares. Appropriate policy design would be impossible without taking these distinctions into account.

An alternative, based on an approach similar to that of Beine, Docquier, and Rapoport (2010), consists of computing the shares of those who entered the United States by age 22 (the standard age of completion of college education) among tertiary-educated immigrants. Table 5.2 shows that close to two-thirds of high-skilled immigrants from many origin countries, mostly those from the Caribbean, entered the United States before the age of 22. For geographically more distant and larger Asian

Table 5.2   Tertiary-educated immigrants in the United States, ages 25–65, 2000 and 2010

Birthplace	2000		2010	
	Total stock	Entered United States when age 22 or younger (%)	Total stock	Entered United States when age 22 or younger (%)
India	566,484	25.8	1,098,625	24.8
Philippines	506,912	26.8	702,063	29.2
China	323,468	22.7	508,855	25.6
Mexico	272,449	49.1	501,114	48.5
United Kingdom	217,582	44.6	249,536	42.4
Jamaica	77,463	60.6	124,447	61.9
Brazil	51,474	26.1	95,791	28.9
Dominican Republic	49,429	43.8	91,562	47.8
Haiti	43,976	55.2	73,338	56.3
Guyana	27,336	51.0	49,974	57.3

Source: Calculated using data from the American Community Survey.

countries, those shares are considerably lower. Nevertheless, even for those countries, the share of migrants who are most likely to have completed their education in the United States varies between 22 and 45 percent. The countries in table 5.2 are some of the largest immigrant-sending countries to the United States, and all these migrants would normally be considered high-skilled emigrants if we looked only at place-of-birth criteria. One may assume that other popular destinations, such as Australia, Canada, and the United Kingdom, exhibit similar patterns. These large gaps imply that more detailed data need to be collected on the educational and professional paths of high-skilled migrants. It also suggests that simple measures of high-skilled emigration vastly overstate the extent and impact of high-skilled emigration in some cases.

Patterns of high-skilled migration

One of the main themes of this report has been that the overall level of global migration has stayed relatively stable. Beneath this stability, however, several key patterns emerge, and high-skilled migration plays a prominent role in this process. The main distinctive features of high-skilled migration can be summarized in three main points.

First, high-skilled migration has rapidly increased over the past two decades, far outpacing overall migration. Second, high-skilled immigrants are very concentrated in a few OECD destination countries, even though they now come from a broader set of origin countries. This concentration is evident not just across destination countries but also within these countries because immigrants tend to be more highly concentrated in large cities and within certain occupations when compared to natives. Finally, the rise in skilled migration has been especially salient among women, who now constitute the majority of all high-skilled immigrants in OECD countries. This final point will likely have important long-term social and economic repercussions in the developing countries from which these highly skilled women emigrate.

High-skilled migration has increased at extraordinary rates since the 1990s. A vast majority of high-skilled immigrants move to OECD countries (Artuç et al. 2015) because these countries have high returns to human capital, provide superior career opportunities, and implement immigration policies to attract a skilled workforce. For this reason, and because of the availability of higher-quality data, most of our analysis in this chapter will be based on OECD destinations.

Figure 5.1 compares aggregate immigrant stocks by education level for a set of 27 OECD destination countries over time. Overall immigrant stocks have increased over time, and a disproportionate share of the increase has come from high-skilled migration. The stock of primary-educated migrants grew by only about 50 percent from 1990 to 2010, whereas the stock of tertiary-educated migrants more than tripled over the same period. Central to this increase has been the role of non-OECD origin countries. From 1990 to 2010, the total number of tertiary educated migrants from non-OECD countries quadrupled, growing from 6.6 million in 1990 to 27 million in 2010.

A particularly important factor contributing to the rise in high-skilled migration is the rise in the number of high-skilled female migrants. Figure 5.2 plots the share of women in immigrant stocks by skill level. Most high-skilled migrants are now women: their share increased from 47 percent in 1990 to 52 percent in 2010.

Complex social and economic reasons account for these patterns and require in-depth analysis. One important explanation is the gap in the demand and supply for high-skilled women in the labor markets of many countries,

Figure 5.1 Skilled emigration, 1990, 2000, and 2010

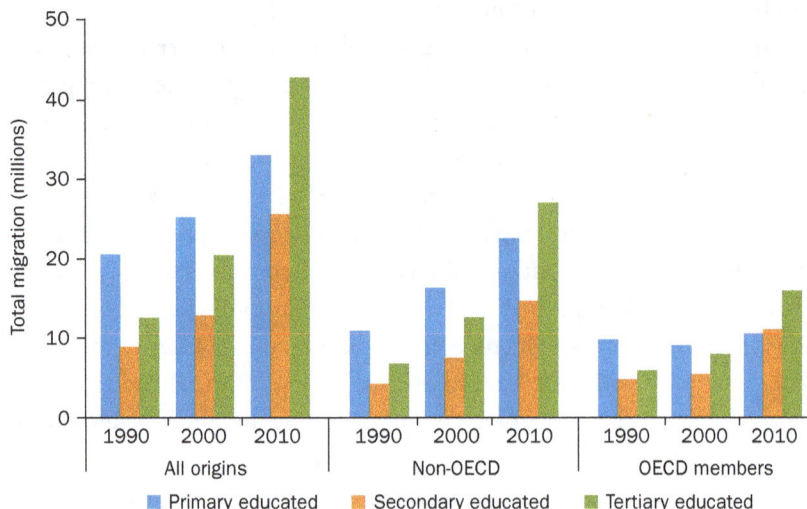

Sources: Data from Docquier, Marfouk, and Lowell 2007 and the 2010/2011 OECD Database on Immigrants in OECD and Non-OECD Countries (DIOC-E).

Note: "Tertiary educated" includes partial tertiary education. Mexico and South Africa treated as non-OECD. OECD = Organisation for Economic Co-operation and Development.

Figure 5.2 Female skilled emigration, 1990, 2000, and 2010

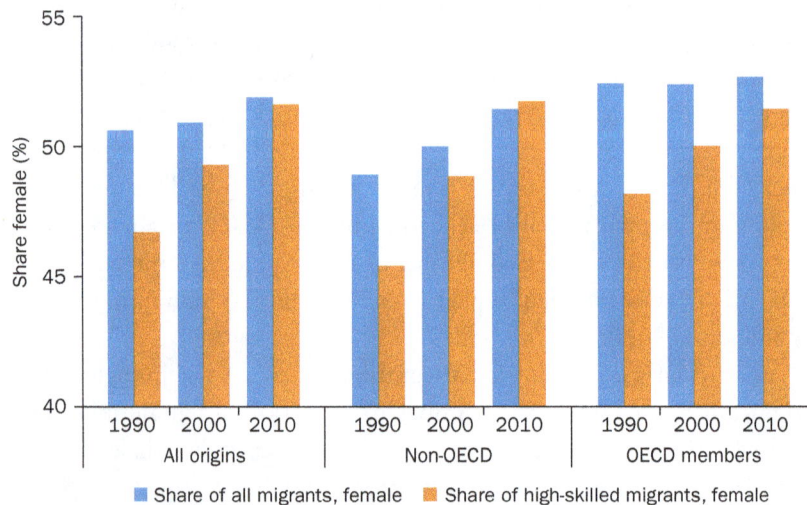

Sources: Data from Docquier, Marfouk, and Lowell 2007 and the 2010/2011 OECD Database on Immigrants in OECD and Non-OECD Countries (DIOC-E).

Note: "High-skilled" includes population with only partially completed tertiary education. Mexico and South Africa treated as non-OECD. OECD = Organisation for Economic Co-operation and Development.

especially lower-income developing countries. Over the last two decades, the share of women in tertiary education increased rapidly, to the extent that women now constitute the majority of university students in a large number of countries, including many low- and middle-income countries (World Bank 2011). However, employment opportunities in the labor market for women have not kept up with this increase. The reasons range from discrimination to cultural conservatism to mismatches between demand and supply of specific skills. In this context, immigration to high-income and culturally more liberal countries provides important opportunities to these highly educated women, which explains why the largest gains in female skilled migration came from non-OECD origin countries. Recent research has shown that differences in women's rights across origin and destination countries have been a driving factor in this trend (Nejad and Young 2014).

The rapid increase in high-skilled immigration has coincided with an increase in the supply of tertiary-educated workers across the world, as well as demand in the labor markets of the OECD countries. Figure 5.3 shows shares of the world population with tertiary education and those of immigrants to OECD countries over the same time periods. The patterns in this

Figure 5.3   Skilled population, 1990, 2000, and 2010

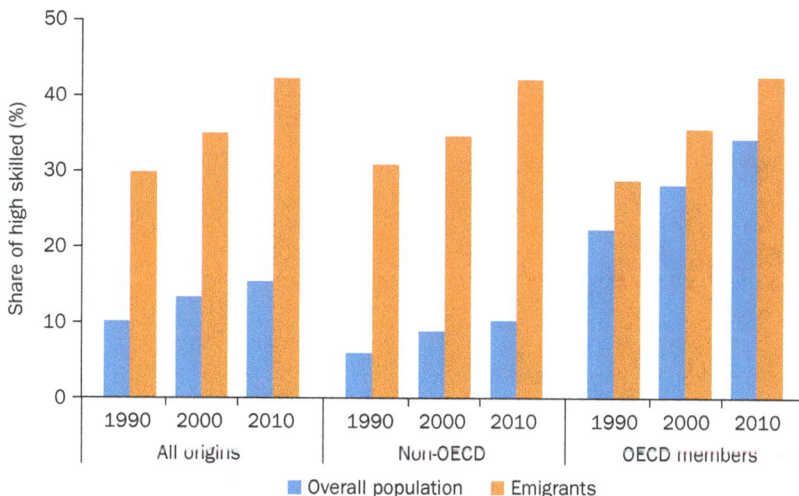

Sources: Migration data for 1990 and 2000 from Docquier, Marfouk, and Lowell 2007; data for 2000 and 2010 from the OECD Database on Immigrants in OECD and Non-OECD Countries (DIOC-E) for 2000/2001 and 2010/2011. Skilled population data from Barro and Lee 2013.

Note: "High skilled" includes those with partially completed tertiary education. Figure shows immigrants to 27 high-income Organisation for Economic Co-operation and Development (OECD) destination countries. Mexico and South Africa treated as non-OECD origin countries.

figure lead to several important observations. First, the share of the tertiary educated among all immigrants moving to OECD countries has been nearly triple that of the education level of the underlying populations of origin countries in each decade. In other words, high-skilled individuals are far more mobile than the average person in the world. Second, the massive increase in high-skilled immigration is primarily driven by the increase in the number of the high skilled in the world population—that is, supply of skills is fueling the process. Third, quite remarkably, both OECD and non-OECD origin countries send similar shares of high-skilled migrants to OECD destination countries despite the fact that the share of tertiary-educated people is three to four times higher in OECD countries. Non-OECD countries in particular experience high rates of high-skilled emigration.

Skill selection is even more evident at the country level. Figure 5.4 plots the share of the tertiary educated (that is, the skill rates) among the

Figure 5.4 Skill rates across emigrants, immigrants, and native-born workers, 2010

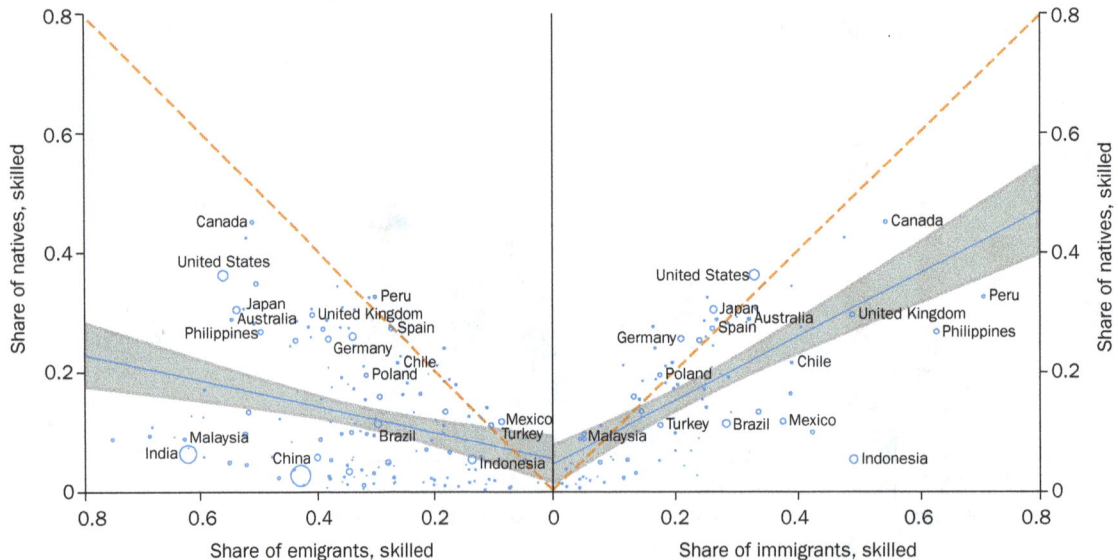

Sources: Migration data from the 2010/2011 OECD Database on Immigrants in OECD and Non-OECD Countries (DIOC-E). Skilled population data from Barro and Lee 2013.

Note: "Skilled" defined as the population with completed tertiary education; shares represent the skilled population divided by the overall popula-tion of interest. For the 88 destination countries included in the DIOC-E 2010/2011 dataset, natives' skill rates are calculated from the native-born population; for all other countries skill rates are calculated from the entire population using Barro and Lee 2013 data. Size of circles are scaled by (log) country population. OECD = Organisation for Economic Co-operation and Development.

immigrant, emigrant, and native-born populations by country. The horizontal axes of the left and right panels show emigrant and immigrant skill rates, respectively, and the left and right vertical axes plot native (nonmigrant) skill rates. Observations below the 45-degree line (orange dashed) indicate higher-skilled emigrants than natives on the left panel and immigrants on the right panel.

As mentioned in chapters 1 and 2, origin countries send a significantly higher share of their skilled work force abroad than of their overall population. Lower-income countries, especially those with smaller populations, experience disproportional emigration of their skilled workers. Destination countries also tend to receive immigrants who are significantly more skilled than the average native-born worker. However, for a number of high-income countries—including the United States—the average immigrant is slightly less skilled than the average native-born worker. These countries lie just above the 45-degree line on the right panel.

Figure 5.5 plots emigration rates of tertiary-educated workers against country populations, where the size of the circles is proportional to

Figure 5.5 Emigration rates, by population and gross domestic product, 2010

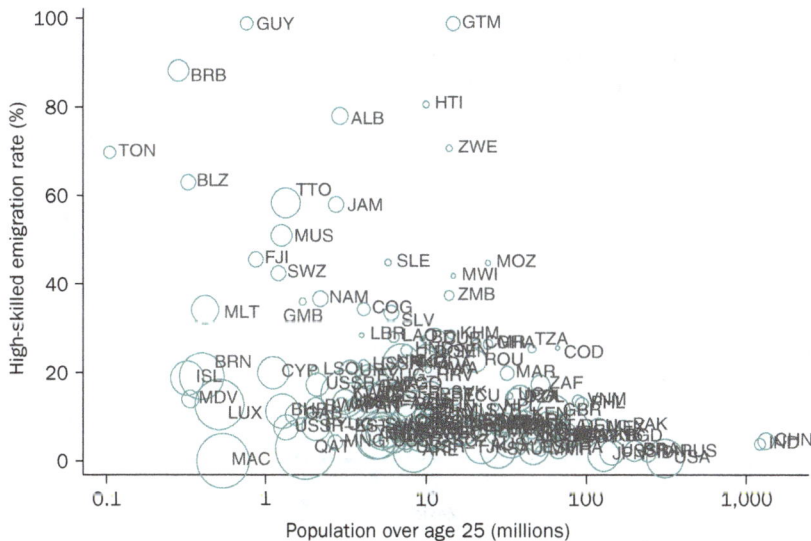

Sources: Data from the 2010/2011 OECD Database on Immigrants in OECD and Non-OECD Countries (DIOC-E) and Barro and Lee 2013.

Note: Emigration rates calculated as the number of emigrants divided by the sum of the remaining population and the number of emigrants. "High-skilled" defined as completed tertiary education. Circles scaled by (log) GDP per capita. GDP = gross domestic product; OECD = Organisation for Economic Co-operation and Development.

per capita gross domestic product (GDP). Countries with larger populations—such as China, India, and the United States—tend to have lower emigration rates. Very small (typically island) nations, in contrast, export nearly all of their skilled workers. For example, Guyana, Guatemala, and Barbados each have skilled emigrant-to-population ratios of 99 percent, 98 percent, and 88 percent respectively.

Most countries in the world, and practically all developing countries, are net exporters of highly skilled or educated people (see figure 5.6). In contrast, only a few, particularly wealthy countries, are significant net receivers of skilled workers. Most notably, these are Australia, Canada, the United Kingdom, and the United States.

The trends discussed above have led to a remarkable concentration of the world's high-skilled population, especially among migrants. Figure 5.7 depicts our familiar cumulative distribution functions of migration for origin and receiving countries by skill level. On the horizontal axis, we rank the countries in terms of the number of high-skilled migrants they send (the dashed lines showing emigration) or receive (the solid lines showing immigration). On the vertical axis, we add up the share of these countries

Figure 5.6 Net importers and exporters of skilled migrants, ordered by per capita gross domestic product, 2010

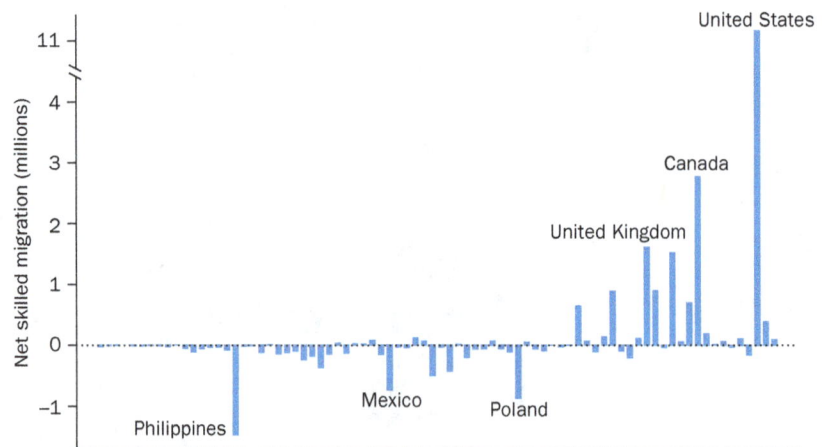

Source: Data from the 2010/2011 OECD Database on Immigrants in OECD and Non-OECD Countries (DIOC-E).

Note: Net migration calculated as total number of immigrants minus total number of emigrants. "Skilled" defined as completed tertiary education. Sample limited to countries with population over 1 million in 2010 with available data. OECD = Organisation for Economic Co-operation and Development.

Figure 5.7 Cumulative distribution function of world migration, by skill

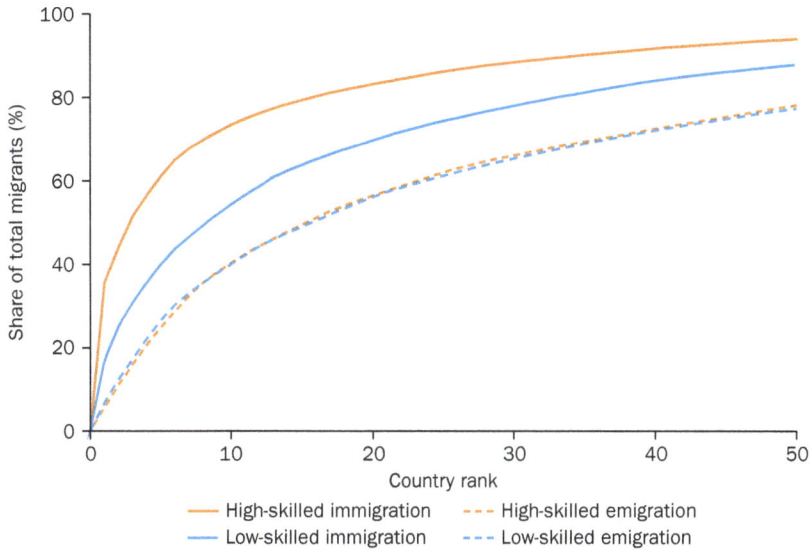

Source: Data from the World Bank Global Bilateral Migration Database (1960–2000).

Note: Countries ranked by size of corresponding population.

in percentage terms. Both high- and low-skilled migrants come from a much broader base of origin countries than destinations, indicated by the dashed lines consistently below the solid lines. For example, top 10 origin countries account for about 40 percent of high- or low-skilled emigrants (dashed lines). In comparison, 60 percent of high-skilled migrants settled in just 4 countries (in order of declining shares these are the United States, the United Kingdom, Australia, and Canada) and almost 75 percent are in 10 destination countries. When looking at those without any tertiary education, although their shares are still concentrated, about 40 percent live in the 5 largest countries and 55 percent are in 10 countries.

These patterns do not end at the national borders but continue within countries where skilled immigrants are also more concentrated than unskilled immigrants and natives. Panel a of figure 5.8 depicts the cumulative distribution functions of immigrants and natives across cities in the United States. Roughly 55 percent of tertiary-educated immigrants live in just 10 metropolitan areas, as opposed to only 25 percent of native-born tertiary-educated workers.

Figure 5.8 Cumulative distribution function of U.S. immigrants and natives, by city and occupation

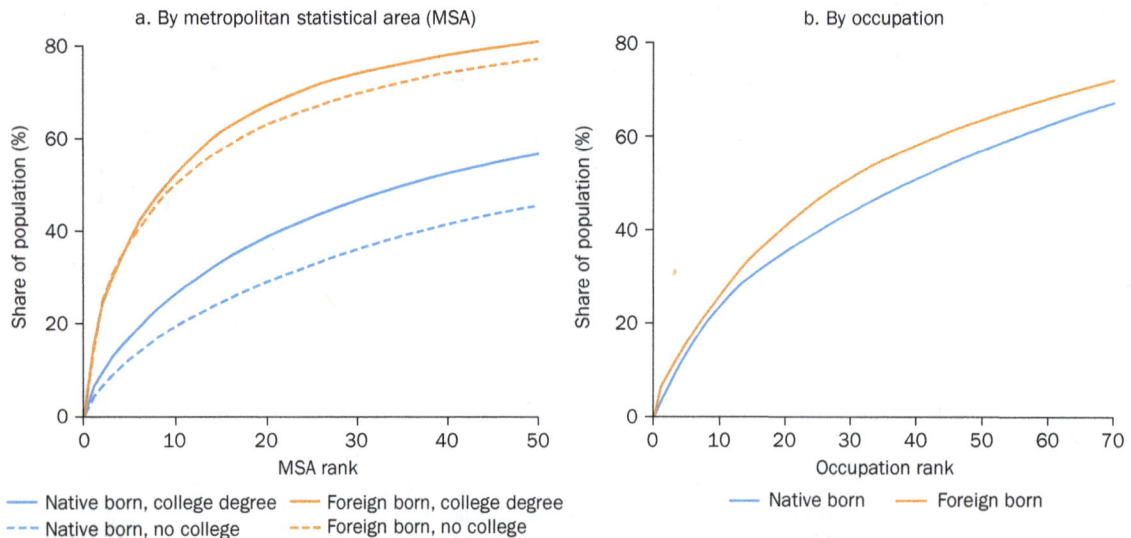

a. By metropolitan statistical area (MSA)

b. By occupation

— Native born, college degree   — Foreign born, college degree
--- Native born, no college   --- Foreign born, no college

— Native born   — Foreign born

Source: Calculated using the five-year American Community Survey 2011–14 from IPUMS (Integrated Public Use Microdata Series) (Ruggles et al. 2017).

Note: Graphs reflect the share (%) of immigrants or natives in the top x MSAs or occupations, where x is indicated on the horizontal axis. Occupations defined using the Standard Occupational Classification system "broad occupation" classification.

When looking across occupations, specifically across high-skilled occupations, we see a similar clustering. For example, academics in many fields tend to locate in just a few cities that host a disproportionate number of universities or research centers; Silicon Valley, Hollywood, and London have, respectively, become hubs for high-tech, entertainment, and finance industries. This locational skill concentration is especially pronounced at the very upper tails of the global skill distribution.

Another interesting example of geographic concentration comes from the Nobel Prizes. Figure 5.9 presents trends in science fields since 1900. The data depict the rise of the United States as a magnet, with scientists in U.S. institutions receiving less than 5 percent of Nobel Prizes in the first 20 years of the 20th century and about 60 percent since the beginning of the 21st century. Playing an important role in this growth has been the rise of foreign-born Nobel laureates who chose to pursue their careers in the United States. They account for more than 60 percent of those winners from the United States in the recent decade. These most talented scientists have chosen to concentrate in the United States because of the availability of generous funding opportunities, research facilities, and the productivity advantage of collaboration and spillovers.

Figure 5.9   Skill agglomeration of Nobel Prize winners, 1900–2016

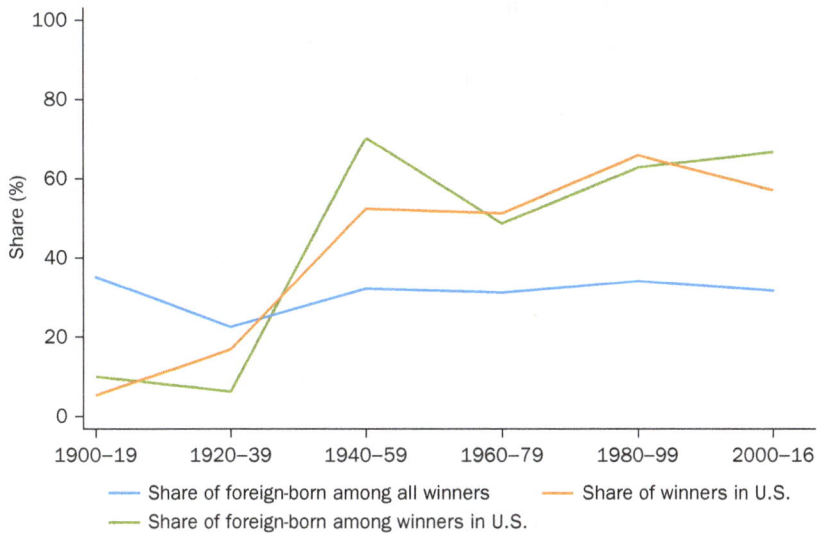

Source: Data from the official website of the Nobel Prize, https://www.nobelprize.org/.

Note: Data include only laureates in chemistry, physics, and medicine or physiology. Shares calculated over 20-year intervals.

Determinants of high-skilled migration patterns

A crucial goal of migration research is to understand the factors that shape migration patterns. Why do skilled migrants flow from poor to rich countries? To put it differently, why does human capital flow from areas of relative shortage to areas of relative abundance? And why are skilled migrants so heavily concentrated in so few countries? The core theoretical framework on human capital mobility dates to at least John Hicks (1932, 76), who noted that "differences in net economic advantages, chiefly differences in wages, are the main causes of migration." This idea gave rise to the textbook models of economic migration used today. Specifically, economic agents consider all the potential costs and benefits of where (and whether) to migrate, and then agents choose the option that maximizes their surplus.

With respect to skill selection in migration patterns, economists often rely on variations of Borjas's (1987) adaptation of the Roy model (discussed in greater detail in the section titled "Who chooses to migrate? Skill composition and the selection of migrants" in chapter 2). These models do relatively well in explaining key patterns in skilled migration. For example, the labor market in the United States, by far the largest destination for high-skilled immigrants, tends to offer a larger skill premium and has a lower marginal tax rate on higher income levels than observed in many other developed countries. Figure 5.10, also presented in chapter 2, confirms the Roy model's predictions that the skill composition of migrant stocks is increasing in wage premiums.

Variation in wages and employment across national labor markets are, however, unable to fully explain the patterns observed in skilled migration flows, most notably the tremendous concentration of high-skilled workers in just a few countries or in certain cities within those countries. Why is it that the Anglo-Saxon countries (Australia, Canada, the United Kingdom, and the United States) have such an advantage in drawing top talent? And why is it that other large, wealthy countries such as France, the Netherlands, and even Japan are unable to attract nearly as many high-skilled migrants? Among the key factors explaining this puzzle include

Figure 5.10   Skill premiums and emigrant skill intensity

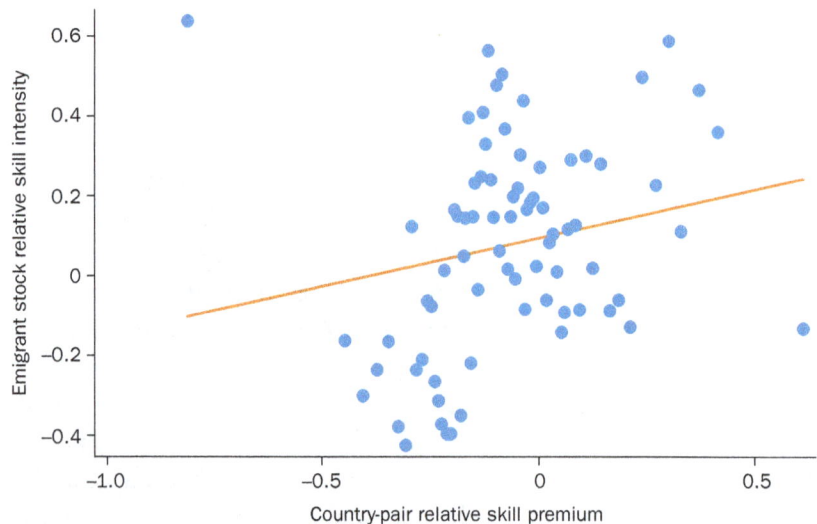

Sources: Data from the 2010/2011 OECD Database on Immigrants in OECD and Non-OECD Countries (DIOC-E) and World Bank International Income Distribution Data (I2D2).

Note: Figure plots the residuals from regressions of the x- and y-axis variables on a set of controls. Controls include origin fixed effects, (log) distance, contiguity, linguistic similarity, (log) average wages, and (log) destination population. Dots represent averages over 100 equally sized bins. Sample restricted to all migration corridors with migrant stocks greater than 1,000 with available data. See annex 2A in chapter 2 for a detailed description of the variables. OECD = Organisation for Economic Co-operation and Development.

geographic clustering of many high-skilled industries and the productivity spillovers they generate; the location of universities, especially of those more focused on research and graduate training; and sensitivity of high-earners to top tax rates.

Skill agglomeration and migration patterns

Geographic variations in wages and available jobs depend on financial and physical capital, technology, complementary financial and legal institutions, and the quality and quantity of workers (Moretti 2012). Related to these factors is the existence of agglomeration effects among highly educated workers in high-skilled occupations. More specifically, high-skilled workers are simply more productive when they collaborate with other high-skilled workers in similar sectors or occupations. For example, Moretti (2004) finds that, as the population in a city becomes more educated, the productivity of firms within that city increases at a faster rate than firms with similar workforces in other cities. That is, the average human capital level within a city also affects productivity above and beyond just the human capital levels of the firm. Additionally, these spillovers are stronger between more similar industries. This may reflect more diffusion of knowledge, benefits from worker mobility across firms, or the agglomeration of investors and venture capitalists.

Agglomeration effects, in essence, increase returns to scale with respect to skilled labor. And the clustering of skilled people in a location leads to greater incentives for others to move there as well. Because these productivity spillovers within a sector depend on geographic proximity as well as economic overlaps, they lead to the rise of geographic hubs of different high-skill industries. Silicon Valley, Hollywood, and Wall Street are just three prominent examples of this phenomenon.

Another critical feature of skill agglomeration is the local production of globally traded products and services. For example, a movie produced in Hollywood is viewed on screens across the world, not just in Los Angeles. Or software developed in Silicon Valley is downloaded by users all over the world within minutes of a release. Bankers in New York City perform transactions for clients on other continents. A global market for its products allows an industry to grow unimpeded in one place because its market is not limited to that physical location. At the same time, the presence of many engineers, scientists, managers, and other professionals leads to employment of others like them as they start new firms or expand existing ones. With agglomeration effects, the presence of high-skilled people in one geographic location—regardless of whether they are native-born individuals or immigrants—may increase the incentives for additional high-skilled people to move there. This pattern can be observed in many high-skilled sectors ranging from science, technology, and academia to entertainment and sports.

Similar trends in agglomeration are evident in many other professions and are not restricted to those that require tertiary education. The key issue is the skill level. Professional sports are another great example. The English Premier League, the world's most popular and profitable soccer league, currently hosts players from over 100 nationalities. German, Italian, and Spanish leagues also each host players from over 50 nationalities. Within these leagues the highest-quality players are concentrated in the top teams. The current Manchester United roster (photo 5.1) has players from 14 different countries. The best players know that, by joining other high-quality players, they will maximize their productivity through joint training

Photo 5.1   Manchester United football team

Source: http://www.manutd.com/en/News-And-Features/Club-News/2016/Oct/Manchester-United-team-photo-201617-download-the-wallpaper.aspx. Used with permission; further permission required for reuse.

and other spillovers. We see a similar agglomeration in the international market for basketball players. In the 1980–81 season, only 1.7 percent of National Basketball Association (NBA) players were foreign-born. This number grew 17 times and peaked at 28.6 percent in 2015–16. Again, basketball players in other countries know that the profitability of the NBA depends on its concentration of high-quality players and that, by moving to the United States, they can take advantage of these spillovers.

Scientists and academics provide another prominent example of this phenomenon. The agglomeration of scientists leads to positive spillovers in research productivity through collaboration and the diffusion of knowledge. Research has shown that German-Jewish émigré chemists to the United States actually increased the productivity of U.S. chemists, resulting in innovation as evidenced by patent filings (Moser, Voena, and Waldinger 2014). Productivity spillovers have resulted in the concentration of scientists from around the world into the top academic departments. The economics department at Harvard University, for example, is home to economists born or trained in 14 different countries, and its pool of graduate students is even more diverse.

The geographic location of academic institutions

The role of academic institutions also provides another driver of skilled migration patterns. The clustering of top academic and research institutions in Australia, Canada, the United Kingdom, and the United States has turned these countries into education and research hubs that attract high-skilled migrant students from around the globe. These four countries currently house 18 of the top 20, and 69 of the top 100, universities worldwide according to the Academic Ranking of World Universities.[1]

The concentration of top universities in a handful of countries, in turn, leads to a concentration of international students. This is especially the case for research universities and students keen to pursue academic and research-focused careers. Figure 5.11 depicts the number of foreign students in tertiary education programs by country for the 12 most popular OECD student destinations. Within this OECD group alone, the top four countries (the United States, the United Kingdom, France, and Australia) represent 70 percent of the total foreign student population.

As important as the concentration of international students is the fact that many of them remain in the destination country after their graduation and enter the labor market. In an extensive study of Indian academics,

Figure 5.11 Non-resident students in tertiary education, by country, 2012

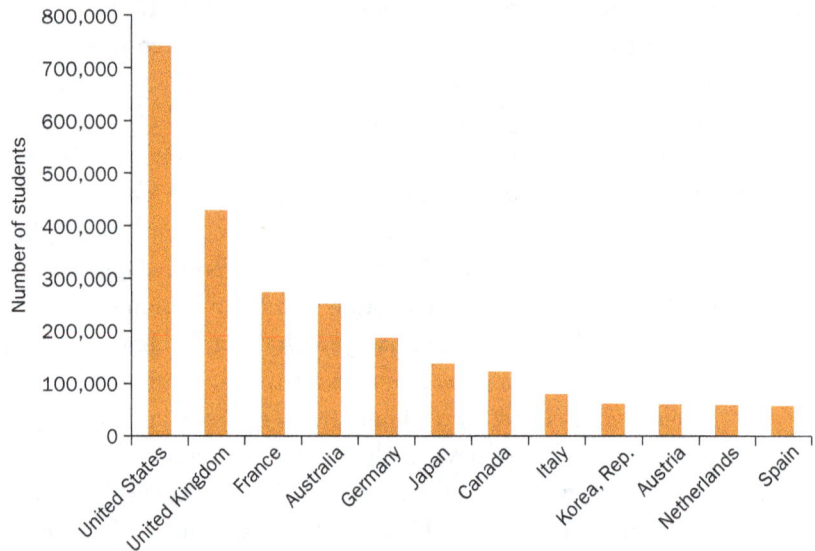

Source: Data from the Organisation for Economic Co-operation and Development.

Note: Data display number of non-resident students in tertiary education programs, except for France, Italy, and the Republic of Korea, which depict non-citizen students.

Czaika and Toma (2016) find significant history-dependence in educational and labor decisions to study and work abroad. Academics who studied abroad in high school are more likely to attend university abroad; those who attend university abroad are more likely to pursue a graduate education abroad. This pattern continues into employment and permanent settlement. Figure 5.12, from Grogger and Hanson (2015), shows the residency and career decisions of foreign-born PhD recipients in the United States: more than 50 percent of these graduates wish to remain. Among those from low-income countries, the share is over 80 percent. The education-career paths combined with the clustering of the top universities in so few countries contribute greatly to the concentration of high-skilled migrants in these same countries.

Top tax rates and the highly skilled

Finally, the way entrepreneurs, innovators, and other high-income-earning immigrants respond to top marginal tax rates offers some evidence on their destination choices. Immigrants start businesses and file patents at higher

Figure 5.12 Post-graduation plans of foreign-born PhD students in the United States, by origin country income level, 1960–2008

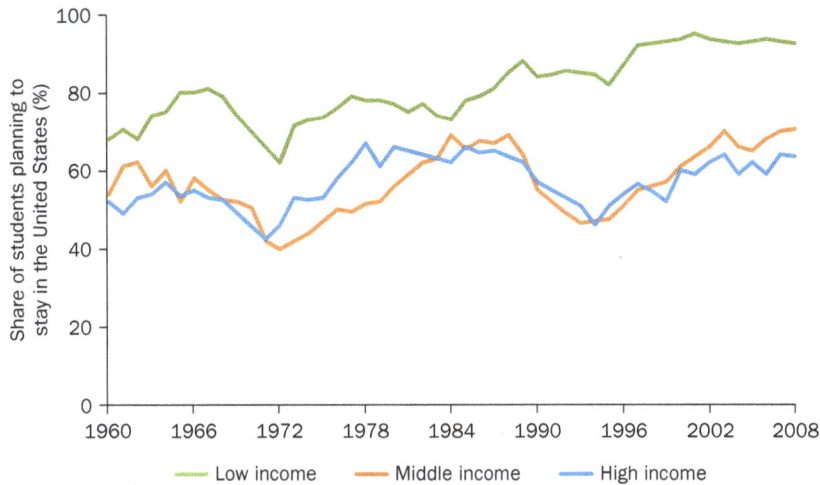

Source: Grogger and Hanson 2015, figure 3. Reproduced with permission; further permission required for reuse.

Note: Share of new foreign-born science and engineering PhDs. "Low income" defined as per capita GDP less than $800, "middle income" as $800 to $8,000, and "high income" as above $8,000, using 1985–94 GDP/capita.

rates than natives. Part of the reason highly skilled migrants migrate to Anglo-Saxon countries is to take advantage of the economic environment that nurtures and financially rewards entrepreneurship and innovation. An important component of this environment is the tax rates, especially for high-income individuals. The impact of the tax rates on migration decisions is an important question, especially for policy makers looking to spur economic growth. Theoretically, the role of taxes in migration decisions should mirror that of wages discussed in chapter 2. Higher taxation should discourage immigration because it will simply lower the net income of all workers.

The evidence confirms that tax rates affect migration decisions. Akcigit, Baslandze, and Stantcheva (2016) study the effect of top tax rates on the migration decisions of "superstar" inventors. Focusing on just the most successful inventors, as measured by the number of citations their patents receive, the authors hope to capture inventors who can drastically affect economic growth. They find the sensitivity of non-migrant inventors to top tax rates to be very low, with an elasticity of 0.03. In contrast, immigrant inventors are highly sensitive to top tax rates, with an elasticity of 1.00.

This implies that a 10 percentage point decrease in the top tax rate from a baseline rate of 60 percent would translate into only a 1 percent increase in the number of domestic inventors in a location but a 26 percent increase in foreign superstar inventors. Similarly, Moretti and Wilson (2017) look at the internal migration decisions of superstar scientists across states in the United States. They find that these superstar scientists are also highly sensitive to the local tax rates, exhibiting migration elasticities between 1.60 and 1.80.

Impact of high-skilled migration on origin countries

The large-scale migration of the highest skilled to high-income countries is generally the focus of the "brain drain" literature, which emphasizes the costs imposed on these mostly low-income origin countries. Ironically, the term brain drain first appeared in the British media to depict the loss of skilled labor from the United Kingdom mainly to the United States after the Second World War (Clemens 2013). And the United Kingdom remains one of the largest source countries of high-skilled emigrants. The earlier literature consisted mostly of theoretical analysis, as exemplified by Grubel and Scott (1966), who provide a framework to examine the implications of high-skilled emigration for economic outcomes in the sending countries. If emigrants take with them the value of their marginal product, welfare loss is irrelevant in competitive and efficient markets. The 1970s saw the emergence of an even more pessimistic view that high-skilled emigration depletes poorer developing countries of their most scarce asset—human capital. Among the most prominent papers, Bhagwati and Hamada (1974) highlight the importance of human capital for productivity and other social externalities. This approach gained prominence at a time when human capital was taking a more central role in development and growth economics. The concern among development officials stems from the externality argument and is that high-skilled emigrants take with them skills—such as technical expertise—that are crucial to the further development of their home countries. This concern also adds to the sense that educational investments aimed at promoting growth may be futile if the recipients proceed to take their newly acquired skills overseas.

Additional issues with high-skilled emigration are its public finance implications. Although migrant-sending developing countries finance the education of their students through public funds, the returns on these investments are reaped by the migrant-receiving, high-income countries. In addition, the sending country is exposed to significant losses of tax revenues from the emigration of people with relatively high earning potential.

The negative effects of skilled emigration may go beyond income losses and productivity spillovers mentioned in the previous section. Certain skill groups, such as teachers, doctors, or scientists, generate certain social externalities through key public services they provide. The earlier literature emphasized the loss of such spillovers with high-skilled emigration, despite scant empirical evidence on the issue. Bhargava, Docquier, and Moullan (2011) analyze the emigration of doctors from Africa and argue that reducing the level of emigration may generate improvements in several health outcomes, but only if accompanied by adequate supporting facilities and other inputs. Although highly relevant and heated, the research and the policy debate on this issue are far from settled. In contrast, Clemens (2007), using cross-sectional data on 53 African countries, finds very little evidence that emigration of medical doctors affects health outcomes, such as child mortality, infant mortality under age one, and vaccination rates and respiratory infections among those younger than age five.

Gains from high-skilled emigration for origin countries

The term "brain drain" conveys a sense of serious loss. Countering this concern, the "brain gain" literature emerged in the 1990s to challenge the assertions of the brain drain literature and show how high-skilled migration might generate welfare gains for the sending countries and the people left behind.

The implications of brain gain are almost the opposite of those emphasized by the effects of brain drain. Whereas brain drain literature argues that emigration leads to the loss of a poor country's human capital stock, brain gain literature postulates that the departure of high-skilled migrants may actually lead to an increase in the human capital levels. Oded Stark and Edward Mountford built a series of theoretical models explaining the potential mechanisms that would underpin this process (see, for example, Stark, Helmenstein, and Prskawetz 1997, 1998; Mountford 1997). Although the returns to education at home may be low, the potential to migrate combined with higher wages abroad increases the incentive for residents of poor countries to invest in education. These incentives will increase overall educational attainment compared to a world with no emigration. If the probability of high-skilled emigration is less than 1, then, under certain assumptions, the final human capital stock of the country might be higher than it would have been without emigration prospects. If the potential gains are high, the cost of education low, and the probability of emigration within a certain range, then we might end up with more skilled people in origin countries.

Beine, Docquier, and Rapoport (2001) bring the data to the theory. They use emigration rates to OECD countries from 37 developing countries to provide empirical support for the brain gain mechanism. Extending their earlier work, Beine, Docquier, and Rapoport (2008) use emigration rates to OECD countries from 127 countries to empirically separate winning and losing sending countries. Whereas sending countries with low levels of skilled labor and low emigration rates stand to gain, those with emigration rates of 20 percent (or higher), or with a share of skilled labor of over 5 percent—or both—are negatively affected. They find a long-run elasticity of about 25 percent between high-skilled emigration and the stock of human capital. In other words, brain gain effects depend on the country and are not foregone conclusions.

Skilled emigration also generates positive externalities through remittances, which are partly used to finance education. Using household data from 11 major migrant destinations, Bollard et al. (2011) find a strong positive correlation between education and levels of remittances: educated migrants remit up to $300 more annually than their less educated counterparts. Yang (2008) provides empirical evidence on the link between remittances and investment in human capital. The paper exploits an exogenous shock to the exchange rate of the Philippine peso against various currencies of migrant-receiving countries in 1997 to show that households receiving positive income shocks, via remittances, experienced more investment in human capital of children.

Other benefits from high-skilled emigration include the diffusion of knowledge and attracting foreign direct investment (FDI) to the sending countries (see Kerr 2008; Mountford and Rapoport 2011). Therefore, a more holistic view of high-skilled emigration implies that the already small negative effect of emigration may be lower than currently believed. It would also suggest that emigration can benefit both the sending and the receiving countries. Saxenian (2005) termed this phenomenon "brain circulation."

Another potential channel of brain gain is how people change their fields of study or occupations when there is a prospect of migration. In a series of surveys of the top high school students in Ghana, Papua

New Guinea, and Tonga, Gibson and McKenzie (2011) found that most students changed their field of study or how much they studied because of potential migration opportunities. For example, students took more foreign language classes and prepared for certain entrance exams. Even the surveyed high school teachers said they covered subjects, such as American history, that were more appropriate for destination countries and that they would not have included in the curriculum in the absence of migration prospects.

These case studies, theoretical models, and empirical analyses are based on two critical assumptions. First, immigration, including high-skilled immigration, must be restricted by the destination country via policy tools, and some people will not be able to migrate even if they would like to. So the brain gain effect à la Stark or Mountford can appear only because some of the potential emigrants are forced to stay behind. Second, the supply of education must be elastic so that the educational system can easily meet the increased demand from potential migrants. For example, although private nursing schools in the Philippines could expand capacity in the face of increased demand, this is unlikely to be the case for publicly funded medical schools in Sub-Saharan Africa. That is why we are more likely to observe the brain gain effect in nursing in the Philippines rather than in medicine in Africa.

Brain circulation and economic networks

In the past five decades, globalization has been accompanied by lower transportation and communication costs, facilitating the movement of people and ideas. With the global competition for talent, skilled migrants now find it much easier, in comparison to their unskilled counterparts, to move from one country to another. This section highlights several other channels through which mobility of highly skilled professionals might generate benefits, especially for their home countries. These gains can best be explained by this quote from former prime minister Manmohan Singh of India: "Today we in India are experiencing the benefits of the reverse flow of income, investment and expertise from the global Indian diaspora. The problem of 'brain drain' has been converted into an opportunity" (Singh 2010).

The first channel through which benefits may be realized, diffusion of knowledge, is frequently repeated in policy circles and the academic literature. As Saxenian (2005, 35) notes, "By 2000, over one-third of

Silicon Valley's high-skilled workers were foreign-born.... These engineers and entrepreneurs, aided by the lowered transaction costs associated with digitization, are transforming technical and institutional know-how between distant regional economies faster and more flexibly than most corporations." Kerr (2008) finds evidence of knowledge transfer between ethnic emigrant groups in the United States and their home countries, in particular among those of Chinese origin. This diffusion of knowledge is found to affect productivity in high-tech manufacturing sectors. Agrawal et al. (2011) provide empirical evidence that India's diaspora has contributed to the development of some of the most important inventions in India.

Closely related to knowledge diffusion is the positive externality of trade stimulated by emigration. The literature on this topic follows Gould's seminal 1994 paper, which posits that movement of people between countries affects movement of goods between them via two channels. First, migrants lead to increased demand for specific goods they would like to consume. Second, migrants facilitate trade between the two countries by lowering transaction costs. The empirical analysis suggests diminishing effects arising from the first channel and nuanced evidence for the second channel. Felbermayr and Jung (2009) find a strong positive elasticity of 0.11 between bilateral stocks of emigrants and bilateral trade, but no evidence exists that the effects differ across educational groups. Migration of the high skilled affects FDI flows as well. At the cross-country level, Kugler and Rapoport (2007) and Javorcik et al. (2011) find a positive relationship between the number of skilled emigrants a country sends to the United States and the level of FDI from the United States to that country.

In addition, a portion of emigrants return to their home countries after a certain period, taking with them the financial capital, technical knowledge, and business experience they acquired abroad (Dustmann and Kirchkamp 2002). Looking at Turkish migrants returning from time in Germany and interviewed in the 1980s, Dustmann and Kirchkamp (2002) find that about 50 percent became entrepreneurs. A similar study by Piracha and Vadean (2010) shows that return migrants to Albania were more likely to start a business than their non-migrant counterparts. Funds accumulated abroad are found to be a significant determinant. Wahba (2015) provides empirical evidence on the wage premium to returnees to the Arab Republic of Egypt after temporary migration: she finds that return migrants earn about 25 percent more than their non-migrant counterparts. All of these studies indicate the value of the human capital acquired abroad.

Comparing different effects of high-skilled emigration

Recent literature provides a comprehensive way to compare various effects of high-skilled emigration on destination countries that we discussed earlier. The overall impact of high-skilled emigration on origin countries will depend on various different channels and their relative importance. The model presented here is designed to highlight these channels and what factors influence their impact. The analysis is based on Docquier (2017), who assumes that the overall economic environment is captured by a constant elasticity of substitution (CES) production function shaped with two types of labor—high and low skilled. This framework is the standard one used in the labor economics literature, especially on migration. Many of the papers we cite in the previous chapters also rely on these assumptions, especially the CES production function.

Using country-level data on the skill composition of the domestic labor forces and the emigration rates of these two skill levels from the global migration databases, we can calculate the impact of skill-biased emigration. Figure 5.13 shows GDP per capita on the horizontal axis and the percentage decline in GDP per capita due to emigration on the vertical axis.

Figure 5.13   **Skill-biased emigration and its effects on gross domestic product**

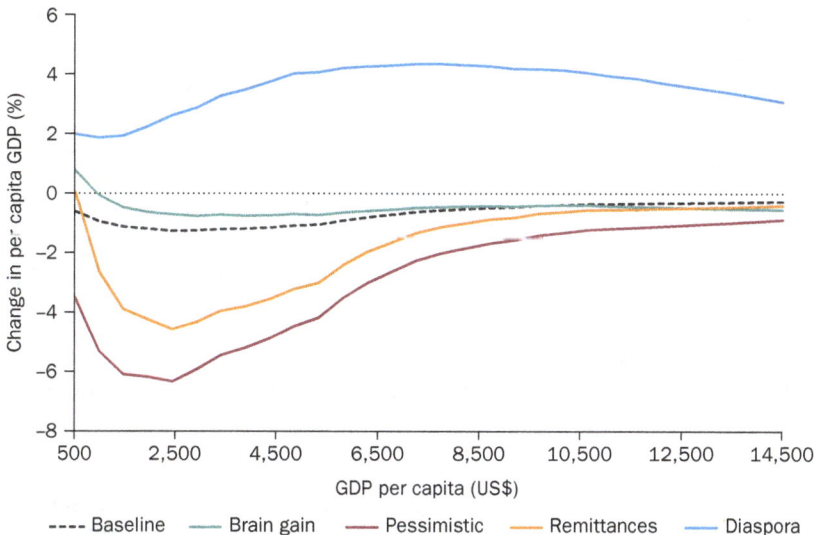

Source: Created using data from Docquier 2017.

Note: The figure shows the effects of skill-biased emigration by GDP per capita for different channels (see text for more detail).

The dashed line shows the decline in the GDP per capita with no presence of externalities. The overall effect is rather small and completely due to the change in average income levels after a larger share of the high skilled emigrate. If the emigration rates were identical between two skill levels, then the total effect would have been zero.

The more interesting scenario (red line) appears when we assume that high-skilled emigrants generate economywide productivity spillovers where the total factor productivity depends on the share of high-skilled individuals in the labor force. In this case, high-skilled emigration imposes a significant negative externality on those left behind. The maximum economic loss is about 6 percent and is realized by those countries with GDP per capita of about $2,500. Compared to lower-income countries, the labor force is more skilled, and a larger share of this skilled group emigrates, resulting in large losses. The loss declines to 3 percent at GDP per capita of $7,000.

The third scenario (depicted by the orange line) assumes emigrants send remittances back home. Remittances reduce the income loss due to high-skilled emigration by about one-third, which represents a significant but partial compensation.

In the next assumption, about the brain gain effects, increased emigration prospects lead to higher long-term education levels. On the basis of the analysis by Beine, Docquier, and Rapoport (2008), we assume that the high-skilled labor force stock has an elasticity of 0.05 with respect to emigration. The green line shows this new scenario and indicates that the brain gain effect almost fully compensates for the brain drain effect but does not lead to actual gains, despite the claims of the theoretical literature. The maximum net loss is about 1 percent.

The fifth and final scenario assumes the presence of diaspora externalities where skilled emigration influences trade and FDI, which in turn affects total factor productivity, as discussed above. The blue line depicts the results of this scenario and the consequent positive net effect of skilled migration. The main beneficiaries are countries with GDP per capita of about $8,000, and the gain is about 4.3 percent. Even low-income countries gain about 2 percent from these diaspora externalities.

This model, like all other models in economics, relies on several assumptions that one can argue are unrealistic or restrictive. However, it is valuable in highlighting various forces in play in the case of high-skilled emigration and identifying the relative impacts. In the absence of remittances, brain gain effects, or diaspora externalities, high-skilled emigration may be quite harmful. The effects are especially strong for lower-middle-income countries, rather than the least developed countries, because they have just enough skilled labor to realize the productivity spillovers and just enough income to finance emigration. Remittances do not fully compensate for losses from emigration, but the brain gain effect does. We should note that education systems must be able to respond to increased demand and expand. If countries have public finance constraints on education, then these positive effects will not materialize. Finally, diaspora externalities can be quite powerful, but are possible mainly for upper-middle-income countries. Low-income and lower-middle-income countries cannot fully take advantage of them.

Effects of skilled migration on destination countries

Even though the policy debate focuses on the impact of high-skilled immigrant workers on their origin countries, the most significant effects are likely to be felt in destination countries. Many of these countries implement policies to attract and retain high-skilled people under the assumption that such immigration will close the shortages in the labor markets, spur innovation and entrepreneurship, and thus lead to economic growth. The main question is on the extent to which high-skilled immigration affects destination economies as well as the native-born workers with whom they directly compete.

The direct effects of high-skilled immigration

Human capital is one of the primary determinants of long-run economic growth (Barro 1991, 2001; Becker, Murphy, and Tamura 1990). For example, Jones (2002) finds that, over the period 1950–93, educational attainment and research intensity account for 80 percent of U.S. per capita economic growth. The concentration of highly skilled individuals, immigrant or native born, may increase productivity through collaboration and diffusion of knowledge. Because they are disproportionately employed in science, technology, engineering, and mathematics (STEM) fields, high-skilled immigrants are an important component of this mechanism in most destination countries.

In the United States, immigrants make up more than a quarter of all STEM jobs in the health care, information, finance, and education industries. Additionally, immigrants represent more than half of all computer scientists, software developers, and software engineers with master's degrees and 60 percent of all STEM workers with PhDs (Hanson and Slaughter 2013). Furthermore, engineering and technology companies founded by immigrants between 1995 and 2005 produced $52 billion in sales and employed 450,000 workers in 2005 (Wadhwa et al. 2008).

Immigrants also play an outsized role in the development of inventions and product innovation. Miguelez and Fink (2013) and Miguelez (2016) document the role of immigrant inventors globally by looking at a database of international patents filed under the Patent Cooperation Treaty. They find that, of about 5 million records available in the database, migrants filed about 10 percent of all patents. This is an astonishing level considering the global population share of migrants is only slightly over 3 percent. Figure 5.14 shows the immigration rate of inventors and those specifically from developing countries across a variety of OECD destinations.

Figure 5.14 Share of immigrants among inventors in OECD countries

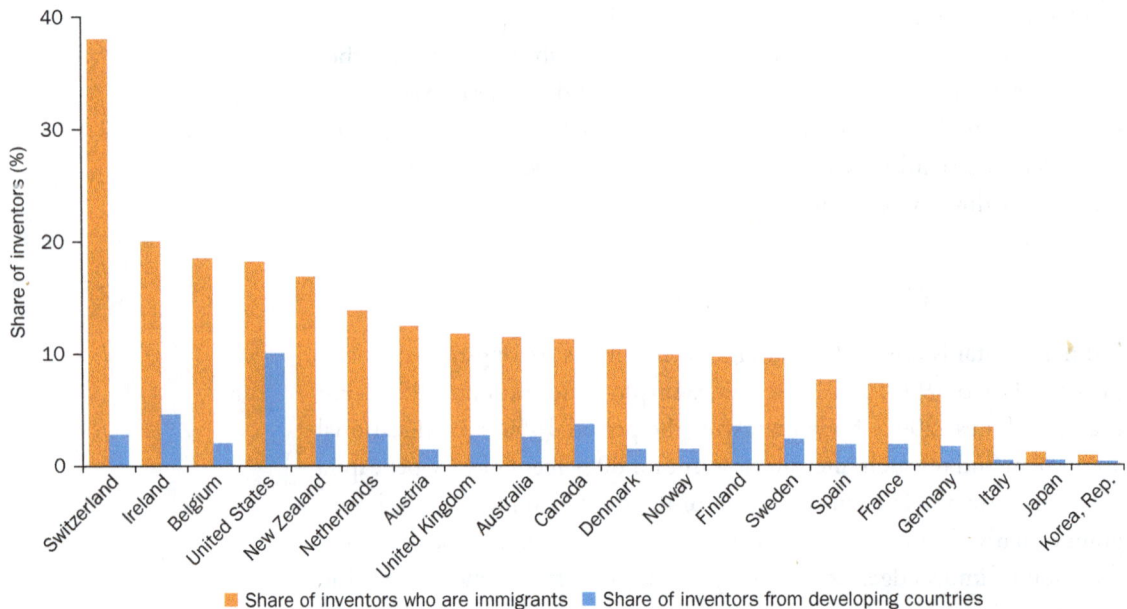

Source: Miguelez 2016, figure 2. Reproduced with permission; further permission required for reuse.

Note: Immigrants are identified via patents filed under the Patent Cooperation Treaty. OECD = Organisation for Economic Co-operation and Development.

Immigrant and native high-skilled workers: Substitutes or complements?

Although it is important to document the overall positive effects of skilled emigrants, it is also necessary to identify the effect on natives who directly compete with these immigrants. Throughout this book, as well as in much of the economic literature, the arrival of immigrants has been treated as an outward shift of the local labor supply, which should result in reduced native wages and employment. These models assume that native-born workers and immigrants are, at least within skill groups, substitutes, possibly imperfectly. When it comes to high-skilled immigration, the validity of this assumption is debatable. For example, because of their collaboration and knowledge sharing, immigrant scientists may actually improve the productivity of native-born scientists. Or the presence of high-skilled immigrants with different expertise than native-born workers could allow each group to specialize by spending more time on tasks in which they have a comparative advantage; in this case both groups can increase the productivity of the other. High-skilled immigration could lead to increased equilibrium wages and native employment if these spillovers are strong enough.

The evidence on such complementarities is mixed, depending on the market, location, and industry. Brucker et al. (2012) look at country-level immigration rates across 14 countries from 1980 to 2005. They find that skilled immigration increases overall employment above and beyond the number of immigrants that actually arrived. They also find an increase in overall capital investment, leading them to hypothesize that educated immigrants may stimulate investment and specialization in skilled sectors. Further evidence of specialization comes from Peri and Sparber (2011), who find that high-skilled immigration to the United States leads to a shift of skilled native-born workers into occupations requiring more communication skills whereas immigrants tend to specialize in occupations requiring quantitative and analytical skills.

A popular approach to evaluating the effects of skilled immigration is to look at the U.S. H-1B visa program. Doran, Gelber, and Isen (2016) find negative employment effects on native-born workers due to the H-1B program. Using firm-level tax and patent data, they evaluate the effect on employment and innovation by comparing firms who won and lost the H-1B visa lottery. Winning firms saw, at most, only modest increases in employment that imply crowding out of native-born workers. They also find some evidence that lottery-winning firms decrease pay, increase profits, but do not change their level of patenting. Kerr and Lincoln (2010), conversely, find that the H-1B has had a net positive effect on science and engineering patenting, specifically from Indian and Chinese immigrants. Additionally, they find no evidence of displacement for patents filed by native-born individuals and even some evidence of increased patenting, implying productivity spillovers.

Perhaps some of the most compelling evidence comes from quasi-natural experiments affecting highly specialized fields. Similar to those described in chapter 3, these analyses rely on sudden shocks of skilled immigration, which are not due to availability of jobs or destination country labor market factors. The unique feature of these studies is that they represent immigration shocks to highly skilled and highly specialized fields (chemists and mathematicians in the following examples), with the variable impact depending on the research focus of the immigrant scholars.

Historical events provide some of the most compelling evidence on such spillovers. For example, Moser, Voena, and Waldinger (2014) look at the effect of German-Jewish chemists expelled from Nazi Germany on the productivity of U.S. chemists. They find that the émigrés spurred innovation by attracting other researchers into their fields, which resulted in the crowding in rather than crowding out of U.S. chemists into those fields studied specifically by the German émigrés. Figure 5.15 shows patenting by native-born chemists in fields that overlap with the German émigrés and those that do not. U.S. patenting in fields closely related to those of the immigrants increased at a significantly faster rate than other fields.

In contrast, Borjas and Doran (2012), look at the arrival of Soviet mathematicians to the United States after the collapse of the Soviet Union. They find no evidence that the influx of mathematicians increased the overall production of mathematical research (measured as the number of academic papers). Instead, the total productivity of U.S. mathematicians decreased, and those with research most similar to that of the Soviet mathematicians saw the largest negative effect. These results stem from U.S. mathematicians changing fields, moving to lower-quality research institutions, and leaving active research positions altogether. Additionally, Borjas and Doran find that competition with the immigrants arose along two dimensions: first, geographically, in competition for jobs at the same universities and research institutions, and, second, in the space of ideas, with competition for publications in the same mathematical fields.

Figure 5.15 U.S. patents per class and year, by U.S. inventors in research fields of émigrés and other German chemists, 1920–70

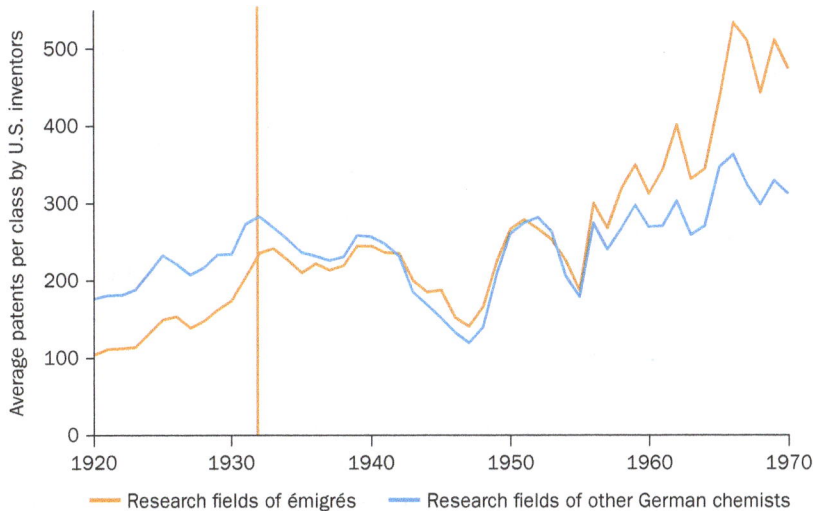

Source: Moser, Voena, and Waldinger 2014, figure 2A. Reproduced with permission; further permission required for reuse.

Note: Data cover 2,073,771 patent-main class combinations by U.S. inventors across 166 research fields defined at the level of U.S. Patent and Trademark Office (USPTO) classes. "Research fields of émigrés" cover 60 classes that include at least one patent between 1920 and 1970 by a German or Austrian émigré to the United States. "Research fields of other German chemists" cover 106 USPTO classes that include at least one patent between 1920 and 1970 by another German chemist but include no patents by émigrés. The orange vertical line (1933) represents when the migration of German-Jewish scientists began with the start of the Nazi regime.

So why did the arrival of German chemists and Soviet mathematicians have such different effects? One explanation may depend on the differing structures of each labor market. The market for mathematicians and mathematical research is subject to much stricter space constraints. It has limited room for research and slots for tenured professors within universities and has limited space for published research within academic journals. Conversely, in the space of chemistry, there is no concrete constraint on the number of patentable ideas; and, in certain cases, groundbreaking innovations may increase the potential for further patentable ideas. So the arrival of Soviet mathematicians crowded out U.S. mathematicians because the demand for mathematicians and their output is relatively fixed. In contrast, the demand for "knowledge products" in chemistry is elastic, and the spillovers lead to productivity gains as well as increased demand for U.S. chemists.

High-skilled migration policies

It should be clear from the evidence in this chapter that high-skilled migration has dramatically affected the global economy. The global stock of high-skilled migrant workers originates from a broad base of countries yet is highly concentrated in relatively few developed countries (see figure 5.7). This concentration has resulted in a world in which many of the most talented individuals from poor countries migrate to a few wealthy countries. Emigrants from non-OECD countries to OECD countries are four times as likely as non-emigrants to have tertiary education (see figure 5.3).

In developed countries, highly skilled immigrants—many from the developing world—make up a disproportionately large share of inventors and entrepreneurs. Looking to reap the benefits of a skilled labor force, countries around the world have implemented policies aimed to either attract or retain high-skilled workers. Destination countries implement policies that favor high-skilled immigrants by giving preference to specific employers, attracting international students, and using points-based immigration systems. Low-income origin countries, international organizations, and destination countries attempt to mitigate the effects of human capital loss by limiting emigration, reducing incentives to leave, and incentivizing return migration.

This section aims to outline the types of policies taken. We will describe the different alternatives that policy makers have in restricting or promoting skilled migration, describe how these policies affect the incentives facing high-skilled workers, and, when possible, present evidence on the efficacy of such policies.

Policies to promote high-skilled immigration

Globally, a clear pattern exists toward the adoption of more skill-selective immigration policies (Facchini and Mayda 2010; see also figure 5.16). With the goal of increasing the productivity of the workforce and spurring economic growth, destination countries use selective immigration policy to positively select economic migrants. Typically, destination countries adopt one of two broad migration policy regimes (Kerr et al. 2016). Demand-driven policies require that incoming migrants first acquire a job in the destination country, therefore prioritizing migrants' almost-immediate employment and giving potential employers and

Figure 5.16 Share of governments whose policy goal is to raise high-skilled immigration, 2005–15

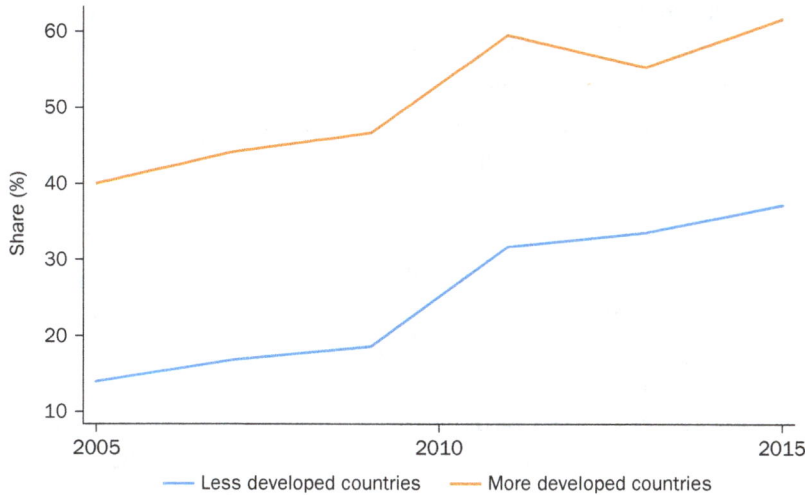

Source: Data from the United Nations World Population Prospects Database.

Note: Figure shows the share of all countries, for which data are available, whose policy is to raise high-skilled immigration.

current labor market conditions a key role in determining who can migrate. Supply-driven policies instead evaluate potential incoming migrants by a points-based system, giving preference to those who possess more desirable labor market characteristics such as younger age, higher education, experience, occupation, and language proficiency. In supply-driven regimes, migrants generally can obtain employment permits without an actual job offer: they tend to migrate first and then look for employment after their arrival.

Australia and Canada, commonly given as the most prominent examples of countries taking supply-driven strategies to immigration policy, have both historically used a points-based system. Their programs select individuals on the basis of their observable education, language skills, work experience, and existing employment arrangements. Each factor is weighted by a formula, and potential migrants receive a score based on their credentials. Those migrants with points above a threshold obtain visas and work permits.

Supply-driven systems are praised for their long-term view and ability to effectively increase human capital levels in the country. Rather than using immigration policy to fill short-term labor market needs, as a demand-driven policy would, supply-driven approaches aim to attract the highest skilled, regardless of existing demand for those skills. Some studies find that these systems effectively attract high-skilled migrants in large numbers (Facchini and Lodigiani 2014).

Points-based policies also have certain disadvantages. Migrants could exaggerate or misrepresent their qualifications. Adverse selection could occur if those who can find immediate employment select into demand-based systems. There is also the risk of immigrant downgrading: talented migrants may end up underemployed because of a mismatch in supply and demand for their skills, with the typical anecdote being a nuclear physicist who is driving a taxi. This underemployment often indicates that the country did not realize the benefits of immigration it sought, tax receipts are lower than expected (because of underemployment), and employers might have preferred someone farther back in the queue. Given the dynamic aspect of labor markets and the typically anemic pace of government bureaucracy, it may not be realistic to expect a points-based policy to keep up with the changing demands of employers. These are some of the reasons why Australia and Canada are transforming their migration policies toward a more hybrid regime.

Demand-driven policies rely on potential immigrants obtaining an offer of employment before being granted a work visa. The United States and most European countries use at least some employer-driven elements. The United States, for example, has the H-1B and L1 visas as primary categories (Kerr, Kerr, and Lincoln 2015). The H-1B visa is a temporary visa to employ workers in specialized fields, with many, but not all, classified as STEM occupations. The visas are employer sponsored, in that migrants have already secured a job offer. The visas are also two of the few with a "dual intent" feature, meaning that temporary migrants can pursue permanent residency while holding their H-1B or L1 visa.

Virtually all H-1B holders have a bachelor's degree or higher, and about 70 percent of the visas in recent years went to STEM-related occupations. India is by far the largest source country: of the over 530,000 H-1B visa holders in 2015, over 250,000 were from India (DHS 2016). Visas, valid for three years, can be renewed once. In order to protect native-born workers, firms need to pay the visa holder wages that are consistent with the current labor market. The mean annual starting compensation for a new H-1B worker was $75,000 in 2014.

A country's choice of a supply- or demand-driven policy depends upon policy makers' priorities when balancing long-term human capital goals and short-term labor supply shortages. In practice, immigration policies tend to comprise a mixture of elements, both demand and supply, which have been termed "hybrid systems" (Papademetriou, Somerville, and Tanaka 2009). Australia and Canada have recently begun to add demand-side elements to their points-based systems—for example, applicants gain additional credit if their occupation is recognized as being in high demand.

In addition to the supply- and demand-driven policies discussed, destination countries have a few other options. Bilateral policies between countries to mutually recognize degrees from their higher education institutions allow high-skilled workers to migrate with less uncertainty. Additionally, destination countries can offer financial incentives, such as local tax exemptions, to high-skilled migrants.

The lack of quality data and the complexity of immigration systems make measuring the efficacy of such systems very difficult, but a few studies attempt this feat. Facchini and Lodigiani (2014) take a qualitative approach by individually analyzing immigration policies of 11 high-income destination countries. They find little evidence of employer-driven programs in attracting high-skilled workers, although the systems perform better for countries that host a high number of foreign students (such as the United States). They find stronger evidence with respect to supply-driven policies, which are more effective in increasing the average skill level of migrants.

In a related study, Czaika and Parsons (2017) look at migration flows to 10 OECD destinations from 2000 to 2012 and attempt to analyze the effects of changes in high-skilled migration policies. They find that supply-driven policies are much more effective than demand-driven in selecting high-skilled migrants. They also find that financial incentives increase the effectiveness of demand-driven policies and that bilateral degree recognition policies also increase the skill composition of migration flows. We should, however, expect these results regarding supply-driven policies because attracting highly educated migrants is the goal of such policies. Demand-driven policies may very well be more effective in attracting more productive migrants because migrants have a better chance of finding a better employer match in the labor market.

Policies to prevent high-skilled emigration

Policy makers in origin countries who are interested in alleviating the effects of high-skilled emigration often approach the problem in three ways. First, they can just eliminate emigration opportunities; this usually takes the form of quotas, emigration bans, and discouraging recruiting by foreign industries. Second, they can seek compensation for any harm to the origin country from emigration—typically by imposing a tax on emigration. Finally, they can attempt to increase the incentives for skilled natives to stay in the origin country or return from a previous migration. These strategies include improving local higher education, international training partnerships, and diaspora engagement.

Policies aimed at restricting emigration are the most direct actions that can be taken. Rather than altering incentives to reduce emigration, policy makers simply take the emigration option off of the table. Destination countries and employers of high-skilled migrants often implement restrictive migration policies to protect the employment opportunities of natives; these policies also act to prevent emigration and have been promoted by economists as such. One example is that of country-specific immigration quotas implemented by destination countries. The United States, for example, does not allow immigration from any single country to exceed more than 7 percent of total immigration. Another example is policies that prevent overseas recruiting in high-skilled occupations. The U.K. National Health Service forbids employees from recruiting from many developing countries. The World Health Organization Code of Practice promotes self-sufficiency in an attempt to encourage the employment of native-born individuals and effectively reduce emigration of health care workers from low-income countries.

Simply eliminating options to emigrate can greatly reduce the returns to pursuing higher education. African doctors or South Asian software engineers would earn only a fraction at home compared to what they could earn in Canada or the United States. Research has shown that economic incentives play a crucial role in the decision to invest in human capital and mitigate the brain gain effect (see the discussion earlier in the chapter in the section titled "Gains from high-skilled emigration for origin countries"). Rather than increase the stock of high-skilled native-born workers, policies restricting emigration could reduce it by hindering overall human capital accumulation. Additionally, restricting high-skilled emigration could reduce other externalities such as knowledge spillovers and remittances.

Another action taken by origin countries is to seek compensation for high-skilled emigration, often in the form of a tax on earnings abroad or a one-time fee for emigration. Supporters often justify this as compensation for training costs (for which the origin country does not reap the benefits) or simply as redistribution from high-earning emigrants to low-earning natives. The foremost advocate of this is economist Jagdish Bhagwati (1976), an early proponent of the tax and the namesake for such proposals (the "Bhagwati Tax").

Opponents of such policies argue that calculating such compensation is too difficult and that, in some cases, benefits to the origin country already exceed the training costs (Clemens 2015). For example, African doctors in Canada or the United States often work in their home country for multiple years before emigrating, and total remittances after migration often outweigh the costs of training (Clemens 2011). Additionally, like the restrictions of emigration decisions, a tax on emigration will reduce the returns from migration, reducing incentives and potentially decreasing overall human capital accumulation.

Finally, the last type of policies intends to raise the benefits of remaining at home or returning home after an emigration. These policies include investing in local higher education institutions to prevent studying abroad, incentive payments and reintegration assistance for skilled workers abroad, and diaspora engagement. The general strategy is to reduce the incentive for high-skilled migrants to leave—not by reducing the returns to human capital investment but by increasing the returns of staying in one's origin country.

Policies increasing the returns to skill at home have shown positive effects. Antwi and Phillips (2013) assess the effects of a policy-induced increase in public sector wages for health workers in Ghana. They find that a 10 percent increase in wages decreases attrition from public sector jobs by 1 percentage point per year; they attribute this lowering of attrition to decreases in international migration.

In a direct evaluation of a tax-incentive scheme, Del Carpio et al. (2016) evaluate the Malaysian Returning Expert Program, which provides tax reductions targeted at high-skilled Malaysians abroad to encourage return migration. The authors find that acceptance into the program increases the probability of return migration by 40 percent for those who apply with a preexisting job offer. A cost–benefit analysis of the program shows that the increased return migration cancels out the reduced tax receipts and that the program roughly pays for itself.

Other programs simply offer one-time lump sums for return migration, called *assisted voluntary return programs*. Limited evidence has found these programs to be mostly ineffective. Increasing the size of the monetary incentive does little to increase return migration (Thiel and Gillan 2010).

Diaspora engagement programs attempt to connect investors and entrepreneurs abroad with investment opportunities at home. These programs attempt to harness the knowledge spillovers discussed earlier in this chapter (see the section titled "Impact of high-skilled migration on origin countries") and to foster the transfer of technology and institutions from abroad. Examples are the Ethiopian Investment Agency, the Mexican Talent Network, and the Lebanese Business Network. The effects of organizations such as these have been well documented (Saxenian 2007), but little evidence supports the effects of government interventions that promote such programs (Clemens 2015).

Despite these perceptions, however, many questions on the issues surrounding high-skilled migration—from its extent to its impact to appropriate policy responses—remain unanswered. Many destination countries aim to design their policies to attract and retain high-skilled workers, but the evidence is also thin on their effectiveness. In addition to the difficulties associated with quantifying policies for empirical analysis, governments tend not to share certain data, on various security and confidentiality grounds, making rigorous analysis almost impossible.

Overall, the evidence and economic theory support the idea that it is better to increase the potential benefits at home (origin country) than to pursue policies that restrict benefits abroad (destination country). Policies that attempt to restrict emigration either directly or through tax programs reduce the incentive to accumulate human capital and are thus inefficient. Instead, increasing the opportunities for high-skilled work at home can reduce emigration (and increase return migration) incentives. Nevertheless, there are many unanswered questions on high-skilled migration policies of both origin and destination countries. The evidence on effectiveness of many policies is incomplete. Existing evidence on some policies indicates that many of the results are context specific and depend on the underlying conditions. One conclusion we can confidently claim is the need for more detailed and rigorous empirical studies.

Note

1. For more information on the rankings, see http://www.shanghairanking.com /ARWU2016.html.

References

Acemoglu, D., and D. Autor. 2011. "Skills, Tasks and Technologies: Implications for Employment and Earnings." *Handbook of Labor Economics* 4: 1043–171.

Agrawal, A., D. Kapur, J. McHale, and A. Oettl. 2011. "Brain Drain or Brain Bank? The Impact of Skilled Emigration on Poor-Country Innovation." *Journal of Urban Economics* 69 (1): 43–55.

Akcigit, U., S. Baslandze, and S. Stantcheva. 2016. "Taxation and the International Mobility of Inventors." *American Economic Review* 106 (10): 2930–81.

Antwi, J., and D. C. Phillips. 2013. "Wages and Health Worker Retention: Evidence from Public Sector Wage Reforms in Ghana." *Journal of Development Economics* 102: 101–15.

Artuç, E., F. Docquier, Ç. Özden, and C. Parsons. 2015. "A Global Assessment of Human Capital Mobility: The Role of Non-OECD Destinations." *World Development* 65: 6–26.

Barro, R. J. 1991. "Economic Growth in a Cross Section of Countries." *Quarterly Journal of Economics* 106 (2): 407–43.

———. 2001. "Human Capital and Growth." *American Economic Review* 91 (2): 12–17.

Barro, R. J., and J. W. Lee. 2013. "A New Data Set of Educational Attainment in the World, 1950–2010." *Journal of Development Economics* 104 (September): 184–98.

Becker, G. S., K. M. Murphy, and R. Tamura. 1990. "Human Capital, Fertility, and Economic Growth." *Journal of Political Economy* 98 (5, Part 2): S12– S37.

Beine, M., F. Docquier, and H. Rapoport. 2001. "Brain Drain and Economic Growth: Theory and Evidence." *Journal of Development Economics* 64 (1): 275–89.

———. 2008. "Brain Drain and Human Capital Formation in Developing Countries: Winners and Losers." *Economic Journal* 118 (528): 631–52.

———. 2010. "On the Robustness of Brain Gain Estimates." *Annals of Economics and Statistics/Annales d'Économie et de Statistique* 97/98 (January/June): 143–65.

Bhagwati, J. N. 1976. "Taxing the Brain Drain." *Challenge* 19 (3): 34–38.

Bhagwati, J., and K. Hamada. 1974. "The Brain Drain, International Integration of Markets for Professionals and Unemployment: A Theoretical Analysis." *Journal of Development Economics* 1 (1): 19–42.

Bhargava, A., F. Docquier, and Y. Moullan. 2011. "Modeling the Effects of Physician Emigration on Human Development." *Economics & Human Biology* 9 (2): 172–83.

Bollard, A., D. McKenzie, M. Morten, and H. Rapoport. 2011. "Remittances and the Brain Drain Revisited: The Microdata Show that More Educated Migrants Remit More." *World Bank Economic Review* 25 (1): 132–56.

Borjas, G. J. 1987. "Self-Selection and the Earnings of Immigrants." *American Economic Review* 77 (4): 531–53.

Borjas, G. J., and K. B. Doran. 2012. "The Collapse of the Soviet Union and the Productivity of American Mathematicians." *Quarterly Journal of Economics* 127 (3): 1143–203.

Brucker, H., S. Bertoli, G. Facchini, A. M. Mayda, and G. Peri. 2012. "The Effects of Brain Gain on Growth, Investment, and Employment: Evidence from OECD Countries, 1980–2005." In *Brain Drain and Brain Gain: The Global Competition to Attract High-Skilled Migrants*, edited by T. Boeri, H. Brucker, F. Docquier, and H. Rapoport. New York: Oxford University Press.

Clemens, M. 2007. "Do Visas Kill? Health Effects of African Health Professional Emigration." Working Paper 114, Center for Global Development, Washington, DC.

Clemens, M. A. 2011. "The Financial Consequences of High-Skill Emigration: Lessons from African Doctors Abroad." In *Diaspora for Development in Africa*, edited by Dilip Ratha and Sonia Plaze, 165–82. Washington, DC: World Bank.

———. 2013. "What Do We Know about Skilled Migration and Development?" Policy Brief 3, Migration Policy Institute, Washington, DC.

———. 2015. "Smart Policy toward High-Skill Emigrants." *IZA World of Labor*, article no. 203. https://wol.iza.org/articles/smart-policy-toward-high-skill -emigrants/long.

Czaika, M., and C. R. Parsons. 2017. "The Gravity of High-Skilled Migration Policies." *Demography* 54 (2): 603–30.

Czaika, M., and S. Toma. 2016. "International Academic Mobility across Space and Time: The Case of Indian Academics." *Population, Space and Place* 23 (8): e2069.

Del Carpio, X. V., C. Ozden, M. Testaverde, and M. C. Wagner. 2016. "Global Migration of Talent and Tax Incentives: Evidence from Malaysia's Returning Expert Program." Policy Research Working Paper 7875, World Bank, Washington, DC.

DHS (U.S. Department of Homeland Security). 2016. *Yearbook of Immigration Statistics: 2015.* Washington, DC: U.S. Department of Homeland Security, Office of Immigration Statistics.

Docquier, F. 2017. "Note on High-Skilled Emigration Externalities." Unpublished working paper, UC Louvain, Belgium.

Docquier, F., A. Marfouk, and B. L. Lowell. 2007. "A Gendered Assessment of the Brain Drain." IZA Discussion Paper 3235, Institute for the Study of Labor, Bonn.

Docquier, F., and H. Rapoport. 2012. "Globalization, Brain Drain, and Development." *Journal of Economic Literature* 50 (3): 681–730.

Doran, K., A. Gelber, and A. Isen. 2016. "The Effects of High-Skilled Immigration Policy on Firms: Evidence from Visa Lotteries." NBER Working Paper 20668, National Bureau of Economic Research, Cambridge, MA.

Dustmann, C., and O. Kirchkamp. 2002. "The Optimal Migration Duration and Activity Choice after Re-migration." *Journal of Development Economics* 67 (2): 351–72.

Facchini, G., and E. Lodigiani. 2014. "Attracting Skilled Immigrants: An Overview of Recent Policy Developments in Advanced Countries." *National Institute Economic Review* 229 (1): R3–R21.

Facchini, G., and A. M. Mayda. 2010. "What Drives Immigration Policy? Evidence Based on a Survey of Governments' Officials." In *Migration and Culture*, edited by Gil S. Epstein and Ira N. Gang, 605–48. Bingley, U.K.: Emerald Group Publishing.

Felbermayr, G. J., and B. Jung. 2009. "The Pro-trade Effect of the Brain Drain: Sorting Out Confounding Factors." *Economics Letters* 104 (2): 72–75.

Gibson, J., and D. McKenzie. 2011. "The Microeconomic Determinants of Emigration and Return Migration of the Best and Brightest: Evidence from the Pacific." *Journal of Development Economics* 95 (1): 18–29.

Gould, D. M. 1994. "Immigrant Links to the Home Country: Empirical Implications for U.S. Bilateral Trade Flows." *Review of Economics and Statistics* 76 (2): 302–16.

Grogger, J., and G. H. Hanson. 2015. "Attracting Talent: Location Choices of Foreign-Born PhDs in the United States." *Journal of Labor Economics* 33 (Suppl 1): S5–S38.

Grubel, H. G., and A. D. Scott. 1966. "The Cost of U.S. College Student Exchange Programs." *Journal of Human Resources* 1 (2): 81–98.

Hanson, G. H., and M. J. Slaughter. 2013. "Talent, Immigration, and U.S. Economic Competitiveness." Compete America Coalition.

Hicks, J. 1932. *The Theory of Wages.* London: Macmillan.

Javorcik, B. S., Ç. Özden, M. Spatareanu, and C. Neagu. 2011. "Migrant Networks and Foreign Direct Investment." *Journal of Development Economics* 94 (2): 231–41.

Jones, C. I. 2002. "Sources of U.S. Economic Growth in a World of Ideas." *American Economic Review* 92 (1): 220–39.

Kerr, S. P., W. R. Kerr, and W. F. Lincoln. 2015. "Skilled Immigration and the Employment Structures of U.S. Firms." *Journal of Labor Economics* 33 (Suppl 1): S147–S186.

Kerr, S. P., W. Kerr, C. Ozden, and C. Parsons. 2016. "Global Talent Flows." *Journal of Economic Perspectives* 30 (4): 83–106.

Kerr, W. R. 2008. "Ethnic Scientific Communities and International Technology Diffusion." *Review of Economics and Statistics* 90 (3): 518–37.

Kerr, W. R., and W. F. Lincoln. 2010. "The Supply Side of Innovation: H-1B Visa Reforms and U.S. Ethnic Invention." *Journal of Labor Economics* 28 (3): 473–508.

Kugler, M., and H. Rapoport. 2007. "International Labor and Capital Flows: Complements or Substitutes?" *Economics Letters* 94 (2): 155–62.

Mattoo, A., I. C. Neagu, and Ç. Özden. 2008. "Brain Waste? Educated Immigrants in the U.S. Labor Market." *Journal of Development Economics* 87 (2): 255–69.

Miguelez, E. 2016. "Inventor Diasporas and the Internationalization of Technology." Policy Research Working Paper 7619, World Bank, Washington, DC.

Miguelez, E., and C. Fink. 2013. "Measuring the International Mobility of Inventors: A New Database." WIPO Economic Research Working Paper 08, World Intellectual Property Organization, Economics and Statistics Division.

Moretti, E. 2004. "Workers' Education, Spillovers, and Productivity: Evidence from Plant-Level Production Functions." *American Economic Review* 94 (3): 656–90.

Moretti, E. 2012. *The New Geography of Jobs*. New York: Houghton Mifflin Harcourt.

Moretti, E., and D. J. Wilson. 2017. "The Effect of State Taxes on the Geographical Location of Top Earners: Evidence from Star Scientists." *American Economic Review* 107 (7): 1858–903.

Moser, P., A. Voena, and F. Waldinger. 2014. "German Jewish Émigrés and U.S. Invention." *American Economic Review* 104 (10): 3222–55.

Mountford, A. 1997. "Can a Brain Drain Be Good for Growth in the Source Economy?" *Journal of Development Economics* 53 (2): 287–303.

Mountford, A., and H. Rapoport. 2011. "The Brain Drain and the World Distribution of Income." *Journal of Development Economics* 95 (1): 4–17.

Nejad, M. N., and A. T. Young. 2014. "Female Brain Drains and Women's Rights Gaps: An Empirical Analysis of Bilateral Migration Flows." IZA Discussion Paper 8067, Institute for the Study of Labor, Bonn.

Ozden, C., and D. Phillips. 2015. "What Really Is Brain Drain? Location of Birth, Education and Migration Dynamics of African Doctors." KNOMAD Working Paper 4, Global Knowledge Partnership on Migration and Development.

Papademetriou, D. G., W. Somerville, and H. Tanaka. 2009. "Hybrid Immigrant-Selection Systems: The Next Generation of Economic Migration Schemes." In *Talent, Competitiveness and Migration,* edited by Bertelsmann Stiftung and Migration Policy Institute, 267–336. Gutersloh, Germany: Bertelsmann Stiftung.

Parsons, C. R., S. Rojon, F. Samanani, and L. Wettach. 2015. *Conceptualising International High-Skilled Migration*. Discussion paper, University of Western Australia, Business School, Economics, Perth.

Peri, G., and C. Sparber. 2011. "Highly Educated Immigrants and Native Occupational Choice." *Industrial Relations: A Journal of Economy and Society* 50 (3): 385–411.

Piracha, M., and F. Vadean. 2010. "Return Migration and Occupational Choice: Evidence from Albania." *World Development* 38 (8): 1141–55.

Ruggles S., K. Genadek, R. Goeken, J. Grover, and M. Sobek. 2017. *Integrated Public Use Microdata Series: Version 7.0* [dataset]. Minneapolis: University of Minnesota. https://doi.org/10.18128/D010.V7.0.

Saxenian, A. 2005. "From Brain Drain to Brain Circulation: Transnational Communities and Regional Upgrading in India and China." *Studies in Comparative International Development (SCID)* 40 (2): 35–61.

———. 2007. *The New Argonauts: Regional Advantage in a Global Economy*. Cambridge, MA: Harvard University Press.

Singh, Manmohan. 2010. "Prime Minister's Remarks at Hiren Mukherjee Memorial Lecture 2010." New Delhi, December 2. http://archivepmo.nic.in/drmanmohansingh/speech-details.php?nodeid=957.

Stark, O., C. Helmenstein, and A. Prskawetz. 1997. "A Brain Gain with a Brain Drain." *Economics Letters* 55 (2): 227–34.

———. 1998. "Human Capital Depletion, Human Capital Formation, and Migration: A Blessing or a 'Curse'?" *Economics Letters* 60 (3): 363–67.

Thiel, D., and K. Gillan. 2010. "Factors Affecting Participation in Assisted Voluntary Return Programmes and Successful Reintegration: A Review of the Evidence." Research Report 29, Home Office, Her Majesty's Government of the United Kingdom.

Wadhwa, V., A. Saxenian, B. A. Rissing, and G. Gereffi. 2008. "Skilled Immigration and Economic Growth." *Applied Research in Economic Development* 5 (1): 6–14.

Wahba, J. 2015. "Selection, Selection, Selection: The Impact of Return Migration." *Journal of Population Economics* 28 (3): 535–63.

World Bank. 2011. *World Development Report 2012: Gender Equality and Development*. Washington, DC: World Bank.

Yang, D. 2008. "International Migration, Remittances and Household Investment: Evidence from Philippine Migrants' Exchange Rate Shocks." *Economic Journal* 118 (528): 591–630.

Migration Data

Migration data are as complex as the policy and research questions of the migration literature. Ernst Georg Ravenstein (1885, 1889), founder of modern research on migration in the 19th century, concluded that high-quality primary data, mainly from national sources, are necessary for demographic, social, and economic research. Since then, researchers in demography, economics, sociology, political science, and geography established various data collection principles via censuses, administrative registers, and nationally representative or special-purpose surveys. The progress has been quite impressive in terms of the variety and quality of data sources available. Yet some of the basic challenges from the 19th century still haunt us with all their vigor. One of the main conclusions of this book is that there is an urgent need for better data collection, dissemination, and analysis efforts in order to answer a wide range of academic and policy questions, some of which we discuss in the chapters.

Migration data almost always come from destination countries because it is difficult for origin countries to collect demographic, labor market, and other personal data on people who are not living in the country. Unlike trade and financial statistics, which are recorded by both transacting parties, the quality of migration statistics depends almost entirely on the rigor with which destination countries survey the migrants within their borders.

Destination countries use a wide range of tools to count and analyze characteristics of migrants within their boundaries. Among these data sources are (1) censuses aimed at capturing all people within borders at a given point; (2) various surveys, such as labor market or specialized and multitopic surveys, that sample a smaller portion of the population but ask more detailed questions; (3) population registers, common in certain countries; and (4) various administrative data sources such as statistics, employment and residency permits, and naturalization records. Typically, migration is not the main focus of each of these sources, and the amount of data and the information available will depend on the original purpose of the data source.

In this report, we rely mostly on databases that have been compiled from hundreds of censuses across countries and years. Thus, we will first examine the design and limitations of such data sources. Censuses attempt to survey an entire population at a single time using a short questionnaire on mainly demographic variables. A "census round" corresponds to a specific decade and includes censuses collected in the five years before and after the start of that decade (for example, the 2010 round includes censuses collected from 2005 to 2014). As noted above, data on migration are not the focus of censuses but are generally a by-product, revealed by questions regarding country of birth or nationality and sometimes about the time of arrival. On the one hand, censuses are highly valuable because they can provide accurate counts of immigrants from even very small origin countries as they attempt to measure the entire population. On the other hand, they have an important drawback. The amount of information on each migrant tends to be limited to a few demographic and labor market statistics. Finally, censuses are among the few sources that are relatively standardized across countries and can lead to more comparable global datasets.

Bilateral migration databases are constructed using censuses gathered from multiple destinations and census rounds. They contain the total migrant stock or flow from a given origin country to a given destination, sometimes disaggregated by age, gender, education level, or labor market status. Such databases are limited by the number of destination countries available, making estimates of total migration difficult. Because the quality and frequency of data collection are correlated with a country's income level and size, the data from Organisation for Economic Co-operation and Development (OECD) and other high-income destinations are much more complete; most data gaps are seen for lower-income and smaller destination countries. Data availability will also depend on the amount of disaggregation required. The United Nations Global Migration Database—which disaggregates bilateral stocks only by gender—has collected data from at least one data source from over 200 destination countries across many years. In contrast, the OECD Database on Immigrants in OECD and Non-OECD Countries

(DIOC-E)—which collects bilateral migration data disaggregated by age, gender, education level, and labor market status—contains destination data for only 88 countries in the 2010 census round: 33 of the 34 OECD member countries in 2010 and only 55 of the more than 180 remaining non-OECD countries (see Arslan et al. 2014 for details). To account for the missing data, researchers often focus on migration patterns into OECD countries so as not to bias results.

Another way to address missing data is to estimate the size of missing corridors using econometric methods that incorporate historical patterns, country-pair characteristics, and patterns observed from other migration corridors. Three such databases that use this approach to impute the missing data are the United Nations' Global Migration Database, the World Bank's Global Bilateral Migration Database (Ozden et al. 2011), and the World Bank's High-Skill Bilateral Migration Database (Artuç et al. 2015). Researchers have many different strategies for imputing data, and the quality of the estimates will depend on the amount of data used and the model used in predicting the migration stocks. These estimates provide researchers with a full matrix of migration corridors and allow us to make statements regarding global migration patterns that would be impossible otherwise.

Relying only on destination data also has shortcomings. The lack of high-quality origin data prevents researchers from answering many important policy questions. Most of these questions concern the impact of emigration on the families and communities that migrants have left behind in their home countries. The effects range from the poverty alleviation impact of remittances to the decline in health and education services when doctors and teachers emigrate. Although censuses and administrative records in origin countries may provide clues on these issues, most relevant data come from surveys with special migration questions or modules.

Datasets used

This book takes advantage of five separate bilateral migration datasets, the use of which will depend on the scope of the question and whether it is beneficial or necessary to use estimated data. We can differentiate the databases along three dimensions: (1) the time frame covered, (2) whether they contain information on education level (and how disaggregated such data are), and (3) whether they cover the full bilateral matrix (that is, whether they contain predicted data). First, the most complete databases (with respect to space and time) are the World Bank's Global Bilateral Migration

Database and the United Nations' Global Migration Database. World Bank and United Nations datasets contain full bilateral matrixes of migrant stocks disaggregated by gender in 10-year intervals from 1960 to 2000 and 5-year intervals from 1990 to 2015, respectively. We use these datasets in chapter 1 to present broad global patterns over time.

Second, because we would also like to present global patterns disaggregated by skill (education) group, we use the World Bank's High-Skill Migration Database. This dataset uses raw and predicted data in a full matrix of global migrant stocks for the age 25 and over population disaggregated into two skill groups (less than tertiary education and at least some tertiary education) for the 1990 and 2000 census rounds. We use this dataset to present global patterns by education level in chapters 1 and 5. See Artuç et al. (2015) for an in-depth description of the dataset.

Finally, two datasets provide raw migrant stock data further disaggregated by education. The OECD DIOC-E has bilateral migration data to nearly every OECD country and many non-OECD countries disaggregated into three education groups for the 2000 and 2010 census rounds. The other dataset, compiled by Docquier, Lowell, and Marfouk (2007), contains similarly disaggregated data for migrant stocks to 30 OECD destinations in 1990 and 2000. Because the datasets define education levels slightly differently, when we present patterns over all three decades, we adjust the DIOC-E data to match education shares from Docquier, Lowell, and Marfouk (2007) in the overlapping 2000 round. We also use the DIOC-E data (sometimes aggregated into one or two education groups) in chapter 2 in investigating the drivers of migration where including estimated data would be counterproductive (because such drivers are also used when predicting missing data). In this case, we use the entire DIOC-E database and investigate immigration to all 88 destination countries (see Arslan et al. 2014 for the details of the latest version of the dataset).

Other migration data challenges

Defining a migrant: The definition of a migrant may vary across datasets, and the definition chosen will depend on the data available. Ideally, an international migrant would be someone who changes his or her country of residence, and for most destination countries that will be the definition. This is identified through a country of birth variable. Unfortunately, for a few countries, the best information regarding migration history is country of nationality, which can be misleading for a variety of reasons.

First, immigrants who have become naturalized citizens will not be counted in migrant stocks, leading to undercounting. This undercounting will depend on countries' immigration policy: countries in which naturalization occurs faster will have higher rates of undercounting. Second, country immigration laws vary—in more restrictive cases, even native-born children of foreigners are not granted citizenship, thus leading to overcounting of migrants. The possibility of holding multiple nationalities complicates matters further. Finally, when migrants, especially refugees and asylum seekers, cannot be assigned to a specific nationality, they are often recorded under an aggregated umbrella heading, leading to ambiguity.

All of these issues plague censuses, population registers, administrative data, and surveys. Thus, it is critical for collectors of data to ask specific questions and for users to be aware of the differences. Ideally, questions should address both place of birth and citizenship status. Many undocumented migrants, however, will refrain from participation in the survey for fear of identification when faced with citizenship questions, which will bias the data collected. If a choice needs to be made on which information to collect, place of birth is preferable.

Defining a country: Even if a survey or a census asks participants about country of birth or citizenship, the definitions of countries change over time. Many countries have gained independence (Eritrea, Timor-Leste, South Sudan, and many other countries in Sub-Saharan Africa), dissolved into smaller states (the Soviet Union, Yugoslavia, and Czechoslovakia), or unified (Yemen, Germany, Vietnam) since the Second World War. Those born in Moscow, but residing in Kiev, would never have been classified as migrants under either of the two most commonly used definitions until August 23, 1991, but they are classified as such in the following censuses. For example, Ozden et al. (2011) show that the sudden jump in international migrants' numbers between 1990 and 2000 is mainly due to the break-up of the Soviet Union. This is especially problematic when comparing data over time.

Changing borders pose problems when analyzing time-series data. One option is to use the countries in existence at that point. Migrants from Africa who came to the United States before the 1970s were recorded under different origin countries in different censuses as their birth countries gained independence. Other changes are subtler. The definition of an "Ethiopian" included Eritreans in the 1970 census but not in the census of 2000. This results in an artificial decline in Ethiopian migrants because some have been relabeled as Eritreans in later years. Researchers need to keep these border changes in mind when performing their analysis and make the necessary adjustments.

Measuring undocumented migrants: Censuses aim to enumerate the entire resident population, whether documented or undocumented (Bilsborrow et al. 1997). This means that, to the extent that the undocumented are found by surveyors and are willing to provide accurate information, they will be included in censuses. One issue is that, for fear of deportation or incarceration, undocumented immigrants have an incentive to avoid being enumerated. Therefore, researchers making predictions about the size of the undocumented must make assumptions about the extent of under-counting by government enumerators. For example, the U.S. Department of Homeland Security (DHS) assumes that enumerators miss 10 percent of undocumented immigrants (Hoefer, Rytina, and Baker 2012). They estimate that, of the 31 million foreign-born residents who arrived between 1980 and 2010, roughly one-third (11 million) were residing in the United States illegally.

Identifying migration dynamics: Migration is often not a one-time event. International migrants can reside in multiple countries before settling in a final destination or even returning to their home country. Most global bilateral migration datasets are based on censuses and population registers of the destination countries where the migrants currently reside. These data sources record only the country of birth or citizenship of migrants. Other important variables, such as the year of arrival or migration status, are not included in most surveys. Detailed migration histories tend to be available only in small and specialized surveys that are not nationally representative. Therefore, data on immigrant stocks will tell only a partial story of the migration decision process. Without comprehensive global data that cover all possible destinations, it is difficult for empirical and analytical papers to explore beyond static models. One option is to combine data on bilateral migration stocks with individual country surveys that contain more detailed information. Artuç and Ozden (2016) use this strategy to research transit migration, the process of migrating across multiple destinations. The researchers combine the bilateral migration data-bases used in this report with the American Community Survey (ACS) that asks questions on country of birth, year of migration, and country of residence one year prior to the survey. Using these data, they identify common routes into the United States and immigrants from which birth countries typically reside in intermediate countries before arriving in the United States.

Refugee data

Data on refugees, asylum seekers, and internally displaced persons (IDPs) come from the United Nations High Commissioner for Refugees (UNHCR) Population Statistics Database. They contain bilateral stocks of refugees (and those in refugee-like situations) and asylum seekers. The data also include country-by-year stocks of IDPs. When possible, the book combines stocks of both refugees and asylum seekers to gain an accurate picture of the total displaced population in a given country. The UNHCR defines each population as the following:[1]

- *Refugees* are individuals recognized under the 1951 Convention Relating to the Status of Refugees; its 1967 Protocol; the 1969 OAU (Organization of African Unity) Convention Governing the Specific Aspects of Refugee Problems in Africa; those recognized in accordance with the UNHCR Statute; individuals granted complementary forms of protection; or those enjoying temporary protection. Since 2007, the refugee population also includes people in a refugee-like situation.
- *Asylum seekers* are individuals who have sought international protection and whose claims for refugee status have not yet been determined, irrespective of when they may have been lodged.
- *Internally displaced persons (IDPs)* are people or groups of individuals who have been forced to leave their homes or places of habitual residence, in particular as a result of, or in order to avoid the effects of, armed conflict, situations of generalized violence, violations of human rights, or natural or human-caused disasters, and who have not crossed an international border. For the purposes of UNHCR's statistics, this population includes only conflict-generated IDPs to whom the UNHCR extends protection or assistance. Since 2007, the IDP population also includes people in an IDP-like situation.[2]

Wage data

We calculate wage data from the World Bank International Income Distribution Database (I2D2). The World Bank I2D2 dataset is a collection of nearly 1,000 individual-level labor force and household surveys from over 100, mostly developing, countries over time. The variables have been harmonized across surveys, thus making the data comparable across countries. The wage data are originally denominated in local currency and have been adjusted for purchasing power parity (PPP) to 2010 U.S. dollars. We calculate average wages for the age 25–64 population as well as averages disaggregated into two education groups, completed tertiary and less than completed tertiary. For the 2010 round of data, we take the average wage across all surveys between 2001 and 2010. In all, we collect wage data for 116 countries.

Other data

Bilateral data on distance, contiguity, and colonial ties come from the Centre d'Études Prospectives et d'Informations Internationales (CEPII) GeoDist dataset (Mayer and Zignago 2011). The distance variable is calculated as the great-circle distance between each country's most populated city. The colony indicator is equal to one if either country in the pair was a colonizer of the other. The variable is not transitive—the variable will be zero even if the two countries share a third colonizer (for example India and the United States will be zero even though they were both colonized by the United Kingdom). The common language index used comes from the CEPII Language dataset and is described in detail in Melitz and Toubal (2014). Country-level data on gross domestic product, employment, and population density come from the World Bank Databank.[3] Data on population for various age groups and dependency ratios come from the United Nations World Population Prospects dataset.[4] Data on country education rates come from the Barro and Lee (2013) dataset.

Regional groupings

Many tables, figures, and maps in the text refer to regions. We use the classification groups shown in table A.1 to create the regions used in the text. The groupings are mostly based on World Bank regions but, when necessary, we created additional groups. More specifically, we split the East Asia and Pacific and the Middle East and North Africa regions into low-income and high-income groups because the two groups exhibit significantly different economic and migration patterns. Similarly, we split the Europe and Central Asia region into three groups: Western Europe,

Table A.1   Country or economy classification

Region	Country or economy
East Asia and Pacific (low income)	American Samoa, Cambodia, China, Cocos (Keeling) Islands, Cook Islands, Fiji, Indonesia, Kiribati, Lao PDR, Malaysia, Marshall Islands, Federated States of Micronesia, Mongolia, Myanmar, Niue, Norfolk Island, Palau, Papua New Guinea, Philippines, Pitcairn Islands, Samoa, Solomon Islands, Thailand, Timor-Leste, Tokelau, Tonga, Tuvalu, Vanuatu, Vietnam
East Asia and Pacific (high income)	Australia; Brunei Darussalam; Guam; Hong Kong SAR, China; Japan; Republic of Korea; Macao SAR, China; Nauru; New Zealand; Northern Mariana Islands; Singapore; Taiwan, China
Eastern Europe and Central Asia (non-EU)	Albania, Armenia, Azerbaijan, Belarus, Bosnia and Herzegovina, Georgia, Kazakhstan, Kyrgyz Republic, former Yugoslav Republic of Macedonia, Moldova, Montenegro, Russian Federation, Serbia, Tajikistan, Turkey, Turkmenistan, Ukraine, Uzbekistan
Eastern Europe and Central Asia (EU member)	Bulgaria, Croatia, Czech Republic, Estonia, Hungary, Latvia, Lithuania, Poland, Romania, Slovak Republic, Slovenia
Latin America and the Caribbean	Anguilla, Antigua and Barbuda, Argentina, Aruba, The Bahamas, Barbados, Belize, Bolivia, Brazil, British Virgin Islands, Cayman Islands, Chile, Colombia, Costa Rica, Cuba, Dominica, Dominican Republic, Ecuador, El Salvador, Falkland Islands, Grenada, Guatemala, Guyana, Haiti, Honduras, Jamaica, Mexico, Montserrat, Netherlands Antilles, Nicaragua, Panama, Paraguay, Peru, Puerto Rico, St. Kitts and Nevis, St. Lucia, St. Vincent and the Grenadines, Suriname, Trinidad and Tobago, Turks and Caicos Islands, Uruguay, República Bolivariana de Venezuela, Virgin Islands
Middle East and North Africa (low income)	Algeria, Djibouti, Arab Republic of Egypt, Islamic Republic of Iran, Iraq, Jordan, Lebanon, Libya, Morocco, Syrian Arab Republic, Tunisia, West Bank and Gaza, Western Sahara, Republic of Yemen
Middle East and North Africa (high income)	Bahrain, Israel, Kuwait, Oman, Qatar, Saudi Arabia, United Arab Emirates
North America	Bermuda, Canada, United States
South Asia	Afghanistan, Bangladesh, Bhutan, India, Maldives, Nepal, Pakistan, Sri Lanka
Sub-Saharan Africa	Angola, Benin, Botswana, Burkina Faso, Burundi, Cabo Verde, Cameroon, Central African Republic, Chad, Comoros, Democratic Republic of Congo, Republic of Congo, Côte d'Ivoire, Equatorial Guinea, Eritrea, Ethiopia, Gabon, The Gambia, Ghana, Guinea, Guinea-Bissau, Kenya, Lesotho, Liberia, Madagascar, Malawi, Mali, Mauritania, Mauritius, Mozambique, Namibia, Niger, Nigeria, Rwanda, São Tomé and Príncipe, Senegal, Seychelles, Sierra Leone, Somalia, South Africa, St. Helena, Sudan, Swaziland, Tanzania, Togo, Uganda, Zambia, Zimbabwe
Western Europe	Andorra, Austria, Belgium, Cyprus, Denmark, Finland, France, Germany, Gibraltar, Greece, Holy See, Iceland, Ireland, Italy, Liechtenstein, Luxembourg, Malta, Monaco, Netherlands, Norway, Portugal, San Marino, Spain, Sweden, Switzerland, United Kingdom

European Union (EU) members of Eastern Europe and Central Asia, and non-EU members of Eastern Europe and Central Asia—again, on the basis of income and migration patterns.

Notes

1. For more information and definitions of other populations of concern, see the UNHCR Population Statistics web page, http://popstats.unhcr.org/en /overview.
2. For global IDP estimates, see www.internal-displacement.org.
3. For more information, see http://databank.worldbank.org/data/home.aspx.
4. For more information, see https://esa.un.org/unpd/wpp/.

References

Arslan, C., J.-C. Dumont, Z. Kone, Y. Moullan, C. Ozden, C. Parsons, and T. Xenogiani. 2014. "A New Profile of Migrants in the Aftermath of the Recent Economic Crisis." OECD Social, Employment and Migration Working Paper 160, OECD Publishing, Paris.

Artuç, E., F. Docquier, C. Ozden, and C. Parsons. 2015. "A Global Assessment of Human Capital Mobility: The Role of Non-OECD Destinations." *World Development* 65: 6–26.

Artuç, E., and C. Ozden. 2016. "Transit Migration: All Roads Lead to America." Policy Research Working Paper 7880, World Bank, Washington, DC.

Barro, R. J., and J. W. Lee. 2013. "A New Data Set of Educational Attainment in the World, 1950–2010." *Journal of Development Economics* 104: 184–98.

Bilsborrow, R. E., G. Hugo, A. S. Oberai, and H. Zlotnik. 1997. *International Migration Statistics: Guidelines for Improving Data Collection Systems.* Geneva: International Labour Organization.

Docquier, F., B. L. Lowell, and A. Marfouk. 2007. "A Gendered Assessment of the Brain Drain." IZA Discussion Papers 3235, Institute for the Study of Labor, Bonn.

Hoefer, M., N. F. Rytina, and B. Baker. 2012. "Estimates of the Unauthorized Immigrant Population Residing in the United States: January 2011." Department of Homeland Security, Office of Immigration Statistics, Washington, DC.

Mayer, T., and S. Zignago. 2011. "Notes on CEPII's Distances Measures: The GeoDist Database." CEPII Working Paper 2011–25, Centre d'Études Prospectives et d'Informations Internationales, Paris.

Melitz, J., and F. Toubal. 2014. "Native Language, Spoken Language, Translation and Trade." *Journal of International Economics* 93 (2): 351–63.

Ozden, C., C. R. Parsons, M. Schiff, and T. L. Walmsley. 2011. "Where on Earth Is Everybody? The Evolution of Global Bilateral Migration 1960–2000." *World Bank Economic Review* 25 (1): 12–56.

Ravenstein, E. G. 1885. "The Laws of Migration." *Journal of the Statistical Society* 46: 167–235.

———. 1889. "The Laws of Migration: Second Paper." *Journal of the Royal Statistical Society* 52: 241–305.

www.ingramcontent.com/pod-product-compliance
Lightning Source LLC
Chambersburg PA
CBHW081430270326
41932CB00019B/3145